The Naked Guide to
Bristol

◆Tangent Books

First published in 2004 by Naked Guides Ltd. Second Edition published 2006 by Tangent Books. Third Edition published 2011 by Tangent Books, reprinted June 2012. Fourth Edition published August 2013. Fifth Edition published 2015. Sixth Edition published 2017. This edition published 2019

Tangent Books, Unit 5.16 Paintworks, Bristol BS4 3EH
www.tangentbooks.co.uk
Tel: 0117 972 0645

Publisher: Richard Jones
Assistant Publisher: Johanna Darque
Design/cover artwork: Joe Burt

ISBN: 978-1-910089-85-9

Photography: All pictures by Richard Jones unless otherwise credited.

A CIP catalogue record for this book is available from the British Library

Printed on paper from sustainable sources.

Thanks and Contributors

Alice Perera, Andy Hamilton, Beccy Golding, Caitlin Telfer, Caitlin Thomson, David Williams, Eva Mason, Evie Steen, Finn Dovey, Gil Gillespie, Jane Duffus, Jim Allum, Johanna Darque, Kevin Brooks, Maggie Telfer, Mark Steeds, Megan Miller-Golding, Mena Telfer, Mike Manson, Naomi Berry, Nicky Coates, Rosemary Wagg, Royston Griffey, Tony Bolger, Tony D'Arpino

Photography and Illustration

Ania Shrimpton, Beezer, Chris Chalkley, Claudio Ahlers, Darren Thompson, Frank Drake, Gage Graphics, Joe Burt, Mat Kauhanen, Mike Manson, Paul Roberts, Pete Maginnis, Rob Daw, Sarah Connolly, Scott Buchanan Barden, Simon Ellis, Simon Holliday, Vince John

The Naked Guide to
Bristol

DISCOVER:
Top sights,
area guides,
in-depth culture,
listings, maps
and more

Not all guide books are the same

On the cover...

1. Tony Benn (p240)
2. Gromit (p239)
3. Wallace (p239)
4. Dr Paul Stephenson OBE (p253)
5. DJ Derek (p153)
6. Cleo Lake (p238)
7. Ursa Bear (p60)
8. Mary Carpenter (p245)
9. Isambard Kingdom Brunel (p244)
10. Blackbeard (p244)
11. George Ferguson (p247)
12. Sherrie Eugene (p247)
13. Grant Marshall (p160)
14. Robert Del Naja (p160)
15. Marvin Rees p178)

Contents

AREA GUIDES

UP CLOSE

LISTINGS

MAPS

Welcome to Bristol

The capital city of the South West of England is a place of contradictions, independence and hidden charms...

Bristol is Britain's happiest city according to research published in 2019; in 2017 it was named the number one city, along Oxford, for general life satisfaction and in the same year it took the UK crown of Best Place To Live in a *Sunday Times* survey. Students love Bristol, it's the home of Massive Attack, Tricky, Portishead, PJ Harvey, Idles and Banksy and (also in 2017) it was named Europe's Trendiest City by *National Geographic Traveller*.

According to *Guardian* research, it is the third most popular city (after Birmingham and Brighton) for people relocating from London and has long been a crossroads attracting people from Devon and Cornwall and those heading over the Severn Bridge from Wales.

However, in a Runnymead Trust report of 2017 it was identified as one of the most racially segregated areas of Britain; historically it's the largest city in Britain not to have a football team in the top division; it was European Green Capital in 2015 yet in 2017 was named the third most congested city in Britain with only London and Manchester suffering worse traffic gridlock.

Bristol is a city of contradictions. Each area has its own distinct character, it's culturally divided by the River Avon, it's not in Somerset or Gloucestershire but is the City and County of Bristol. It's an odd place, in a laid-back kind of way. We love it. We hope you will too.

Richard Jones
Author and publisher of the Naked Guide To Bristol
Richard Jones grew up in Kingswood, east Bristol. His first proper job was as a trainee reporter on the South Gloucestershire Gazette. He went on to work as a sub-editor on the Western Daily Press and was a features sub-editor and music editor of the Bristol Evening Post before working at Future Publishing in Bath as a football magazine editor. He founded Tangent Books in 2004.

Mild Mild Mild West, Banksy, Stokes Croft © Richard Jones

Ursa, Bearpit © Jamie Gillman

Bristol at a glance

Trade rather than industry has been at the heart of Bristol's identity from the Saxons to the present day...

Bristol is the largest city in the South West of England with a population of 457,300 in 2017 according to Bristol City Council estimates. The number of people living in Bristol is expected to reach 500,000 by 2027 say the bean counters.

Its roots go back to an Anglo-Saxon settlement near the modern day Bristol Bridge although there is also evidence of earlier iron age forts and Roman villas around Bristol and at Abona – the present-day Sea Mills. Abona was a third-century Roman port connected by road to Bath. Archaeological excavations at Abona have found a street pattern, shops, cemeteries and wharves. There were also isolated villas and small settlements throughout the area, notably Kings Weston Roman Villa and another at Brislington. However, the significant local Roman presence is at Bath, not Bristol.

The origins of the city go back to the Saxon era when a settlement was founded on a low hill between the rivers Avon and Frome on what is now Castle Park next to Bristol Bridge The main evidence for this is a coin of Aethelred issued in about 1010. This shows that the settlement must have been a market town and the name Brycg stowe indicates 'place by the bridge'. As sea trade developed Bristol became an increasingly important city, but all the way back to Saxon times it has been associated with slavery. It was a leading centre for the Anglo-Saxon slave trade with men women and children kidnapped and shipped from Bristol to the slave markets in Dublin and then sold on throughout the Viking empire.

In 1552, 'The Master, Wardens and Commonalty of Merchant Venturers of the City of Bristol' received their first Royal Charter from Edward VI. The Society of Merchant Venturers still exert considerable influence over Bristol and for centuries held a monopoly on sea trade from Bristol Docks – most notably the slave trade. Between the late seventeenth century and the abolition of the slave trade in 1807, it is estimated that Bristol merchants traded at least 500,000 enslaved Africans. The city you see today is founded on money from the slave trade and its associated industries, particularly tobacco, sugar and chocolate.

© Destination Bristol

The legacy of the slave trade still dominates Bristol's identity, yet there is no memorial or public recognition of the trade other than a permanent exhibition at the M Shed museum. Instead, one of the leading figures of the London and Bristol slave trade, Edward Colston, is celebrated with a prominent statue in the city centre overlooked by the Colston Tower. There are schools, pubs and at least a dozen road named after Colston. Until recently the city's major concert venue was called the Colston Hall.

Bristol's significance as a port began to decline in the early 19th century, partly because of the abolition of slavery, but also because the city docks were too small and ships had to navigate the river Avon with its large tidal range in order to reach the port.

Very little remains of the old city of Bristol. It was destroyed between 1940 and 1941 by German air raids in the Second World War. The most devastating raid was on November 24, 1940 when the remains of the medieval city were blitzed. Castle Street and St Mary Le Port Street, once the centre of Bristol which linked St Nicholas Market and Old Market, were engulfed in a fire storm and little trace of them remains.

In many ways, trade (particularly the slave trade) and the Second World War are two of the biggest influences on the development of modern Bristol. The obvious wealth of areas such as Clifton are a visible expression of the huge profits from the slave trade while the working-class terraces of Southville, Ashton and Bedminster housed tobacco workers and were dominated by the red-brick Wills cigarette factories for most of the 20th century.

The old city was replaced by the 1950s Broadmead shopping centre and the bomb sites remained mostly undeveloped until the 1980s, many inner-city working class areas such as St Philip's and the Dings were badly bombed and then demolished by city planners. The result was that inner-city Bristolians were relocated to the new suburbs such as Hartcliffe and Southmead leaving the city centre eerily empty once the office workers had departed.

This emptiness was reinforced by the decline of the city docks in the 1960s and eventual closure in the early 1970s when shipping operations moved to the Royal Portbury Dock in Avonmouth. And yet, Bristol has maintained a strong independent identity partly because of its civic status as city and county – despite the apparent geographical evidence to the contrary, Bristol is neither Somerset nor Gloucestershire, but fiercely Bristol!

In its 1980 review of Bristol's post-war planning strategy, Bristol Civic Society said: 'By the 1960s the central area was still in ruins. Except for Broadmead, nothing had happened... The city did not appear to have a heart any more.' (The Fight For Bristol: Planning and the Growth of Public Protest (Bristol Civic Society and Redcliffe Press, 1980, 0-905459-25-3)

In the 70s, 80s and 90s, before the appearance of the luxury harbourside apartments and influx of London money, an underground culture developed among young people in the city centre and particularly St Paul's. The results of this, it can be argued, helped define the anti-establishment reputation of modern Bristol as expressed through the music of Massive Attack and others and in the art of Banksy and his contemporaries. In a strange way Bristol's current reputation for art, music, independence and all round coolness was nurtured by that civic neglect in the 70s and 80s – the DIY attitude was already prevalent in Bristol's sub-cultures before punk rock kicked down the front doors... and the grown-ups hadn't even noticed.

Bristol in numbers

- **456,000** Bristol population 2018 estimate
- **22%** of residents identify themselves as Non-White British
- **91** languages spoken
- **180** countries of birth
- **45** religions
- **52,000** University and UWE students (2016)
- **£276,000** average house price (2016)

All stats from State of Bristol Key Facts 2017/18, Bristol City Council

Bristol in 3 objects

A port city of trade with its own currency, a ship on its coat of arms and a city flower originally from the Middle East...

Bristol Pound

The Bristol Pound is a local currency set up in 2012 to encourage people to spend their money with local independent businesses. Businesses can also trade online with Bristol Pounds and they can be used to pay council tax, rates and other local authority bills. The city's first elected mayor, George Ferguson took his £65,000 salary in Bristol Pounds. The 'currency' is effectively a voucher. If you are given Bristol pounds in your change, check that they are still valid by locating the date they run out next to the metallic strip on the side of the note. For a full list of where you can spend Bristol pounds, visit www.bristolpound.org.

Flower of Bristol

The Scarlet Lychnis (Lychnis Chalcedonica) or Nonsuch has been associated with Bristol since the Middle Ages when it was known as the Flower of Bristowe. It is thought the flower is native to the Middle East and was imported to Bristol by sea traders or returning crusaders. The association of the flower with the city is recognised by Bristol University in the choice of its distinctive red colour for academic hoods.

Coat of Arms

Until 1569,the Bristol Coat of Arms was only the shield. The coat of arms with the unicorns and crest was granted to Bristol in 1569 by the College of Arms. The background to the shield is red with a golden ship sailing on blue waves out of a silver castle which stands on a green mound – all signifying Bristol's huge importance as a major port.

Above the shield is a silver helmet, a red wreath and two crossed arms holding a green serpent and golden scales representing wisdom and justice. The unicorns are a symbol of extreme courage, virtue and strength. The motto translates as: 'By virtue and industry'.

Arriving in Bristol

By plane

Bristol Airport is located 8 miles to the south west of the city at Lulsgate Bottom.

TAXIS

Arrow Cars is the airport's official; private hire partner. The office is directly opposite the main entrance to the terminal building. You will be quoted a fixed fare and pay when you book. Expect the fare into Bristol to be about £30. Journey time is 25-30 min.
Phone: 01275 475000
Online: www.arrowcars.co.uk
App: Arrow Cars Bristol, Android/IoS

BUS

Two bus services connect Bristol Airport to the city centre, both are operated by First Bus.

A1 Airport Flyer: New First Bus route that started operating in January 2019. It brings you into Bristol on the new Metrobus link road through Long Ashton and then along Cumberland Road via the SS Great Britain. There are good views of the suspension bridge as you approach Bristol and because much of the route is bus lane only, journey times should be less affected by traffic. Allow 35 minutes to bus station. Adult single ticket £7; return £11 www.firstgroup.com

A2: Buses run every 30 minutes 7 days a week from 3.10am to 11.15pm. You approach the city via Bedminster, which is not the most scenic way into Bristol. Allow 35 minutes to the Centre in average traffic. £4.50 single. www.firstgroup.com

CAR HIRE

There are eight national car hire companies at the airport. www.bristolairport.co.uk

By bus and coach

Bus Station and Megabus: If you are arriving in Bristol or continuing your journey by bus or coach, First Bus and National Express operate a full range of local and national services from the bus station in the heart of the city: Marlborough Street, BS1 3NU. There's a taxi rank outside on Whitson Street. www.nationalexpress.com; www.firstgroup.com.

Megabus offers bargain fares and is a decent alternative to National Express. The bus stop is on Bond Street, an easy five-minute walk from the bus station. www.uk.megabus.com

By train

Parkway: Parkway station is on the main South Wales-London line and is situated on the northern border of Bristol and South Gloucestershire in Stoke Gifford. It was opened in 1972 and was the first in the new generation of park and ride commuter stations. If you should arrive at Parkway, it's perfectly possible to get a bus, taxi or hire a bike to get into Bristol, but you are for more likely to hop onto one of the regular services to Temple Meads. Your ticket should cover you unless you leave the station. www.nationalrail.co.uk

Massive Attack by Haka.

Temple Meads: Arriving at Temple Meads is straightforward. Leaving it less so. Bus connections to the rest of the city aren't great and it's a 25-minute walk to the bus station. The easiest option is to walk to your destination or get a cab. There is a ferry stop behind the station. Taking the boat across the floating harbour is an option if you are heading towards the centre and Hotwells.

Tourist information centre

Bristol Visitor Information Centre is next to the Watershed. Here you will find free maps, free wi-fi, left luggage, a wide range of Bristol gifts and information about accommodation, transport and events. You can buy tickets here for local and national buses, ferries and walking tours at Bristol Visitor Information Centre, E Shed, Canons Road, Bristol BS1 5TX; www.visitbristol.co.uk

Getting around

By bus

Despite the many criticisms of Bristol's commuter bus network being slow, unreliable and expensive, the bus is an excellent way of exploring Bristol as a visitor. First Bus run almost all the services and the best way of exploring the city and surrounding area is to download the App and buy day tickets for the inner and outer zones. At the time of writing First Day tickets bought on the app were £4 for the inner zone and £6 for the West of England zone. The tickets can be used on the Metrobus network. For more details visit www.firstgroup.com.

The Bristol Insight Tour Bus runs from the beginning of April to the end of September and offers an excellent way of getting round the city with a hop-on, hop-off Explorer Ticket. Book online for the best deal and look out for bus/ferry combo offers. www.bristolinsight.co.uk

By train

Bristol does not have a good local train network so the only line that is of any real use is the Severn Beach service from Temple Meads that stops at Lawrence Hill, Stapleton Road, Montpelier, Redland, Clifton Down, Sea Mills, Shirehampton, Avonmouth and Severn Beach.

By bike

Despite being named England's first Cycling City in 2008 and receiving more than £11 million from Central Government to improve cycle networks and training, Bristol isn't a great city for cycling. A combination of traffic and hills make for hard work unless you stick to the central areas. YoBikes operate a cycle rental scheme in central areas for £1 an hour. Download the App to get started.

By ferry

Taking a ferry around the floating harbour is one of the essential experiences for a visitor to Bristol. It's also a reasonable way of getting around the floating harbour. There are two main ferry operators, No. 7 Boats and Bristol Ferry Boats who offer a range of fares. The all-day ticket is good value. www.bristolferry.com and www.numbersevenboattrips.com

On foot

About 20 per cent of Bristol residents walk to work, the highest proportion of any large UK city and the number increased by 40 per cent between 2001 and 2011 according to Bristol Walking Alliance, a pressure group campaigning to make Bristol the best city for walking in the world. It's easy to visit most of the Bristol attractions on foot and large areas of the harbourside and city centre are pedestrianised. www.bristolwalkingalliance.co.uk

A note on the lingo

Do not be alarmed the first time you encounter someone speaking in a broad Bristolian accent. They are unlikely to harm you. As with all accents there are subtle variations across the city, the most obvious being between a Gloucestershire accent (north Bristol) and the Somerset burr from south of the river.

The main linguistic features of the great Bristolian accent include:

● **The post-vocalic 'r':** pronouncing the 'r' where it occurs after a vowel as in caRt, paRty, AlaRm, neveR. Asder (ASDA)

● **The add-on 'er':** Most commonly heard in lover (love), slider (playground slide).

● **Rising Intonation:** When a statement Is made to sound like a question.

● **The Bristol 'l':** Adding an L to the end of words that end in an unstressed vowel as in Australial (Australia), ideal (idea) and areal (area). Also sometimes heard in the middle of words as in drawling (drawing).

For years, speaking in a Bristolian accent was regarded as a sign of simplicity. Indeed, there have been stories over the years of Bristol footballers having to leave teams from outside Bristol because they or their partners and families got the rise taken out of their accent so badly. But, all that has changed, thankfully. The three main champions of the Bristolian accent are football manager Ian Holloway, Little Britain's Vicky Pollard character and clothing shop Beast, whose Bristolian T-shirts, socks and underwear are spreading the word across the world. Here are a few key phrases to help you get the most out of your visit by engaging with the locals:

● **How are you?** How bist?

● **Can I try a pint of cider please?** Zider I up lanlord.

● **Good morning/afternoon/evening.** Awlrite.

● **Listen to/look at that** Ark at ee.

● **Thank you.** Churz.

● **No thank you.** Nah.

● **Thank you for the lift.** Churz drive.

A Dictionary of Bristle

A Dictionary of Bristle by Harry Stoke and Vinny Green is available from Tangent Books for £5.95 from discerning bookshops and from www.tangentbooks.co.uk

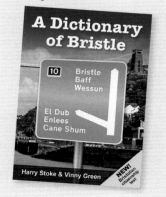

15

30 Things To Do In Bristol

© Destination Bristol

1 Bristol Museum & Art Gallery
Queens Road BS8 1RL | www.bristolmuseums.org.uk

This impressive Edwardian building was gifted to the city by Sir William Henry Wills and designed by his cousin Sir Frank William Wills. It opened in 1905 as the Art Gallery and Museum of Antiquities and now houses a world-class collection in 19 galleries. The city Art Gallery is home to an outstanding collection from medieval to contemporary art. It also boasts one of the finest collections of Chinese glass outside of Asia as well as Ai Weiwei's 'A Ton Of Tea' conceptual piece.

Free entry, donations encouraged, open 10am-5pm, closed Mondays except Bank Holidays.

2 M Shed
Princes Wharf BS1 4RN | www.bristolmuseums.org.uk

Originally a 1950 dockside transit shed, the M Shed tells the story of Bristol from prehistoric times to the 21st century with the emphasis being on it being a 'living museum' where the stories of the past inform present-day Bristol and the future city. The three galleries over two floors are themed around People, Places and Life. Check the website for details of regular special exhibitions.

Free entry, donations encouraged, open 10am-5pm, closed Mondays except Bank Holidays.

© Visit England

3 Red Lodge
Park Row BS1 5LJ | www.bristolmuseums.org.uk

Built in 1590, this Elizabethan home was originally a Tudor lodge and home to a number of families over the years. Fortunately, the last people to live here seem to have gone in a hurry and left their furniture exactly as it was. As you tiptoe around, you half expect them to come bursting through the door at any minute demanding to know what you are doing in their house. A paternalistic group of artists, musicians and writers called the Bristol Savages (formed in 1894) hold their club nights in the gardens of the Red Lodge in a building called the Wigwam.

Open 11am-4pm Saturday-Tuesday, April 1-Dec 31. Students and under-25s free, joint tickets for Georgian House available, see website for prices.

5

© Visit England

4 Georgian House
7 Great George Street BS1 5RR | www.bristolmuseums.org.uk

No. 7 Great George Street is unlike any of its neighbours' houses. There are no Ikea sofas, no washing machines, not even a dimmer switch. This place remains exactly as it was when it was built in 1790. And if you think this is taking retroism too far, fear not, it's a museum, not a deliberate attempt to live uncomfortably. And like its first resident, Bristol slave trader and sugar merchant John Pinney, you can call in and wander around four of the six storeys from kitchen to bedroom as if you own the place. Austerity dominates throughout but there are a few elegant pieces of furniture and some detailed plasterwork to admire, if you like that sort of thing. The Georgian House was home to Pero, an enslaved African Pinney brought back to Bristol from the Montravers Plantation on Nevis in the West Indies. The bridge over the Floating Harbour is named after Pero.

Open 11am-4pm Saturday-Tuesday, April 1-Dec 31. Students and under-25s free, joint tickets for Red House available, see website for prices.

5 Clifton Suspension Bridge
Bridge Road, Clifton BS8 3PA | www.cliftonbridge.org.uk

The world famous Clifton Suspension Bridge was designed by the great Victorian engineer Isambard Kingdom Brunel – or was it? In 2016, new research appeared in the Oxford Dictionary of National Biography suggesting that Brunel had based his design on a patent filed by the great female inventor, engineer and resident of Bristol Sarah Guppy (1770-1852). There's no doubt that Guppy was a significant influence on Brunel and also communicated with Thomas Telford whose Menai Bridge was completed in 1826, but was she the designer? Who knows?

Work began on the Bridge in 1831, but the project was dogged with political and financial difficulties, and by 1843, with only the towers completed, work was abandoned. Brunel died aged only 53 in 1859, but the Clifton Suspension Bridge was completed as his memorial and opened on December 8, 1864. Designed for light horse drawn traffic, it still meets the demands of 21st century commuters with 11-12,000 vehicles crossing it every day.

Walking over the Bridge is a must for any visitor to Bristol. Combine it with a visit to Clifton village and or Ashton Court/Leigh Woods on the other side. There's an excellent visitor centre on the Leigh Woods side of the Bridge.

© Destination Bristol

6 **Where The Wall Street Art Tour** | www.wherethewall.com
Founded by the legendary 'Godfather of Graff' John Nation, Where The Wall street art tours are hugely popular and have won numerous visitor and tourism awards. They run throughout the year on Saturdays and Sundays starting at 11am from College Green next to Banksy's 'Well Hung Man'. The route takes you through the centre of Bristol ending in Stokes Croft. The guides are super-knowledgeable about all aspects of the work and the artists. Where The Wall also offer Upfest tours of South Bristol, private bookings and Introducing Stencil Art Spray Sessions. Booking in advance is essential. **Scan QR code to download Banksy Tour app.**

7 **Underfall Yard**
Cumberland Road BS1 6XG | www.underfallyard.co.uk
Underfall Yard is a working boat yard and also the historic control centre that manages the level of water in the Floating Harbour and removes silt by way of an ingenious system of underwater sluices. The visitor centre features excellent explanations and demonstrations of how the hydraulic sluice system works and there are also hydraulic pump demonstrations using the restored pumps that date back to 1907. The slipway known as a 'heave-up slip' can lift vessels from the water up to 32 metres long and up to 180 tonnes in weight.
The café is a lovely spot to sit outside and take in fine views of the Floating Harbour.
Free entry. The boatyard is open seven days a week all year between 7.30am and 9.30pm (Easter-October) and 9am-5pm (October-Easter). The visitor centre and café is closed Mondays. Opening hours 10am-5pm (Easter to October), and 10am-4pm (October-Easter).

19

8

© Destination Bristol

8 Ferry Trip/Floating Harbour
www.bristolferry.com | www.numbersevenboattrips.com | www.bristolpacket.co.uk

A leisurely stroll around the Floating Harbour is one of the high points of a visit to Bristol. It's traditional to start the day with tea and a bacon sandwich at Brunel's Buttery just past M Shed and see where your perambulations take you. Combine your walk with an all-day ferry ticket to enjoy the harbour by land and from the water.

9 Bristol Zoo
Guthrie Road, Clifton BS8 3HA | www.bristolzoo.org.uk

Zoos, of course aren't for everyone, but if you do visit, you'll find 12 acres of award-winning gardens and 400 species of animals, many of them endangered species. The nine under-cover animal houses makes the zoo an all-weather family option. Some of the favourite attractions include the 180 degree view gorilla house, twilight world the seal and penguin coast, monkey jungle, bug world, meerkat lookout and the aquarium.

ZooRopia is a high ropes course around the zoo gardens that ends with a zip wire, there's an adventure playground, animal encounters sessions and several cafes, although taking a picnic is a good option.

Plan your visit in advance via the website to see animal feeding sessions and to get discounts on tickets.

Open 9am-5pm every day except Christmas Day.

10 Wild Place Project
Blackhorse Hill, Bristol BS10 7TP | www.wildplace.org.uk

Set in park and woodland to the north of Bristol near the M5, the Wild Place Project is Bristol Zoo's conservation park where you'll find okapi, reindeer, bears, wolves, lemurs, giraffes, baboons and more. The aim is to keep the animals in as natural an environment as possible. There's also a Leap of Faith climbing and giant swing feature for kids. Check the website for details of events and animal talks and to save money on tickets. Joint tickets are available with Bristol Zoo and the annual membership is excellent value.

Open 10am-5pm every day except Christmas Day.

© Destination Bristol

11 Cabot Tower/Brandon Hill
Between Park Street and Jacob's Wells Road

The Cabot Tower is a 105ft tower built in 1897 to commemorate John Cabot's voyage from Bristol and the continent of North America in 1497. It's set in the grounds of Brandon Hill, Bristol's oldest park which was granted to the city in 1174 by the Earl of Gloucester. Climbing Cabot Tower to enjoy the panoramic views of Bristol from the top is one of the highlights of a visit to the city. Brandon Hill is a lovely city centre park with ponds and a nature reserve and fine views over the city for those not able to make it up the tower.

Free entry. Cabot Tower is open to visitors from 8.15am-4.30pm every day apart from Christmas Day and New Year's Day.

12 George Müller Museum
Müller House, 7 Cotham Park BS6 6DA | www.mullers.org

Tucked away in Cotham, this one-room museum is housed in the charity offices of the Müllers charitable trust. Their history is traced back to their founder, Christian evangelist George Müller who cared for 10,000 orphans in Bristol at orphan houses in Ashley Down from 1836. The museum houses photographs, artefacts and records from the orphanages.

Free entry. Open 10am-4pm Monday-Friday. Visits must be booked in advance by calling 0117 924 5001 or emailing admin@mullers.org.

© Destination Bristol

13 We The Curious
Anchor Road, Harbourside BS1 5DB | www.wethecurious.org

We The Curious (formerly At-Bristol Science Centre) features more than 300 exhibits encouraging youngsters to explore and interpret science and the natural world, aiming to remove boundaries between science, art, people and ideas. Many of the exhibits are interactive and include an Aardman exhibition where you can become an animator for the day; a walk through a tornado; how to create your own TV show and the UK's first 3D planetarium with full surround sound and awe-inspiring sights from around the universe. Details of regular special events are on the website.

Open daily except Christmas Day. Weekdays 10am-5pm, weekends, school holidays, bank holidays 10am-6pm.

14 Observatory & Durdham Downs
Litfield Road, Clifton BS8 3LT | www.clifton observatory.com

Enjoy a stroll around the Downs which boasts fantastic views over the Avon Gorge from Sea Walls on Circular Road and then take a look at one of Bristol's more curious attractions, the camera obscura and observatory near the Suspension Bridge. Originally a snuff mill, the building was partially destroyed during a gale in 1777. Apparently the sails went round so fast in the storm that the machinery caught fire.

The old mill was rented to the artist William West in 1828 for use as his studio. He installed the camera obscura and cut the underground passage to Ghyston's Cave, sometimes known as the Giants' Cave or Foxhole. The cave's visiting platform can be seen clearly from the Clifton Suspension Bridge, set within the sheer 250-foot cliff face. The camera obscura projects a panoramic view of the surrounding area onto a white surface inside a darkened room. A box on top of the building contains a lens and sloping mirror. Light is reflected vertically downward onto the table, giving a true (not mirror) image. The technique, which originated in the 16th Century, gives best results on bright days. Odd but fascinating.

Entry £4 for adults. Buy online for a discount. Open all year from 10am-4pm (Oct-March), 10am-4pm (April to September. 360 Café open in summer months.

© Philip Vile

15

© Philip Vile

15 Bristol Old Vic
King Street BS1 4ED | www.bristololdvic.org.uk

Built in 1766, Bristol Old Vic is the oldest continuously working theatre in the English-speaking world, and is obviously a great theatre with a wonderful programme in the main auditorium and studio. And since a multi-million pound foyer and front-of-house project was completed in 2018, it's become a destination. For the first time since it was built, the original theatre outside wall has been exposed and forms the centrepiece for the 1766 bar and café that also features a performance area. The ideal place to begin your exploration of King Street, Welsh Back and Queen Square.

16 Ashton Court
Long Ashton BS41 9JN | www.visitbristol.co.uk

The Ashton Court Estate was once the home of the Smyth family, and is now a historic park just across the suspension bridge. It covers 850 acres of woods and grasslands designed by Humphry Repton and features mountain biking courses, pitch and putt and a gold course, a miniature railway and deer park.

17 SS Great Britain
Great Western Dockyard, Gas Ferry Road BS1 6TY | www.ssgreatbritain.org

17

© Destination Bristol

Bristol's leading visitor attraction is also amazingly good value if you plan to return because a ticket gives you free entry for a year after the original visit. Built in Bristol by Isambard Kingdom Brunel, the SS Great Britain was the world's first iron-hulled, screw propeller-driven, steam-powered passenger liner and the only surviving 19th-century example of its type. Launched in 1843 as the world's greatest ocean-going passenger liner, the Great Britain ended her life in 1886. She had been converted to a cargo vessel and was badly damaged in storms off Cape Horn. Her captain, Henry Stap, managed to take shelter in the Falkland Islands, but the ship's owners decided that the cost of repairs were too great and there the SS Great Britain remained. A rescue attempt failed in 1933, but in 1970 a team led by naval architect Ewan Corlett managed to refloat the Great Britain and sail her 8,000 miles across the Atlantic in a floating pontoon pulled by tugs. More than 100,000 people lined the banks of the River Avon on July 19, 1970 to watch the Great Britain return to the dry dock where she was built.

Today the SS Great Britain is a wonderful visitor attraction and museum. You can see the ship from all angles including from below the glass 'sea', tour the weather deck, promenade, dining saloon and inspect the steerage, galley, engine room and holds. You can even climb the mast (in a secure harness). You'll enjoy a real sense of history on board the SS Great Britain, while the Being Brunel museum (opened in 2018) puts on display for the first time many documents and artefacts celebrating the engineer's life and legacy.

See website for ticket details: Open every day except Christmas Eve and Christmas Day. November-March 10am-4.30pm, April-October 10.30am-6pm. Last entry an hour before closing.

18 Snuff Mills
River View, Stapleton BS16 1DL | www.fromewalkway.org.uk

The Frome Valley Walkway follows the river for 18 miles from Castle Park to close to its source near Old Sodbury in the Cotswolds. It's possible to join the Cotswold Way from Old Sodbury, but unless you are a committed hiker, the section of the river at Snuff Mills and Oldbury Court is the most realistic option for a riverside walk. Start the walk at Snuff Mills from the car park at River View. It's a peaceful wooded riverside retreat in the heart of the city with a very special sense of calm and history.

19 People's Republic of Stokes Croft

35 Jamaica St, Stokes Croft BS2 8JP
| www.prsc.org.uk

PRSC is the epicentre of the alternative, radical, political culture and activism that has made Stokes Croft famous around the world. PRSC was founded by Chris Chalkley in September 2007 as a community organisation committed to anti-consumerism and using art (specifically street art) to promote a sense of community ownership, respect and tolerance. PRSC is home to the Outdoor Gallery wall, a screen printing studio and PRSC Radio.

Stokes Croft China is the ceramics faction of the PRSC movement and the kiln and shop are based in Hillgrove Street next door to The Space – a performance and community gallery and bar with a full programme of events, usually with a radical and community focus.

China decorating workshops are held at 14 Hillgrove Street. See website for details.

20 Blaise Castle House and Estate

Henbury Road, Henbury BS10 7QS | www.bristolmuseums.org.uk

There are four distinct attractions on and near this 400-acre estate to the north of Bristol: Blaise House, the grounds and adventure playground, the 'castle' and the remains of nearby Kings Weston Roman villa at Long Cross.

Blaise House is a 19th century mansion, set in 400 acres of parkland, and is home to the city museum's social history collection. Discover everyday objects from centuries past, including Victorian toilets and baths, kitchen and laundry equipment, model trains, dolls, toys and period costume in the museum. The magnificent Picture Room is hung with paintings from the museum's collections.

You can walk along the Hazel stream (quite marshy and spooky even on a bright day) for about 20 minutes as far as the rocky outcrop where you'll find the folly castle built on the site of an Iron Age fort. The castle is opened by volunteers on some summer Sundays. Look out for the flag flying on top of the castle and enjoy panoramic views of the area from the castle roof. The castle was built as a summer house in 1766 by owner of the estate Thomas Farr. He became Master of the Society of Merchant Venturers in 1771 and in 1775 became Mayor of Bristol. Farr was declared bankrupt after the American War Of Independence in 1778.

Pick up the key at Blaise House to visit the remains of the Roman Villa at nearby Long Cross. Entry is free but there's a £10 deposit on the key.

Free entry. Donations encouraged. House open April-December, 11am-4pm.

21 The Matthew
Princes Wharf BS1 4RN
www.matthew.co.uk

© Visit England

The Matthew is a faithful reconstruction of the Tudor ship that put North America on the map when John Cabot sailed from Bristol and discovered Newfoundland in 1497. The stunning replica was built in Bristol to mark the 500th anniversary of Cabot's voyage, and upon her completion she set sail to reconstruct Cabot's original journey. On this historic journey, the Matthew followed the same course to Newfoundland as John Cabot had in 1497, carrying the same number of crew members and taking exactly the same amount of time to complete the crossing. On June 24 1997, the replica of the Matthew was welcomed into port at Bonavista by Queen Elizabeth II.

Today, The Matthew is moored outside M Shed and is open to visitors when in port. There are regular trips from the Floating Harbour through the locks and onto the Avon to Avonmouth which are highly recommended. Check website for details.

22 Aerospace Bristol
Hayes Way, Patchay BS34 5BZ | www.aerospacebristol.org

Abandoned on a disused runway at Filton, north Bristol for more than a decade, the last Concorde to be built now takes pride of place in the £19m Aerospace Bristol Museum that opened in October 2017. Visitors can now follow in the footsteps of world leaders, rock stars and royalty when they step onboard Concorde G-BOAF also known as Alpha Foxtrot.

Filton was the home of Concorde, the Anglo-French supersonic plane that crossed the Atlantic in less than three hours on the edge of space. The planes were built and maintained in Filton, but since their retirement, Concordes in the fleet have been placed in museums around the world. Alpha Foxtrot had remained exposed to the elements since its final flight in 2003.

It's not all about Concorde though Aerospace Bristol takes you from the beginnings of the British and Colonial Aeroplane Company in 1910 to the modern day celebrating the city's long connection with the aviation, aerospace and (more controversially) arms industries.

Open seven days a week apart from Christmas Eve, Christmas Day and Boxing Day, 10am-5pm, last entry 4pm. Like the SS Great Britain, the ticket price includes free return visits for a year. See website for details.

23 Arnos Vale Cemetery
Bath Road, BS4 3EW | www.arnosvale.org.uk

This magnificent 45-acre site opened as a cemetery in 1839 as a 'garden cemetery' inspired by Pere-Lachaise cemetery in Paris and Kensal Green in London. By the time it stopped operating as a cemetery in the 1980s it was the last resting place for more that 300,000 people, but quickly fell into neglect.

Today the cemetery is run by a charitable trust who have gradually cleared overgrown areas, restored the chapels, created a visitor centre, shop and café and organised regular history and nature tours of the cemetery. It's a wonderful green space in the heart of the city packed with history and wildlife.

Free admission. Gates open 9am-5pm every day. Cafe, gift shop exhibitions open 10am-4pm.

24 Palestine Museum and Cultural Centre
27 Broad Street BS1 2HG | www.palmuseumbristol.org

Founded in June 2013, this is the only Palestine museum in Europe. The permanent display of Palestinian heritage, culture and political life takes you on a journey through the history of Palestine, from the late 19th century through to current day events. The museum also highlights the Bristol connection with Palestine, through the Easton Cowboys and Cowgirls football tours and Banksy's work at the Walled Off Hotel and his pieces highlighting the plight of Palestinians. There is a wide range of fair trade Palestinian products for sale, including olive oil, dates, za'atar and crafts.

The vegan Resbite Café is open Monday-Saturday 11am-4pm (5.30pm Weds). Free admission. Donations welcome, Open Saturdays & Sundays 11am to 6pm and on weekdays by special arrangement.

25

© The New Room

25 New Room/John Wesley Chapel
36 The Horsefair BS1 3JE | www.newroombristol.org.uk

Built in 1739, The New Room (John Wesley's Chapel) is the oldest Methodist building in the world. The building is an oddity in the middle of the concrete surroundings of Broadmead – everything around it was destroyed in the Blitz, but the New Room escaped with just a few dislodged roof tiles and broken windows.

It's a fascinating place, steeped in history and atmosphere, but never really seemed to be accorded the importance it deserves as the cradle of Methodism. Then, early in 2015, the New Room was awarded a £2.6 million Heritage Lottery Fund grant having already secured £1.4 million from the Bristol Methodist District. Work began almost immediately on The Horsefair Project – a new visitor centre and entrance to the New Room on the Horsefair side of the site which was officially opened in July 2017.

It's a triumph. The atrium-style building covers the original courtyard giving a sense of being outdoors. There's a bookshop and café, library and study centre and the 12-room museum above the chapel has been completely revamped to provide an excellent insight into the Wesleys and the early days of Methodism. It's one of the most successful new developments in the city and a visit is highly recommended.

There are regular Friday Communion and other services in the chapel and a full programme of events. Check website for details.

Open Monday-Saturday 10.30am-4pm Last entry to Museum 3.30pm. Admission £7 adults, £6 students and seniors, £4 children.

Bristol Cathedral © Visit England

26 Cathedral
College Green BS1 5TJ | www.bristol-cathedral.co.uk

A church has almost certainly stood on the site of Bristol Cathedral for more than 1,000 years, but it came to prominence in 1140 when Robert Fitzhardinge founded the Abbey of St Augustine. The Chapter House and Abbey Gatehouse remain clear to see, and the other remains are to be found within Bristol Cathedral School.
The eastern end of the Cathedral, especially in the choir, gives Bristol Cathedral a unique place in the development of British and European architecture. The nave, choir and aisles are all the same height, making Bristol Cathedral the major example of a hall church in Great Britain and one of the finest to be found anywhere in the world. The famous architectural historian Nikolaus Pevsner described the eastern end as 'superior to anything else built in England and indeed in Europe at the same time'. Guided tours are available on Saturdays, or as arranged directly through the Chapter Clerk.

Free admission. Open every day 8am-6pm Monday to Saturday and 7.20am-5pm on Sundays.

27 St Mary Redcliffe Church
Redcliffe Way BS1 6RA | www.stmaryredcliffe.co.uk

St Mary Redcliffe is a masterpiece of Gothic architecture. The present building dates back to 1292 when it was founded by Simon de Burton, three-times Mayor of Bristol. There is evidence of an earlier church on the site dating back to Saxon times. William Canynges completed the building of the church in the late 14th century and it was famously described by Elizabeth 1 on her visit to Bristol in 1574 as 'The fairest, goodliest, and most famous parish church in England.' St Mary Redcliffe is packed with Bristol history commemorated in its stained glass, tombs and statues.

Free admission. Open 8.30am-5.00pm, Monday to Saturday, and 9.00am-4.00pm on bank holidays. During certain festivals, the Church is only open for worship.

29

© St Nick's Market. Visit England

28 St Nicholas Market
Corn Street, Bristol BS1 1JQ | www.stnicholasmarketbristol.co.uk

Bristol is unusual in that it doesn't have a large Victorian covered market like most UK cities. Instead, we have St Nick's which was established in 1743, almost 100 years before Victoria took the throne. The market is home to more than 60 traders selling everything from flowers to Bristol T-shirts and socks and second-hand records to hot chilli sauce. It's divided into three parts, the Exchange Hall that features a broad selection of items for sale, the Glass Arcade with its excellent take-away world food stalls and the Covered Market, a series of individual shops and alleyways.

29 Gloucester Road & St Mark's Road
www.sweetmart.co.uk | www.glosrdcentral.co.uk

Two of Bristol's most characterful shopping streets. Gloucester Road claims to be the longest street of independent traders in Europe, while St Mark's Road is a hub for Bristol's Asian community with Bristol Sweet Mart at its centre. Check the websites for details of Mayfest and Christmas markets on Gloucester Road, while St Mark's Road is the venue for one of the country's leading Iftars – a festival to celebrate the end of Ramadan.

Robert Louis Stevenson's

Treasure Island Trail
Audio App from the Long John Silver Trust

Image courtesy of Mervyn Peake Estate

A The Treasure Map
Merchant Venturers Almshouses
B The Black Spot
Llandoger Trow
C The Captain's Papers
Welsh Back
D At the Sign of the Spy-Glass
The Hole in the Wall

E What I Heard in the Apple Barrel
Redcliffe Wharf
F The Man of the Island
Redcliffe Caves
G Israel Hands
The Ostrich
H The Fall of the Chieftain
Merchant's Landing

www.longjohnsilvertrust.co.uk

30 Treasure Island Trail
Starts outside Merchant Venturers' Alms House, King Street BS1 4ED
www.longjohnsilvertrust.co.uk | **Scan QR code to download audio app**

The early part of Robert Louis Stevenson's Treasure Island is set in Bristol. Long John Silver was landlord of the Spyglass (the present-day Hole In The Wall pub) and the Hispaniola set sail from Bristol. The Treasure Island Trail is a series of eight barrels around the Floating Harbour which mark a significant place in Treasure Island or are relevant to other books in Bristol's literary heritage such as Robinson Crusoe and Gulliver's Travels. Apart from being a hugely informative literary trail, the barrels also mark a pleasant route around the Floating Harbour. To get the most out of the Treasure Island Trail, download the App that features an audio guide to the trail. It's available from www.treasureislandtrail.cactus.co.uk.

Events Calendar

January/February

Slapstick Silent Comedy Film Festival
www.slapstick.org.uk
Laurel and Hardy, Harold Lloyd, Charlie Chaplin and Buster Keaton blowout at various venues. Usually end of January/ beginning of February.

March

Beer Festival
www.camrabristol.org.uk
Now settled into a long-term venue at the Brunel Passenger Shed at Temple Meads station, the Bristol Beer Festival is usually held on the last weekend in March. At the last count it featured more than 125 real ales and about 40 ciders.

International Jazz & Blues Festival
www.bristoljazzandbluesfest.com
From humble beginnings in 2012 the festival has grown hugely to become one of the city's biggest music events fuelled by a mission to make jazz and blues accessible to people of all ages and from all walks of life.

April

Storytelling festival
www.bristolstoryfest.org
Storyfest aims to bring people together by harnessing the power of storytelling.

May

Cheese Rolling
www.gloucestershirelive.co.uk
In a tradition that dates back to the 1700s, country folk congregate at Coopers Hill near Brockworth between Cheltenham and Stroud and chase a bloody great big Double Gloucester down the hill. The event takes place on Whit Bank Holiday Monday despite annual health and safety attempts to prevent it.

Crimefest
www.crimefest.com
One of the biggest crime fiction events in Europe.

Dot To Dot
www.dottodotfestival.co.uk
New music festival held across small venues in Bristol, Nottingham and Manchester usually over the last weekend in May.

Folk festival
www.bristolfolkfestival.org
Held for the first time in 32 years in 2011 and now a regular event at various venues across town. Usually the first full week of May.

Foodies Festival
www.foodiesfestival.com
One of the biggest food events in the country is held on the Downs, over a long weekend in mid May.

Jack in the Green
www.home.freeuk.net/bristoljack

Pagan frivolity featuring a procession of musicians and dancers dawdling behind Jack from the Harbourside to Horfield Common in a celebration of summer. Expect Morris dancers. Held on the first Saturday in May.

Love saves the day
www.lovesavestheday.org

Bristol's biggest party. Held in Eastville Park at the end of May, Love Saves the Day launched in 2011 and swiftly established itself as *the* Bristol Festival.

Mayfest
www.mayfestbristol.co.uk

Biennial (even number years) festival of contemporary theatre with a broad range of unusual, playful and ambitious work from leading theatre makers from Bristol, the UK and beyond. Produced in collaboration with Bristol Old Vic and works in partnership with other key arts venues across Bristol. Usually held last two weeks of May.

Model Railway Exhibition
www.bristolmodrailex.co.uk

One of the biggest and widely attended model railway exhibitions in the country, the Bristol show has been held since 1968. It takes place over the first weekend of May at Thornbury Leisure Centre. Among the notable visitors over the years is devilish pop supremo and steam locomotive owner Pete Waterman.

Walkfest
www.bristolwalkfest.com

More than 150 walks and events for all ages and all abilities. The month-long festival is the UK's largest urban celebration of walking. Takes place throughout May.

June

Bike Fest
www.bike-fest.com

Increasingly popular bike racing event at Ashton Court. Usually end of June.

Craft Beer Festival
www.bristolcraftbeerfestival.co.uk

Began life in Motion at the back of Temple Meads, but in 2018 the 'carnival of craft beer' moved to Harbourside and became mega.

Festival of Nature & Big Green Week
www.bnhc.org.uk

Centred around the Millenium Square and Queen Square, the festival is organised by the Natural History Consortium and features talks, walks, animal encounters, cookery, real food, green markets, books, art and much more. Usually the second weekend in June at the beginning of Big Green Week.

Refugee Week Big Fun Day
www.bristolrefugeefestival.org

Festival of dance, music, art and food in Queen Square celebrating the contribution to Bristol's community of asylum seekers and refugees.

Upfest Urban Paint Festival
www.upfest.co.uk

There's no Upfest in 2019, but Europe's largest (free) urban paint festival is set to return in 2020.

July

Harbour Festival
www.bristolharbourfestival.co.uk

Bristol's biggest party. In recent years organisers have tried to re-focus the event on Bristol's maritime heritage because it was in danger of becoming a huge piss-up in Queen Square. Music, events, stalls, performance all set around the Floating Harbour.

Jamaica Street Studios Open Day
www.jamaicastreetartists.co.uk
This Stokes Croft studio with a big reputation throws open its doors in July.

Pride
wwbristolpride.co.uk
The LGBTQ celebration has moved to different sites as it has grown in popularity and now takes place on the Downs.

Priddy Folk Festival
www.priddyfolk.org
Mendip folk festival usually held early July. The Priddy Festival started in 1991 as a Parent Teacher Association fundraiser for the village hall and although it is now a major event on the folk circuit, funds are still fed back into the village.

St Paul's Carnival
www.stpaulscarnival.net
Legendary street fun in the multi-cultural heart of Bristol. Floats, PA battles, lots of food, drink and nocturnal liveliness. First Saturday of July.

St Werburgh's City Farm Summer Fair
@stwerburghscityfarm
Music, craft workshops, carnival procession. Big fun. Usually late June/ early July.

August

Amnesty International Garden Party
www.sites.google.com/view/amnestybristolgroup/home
Fundraiser for the very active local Amnesty International group and a wonderful and rare opportunity to explore the grounds of Goldney House, one of Bristol's best preserved 18th-Century houses, famous for its grotto. Usually held on the first Sunday in August.

Balloon Fiesta
www.bristolballoonfiesta.co.uk
If the tacky cynicism of the funfair and the squawkings of the wannabe 'pop' acts don't appeal, go instead to the Avon Gorge Hotel's patio bar and watch Europe's finest hot-air balloons drift majestically by. Mid August at the Ashton Court Estate

Islamic Cultural Fayre
www.bmcs.org.uk
Since its beginnings in 1998, the Islamic Cultural Fayre has grown into a large family funday in Eastville Park with food, craft stalls, performances and a five-a-side football tournament.

Redfest
@redfestbristol
Held in St George's Park, this annual arts festival includes music, art, kids stuff, circus performances and theatre.

Valleyfest
www.valleyfest.co.uk
Lovely, laid-back (but fast-growing) festival on farmer Luke Hassell's land overlooking Chew Valley Lake.

September

Doors Open Day
www.bristolopendoors.org.uk
Popular event in which the finer private, closed and inaccessible buildings and spaces of Bristol are opened to the public in mid September.

Encounters Short Film Festival
www.encounters-festival.org.uk
Showcases the best in UK and international short filmmaking. Cool scene for aspiring industry types, schmoozers and blaggers.

Half Marathon
www.greatrun.org
13-mile jog which is sometimes sponsored by BUPA but which costs the NHS a fortune in ferrying out-of-breath, blistered people to hospital and treating them. Mid-September.

Tokyo World
www.tokyoworld.org
Drum 'n' bass, hip-hop and grime are at the core of this Eastville Park event which increasingly expands its horizons to include more live bands and new artists.

October

Cajun and Zydeco Festival
www.bristolcajunfestival.com
A weekend of Louisiana-style music, dance, food and drink at the Folk House. Started in 2004 and seems to have selected a mid October regular date.

Festival of literature
www.bristolliteraturefestival.org
Grass-roots literature festival aimed at celebrating the city's authors, novelists and poets.

Royal West of England Academy Autumn exhibition
www.rwa.org.uk
There are exhibitions here all year, but one of the highlights is the annual Autumn Exhibition between October and December when more than 600 works of painting, printmaking, sculpture and architecture are selected by open submission.

Wildscreen
www.wildscreenfestival.org
Biennial filmfest for the wildlife media industry held in even number years (2020)

November

Front Room Art Trail, Totterdown
www.frontroom.org.uk
Go and look at art in people's front rooms, in their cellars, in their kitchens and even in the pub. The Totterdown trail was the first one, now just about every area of Bristol has followed suit. Usually held the third weekend in November.

December

Marshfield Mummers
This ancient mystery play is performed on Boxing Day (unless it's a Sunday) by Marshfield villagers wearing costumes made from torn up newspaper. There's carol singing at 10.30am before the Mummers perform the play four times at different points in the village and then adjourn to the Catherine Wheel.

Festival of Ideas
Bristol Festival of Ideas is the city's leading cultural entity staging talks and events throughout the year. It was established in 2005 and gathered momentum as part of Bristol's (failed) bid to be Capital of Culture in 2008. Andrew Kelly, who led that bid, is the driving force behind FOI which is an initiative of Bristol Cultural Development Partnership which is backed by the council, BusinessWest, Bristol University and the University of the West of England.
www.ideasfestival.co.uk

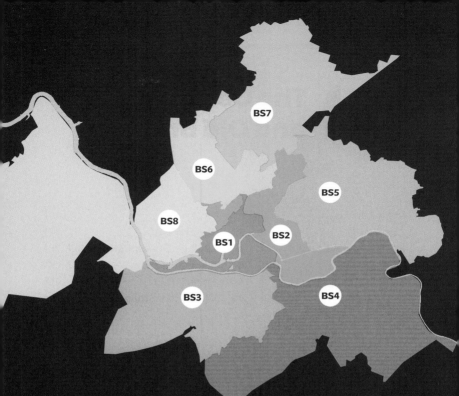

Area Guides

BS1 The Centre and Old Bristol

Earthquakes, floods, riots, slavery, bandits, bombs and the most severe traffic congestion anywhere outside London. The square miles that make up Bristol's heartland have seen it all since their Saxon beginnings. Little pieces of history lurk in every corner...

The Centre

The Centre (so named because it used to be the old tram centre) has undergone several facelifts and traffic reorganisations in recent decades. These were all looked down on by the landmark Bristol Hippodrome which was built by Oswald Stoll in 1912 and is one of the largest stages in England outside of the West End. Cary Grant worked there before he joined a travelling troupe and went to America to seek his fortune.

Years ago, the Hippodrome used to have an illuminated board on the roof that displayed messages. So it was traditional to arrange for your Uncle Bill to be on the Centre while 'Happy Birthday Uncle Bill' was displayed on top of the Hippodrome. Oh, for the simple pleasures...

The Centre is now a semi-pedestrianised playground, complete with cobbles and sculptures. The not-very-convincing fountains were once described by a Lord Mayor as being 'Like a bunch of old men peeing.' and are now routinely boarded over when events take place. But while we're on the subject of peeing, beware the notorious cab queue on St Augustine's Parade.

The Centre, as you see it today, is one of the most controversial developments in Bristol's recent history. Until 1892, the River Frome flowed through the Centre and into the Floating Harbour. It still does, but the Centre was built over it. The City Council decided to redevelop the Centre for the millennium and considered bold plans to re-open the Frome and ban cars. Instead, they opted to redirect traffic around the Centre, making it a car-snarled bottleneck.

Further traffic changes were put in place in 2018 and the Centre is actually a lot better than it used to be. The fountains, which dribble so unconvincingly, are supposed to provide a cascade of water dancing in coloured lights. Two years after they were installed, the City Council claimed that the constructors had still not provided the software package to create this effect.

Once, the excellent Falafel King was the only street food outlet but now regular stalls are starting to make the Centre more than just somewhere you walk across. The Electricity House end of the Centre was redeveloped in 2017/18 as part of the MetroBus reorganisation. It's effectively created a large skateboard area and has also given added prominence to the statue of slave trader Edward Colston which sits beneath the Colston Tower, just yards from where the slave ships set sail.

Harbourside & Cargo

Fountains and dickheads apart, the whole Harbourside has been transformed in recent decades as part of the area's massive regeneration programme. The Harbourside is certainly a whole lot better than it used to be – and you'd have a right to expect that because the 11-acre redevelopment cost more than £450 million. We The Curious (previously called At-Bristol), The Aquarium and M Shed

Past Notes
1140 Building of St Augustine's Abbey, later to become Bristol Cathedral.
1239 River Frome diverted to increase trade at the port.
1654 Destruction of Bristol Castle by Cromwell.
1702 Queen Square built.
1831 Riots in Queen Square. Mansion House and Customs House destroyed.

Cargo at Wapping Wharf is one of Bristol's more imaginative recent developments

showpieces are the main attractions in the tourist brochures. But At-Bristol/ Wildwalk wasn't an immediate financial success and had to be bailed out with a £500,000 City Council sub in 2003, so let's not forget about the other places that have propped up the Harbourside for so long.

There are those old favourites, the Watershed, Architecture Centre, YHA and the refurbished Arnolfini which are linked by the 'ear-trumpeted' Pero's Bridge. Designed by Irish artist, Eilis O'Connell, the bridge is named after an enslaved African who was brought to Bristol from Nevis Island in the 17th Century. If it's heritage you're after, the SS Great Britain, the Matthew, and the £27 million M Shed (the old Industrial Museum) which opened in June 2011 will plunge you deep into the depths of Bristol's maritime past. If this doesn't satisfy your lust for the sea, try a guided tour offered by the Bristol Ferry Boat Company and Bristol Packet.

The most recent addition to the Harbourside is the Wapping Wharf housing development behind M Shed and the foodie and shopping area of Cargo and Cargo 2. Based on the London Boxpark model in Shoreditch and Croydon, Cargo combines permanent structures with units housed in shipping containers. The retailers include some of Bristol's finest independent brands such as Fig.1 Interiors, Mabboo clothing, Bristol Cider Shop, Biblos Calypso Kitchen, Box-E, Oliver's Ice Cream, the Wild Beer Bar, the Pickled Brisket and Salt 'n' Malt to name but a few.

Of course, it's all achingly trendy and everso Shoreditch hipster, but compared to the mediocrity of most of the Harbourside development, it's an interesting and lively destination with a sense of space and confidence.

The other major development on Harbourside is the restoration of Underfall Yard at the far end of the Floating Harbour between the Nova Scotia and Cottage pubs. To understand the importance of Underfall Yard you'll need to know a bit about the history of Bristol Docks. The original city docks were tidal and because the Avon has one of the highest tidal ranges in the world (up to 15 metres), ships would float at high tide and sit in the mud at low tide. By the mid-eighteenth century Bristol was beginning to lose trade because of the inconvenience of the ships being grounded and the risk of fire spreading from ship to ship at low tide.

Various plans were suggested to create a non-tidal harbour, but it wasn't until 1802 that civil engineer William Jessop was engaged to come up with a solution. That solution was the New Cut, the 1.8-mile artificial waterway that runs from the Underfall sluices at Cumberland Basin to the Netham Weir and Totterdown Basin.

It took thousands of Navvies from May 1804 to May 1809 to dig the channel. At the celebration dinner at Spike Island, 1,000 Navvies were each given a gallon of strong beer and the almighty piss-up descended into an mass punch-up then into a riot which was eventually suppressed by the press gang.

So by diverting the Avon, a Floating Harbour was created, but it suffered from severe silting and in the 1830s Brunel developed an underfall sluice system as a solution and Underfall Yard became the dock maintenance centre for controlling the sluices. In the 1880s, under docks engineer John Ward Girdlestone, the whole yard was rebuilt to provide a single site for the workforce who maintained the Floating Harbour including plumbers, electricians, divers and engineers. It is one of the few surviving Victorian dock workshops in the world, but by the 1990s it was derelict and only the efforts of the Underfall Yard Trust saved it from being lost altogether. They secured £3 million of Heritage Lottery Funding and by 2016 they had renovated the historic slipway, built a visitor centre around the pump room, restored the buildings, opened a café and created a calendar of Floating Harbour-related events. It's a fascinating place. Don't miss it.

The Harbourside is one of the best things about Bristol, not so much for the corporate regeneration, nor the profusion of theme bars and clubs, but because it's a lovely place to stroll around the water. On warm evenings, drinking outside the Arnolfini is still the venue of choice for Bristol's budding bohemians and artists.

A Tour Of Old Bristol

The secrets of the medieval city revealed...

1. St Nicholas Church, St Nicholas Street

Site of an odd annual ceremony in which school girls pay homage to their 17th-century male benefactor. The pupils from Red Maids School hold a service in front of an effigy of John Whitson in the church's medieval crypt. Whitson, merchant, Mayor and Member of Parliament for Bristol, died in 1629 after falling off his horse. He bequeathed cash for a hospital for '40 poor women children' to be 'apparelled in Red Cloth'.

2. Victoria Fountain, St Nicholas Street

Designed by the Coalbrookdale Iron Company of Shropshire in 1859 to mark Queen Victoria's 40th birthday.

3. Veiled Lady, St Nicholas Street

If you face the Boardroom bar and look at the shop to the right, you'll spot a row of four figures on the wall. The second from the right appears to have no face. This is the Veiled Lady. Nobody knows who she is or what she signifies.

4. Corn Exchange and Nails, Corn Street

John Woods designed the Palladian-fronted Corn Exchange in 1743, when the corn trade was at its height. The bronze pillars outside are the nails. Traders did business over the nails before the Corn Exchange was built. When the deal was done, the merchants handed over their groats and guineas and literally 'paid on the nail.'

5. Commercial Rooms, Corn Street

It was in the Commercial Rooms that merchants flexed their political muscle. In 1811, John McAdam (who invented Tarmac) became the first president of the Commercial Rooms. The three statues outside represent the City, Commerce and Navigation; the relief over the door shows Britannia with Neptune and Minerva receiving tributes.

6. Harbour Hotel, Corn Street

Opposite the Corn Exchange, originally a Lloyds bank built in 1857 and based on the Library of St Mark's in Venice. It is the city's best example of Victorian High Renaissance style. Check out the frieze on the wall. It is believed this is the site of the Bush Inn portrayed by Charles Dickens in *The Pickwick Papers*.

7. All Saints Church, Corn Street

One of three churches at the crossroads of the Medieval city. There has been a church here since 1066. The tower and cupular were built between 1712 and 1717. All Saints is now a Diocesan Education and Resource Centre and is not usually open to the public. The church houses a monument to Bristol slave trader Edward Colston, sculpted by Rysbrack, who did the William lll statue in Queen Square.

8. Christ Church, Broad Street

The original Christ Church St Ewan was first mentioned in the 12th Century, but the current one was built in 1790 by William Paty. The church is best known for its clock (Henry Williams, 1883)

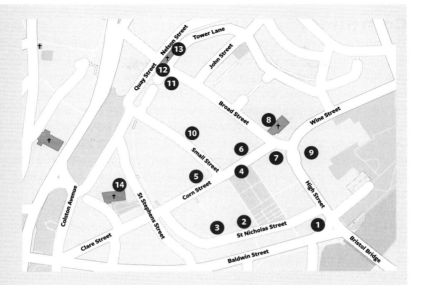

where two quarterjacks dating from 1728 strike the bells every 15 minutes.

9. High Cross
The site of the original Medieval High Cross. A replica of the High Cross now sits in Berkeley Square, off Park Street.

10. Old Guildhall, Small Street
The site of Judge Jeffreys' Bloody Assizes, held after the Monmouth rebellion of 1685. Six people were hanged and Judge Jeffreys called the Bristol rebels 'mere sons of dunghills'.

11. Edward Everard Building, Broad Street
The facade of Carrera marbleware was inspired by the William Morris arts and crafts revival. It was built in 1900-1901 as Edward Everard's Printing Works. Figures on the front are of Gutenburg, who invented a printing process in the 15th Century, and Morris, who helped revive fine printing in the 19th century.

12. St John The Baptist, Tower Lane
The church of St John the Baptist or St John on the Wall incorporates the only surviving Medieval gateway on the city walls. The existing church dates back to the 14th Century. Inside, there's an Upper Church and a Crypt. The figures on the outside wall are Brennus and Belinus, legendary founders of Bristol.

13. St John's Conduit, Nelson Street
This 14th century water supply carried water from Brandon Hill to a Carmelite friary. The parishioners of St John's were allowed to use the overflow from the system. For a short time in World War Two, this was the only water supply for the city centre.

14. St Stephen's Church
The magnificent 152-foot Gothic perpendicular tower dates back to 1470. It has been restored three times following storm damage in 1703, 1914 and 1970.

Corn Street

The rebirth of a city was never going to work on the strength of a few flashy multimedia projects alone. It's the sudden explosion in the centre's nightlife that has really put the spring in its heels. Now dizzy with pseudo-sophisticated style-bars, Corn Street used to be the place where most of the city's business dealings were conducted before the Corn Exchange was built. Transactions were carried out on four flat-topped bronze pillars called the nails. The bronze pillars still stand in Corn Street today and are the origin of the phrase 'to pay on the nail'. Bath, and some other towns with nails, also claim ownership of this phrase. Two of the nails on Corn Street are Elizabethan (1594). The others date from 1625 and 1631.

More recent history can be found on Broad Street, home to the Grand Hotel which has never lived down the day in 1964 when it refused entry to The Rolling Stones because they weren't wearing jackets and ties. 'I realised the young gentleman was something of a celebrity,' said head waiter Dick Court of Mick Jagger, 'but I would feel compelled to refuse anyone – even a king – if he did not dress correctly'. Mick and the boys probably headed off to King Street, an ancient pub-strewn badlands with many a story to tell.

St Nicholas Market

St Nick's Market dates back to 1743 and looks even older. It is divided into three parts – Exchange Hall, Glass Arcade and Covered Market. You'll find flowers, Beast's Bristol T-shirts, Wanted Records, excellent take-away food, vintage clothes, jewellery, second-hand books, crockery, sweets, a milliner, many cafes, old prints and a stall specialising in hot chilli sauce. The market is undergoing a resurgence – particularly for food. The Spice Up Your Life curry cafe in All Saints Lane is outstanding, the Moroccan Al Madinha does tasty tagines, Portuguese Taste offers authentic Iberian stews, there's Caribbean and Italian food, falafel, sausages, Pieminister pies and more. Outside in Corn Street, there's a Farmers' Market on Wednesdays. St Nick's was originally built to get traders off the cluttered streets and has been added to over the years. Its last renovation in 2003 cost more than £300,000.

King Street

King Street runs parallel to Baldwin Street, next to Queen Square. It's now Bristol's theatreland but once led down to the thriving docks at Welsh Back. The Llandoger Trow pub dates from 1664 and used to be the sort of place you went to if you were fond of wearing eye patches and carrying parrots on your shoulder. Originally, the pub occupied one of five buildings on the current site and was built on marshland that covered the area between the Centre, Welsh Back and Queen Square. The pub's odd name comes from Captain Hawkins who retired to run it after sailing a trow – a flat-bottomed sailing barge – between South Wales and Bristol. The Llandoger part comes from Llandogo, a village on the Wye, perhaps Hawkins' home. Robert Louis Stevenson apparently used to drink there and it's possible that it's the basis for the Spy Glass in Treasure Island whose landlord was Long John Silver, though the nearby Hole in the Wall is a far more likely contender. It's said that Daniel Defoe met Alexander Selkirk in the Llandoger and Selkirk's tale of being shipwrecked and marooned was the inspiration for *Robinson Crusoe* (published in 1719). It's more likely that the two met in a long-gone inn called the Star near Bristol castle. It's also likely that Edward Teach of Redcliffe (aka Blackbeard) may have been a regular when he wasn't pirating. The pub closed in May 2019 with its future in doubt.

Certainly, Woodes Rogers, the privateer, explorer and colonial governor who lived in Queen Square, popped in for a quick grog. There was a network of tunnels leading to the waterfront that would have been used by smugglers, or by customers fleeing the press gangs. The remains of one tunnel were found but destroyed during refurbishment in 1962. Legend has

---

Five Old Bristol Streets

1. Johnny Ball Lane: Not, as most people think, a misplaced homage to Zoe's dad. This dodgy looking alleyway near Christmas Steps is actually named after an 18th-Century local character of the same name.

2. Nelson Street: Found itself the subject of a campaign by Venue magazine who wanted it restored to its original medieval name: Gropecunt Lane.

3. Pitch and Pay Lane: Used as a line of segregation between the infected city and the countryside during the Black Death. Villagers threw their produce over to the townsfolk who threw back their coins in payment.

4. Wade Street: Named after an extremely unpopular bloke called Nathaniel Wade who was a conspirator with the Duke of Monmouth in the rebellion of 1685.

5. There and Back Again Lane: Appropriately blunt name for the pointless little cul-de-sac opposite Pizza Express just off Park Street. Also the title of a Bristol-based Sarah Records compilation album featuring such luminaries as the Field Mice and the Sea Urchins.

The Llandoger Trow. What does the future hold for Bristol's famous dockside inn?

it that the original pub's ceiling was painted with scantily-clad women but no evidence of this has been found.

King Street is also home to the Theatre Royal and the Bristol Old Vic. The Theatre Royal was opened on 30 May 1766 and survived plans in World War Two to turn it into a fruit warehouse. In 1946, the Old Vic Theatre Company made its home there and the entire theatre complex is now known as the Old Vic, encompassing the Theatre Royal and the New Vic Studio. It is the oldest continuously working theatre in England and one of the first theatres to be based on a horseshoe-shaped auditorium.

A major refurbishment of the Georgian auditorium was completed in 2012. In 2018 a two-year £25 million project to transform the foyer, create a new studio and restore the Cooper's Hall as an event space was completed. The project exposed the original theatre wall and created an excellent bar, café and performance space that should be on your list of places to visit regardless of whether or not you intend to take in a show.

King Street also has a rich musical heritage. Not only is it home to legendary jazz venue the Old Duke but the old Granary nightclub (now Loch Fyne) on Welsh Back used to attract names such as Muddy Waters, Thin Lizzy and Led Zeppelin. The Granary had the worst toilets this side of Glastonbury – dimly lit and wet, with a door that stuck.

King Street is the craft beer centre of Bristol (or the Beermuda Triangle) with Small Bar, the Beer Emporium, the Naval Volunteer and King Street

Brew House all specialising in expensive brews.

At the bottom of King Street, Welsh Back boasts a raft of new hotels, bars and restaurants. Step out of the stylish Brigstow Hotel opposite the Glass Boat restaurant and stroll along the cobbles past the Spyglass and Apple cider boat, past the Granary (Loch Fyne) and take a right turn into the restored and traffic-free Queen Square. Check out the equestrian bronze statue by Rysbrack of William III, which dates from the 1730s. During World War Two, it was removed for safety to Badminton Park, home of the Duke of Beaufort. It was replaced in the Square after repairs in 1948.

Head through the gap in the buildings on the left of Queen Square and you'll come face to face with hip dockside eateries Riverstation, Severnshed and the award-winning Mud Dock Cafe or the still-floating Thekla nightclub.

The Thekla has a glorious past. Ki Longfellow-Stanshall and her surrealist performer husband Viv Stanshall (of Bonzo Dog Doo Dah Band and Sir Henry Rawlinson fame) found the German-built boat in a dockyard in Sunderland.

Ki restored her and sailed her round Britain to Bristol with a rookie crew and no insurance. The Thekla (which had been renamed the Old Profanity Showboat) was opened in 1983 as a music venue. In December 1985, the couple staged the English comic opera Stinkfoot on board the Thekla. This truly remarkable piece of theatre was described by *Evening Post* theatre critic, the late David Harrison, as: 'a wondrous collection of bizarre characters, eccentric ideas, and at least one top ten contender among the songs'. Stanshall's daughter Sydney promoted at the Thekla into the 1990s. Viv Stanshall died in a fire at his London home in 1995 and the rest of the family now live in America. The Thekla remains a cutting-edge music venue.

St Thomas

The area on the other side of Bristol Bridge from Baldwin Street was part of Bristol's original medieval settlement with remains of buildings dating back to the 12th century discovered in excavations for various building projects. It has long been a barren collection of half-finished developments, corner shops, billboards and bathroom showrooms.

Since the 1990s, the old dockside warehouses have been developed into (even more) posh apartments and in 2016 work began on a huge building project to transform the neglected area into the Redcliff Quarter (some place names are Redcliff, others Redcliffe) which according to the developers will be 'a bustling new neighbourhood for Bristol, bringing together a unique mix of artisan cuisine, an urban lifestyle hotel, characterful apartments and offices.' The centerpiece is the 22-storey Redcliff Tower hotel development.

The old Courage Brewery that looks over the Floating Harbour to Castle Park now houses 38 apartments and one- and two-bedroom flats – the 'prem lofts' would set you back about £500,000 when they went on the market in 2004, but a one-bed apartment was a mere £170,000. Local CAMRA real ale activists from the *Pints West* publication suggested the site be converted into a museum and visitor centre celebrating the tradition of beer-making in the city. The Council decided flats were a better idea.

There are several decent pubs in St Thomas including the Cornubia and King's Arms. Ye Shakespeare (78 Victoria Street) claims to be one of the oldest (built in 1636) and the Fleece and Firkin (12 St Thomas Street) has been one of Bristol's leading live music venues since the early 1980s. The Seven Stars next door to The Fleece was the setting for a series of hearings held by anti-slaver Thomas Clarkson in 1787 that helped lead to the abolition of slavery.

Redcliffe

Redcliffe used to comprise a tower block development, St Mary Redcliffe Church, a couple of hotels, three pubs, a school and traffic-snarled dual carriageways. But then the old General Hospital was developed into fancy flats and Westbury-on-Trym's Michelin-starred restaurant Casa Mia opened at The General. In 2016, the Pi Shop pizza restaurant and Paco Tapas opened next door.

Despite the foodie invasion, Redcliffe will always be best known for St Mary Redcliffe Church. The church was effectively put in the middle of a roundabout, flanked on all sides by major roads, as part of the dreadful outer circuit scheme of the early 1970s. In the Middle Ages, Redcliffe was outside the city walls and there was great rivalry with the port of Bristol on the opposite side of the river. The area is steeped in history but sadly, apart from the church, very little remains thanks to a combination of the Luftwaffe and the city planners. The church is still one of the finest sights in Bristol. The present building was founded in 1292 by Simon de Burton, three times Mayor of Bristol, although there was an earlier church on the site. William Canynges Senior completed the building of the church, which was then known as St Mary de Radeclive, back in the late 14th Century.

In 1446, the church was struck by lightning and badly damaged. Canynges' grandson, William, was responsible for funding much of the necessary rebuilding. His first celebration of mass at the church in 1468 is still commemorated annually. At this ceremony, called the Rush Service, the church floor is strewn with rushes and rosemary in memory of those ancient times. There is a richly-decorated Canynges tomb where his wife is buried and also a simpler one showing him in his priest's robes.

We will resist the temptation to mention the over-used quotation by Queen Elizabeth I about St Mary Redcliffe and instead mention some more recent history. During an air raid in 1941, a bomb threw a tram rail into the air and it became embedded in the churchyard turf. It remains there today, complete with a plaque.

Broadmead

Castle Street and St Mary Le Port Street used to connect Old Market and St Nick's Market and was the centre of Bristol until the area was completely destroyed by German bombs in 1940. The remains of the old city were cleared after the war and replaced with the Broadmead shopping centre. Despite various efforts to invigorate it over the years, dreary Broadmead has struggled and in 2006 work began at the bottom of the M32 on realising the planners' vision for 21st-Century shopping in Bristol. Concrete crumbled, bridges were dismantled, carpet showrooms sacrificed, all in the name of the new Broadmead (or the Merchants' Quarter, as it was going to be called, until the developers eventually admitted it was a crap name and called it Cabot Circus).

Cabot Circus opened in Autumn 2008 – just in time for the credit crunch. The £500 million makeover attracted more than 100 new shops, a state-of-the-art cinema complex, as well as student housing, bars, restaurants and thousands of parking spaces. Harvey Nicks is the flagship store which nestles under a 17-storey apartment block.

The Broadmead redevelopment sparked a fierce debate that typifies criticism in some quarters that Bristol City Council has handed the city over to developers at the expense of the interests of long-standing residents. In December 2002, the City Council gave the go-ahead for the regeneration of the area promising a '24-hour living city'. The plan relied on rerouting the bottom of the M32 to allow Broadmead to expand towards St Paul's.

The Council would claim that this is an example of visionary inner-city regeneration in partnership with blue-chip developers. In reality, however, it meant that people who live in rented homes in St Paul's (the largest concentration of rented homes in Bristol) would be kicked out to accommodate well-heeled newcomers when the area became prime real estate. The population of St Paul's had already seen much of its community

John Wesley's New Room

Hidden in Broadmead is the birthplace of Methodism...

Built in 1739, The New Room (John Wesley's Chapel) is the oldest Methodist building in the world. The building in an oddity in the middle of the concrete surroundings of Broadmead – everything around it was destroyed in the Blitz, but the New Room escaped with just dislodged roof tiles and broken windows.

Much of what developed into the Methodist movement was initiated at the New Room. In his definitive study, *The Cradle of Methodism* (New Room Publications) G.M. Best, former Warden of the New Room, says: 'Among other things the building acted as a food bank, as a school for the poor and as one of the first free medical dispensaries, and its early members championed prison reform in Bristol. From it John Wesley attacked the consumerism that was creating a huge gulf between the rich and the poor, spoke out for a living wage for workers, encouraged women to take leadership roles and vigorously campaigned against the slave trade.'

Despite its huge historical significance, the New Room, never seemed to be afforded the respect it deserves. Then in February 201S it was awarded a £2.6 million grant by the Heritage Lottery Fund having already secured £1.4 million from the Bristol Methodist District from the sale of Methodist International House in the city. Work began almost immediately on the Horsefair Project – a new visitor centre and entrance to the New Room on the Horsefair side of the

site and it was officially opened in July 2017. It's a triumph. The atrium-style building covers the original courtyard giving a sense of being outdoors. There's a bookshop and cafe on the ground floor, seating in the courtyard and a door leads into the chapel.

The wide doorways and lifts mean that for the first time the entire building (including the upstairs) is accessible to wheelchair users. On the first floor there's an education room and library with 12 stacks. This houses the existing New Room archive and should attract Methodist collections from throughout the UK and perhaps the world.

The second floor museum takes you into the rooms above the chapel where Wesley lived. The designers of the new museum, Cod Steaks (an award-winning Bristol-based design and build company), have retained the simplicity or the original, but added so much in terms of content and context. Although it's a small museum it's packed with information and heritage. There's no hi-tech gadgetry, although audio guides are available.

There's a deep sense of history in these rooms, perhaps best captured in the windows looking down onto the pulpit in the chapel below. Those early Methodists scratched their names into the glass and they are still there today.

● *John Wesley's Chapel, 36 The Horsefair BS1 3JE. For details of opening times and entrance price to museum, go to www. newroombristol.org.uk.*

destroyed to build the M32 and a wave of gentrification has put more pressure on the well-established community.

College Green, Cathedral and Central Library

College Green at the bottom of Park Street is where the skateboarders congregate after tearing down the hill. It's also a pleasant spot to enjoy a lunchtime sandwich. It's dominated by the Cathedral, Central Library and City Hall (formerly the Council House or 'Counts Louse' in Bristolese) which was commissioned in 1935 when the local authority outgrew its Corn Street base but, because of the war, was not finished until 1956.

Brunel House behind the Council House was originally called the Royal Western Hotel, it was constructed by Brunel as a hotel for passengers disembarking from the Great Western Railway to stay overnight before boarding the SS Great Britain to sail to America. A proposed station near the Cathedral was never built and the hotel eventually became council offices.

There has been a religious building on the site of the Cathedral for more than 1,000 years. The history of the existing cathedral dates back to 1140 when wealthy merchant Robert Fitzhardinge invited monks to set up residence in what was then known as St Augustine's Abbey. Since then, the history of the Cathedral has been one of gradual religious and aesthetic progression. The Cathedral itself was established in 1542 and finished by architect George Edmund Street in 1868.

Just along from the Cathedral sits the Central Library, one of the greatest public buildings in the country. The first recorded public library in Bristol was founded in 1613 when a merchant called Robert Redwood gave his home in King Street to the city for conversion into a library. In 1740, a new Library was built on the same site and, in 1906, the Central Library was moved to its current site next to the Cathedral. There is a room at the library called the Bristol Room which is a copy of the old King Street library. It is not open to the public, but you can request a visit.

The library was designed in 1902 by Charles Holden, who later gained fame as the architect of many London Underground stations. Building work was funded by a bequest of £50,000 from Vincent Stuckey Lean. Although its influences are Medieval/Tudor, this stunning building is regarded as an example of the early modern movement. The three large windows at the front hold sculptures by Charles Pibworth and depict Chaucer with the Canterbury Pilgrims, The Venerable Bede with Literary Saints and King Alfred. Inside, the theme is more classical and the most immediately striking feature is the grand staircase which is made of white Sicilian marble from Carrara. The staircase sweeps you up to the reference library, one of the must-visit places in the city. The tunnel-vaulted skylight ceiling filters through a mellow light onto the original teak, leather-topped reading desks and white pillars. The room's design was inspired by the high chambers of the bath buildings of imperial Rome and its most spectacular features are the two great oriel windows at either end of the north wall, ornamented with heraldic panels commemorating figures from Bristol's past.

College Green is also home to the Lord Mayor's Chapel, an ancient house of worship, formerly known as St Mark's Church and originally as the Chapel of the Hospital of the Gaunts. It was founded in 1220 by Maurice and Henry de Gaunt, grandsons of Robert Fitzhardinge who, in 1140, built the Abbey of the Black Canons of St Augustine, where the Cathedral now stands. The tower was a later addition in 1487. The building was originally built as a hospital. The nephew of the de Gaunts, Robert de Gournay, also had a hand in its endowment. Visitors should look out for the grotesque carvings that decorate the exterior of the tower and nave.

Wills Memorial Building

If you've never set foot inside the skyscraper-high building at the top of Park Street, you really should take a detour next time you're walking by. Push open the huge double doors and you will be greeted by a sight so opulent it would make a peacock blush. There are two sweeping stone staircases which drop elegantly from the cavernous ceiling, while the grandest wooden entrance hall you've ever seen stretches out beneath. You don't get this sort of learning environment at Soundwell Tech.

Cigarette tycoon Henry Overton Wills put up £100,000 for the building in 1908 and over the years the Wills family donated the equivalent of £100m to the University. The Wills Memorial Building was opened by King George V and Queen Mary in 1925. The final cost was £501,566 19s 10d. At 215 feet tall, it is twice the height of the Cabot Tower.

The Wills tower, designed by George Herbert Oatley, is constructed from Bath and Clipsham stone. It has been called the last great Gothic building to be constructed in England. The bell inside the tower is called Great George and strikes every hour. It weighs over ten tons and is the fourth largest bell in Britain. The tower, which is covered in grotesque carved heads, was constructed to amplify the sound of the bell striking.

The Mauretania sign was restored in 2019. Wills Memorial Building in the background

Park Street

It may have lost some of its appeal since the compact formula multinational convenience stores decided to move in, but Park Street is still one of the most elegant places to shop in the land – and one of the steepest. Standing at the top, looking down, you can't help but be impressed. We might take these things for granted, but this is one of the reasons so many visitors fall in love with Bristol.

To the right, as you descend Park Street, is Brandon Hill and on top of that is Cabot Tower. It's hard to believe it now, but both have had their moments of controversy. In the late 19th century, the breathtakingly landscaped hill was criticised by a local councillor as being 'a resort of lazy, idle, loafing persons' while the 105-foot tall monument to the explorer was described as 'a complete waste of money'. In fact, Brandon Hill was a gathering point for political meetings in the 18th and 19th century and a key site in the Chartist movement. In 1832 wealthy Bristol businessmen held a Great Reform Dinner on Brandon Hill. Almost 6,000 tickets were sold for the event, which was disrupted when 14,000 less well-off Bristolians stormed the barricades, ate the food, drank the beer and danced on the tables. Barrels of beer were rolled down the hill to the poorer districts and a wagon of dumplings was hijacked on Hotwells Road.

With this in mind, every visitor should climb up the spiral staircase of the Cabot Tower and take a look at the most spectacular view Bristol has to offer. Do not attempt this on very windy days or when drunk. As inspiring as this sounds, however, it's not the reason the crowds flock to Park Street every Saturday. Unlike the Mall and Broadmead, many of the shops here are still independent and variety is still an option and the Folk House remains one of the most pleasant places for lunch or tea and cake in town. It's also worth mentioning that a more leftfield shopping experience can be unearthed on Park Row. To go from the glassy-eyed optimism of the Crystal Shop at the top of Lodge Street to the full metal hardware of Militaria on Lower Park Row takes only a handful of paces but is one hell of a cultural leap.

Christmas Steps

There is a plaque at the top of Christmas Steps that reads 'This streete was steppered done in 1669' but anyone using it back in those days took their life in their hands. Old public records tell of a dangerously steep and muddy path that sent pedestrians hurtling down towards the Centre at breakneck speeds.

And if the conditions underfoot didn't get you, the dagger-wielding muggers would. It used to be known as Knifesmith Street, though this was because the city's knife makers worked here. It was also referred to as Cutellare (cutlery) Street in records dating back to 1389, but by the end of the 16th Century, it had become Christmas Street and Christmas Steps when the steps were built in 1669. Condemned prisoners were dragged up the 49 steps from Bristol gaol to be hanged on St Michael's Hill.

Christmas Steps is home to the mighty That Art Gallery and at the top on Colston Street, there's a thriving community of independent shops. Blaze is an artist-run co-op with loads of bespoke hand-made things and a fine selection of hats. Bloom & Curll is a lovely second-hand bookshop and you can get a haircut in Mack Daddy's before buying a bike at the Bristol Bicycle Workshop.

BS2

Stokes Croft to Old Market

Only an estate agent would describe Montpelier as Bristol's Notting Hill but this is where the city's leafier crowd hang out. Don't be fooled by the five-storey Regency terraced houses, Montpelier is full of what we used to call Jitters. Linking this counter-culture enclave to the world outside is Picton Street...

Stokes Croft

When Chris Chalkley and a group of like-minded adventurers set up The People's Republic of Stokes Croft in 2007, they could hardly have realised the local, national and international impact that PRSC would have. PRSC is based next to the Bell pub on the corner of Hillgrove Street and Jamaica Street and is home to (among others) PRSC Radio, the Bristol Cable newspaper, a screenprint studio, a ceramics studio and kiln, the Space

Past Notes

1873: Residents complain about the filthy state of Richmond Road. One local talks of a 'muddy ditch impassable for pedestrians.'

1874 The Cheltenham Road Viaduct, better known as The Arches, is built.

1882: The Montpelier Hotel begins its 100-year lifespan.

1993: Dozens of 'Picton Street Against The War' posters fail to prevent the invasion of Iraq.

The artwork at Turbo Island is designed to distract from the corporate messages on the billboard

events area and bar and the Stokes Croft China shop.

Chalkley started the ball rolling by inviting artists to create visual art for the streets. The impact of this was massive, effectively turning the whole area into an outdoor gallery. For a few years there was a buzzing, alternative art and cafe culture in Stokes Croft giving the area a modern bohemian European feel in the evenings when politicos, artists, poets and passers-bye spill out onto the streets from the bars and cafes no doubt plotting revolution and burning their Tesco Club Cards, no matter what the consequences for their points tally. More recently, it's become party central for middle-class Bristol University students who get away all-night street parties that wouldn't be tolerated in they took place just round the corner in St Paul's. Yet Stokes Croft has retained much of its character typified by Rita's still essential late-night take-away, and the universally-loved Pieminister. Even though, the upper crust, it seems, have replaced crusties.

People's perceptions of this long-neglected part of town have changed, and it is now an example to radical communities around the world of how local people can take control of their own futures. Like so many of the best things in Bristol, Stokes Croft has thrived because creative, free thinkers have stepped into the vacuum left by years of civic apathy and neglect.

However, developers and franchise stores are desperate to get a piece of the action in the hippest and fastest changing part of Bristol, but fail to realise that if they move in, they will destroy the very thing that makes

The Battle against Tesco

When Stokers Croft rioted in 2011 it came as no surprise that Tesco got trashed

The battle against the siting of a Tesco's Metro store in Stokes Croft was long and acrimonious and culminated in a riot on the evening of Thursday April 21, 2011. For those who had followed the No Tesco campaign closely, the trashing of Tesco's was entirely predictable. For more than a year 24-hour security guards had sat behind razor wire on the flat roof of the Tesco store to protect the site from protesters and squatters.

It was terrible PR for the supermarket giant who seemed completely unaware that its brand contradicts everything that Stokes Croft stands for – independence, support for local businesses and a readiness to wave two fingers at any form of authority should it dare to cross Turbo Island.

For over a year the local community worked hard to peacefully campaign to stop Tesco from opening – 2,500 people sent postcards to Bristol City Council objecting to Tesco, thousands more signed petitions and 96 per cent of 700 people surveyed said they don't want a Tesco in Stokes Croft – technically the store (on the old Jesters' Club site) is just outside Stokes Croft.

Throughout the campaign against Tesco, some of the organisers felt they were given assurances by councillors that the planning application would be refused. On planning grounds alone, the No Campaign had a strong case.

The Tesco store would require at least 42 lorry deliveries a week and the only place a lorry can park is across a cycle lane and a bus lane close to a busy junction on one of the main routes into the city. Of course, with 96 per cent of local people objecting to the Tesco application, those little things called Democracy and Accountability might also have had a role to play. But this is Bristol City Council. Many campaigners felt cheated when the City Council planning committee voted 4-3 in favour of the retail giant that spends millions on advertising in the local and national press and which has oodles of money to spend on planning appeals. And then came the riot.

As with the St Paul's riots 30 years earlier, cack-handed policing was the immediate cause of the unrest. The word on the street is that it all went something like this.

At some point in the day, a squatter in Telepathic Heights directly opposite Tesco let it be known to staff at Tesco that he had made petrol bombs and they had Tesco's name on them. At the time of writing there is no evidence that any petrol bombs actually existed. It has been suggested that the squatter was a person with some form of learning difficulty. Whatever, concerned Tesco staff understandably called the Old Bill.

This is where the police had to make a decision. The information in front of them is that a person living in a squat opposite Tesco has petrol bombs and has threatened to chuck them at Tesco. Given the strong tension in Stokes Croft and the feeling that the democratic process had betrayed the local community do you...

a) Send in plain clothes officers in unmarked cars, snatch the person in question grab the alleged petrol bombs and get the hell out of Stokes Croft.

b) Send in 16 riot vans packed with coppers from South Wales and Wiltshire who don't know the area and storm Telepathic Heights? Oh and let's stick a helicopter directly above Tesco, just in case people on the other side of town don't know what's going on.

So the riot vans packed with coppers from outside Bristol cut through the early evening crowds of people gathering in Stokes Croft for an evening out before the Easter weekend. Other people were still returning from work. Stokes Croft was busy. Naturally, the 16 riot vans and helicopter attracted a crowd, scuffles broke out and pretty soon they had escalated into an all-out battle outside Tesco's.

At some point the police thought it would be a good idea to send in horses and to charge the crowd. Again it's a question of choices.

a) Do you disperse the crowd into St Paul's which has a history of rioting and into Montpelier, home of many of the people most narked off with the whole Tesco thing.
Or

b) Try to disperse the crowd into the leafy residential areas of Redland and Cotham.

So then it kicks off in St Paul's and in Picton Street in Montpelier. It seems that one of the main issues once the police had decided on option b) above, was that people coming out of their homes in St Paul's and Montpelier to see what all the fuss was about quickly found themselves on the wrong side of police lines and unable to return home. Requests to be allowed home were allegedly met with violence as the police successfully opened a second front of unrest.

There have been many complaints made against the police and one friend of the Naked Guides who was trying to negotiate with officers to allow people home was among a group near Picton Street who were charged by police horses without warning. He was then brought down by two police Alsatians and a dog handler also unleashed a Rottweiler on him. Unlike the Alsatians, the Rottweiler went bonkers and tore a chunk of flesh from under his arm.

Having by now seriously pissed off large parts of the community in Stokes Croft, St Paul's and Montpelier, the police eventually made the right decision and retreated leaving 'our popular local store' to quote a Tesco spokesperson, to be trashed.

Stokes Croft special. Bristol City Council seem at odds with the PRSC vision even though it is a big factor in selling the city to visitors and students. Early in 2019 it seemed that the universities and developers would achieve their vision of rebuilding Stokes Croft and creating a 'smart city' based on functionality – something Stokes Croft has never been very good at.

Seebright printers had moved out, the Blue Mountain Club announced its closure (then said it was staying open), plans were revealed for housing at Hamilton House and long-term management company Co-exist were kicked out, the Carriageworks and Westmoreland House were being redeveloped and the Lakota night club and old Coroners' Court sites were up for sale. Most of the real estate in Stokes Croft was up for grabs and the future looks dull. Enjoy Stokes Croft while you can.

But Stokes Croft isn't all about these bold nouveau enterprises, y'know. Some things have been around since the first alarm clock went off on the morning of the dawn of time. Take the heroically-named Everest Secretarial Services, for example. If you need a dissertation, CV, business proposal, manuscript or shopping list typed then look no further. Founded by Mrs Everest, yes really, it is a beacon of traditionalism where typists sit in a pool and quite possibly still buy their nylons off the black market. And their shoes in KBK by the Arches.

One site of historical importance is the building opposite the Here shop at the top of Picton Street. In the early 1980s, this was the legendary Demolition Diner, an anarcho-punk, peace-crazies squat and a centre for unruly music and even unrulier politics. The night when it was first squatted, police took dogs onto the roof to try and oust the new residents by entering via a skylight. But the dogs got scared and couldn't get down. After some hard bargaining, the police and their dogs were escorted through the skylight and allowed to leave via the front door.

Bus Station

The redeveloped Bristol Bus Station was an indication of what we could anticipate from the rest of the Broadmead redevelopment – something functional and characterless where you have to pay 20p to take a leak. Admittedly, the bus station, which was completed early in 2006, now boasts some natural light and doesn't stink of piss. This is a significant improvement on the previous terminus which was built in 1958 and, it is popularly believed, wasn't properly cleaned between 1959 and 2004.

The old bus station, y'see, was probably one of the most unpleasant first impressions of a city anywhere in Europe. The new one is deeply uninspiring, but clean and functional. Its functionality is only marred by the fact that it doesn't have a car park and it's nowhere near the train station at Temple Meads. Don't expect to get a parking place in the small lay-by on the side road behind the bus station, head to the NCP instead.

The only interesting thing about the bus station is the plaque commemorating the successful Bristol Bus Boycott campaign in 1963 against the Bristol Omnibus Company policy of not allowing black people to work as drivers or conductors. The plaque was funded by Mayor George Ferguson, First Bus and the University of Bristol and unveiled in 2014.

During the rebuilding of the bus station, the City Archaeological Unit uncovered part of the cloister and other original remains of the Benedictine Priory of St James. Founded in 1129 by Robert, Earl of Gloucester (the natural son of Henry I of England), the Priory is almost as old as the city itself and appears in the earliest maps of 'Brigstowe'. When St James' Priory was excavated in 1995, part of the original east end of the church was revealed along with more than 200 human remains from the adjoining burial ground. This site is now covered by an office block on Cannon Street right next to the bus station.

Bearpit

It may appear to be only a large roundabout with pedestrian tunnels and a sunken central area, but the Bearpit has a significance that goes way beyond its traffic management functionality. In the late 70s and early 80s the Bearpit was one of the hotspots on the cultural map of Bristol that culminated in the Bristol Sound and helped shape the city's reputation as a street art capital.

Back in 1977, local post-punk revolutionaries the Pop Group were managed by Alan Jones who had been in the music business since being a member of 60s welsh band Amen Corner. Jones was well connected with the nascent London punk fashion scene on the King's Road and in Kensington Market and opened a fashion shop called Paradise Garage in the Bearpit. One of the young punk shop assistants was Miles Johnson, AKA DJ Milo, one of the founders of the Wild Bunch hip-hop crew who later evolved into Massive Attack.

Miles recalls: "Paradise Garage was the epicentre of every band around at the time from the Pop Group through to the Wild Bunch/Massive Attack. I became friends with Daniel Day Lewis in Paradise Garage back in the early 1980s as he was a friend of Rich Payne's who ran the shop and I always hung out down there.

Protesters gather at City Hall to present a 4,000-signature petition to save Ursa. Inset: Jamie Gillman built the bear

"Eventually I worked for them in London's Kensington Market. I met Daddy G and 3D down there at separate times. Everyone who was into the punk and funk scene went to Paradise Garage every weekend. Without doubt the Bearpit was pivotal to the Bristol music and fashion scene."

It was also the home of the city's original Virgin Records shop that boasted the best selection of punk vinyl in the west country and of a second hugely influential clothes and shoe shop Bonie Maronie run by Robert and Basia Andrews.

Trading in the Bearpit became impossible due to ridiculously high levels of burglary and assault and Bonie Maronie eventually moved out in 1994. The Bearpit became a no-go area until the Bearpit Improvement Group formed in 2012 and the space was declared a Community Action Zone which effectively gave BIG the power to implement various improvements, hold markets, organise public art and undertake gardening projects.

The improvements were impressive, but in 2016 a split occurred between the traders and the rest of the BIG team. Bristol City Council handled the schism badly playing one side off against the other before coming down on the side of the traders and sending in Bristol Waste to cover the walls with anti-graffiti paint. BIG dissolved in 2017 and the council 'took back control'. The traders ceased trading, the public toilets were closed, the markets stopped and the Bearpit once again became an unloved and neglected public space.

At the time of writing, the council were attempting to remove all evidence of BIG from the Bearpit. The Cube alternative billboard was ripped down and, in the face of substantial public opposition, Bristol City Council launched a legal process to remove the iconic Ursa bear statue from its plinth overlooking Bond Street. For more on the formation of the Bearpit Improvement Group go to www.convivialspaces.org

Montpelier

It's fitting that Picton Street, Montpelier's main artery, is a Georgian raggle-taggle, car-unfriendly lane because this is the historical home of Bristol's counter-culture. There are also several wonderful places to eat and drink too: Bell's Diner (1-3 York Road) is one of Bristol's most inspirational restaurants, the Bristolian (2 Picton Street) is one of the city's best café diners, the One Stop Thali Cafe (12 York Road) is renowned for its veggie Indian street food, Mela (19 York Road) is an excellent Indian take-away, Licata (36 Picton Street) is an authentic Sicilian deli, Herbert's Bakery (Wellington Avenue) is one of Bristol's finest bread-makers, Radford Mill Farm Shop (41 Picton Street) is a top organic and community wholefood shop while the Wai Yee Hong Supermarket (4 Station Road) is a warehouse full of unusual delights from the Far East.

If you want a drink stop, why not savour the friendly local atmosphere of the Star & Garter (Brook Road) which reopened in 2019 following the death of long-time landlord Dutty Ken or The Beaufort (York Road). For a livelier time, head up the unassuming Richmond Road until you come to the legendary Cadbury House. Until 2003, when the New Prince of Wales on Gloucester Road took the honours, *Venue* magazine readers voted the Cadbury House the best pub in Bristol for something like the previous ten years running. And it's easy to see why. It's one of just a handful of unique local landmarks that give underground Bristol its identity. You won't find anywhere like it in any other city.

St Paul's

In the 1980s something remarkable happened in St Paul's, the consequences of which we are still experiencing today in the continued success of Massive Attack, Banksy, Tricky, Portishead and the hugely successful New Circus movement of which Bristol could lay a justifiable claim to being the international capital.

Until recently, whatever cultural collision took place in St Paul's after the cold punches of Thatcherism resulted in the riots was almost entirely unrecorded. There wasn't a plan and there were no leaders. Its only real voice were the long-gone pirate radio stations such as FTP, Emergency Radio and others.

In their book *Art & Sound of the Bristol Underground* (Tangent Books) Chris Burton and Gary Thompson identify the birth of the free party scene as the arrival of hip-hop from New York. Punk and reggae had become mainstream. Black and white kids across town wanted a new beat for the sub-culture and it came in the form of hip-hop which Bristol embraced like no other UK city. To be a viable hip-hop crew you needed the four disciplines of a DJ, MC, break-dancers and a graffiti writer. Enter the Wild Bunch, a loose collective of young men that included DJ Milo (Miles Johnson), DJ Nellee (Nellee Hooper), graffiti artist and MC 3D (Robert Del Naja), MC Daddy G (Grant Marshall), Willie Wee (Claude Williams) and an associated

St Paul's Uprising, April 2, 1980

The riots that broke out on Grosvenor Road 'Front Line' in 1980 were the most serious in modern British history and the precursors of the summer riots that swept through Britain's inner cities in 1981. A lot has been written about the social causes for the disturbances and certainly the uprising had a lot to do with the black and the white community of St Paul's expressing its anger at heavy-handed policing, unemployment and poor housing. And yet the immediate cause of the riots, according to Bristol urban legend, was all to do with a ripped pair of trousers.

The trouble started at the Black and White Cafe in Grosvenor Road. The Black and White was run by Stephen Wilks and his partner Shirley Andow. Wilks was a Jamaican national who came to Britain in the early 1960s, settled in Oxford and then moved to Bristol where he took over the Black and White in 1971. The cafe was well known as a haven for drug dealers. Some would say that it was fairly

harmless – a few people indulging in small-time marijuana dealing. But others claimed it was actually the base for one of Britain's most serious drug operations.

What is beyond doubt is that the Black and White was a significant centre for a section of the black community. Detectives raided it on April 2, 1980, but had failed to warn either local uniform police or community leaders. Police met such violent resistance that they were forced to withdraw entirely for several hours and 19 officers were wounded.

However, according to the rumours in the following weeks, in the process of searching for drugs, police ripped one of the customer's trousers. He demanded immediate compensation, the police refused, a scuffle followed that spilled out onto Grosvenor Road and... Bingo! Within hours, several thousand people were fighting a pitch battle with police. There were further disturbances in St Paul's in January 1982 and May 1987.

crew of breakdancers. The Wild Bunch weren't the only exponents, FBI, UD4, City Rockas and others were just as popular, but it was Wild Bunch who formed the basis of Massive Attack with the arrival of Mushroom and the departure of Milo and Nellee.

The young crews typically played house parties, often breaking into derelict buildings or being invited into squats, sometimes hooking up power from neighbouring buildings and hiring PAs from the reggae sound systems. The parties were publicised by flyers in the New York tradition, designed by young wannabe artists such as 3D, Inkie, Nick Walker FLX, Chaos and others. The link from Banksy to 3D is well established and recorded in Felix (FLX) Braun's book *Children of the Can* and in *Banksy's*

St Paul's Carnival

Bristol's biggest street party is usually held on the first Saturday in July. It aims to promote and celebrate the culture and community of St Paul's – home to much of the city's African-Caribbean population.

The Carnival started in 1968 and has been held every year since, apart from 2002 and 2006. In 2002, it was cancelled following pressure from the police who were concerned about crack gangs looking for revenge for some non-fatal shootings after the 2001 event. There were certainly problems after the 2001 event, but in many quarters, it was considered a disgrace that one of Bristol's longest-established, most vibrant and creative community-based cultural events was banned at the height of Bristol's bid to become European City of Culture in 2008. In 2006, it took a year off to undergo a major revamp.

St Paul's Carnival attracts thousands of people to Grosvenor Road and the surrounding streets. Everybody in Bristol who likes partying turns up and increasingly those from much further afield make the trip. During the day Red Stripe, jerk chicken, fried fish and goat curry abound; after dark the music party moves up a few notches. Cultural events throughout June lead up to the Saturday event at which you'll find costume processions by local schools, community groups and anyone else with access to a float, as well as DJs, sound systems and bands, all blasting out reggae, hip-hop and dub.

For kids, there are two parks (St Agnes and St Paul's Adventure Playground) where they can see puppet shows, do face painting, listen to story-telling, join in drumming workshops and jump up and down on bouncy castles. Carnival has changed very little over the years. It's got bigger, but essentially the form on Carnival day remains the same: watch the procession, eat, drink, listen to music and walk up and down Grosvenor Road until it's time to go home.

St Paul's Carnival is one massive party for all ages and consequently gets very busy, so not one for claustrophobics.

St Paul's Carnival runs from 1pm to 2am and is usually held on the first Saturday in July.

Roy Hackett, one of the founders on St Paul's Carnival in 1968, was 90 years in 2018 when Carnival celebrated 50 years

Bristol by Steve Wright (both Tangent Books). New Circus entered the mix when travellers tired of battling the police in the countryside (most notably in The Battle of the Beanfield near Stonehenge in 1985) and retreated into the inner city where they quickly became part of free party scene.

Although it was based in St Paul's the scene attracted like-minded kids from across Bristol including Fresh 4 from Knowle West and Krissy Kriss and his comrades from Southmead.

For an area that has given Bristol more than any other in terms of music and character, St Paul's doesn't seem to get a lot in return. The Western Star Domino Club? Closed. Ajax Blues Bar? Shut down. And what happened to the club nights at the Malcolm X Centre? Early in 2004, the community was attempting to make the Black and White cafe the centre of a regeneration programme. Steve Wilks, owner of the Black and White, told a public inquiry that closing the cafe wouldn't solve the St Paul's drug problems. Wilks, 34, whose father opened the Black and White in 1971 said: 'We want the cafe to stay. We want it to be part of the rejuvenation programme for St Paul's'. However, the cafe was closed and has now been demolished and replaced with low-cost homes.

In the early 1990s, St Paul's was beginning to buzz again. Anyone looking for after-hours activity of the alcoholic kind would head down to the Jamaican Good Food after midnight and choose from the vast array of Red Stripe on offer. Or you could get a late one in the Criterion on Badminton

Smith & Mighty

Meet the originators of the Bristol Beat...

Rob Smith and Ray Mighty are the masters of the Bristol Beat, the street sound of St Paul's. They've also been hailed as the originators of drum 'n' bass. Rob and Ray are from radical funk and roots reggae backgrounds; they became Smith & Mighty after meeting up in a funk outfit called Sweat in 1986. They built a studio above a Blues Club just off Ashley Road and by 1988 Three Stripe Records had been born.

After a brief collaboration with Mark Stewart from The Pop Group, Smith & Mighty released their sublime broken beats version of Burt Bacharach and Hal David's Dionne Warwick classic *Anyone Who Had a Heart*. This was followed in 1988 by the excellent ultra-mellow, bass-bubbling Jackie Jackson version of *Walk On By*.

They then teamed up with singer Carlton and the people who were to become Massive Attack when they remixed the Wild Bunch cover of the Bacharach classic *Any Love* – a hauntingly minimalist counter to the richness of their Three Stripe work. Rob and Ray were gods of the nascent dance scene, their *Steppers' Delight* 12-inch is credited as being the birth of Jungle. They teamed up with Fresh Four for the Knowle West outfit's Top 10 version of *Wishing On A Star*. Although this track is their only mainstream success to date, it's hardly representative of the depth and diversity of their outstanding work. The major labels were on the prowl for Smith & Mighty. Virgin got short shrift when Ray Mighty said of Richard Branson: 'We just don't like his style and the way Margaret Thatcher portrayed him as the ideal business mogul. Maybe it's got something to do with the fact that we used to be punks.'

Smith and Mighty eventually signed to ffrr (London Records) in 1990 but then hardly released a beat for five years. Sadly their legendary *Bass is Maternal* album was never released in its original form; it remains one of Bristol's lost musical treasures. Outtakes from those sessions revealed a work of sparsely interwoven beats, dub, soul and space (silence). A dub reggae version of the album was eventually released, but not until several years later.

After sitting out their contract and then parting company with London, Smith and Mighty added Peter D Rose as a third member and introduced the world to their More Rockers project. Their first album in this new formation was *Dub Plate Selection Volume 1* which is an uplifting gathering of dub and drum 'n' bass. More Rockers went further down the dub reggae path in their work with Henry and Louis (lovely stuff) and continued to record and tour in their own right.

In 2018 Smith & Mighty issued a retrospective of previously unreleased work from 1988-94. *The Ashley Road Sessions* is on Bristol's Punch Drunk label.

The Windrush mural on Campbell Street, St Paul's, celebrates the arrival of people from the Caribbean in the early 1950s

Road. And just around the corner from there is the defiantly original Star & Garter, still shaking its floorboards after all these years.

The underground sub-culture that St Paul's nurtured has now moved a few hundred yards to Stokes Croft where it has a far more visible presence. Although St Paul's now lacks some of the energy of the 1980s, it remains the area that shaped much of Bristol's contemporary culture.

St Werburgh's

Narroways Hill, the area of steep wasteland that separates St Werburgh's from Ashley Hill, has a history that far exceeds its humble appearance. In the early part of the last century, for example, it was the scene of a terrible murder of a woman called Ada James by her boyfriend Ted Palmer. Once carved into pieces by railway tracks, its junction was a target for Nazi bombs during the war. More recently, British Rail put the land up for sale and local residents decided to raise the money to buy it. Finally, Avon Wildlife Trust registered the land as a nature conservation site.

This is in keeping with the character of the people of St Werburgh's; why else would the suburb have been chosen as the site for the St Werburgh's City Farm? The Farm pub is a welcoming place with good food and hip-hop and beats DJs on Friday and Saturday nights. The Miners' Arms in Mina Road is the favoured watering hole of middle-aged musos and the Duke of York (Jubilee Road) is difficult to find but worth the effort for its homely atmosphere and excellent selection of real ales and ciders.

The other St Werburgh's pubs used to resemble hostels for mostly drunk but mostly amiable old fellas. St Werburgh's has a strong sense of community and the arrival of the uber-organic Better Food Company at the bottom of Ashley Down Road coupled with a retail revamp on Mina Road added interest to the area.

More recently, a new generation have continued the alternative business theme with arrival of the Cauldron firepit grill restaurant in Mina Road (www.thecauldron.restaurant), Extract Coffee Roasters in Gatton Road (www.extractcoffee.co.uk) and two microbreweries with tap rooms, Wiper and True in York Street (www.wiperandtrue.com) and Fierce and Noble in Mina Road (www.fierceandnoble.com). Add to the mix the excellent Neck Of The Woods community café in St Werburgh's Community Centre in Horley Road (www.stwerburghs.org.uk) and St Werburgh's continues its claim to be Bristol's most interesting area. Strangely, it's also Bristol's climbing epicentre with indoor walls/climbing gyms at the Climbing Academy in St Werburgh's Church on Mina Road (www.theclimbingacademy.com) and Clip 'n' Climb in Gatton Road (www.clipnclimbbristol.co.uk)

It wasn't that long ago that there wasn't all that much to get excited about and St Werburgh's was essentially Montpelier with a motorway running past.

Old Market. A capital of 'cool'

Finn Dovey takes an in-depth look at a Bristol area that received an unlikely accolade...

In 2018 Old Market was described by the *Sunday Times* as the second coolest neighbourhood in the UK. Whilst the *Sunday Times* probably doesn't have the strongest grasp on what makes an area cool, it certainly has an aptitude for highlighting spaces on the cusp of a coffee shop invasion. Although Old Market does now boast a salon crossed with a music venue, art gallery and coffee shop, it's certainly retaining the charming smoggy delight that has the *Sunday Times* describing as somewhere your parents wouldn't want to leave their car.

At night the pavements become hectic, with multiple tides outside the 24 hour shop, a combination of intoxicated students and veteran drunks, the gay clubs' cabaret costumes spill out onto the sidewalk. It's a diverse range of disorderly crews,

a strong mix of old and new that seems to be working, for now. The best way I can describe the street is a head shop, next to a dentist, next to a massage parlour. This merging of old and new crowds on one strip of road no doubt is linked to the entanglement of vastly different but complementary independent spots, separate from the corporate Cabot Circus development bubble adjacent.

The Stag and Hounds' fixtures smell old in a cosy way, hosting top bands on the weekend. Next door is the Exchange a newer feeling venue, still sporting the same love for music with an eclectic record store, recently it successfully raised £250,000 from a Community Share Issue to become Bristol's first community-owned live music venue. Next up, Elmer's Arms, complete with sincere 60s feeling and mutton chops, a living room sized dance floor with some great charged musicians playing throughout the week, and a jukebox filled with nostalgia when there's not. Elmer the owner has created a magic watering hole, and for that, Old Market residents regard him as a jewel of the pavement, loved by all.

The next block houses two LGBTQ venues almost opposite each other. Bristol Bear Bar and the Old Market Assembly definitely inject some flair into the otherwise dishevelled landscape, fun for all, most fun if you're gay. The Assembly also doubles up as the Wardrobe Theatre, the most relaxed performing arts venue I've been to. Sitting at the lower end of Old Market is the Trinity Centre, a holy institution for dub, arts and culture. It is the pinnacle of the Old Market pilgrimage, make sure you get down for the legendary day party, that has queues around the block, eagerly awaiting infamous Bristol DJs and finest samosas. The place is changing, but these venues are not going anywhere without a fight.

Stag & Hounds
74 Old Market Street BS2 0EJ
www.stagandhoundsbristol.co.uk
The 'Slag' hosts Pete Bennet Karaoke, live music every weekend and a certain feeling that this pub still looks the same as it did 40 years ago.

The Exchange
72-73 Old Market Street BS2 0EJ
www.exchangebristol.com
Vegan kebabs, but more importantly punk and specialist records upstairs and a thriving venue at ground level. The Exchange is run by Paul Horlick, a legend of the Bristol music scene.

The Long Bar
70 Old Market Street BS2 0EJ
The sign outside says 'No children or shop lifters, dogs welcome' which tells you a lot about who lives within. Outstanding ales and an older relaxed crowd, good for a mid-week pint.

Old Market Tavern
29-30 Old Market Street, Bristol BS2 0HB
www.omtbristol.co.uk
A friendly and certainly homely pub with an exceptional beer garden. A good choice for a mid-day meal or a beer in the sun. Up there with the best LGBTQ pubs in Bristol in true Old Market fashion.

Hydra Books
34 Old Market Street BS2 0EZ
www.hydrabooks.org
A great alternative to the never-ending street filled with Costa and Caffe Nero. Totally volunteer run, it is an anarchist micro society. A bookshelf to rival that of any University of Bristol postgrad. The shop lease runs out in 2019, so its future is uncertain.

Volunteer Tavern
9 New Street BS2 9DX
www.volunteertavern.co.uk
Slightly out of the way of the Old Market strip, this pub is a true gem, huge selection of ales and stouts an ever-changing food menu and spectacular garden seats for the smokers.

Elmer's Arms
53 Old Market Street BS2 0ER
@theelmersarms
Next door to a dentist and massage parlour, the windowed front says; 'Good music, Good people, Good Ales, Good

spirits'. It's all true, Elmer has created a totally unique pub the size of a living room.

Bristol Bear Bar
2 West Street BS2 0BH
www.bristolbears.co.uk
Its smoking area spilling out onto the street, this place is all lasers, smoke and cheap drinks. Expect cheesy music and fabulous people.

Old Market Assembly
25 West Street BS2 0DF
www.oldmarketassembly.co.uk
This place is a popular LGBTQ haunt, the music and performance here is for everyone, with a huge variety of evenings to get down with. Extremely friendly crowd, the pride flags fly proud.

Wardrobe Theatre
25 West Street BS2 0DF
www.thewardrobetheatre.com
Retaining the feeling that Old Market Assembly creates of a relaxed environment with a terrific crowd, this is the most chilled-out theatre in Bristol. 25 West St, Bristol BS2 0DF

Dare To
1 Alfred Street BS2 0RF
www.daretoswing.co.uk
The ultimate of seedy venues, an old sex club which often gets hijacked by Bristol-based techno collectives. If the walls could talk you probably wouldn't go there.

Trinity Centre
Trinity Centre, Trinity Road BS2 0NW
www.3ca.org.uk
One of the best venues in Bristol let alone Old Market. Bristol collectives aplenty perform here. A perfect

combination of old and new Djs, don't miss Teachings in Dub!

The Jam Jar
Little Ann Street BS2 9EB
www.thejamjarbristol.com
Part of the Old Malt House complex, they regularly hold some splendid hedonistic parties. Back with a bang after nearly being closed down due to noise complaints a few years ago.

Fi Real
57 West Street BS2 0BZ
www.fireal.co.uk
An awesome array of vegan Caribbean food, topped off with some exceptional homemade smoothies. A proper independent Bristolian spot with great staff.

Bagelicious
24 Old Market Street BS2 0HB
Who knew so much could be done with a bagel, great local cafe for anyone on the move needing a quick snack, some serious vegetarian and vegan options.

BS3 & BS4

Knowle West to Southville

We've lumped BS3 and BS4 together because this is the South Bristol chapter. If you're feeling adventurous enough to cross the river, read on...

The South Bristol Story

It could all have been so different... If, in 1835, John Miller, Vice-President of the Society of Florists, had gone ahead with his plan to build Bristol Zoo on land at Arnos Vale, then Totterdown and Knowle could now be affluent, sophisticated, leafy suburbs with the zoo and its magnificent gardens at their centre. A bit like Clifton perhaps.

It seemed certain that the zoo would be built on the site that Arnos Vale Cemetery now occupies: in March 1835, the *Bristol Journal* reported that 'the planting of the Zoological Gardens, eight acres in extent on Pylle Hill near this city has just been commenced by Mr John Miller.' But the Zoo was built on its current site at Summer Trenmoor near Clifton Down. It now seems an obvious location for such a major project, but back in 1835 Arnos Vale was a pleasant and unspoilt area of open countryside, whereas the Downs were populated by vagabonds and highwaymen swinging in the wind from gibbets.

South Bristol lost out. In fact, South Bristol always seems to lose out. One suspects that when the Romans arrived in Bristol, they decided to make

Knowle West and Hartcliffe the leisure capital of their European empire. The first stone was probably about to be laid when a breathless centurion jogged up Hartcliffe Way and gasped: 'Hang on a minute, I've found this place called Aquae Sulis down the road. You should have a look there first.'

Successive attempts to make South Bristol trendy have failed. One theory for the lack of anything much happening in South Bristol is that the secondary schools perform badly in the league tables, so parents who can afford it move to different catchment areas where the schools are better when their children reach Year Six, leaving behind those families who aren't in a position to evacuate the area. That's all changing and much of south Bristol is now properly gentrified. And yet... along with Easton and St Paul's, South Bristol has one of the strongest and friendliest communities in the city.

Knowle West

Knowle West is changing. The estate once had a reputation for gang violence and drug-related crime, but in recent years an increasing number of professional people are moving into the former council houses on its fringes because it's one of the last affordable areas close to the city centre. The main council estate was built in the 1930s to house people moved from poor inner-city accommodation. It was constructed on Garden City principles with wide roads, large gardens and with low-rise houses arranged in order to encourage communities to prosper. It has produced three of Bristol's best-known characters: footballer Julian Dicks, hip-hop maniac Tricky (Adrian Thaws) and drum 'n' bass supremo Krust (Keith Thompson). Knowle West was also home to one of Bristol's first skiffle/rock 'n' roll bands, the Eagles, and produced a band that achieved one of the highest chart positions by a pre-Massive Attack Bristol outfit when Fresh Four reached number 10 in 1989 with *Wishing On A Star*.

There's certainly a link between Dicks and Tricky: they're both hard bastards. Dicks (whose nickname is the Terminator) was the most

Past Notes

1080 Bedminster is listed as a royal manor in the Domesday Book.

1748 An angry agricultural mob trash the new Totterdown toll gate.

1900 First section of the Totterdown YMCA is opened. The Village People's great grandfathers rumoured to be delighted.

1988 Estate agents label Southville Lower Clifton in an effort to make the area more appealing.

Mid 90s Locals start Easter Sunday tradition of rolling hard-boiled eggs down Vale Street, the steepest residential streets in Britain.

Wild Westers

Don Robbin gets nostalgic for the 'bad old days'...

You have to climb a hill from anywhere in Bristol to get to Knowle West. High above Victorian Bedminster on the southern fringes of the city, where the wind draughts in from the Dundry Beacon, it's always one or two degrees colder than the rest of town. The irony is that the families who were transplanted to Knowle West in the 1920s were brought from the slums behind Bristol Temple Meads railway station. These were built so close together that the area was always several degrees warmer than its surroundings.

They built Knowle West like a spider's web. Or so it appears from the map, and so it appears from the road. Every street and avenue looks the same and they're all littered with speed bumps. This is where BMX meets joyriding. Certainly, the natives seldom venture out of the estate for any length of time, except to go to Weymouth for their annual Courage Best and Ambre Solaire shandy – or to make it cautiously into the town centre for a little light pillaging, for the crime rate here is high.

At the middle of the web lies Filwood Broadway. Shut-down shops and boarded-up windows face a prevailing wind so strong you can hardly walk against it. Downtown Beirut it's called. Tricky grew up here, as did Julian Dicks. They say the reason Tricky never lifts his head from his microphone is a childhood fear of having his hat blown off. Then there's the graffiti: Sharon-4-Chris, Steve+Tracey4Ever, PIGS (defiantly), and Bruno. He gets everywhere does Bruno. If it's flat, Bruno has signed it. With spray paint and some jumbo markers.

At the edge of the web are the former council houses bought by Thatcher's property-owning democrats. All have storm porches. Some have stone cladding. A few have stone-clad storm porches. Here they have trees, and shelter. And hedges. And double-glazing. Elsewhere they have poverty and drugs, and stripped down Capris in the garden. And utter, utter hopelessness. I don't know where Julian Dicks would have gone to learn how to play football around here. In the street? On the rare patches of green? Or in the park at the end of Broadway? There's not much in the way of leisure facilities for the young in Knowle West.

But Filwood is on the up. The developers are moving in and parts are looking better. The double-glazing is on its way – new flats, new community spirit, rumours of a supermarket to replace the derelict shell at the end of the road, and new shop fronts. New flat surfaces. Bruno will like that.

Four Famous Westers
1. Tricky 2. Julian Dicks
3. DJ Krust 4. Suv (Full Cycle)

This piece first appeared in Total Football magazine as part of a profile of the footballer Julian Dicks who is from Knowle West.

feared left-back of his generation at Birmingham City, Liverpool and, most famously, West Ham United; while Tricky was responsible for the most hard-edged, dysfunctional, alienated sounds of the 1990s. Krust too shows glimpses of the urban chaos that surrounded him in Knowle West particularly in his breathtaking *Coded Language* album from 1999.

Tricky was christened 'the YTS Kid' by Massive Attack when he worked on their classic *Blue Lines* debut album because he was on a retainer of £25 a week. He was a feature at all the parties in town in the early 1990s and was known to one and all as 'the stoned kiddie from Knowle West'. Tricky's mother Maxine Quaye (after whom his 1995 debut album was named) died when he was four. His father had already left, so Tricky spent his childhood living with relatives around Bristol. He worked briefly with Krust in Fresh Four before moving into a squat with ex-Pop Group main man Mark Stewart, who at the time was working with On-U-Sounds producer Adrian Sherwood and Barton Hill hard case Gary Clail on a series of heavyweight dub reggae projects. In an interview with *Venue* magazine to promote his album *Never Trust a Hippy*, Sherwood claims that Tricky lived in a cupboard under the stairs in Stewart's squat. It may be coincidence, but Kat Day, guitarist with Bristol's finest guitar band of the early 1990s, the Seers, is also from Knowle West. Like Tricky, he sometimes wore a dress on stage. A trend that didn't catch on.

Fresh Four comprised Knowle Westers Judge, Suv, his brother Flynn (of Flynn and Flora) and Krust. Their singer was Liz E, a Bristol teacher. Tricky was in the same class as Flynn at Knowle Juniors and Merrywood Boys' School. Although *Wishing On A Star* propelled them into the top 10, the follow-up *Release Yourself* disappeared without trace, and so did Fresh Four. (See Bristol Beat).

Brislington

Once considered merely a boring suburb of Bristol, the Sandy Park side of Brislington is developing a more urban attitude as younger people move in attracted by affordable housing. Eventually, it will be on the fringes of the huge enterprise zone development that will spread from Temple Meads to Paintworks and completely change the shape of South Bristol.

Brislington is the only part of Bristol to have a strong connection with the Romans, with its own Roman villa discovered on Winchester Road in 1899. It is believed that the villa was part of a whole estate, which was burnt down during a giant fire in 270-300 AD, following a raid by Irish pirates. Brislington's history doesn't end there though. Its name was given to it

Outer Circuit Road

How Totterdown is recovering from a planning disaster...

Residents of many English cities claim that what the Luftwaffe didn't destroy in the 1940s, the town planners blitzed with far less imagination in the 1960s and 1970s. This is certainly the case with Totterdown.

It's difficult to imagine now that the famous Three Lamps signpost (one of the best examples of early 19th Century signs in Britain) at the junction of the Bath and Wells Road once marked the gateway to a vibrant inner-city community and one of Bristol's main shopping centres.

The Three Lamps sign is still there, but that's all that remains of that part of Totterdown. It all went horribly wrong for the area in the 1960s when Britain was obsessed with bulldozing cities to make room for new roads. On 15 December 1966, the Ministry of Transport approved a Bristol City Council plan for a £30 million outer ring road, or urban motorway. The brainwave of the Planning Committee and its chairman Alderman Wally Jenkins (or 'Mr Traffic', as the *Western Daily Press* dubbed him), the plans were truly devastating. Essentially, the planners wanted to drive a dual carriageway-cum-motorway from what is now Junction 3 of the M32 through Easton and St Philip's, over the Feeder behind Temple Meads, across the Three Lamps Junction, through Totterdown, across Victoria Park and through Bedminster.

It got worse. The motorway would then head across the Floating Harbour, skirting the Cathedral and heading through Jacobs Wells to the Victoria Rooms. The precise route of this section is unclear: certainly there were proposals to turn Park Street into a dual carriageway and there were alternative plans for a flyover to Brandon Hill and a tunnel underneath the Cabot Tower.

From the Victoria Rooms this monster road would demolish Cotham on its way to Montpelier, where it would stop for breath before bulldozing St Paul's and rejoining the M32 (or Parkway as it was then called) at Junction 3. The plans also included surrounding St Mary Redcliffe Church with dual carriageways and driving a main road straight through the middle of Queen Square. In a word: it was madness.

Giant interchange

But to the everlasting shame of the City Council, the area of Totterdown above the Three Lamps between the Bath and Wells Road was demolished in 1972 to make way for a four-level spaghetti-junction motorway on stilts.

Between Three Lamps and Temple Meads, would be a giant interchange centre about the size of Broadmead where happy motorists would jump on fleets of buses to complete their journey into what was left of the city. Communities, shops and pubs were flattened to realise this nightmare. A total of 500 homes and 40 shops and pubs were demolished. Places like the Lahore Cafe and Club, the Three Lamps Canine and Feline Beauty Centre, the Maypole Dairy, the Bristol

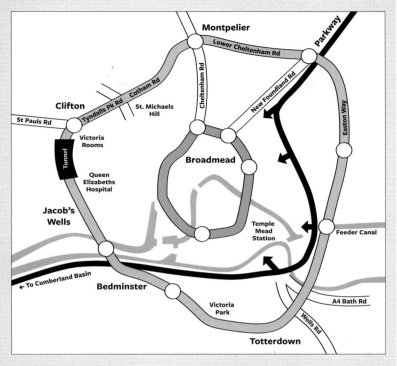

Co-operative Society, the Prince Rupert, the Totterdown Hotel and the Phoenix were lost.

Thankfully, the full awfulness of that road scheme was never realised; North Bristol was spared, Totterdown was destroyed but the road was never built. Easton suffered terribly. Ironically, new flats and houses were built on the Totterdown site in the 1990s, but the community has been lost for ever.

Road to nowhere
This map of the proposed route of the outer circuit road is based on an illustration that appeared in the *Bristol Evening Post* on Friday 15 October 1971. The black line shows the route proposed by *Evening Post* reader Paul

Chadd, which would have taken the traffic through the largely derelict area of St Philip's.

The grey line is the route preferred by the City Council which was to join the M32 at Junction 3. Much of Easton was demolished to build the first section of the outer circuit road and the lower part of Totterdown was bulldozed in 1972 to make way for it.

It is worth noting the tunnel which would appear to go either under Brandon Hill near the Cabot Tower or under the area of Clifton opposite QEH School on Jacobs Wells Road, before emerging near the Victoria Rooms and ploughing straight through Cotham.

by the Saxons and it was part of the manor of Keynsham. Later, however, it became a manor of its own when William the Conqueror gave it to his nephew.

It has always been viewed as separate to Bristol, whether it is a suburb or just a village you pass on the way to Bath (in the 19th Century it was known as the most beautiful village in Somerset). It is connected to the city centre now more obviously by the addition of places in between like Paintworks, Avon Meads and the ITV studios.

Sandy Park Road is a terrific high street, which is quickly evolving into a hip and exciting place with the arrival of the Grounded cafe/bar replacing the T-Cup cafe. Grounded bars were designed to bring new life into areas just outside the city centre and others exist in Bedminster, Redfield and Horfield. They've all brought a trendy vibe with their coffee shop/live music crossover.

Sandy Park is also home to many takeaways, corner shops, beauty salons and all the other shops that you would expect on a small high street. It also treasures the scary Sandringham pub, which has a strict 'locals-only' feel and even if you are local, you have to be a certain type of person to be accepted. Once, a van went accelerating past the pub and accidentally tipped over due to the chaotic speed it was travelling, spilling its entire cargo of marijuana onto the street by the side of the Sandringham. Most of it was removed by the police, but it is believed that a lot was sneakily taken off the scene by members of the public.

Avon Meads is one of the destinations if you live in the Brislington area, with an array of activities to keep you entertained. You can tour the fast food joints – from McDonalds to Greggs – go bowling, watch a film or just browse through the shops. It may not be the classiest or the hippest place in Brislington, but it's definitely a key part of it and if you lived in the Brislington area, you'd eventually grow to love it.

The RSPCA Cats and Dogs Home and Animal Rescue Centre (www.bristolarc.org.uk) on Albert Road is a friendly and welcoming place, which allows you adopt animals and also walk the dogs at the home. The policy used to be that anyone could just come in and walk a dog. However, that has now changed and you will have to do a short training course before you can walk the dogs.

Bristol Blue Glass (www.bristol-glass.co.uk) is a fun place to go on Open Doors Day, as you get the chance to blow some of your very own blue glass! There are also lots of attractive blue glass creations to purchase. The factory was voted 'Best Tourism Activity of the Year' by Destination Bristol in 2011. It is now opposite the entrance to Arnos Vale Cemetery on Bath Road having moved from its former home in Whitby Road.

One of the coolest things to see around Brislington is the Black Castle. It was built in 1745-1755 from blocks of slag, which were cast from waste. It was merely a folly construction, belonging to a local Quaker and businessman. William Reeve also had a number of other decorative structures such as the large walls with the statues by the Lloyds bank. When he went bankrupt, he had to sell his business and the castle to the Tonge family, who were slave traders. It's strange and just seems out of place next to a Sainsbury's and opposite a Shell garage, but adds a kind of quirky edge to Brislington, which helps attract more quirky people. And nothing makes an area like a castle, even if it does have a very poorly rated pub in the middle of it.

Near the castle, there is a large structure decorated with statues, which, like the castle, has a very medieval feel but is actually the old gate to the Arnos Estate stables.

Spark Evans Park may be perfect for dog walking but it was also home to many all-night raves, which could be heard from afar and attracted many people.

Nightingale Valley between Brislington and St Anne's is a deceptively large area of wildlife. It boasts beautiful scenery and also some interesting animals such as slow worms, lizards and kingfishers. It really is one of the prettier sides to Brislington and Bristol as a whole.

Totterdown

Totterdown is split in two by the Wells Road. On the left going out of Bristol is Arnos Vale; on the right is the area most Bristolians would call Totterdown. The Arnos Vale side is residential but there is a bohemian element to the community which blends in with the established South Bristol vibe. There have been several welcome arrivals on Wells Road including the Al Waha take-away, the Assilah Moroccan restaurant (www. assilahbistro.com), Acapella deli and café (www.acappellas.co.uk), Eat Your Greens vegan restaurant, a trendy bar called Southside, the marvellous Farrows chip shop and Bristol's best flower shop Floriography. Down the hill on the Bath Road the Thunderbolt (www.thethunderbolt.net), is an excellent live music venue.

The other side of Wells Road is a far livelier proposition and features two excellent pubs the Shakespeare, the Oxford, as well as the Banco Lounge in the old Lloyd's bank/YMCA building. There's also a mosque on this side of Totterdown: the Bristol Jamia Mosque in Green Street which

Arnos Vale Cemetery

A remarkable 45-acre green space in the heart of the city...

Restoration work at Arnos Vale Cemetery was officially completed in April 2010, but before an army of volunteers and contractors had spent years repairing and restoring this fascinating site had been in a state of neglect for 25 years. In 2003 the cemetery was runner-up in the BBC's *Restoration* TV series. In 2005, Arnos Vale was handed a £4.8 million grant by the Heritage Lottery Fund. Work started immediately on clearing and renovating the cemetery, setting up a visitor centre and introducing educational, wildlife and conservation programmes.

The 45-acre cemetery was owned by Anthony Towner, head of the Bristol General Cemetery Company. In 1987, faced with falling revenue, Mr Towner announced that he wanted to sell a large part of the cemetery for residential development. A public meeting was arranged and the Campaign to Save Arnos Vale Cemetery was formed. Within weeks 20,000 people had signed a petition against the proposed development plans.

In 1998, the City Council refused Mr Towner a cremation licence because the crematorium failed to meet the regulations of the Environmental Protection Act 1990. So the crematorium ceased to operate and Mr Towner threatened to lock the gates. An angry crowd besieged Mr Towner in his office at the cemetery; the gates remained open and the Friends of Arnos Vale (led by the late Richard Smith MBE) took charge of the cemetery, unlocking and locking the gates every day and doing their best to maintain the site.

Bristol City Council was granted a Compulsory Purchase Order for the cemetery in April 2001 and a public inquiry was held in May 2002 to hear the evidence in connection with Mr Towner's objections. The inquiry ended early when the company withdrew its objections. The Council bought the cemetery under the CPO and handed it over to The Friends of Arnos Vale Cemetery.

Arcadian Garden

The cemetery was founded in 1837 when a private Act of Parliament established the Bristol General Cemetery Company. It was planned as a Greek-style Necropolis and was landscaped using trees and plants noted in classical legend. Its Grade II listed Arcadian Garden contains four buildings designed by the architect Charles Underwood: two neo-Greek Doric entrance lodges (both are Grade II listed buildings), an Anglican Mortuary Chapel and a Non-Conformist Chapel.

Arnos Vale is the final resting place of several Lord Mayors of Bristol, an American consul, members of the Wills and Robinson families, George Muller and possibly Mary 'Princess Caraboo' Baker, who managed to persuade the Squire of Almondsbury that she was an Eastern Princess. Further down the Victorian social scale, you'll find the unmarked mounds of the common graves of the poor and the flat markers of the guinea graves of those whose relations had managed to collect 21 shillings (£1.05) to avoid a pauper's burial.

The grave of Mary Carpenter, the Victorian pioneer of juvenile care, was lost in the undergrowth until it was discovered when part of the graveyard was being cleared of brambles. At least two survivors of the Charge of the Light Brigade are buried at Arnos Vale, as is a police officer who was murdered in Old Market whilst trying to intervene in a fight over the ill-treatment of a donkey.

Raja Rammohun Roy

Arnos Vale also contains a considerable number of individual war graves, a small military cemetery with a Cross of Sacrifice, and a World War One memorial classical stone arcade built into the hillside close to the main entrance. Approximately 250,000 burials have taken place in 50,000 graves and 750,000 cremations have also been carried out, with most of the cremated remains scattered in the Arnos Vale Gardens of Rest.

The most famous resident of Arnos Vale Cemetery is Raja Rammohun Roy, the great Bengali social reformer who died from meningitis on 27 September 1833 while he was staying with friends at Beech House in Stapleton (later to become Purdown Hospital and now a residential development).

Rammohun Roy was a scholar fluent in many languages including Greek, Hebrew and Latin. He wrote books on grammar, geography and geometry and published newspapers and is especially remembered for his campaign to end the Hindu custom of 'sati', the burning of a widow on her husband's funeral pyre. As head of the

Atmiya Sabha he spearheaded reform on all fronts: he was against polygamy and the caste system and was a supporter of education for women. The 19th-Century Indian social reformer Ranade called him the 'father of modern India' and Indian academic Professor Brajendraneth Shil described him as 'the pioneer internationalist'. There's now a statue of him outside the Central Library on College Green.

On his death, the Raja was buried in the garden of Beech House. Ten years later, in 1843, his body was moved to a permanent burial site at Arnos Vale so that the public might have access to it. The canopy over the tomb was styled by a Calcutta designer and there are plans for it to be restored to its original glory.

- The Arnos Vale Cemetery Trust is continuing to raise money through its Guardian Angel scheme.
- Arnos Vale Cemetery Trust, West Lodge, Bath Road
- Tel: 971 9117
- www.arnosvale.org.uk

'Totterdown' by Gage Graphics on the Bath Road at the bottom of Thunderbolt Steps

was the first mosque in Bristol when it opened in 1968 on the site of the former St Katherine's Church which closed in 1964.

In the 1980s and 1990s, the Shakespeare was run by Mad Ern (Vernon Somers) and his wife Sane Joan. Ern was one of Bristol's greatest characters and the Shakespeare exuded his extravagant personality. The walls and ceiling were completely covered with postcards, posters, witticisms and house rules. You never needed to take anything to read: you could just work your way around the walls and ceiling. In the midst of this chaos, Ern built himself a DJ den from where he and his mates would treat customers to an eclectic mix of tunes. Ern left in 2000 and a pub full of tat left with him. Mad Ern passed away in August 2011 and with him went a piece of Totterdown history.

PJ Harvey used to live in Totterdown and it is rumoured that Polly enjoyed her 'creative liaison' with Nick Cave in a house in Stevens Crescent. She certainly played the Coup d'Etat acoustic music club upstairs at the Cumberland (now the Star and Dove). Coup d'Etat was run by much-respected local muso Dave McDonald who is now at the Thunderbolt.

Totterdown made a national name for itself for its Front Room Art Trail which began in 2000 and, by 2019, featured about 100 artists, 50 houses, four pubs and attracted 4,000 visitors over two days in November.

Paintworks

The left side of Bath Road is the self-styled 'Creative Quarter', not exactly abuzz with life but it does house some serious players in Bristol's creative industries such as Wildfire media, Bristol 247 and (ahem) Tangent Books. It's also home to Bocabar, one of Bristol's biggest bars. Bocabar is one of the few South Bristol destinations. It serves excellent food and is particularly famous for its pizzas. The staff are outstanding and it's popular with families with young children. Photographer Martin Parr a member of the prestigious Magnum Photos is based at Paintworks as is the Royal Photographic Society.

On the other side of the river in St Philip's is Bristol Fruit Market, the biggest wholesale outlet to the fruit, veg and flower trade in the South West. On Sundays, there's a 'cheap cuts, CDs and clothes market' on the site. You'll also find Charles Saunders, the city's main fresh and frozen fish wholesaler, down this way too. Underneath the bridge from Bath Road to St Philip's behind the old Esso Garage site is a wall loved by the city's graffiti artists.

Victoria Park

Victoria Park lies between Totterdown and Windmill Hill and boasts fine views over the city. The park may lack a central feature, such as a lake but, is being increasingly used by the local community for fun days, sponsored cycle rides and dog shows. There's an active Wildlife Group which has initiated various conservation schemes.

The park is home to St Mary Redcliffe Primary School and a water maze. The maze, on the Totterdown side of the park, is on the original course of the St Mary Redcliffe pipe, which supplied the citizens of Bristol with clean water in the 12th Century. Since 1984, the water has flowed from Knowle into the maze, which is built in brick as a replica of a medieval roof boss in St Mary Redcliffe Church.

Windmill Hill

Like Totterdown, Windmill Hill was a semi-rural area until the railway line from Bristol to Weston-super-Mare and beyond was built in the mid 19th Century. Windmill Hill takes its name from the fact that there was a windmill there – another one faced it across the valley in Totterdown, probably on School Road. Historically, Windmill Hill housed railway and tobacco workers.

The Hill is a curious area. It has got a trendy element, but it took the refit of the Windmill in 2006 to give it a decent pub with good food. In 2010 the Raymend was relaunched as the Victoria Park gastro pub.

Windmill Hill City Farm is its main claim to fame. The Farm was formed in 1976 by a volunteer group of local residents determined to see a piece on inner-city wasteland put to more productive use by farming in the heart of the city. It's a great place, particularly for kids and families, with a farmyard with chickens, pigs, ducks and goats and a great café.

A curious item of south Bristol folklore involves Bristol philanthropist John James who was born at 96 Phillip Street on the main road in front of the farm. The bomb-damaged houses were demolished after the Second World War. John James was one of the Farm's earliest supporters and donated £1,000-a-year to the project. In return he asked that a cabbage should be grown every year on the site of his childhood home. The John James Room was opened in 1998 in recognition of his support.

Bedminster

Bedminster is older than Bristol and probably takes its name from a monastery or church founded by the monk Beda, or from the old English word 'bedydd', which means baptism. In the 15th Century, this is where the lepers came to live.

Bedminster is separated from the rest of the city by the New Cut. This was dug between 1804 and 1809, when the Floating Harbour was built to carry the River Avon around the Harbour. It runs from Hotwells to Totterdown. When the Cut was built, Bedminster was part of Somerset; it was included in the Bristol boundaries in 1897, by which time it was an important industrial area with a coalfield, engineering works, tanneries,

The Smythes

John Smythe bought the Ashton Court Estate and large areas of South Bristol in the 16th Century. He is usually referred to as 'a successful Bristol merchant'. However, there is some evidence that he was actually a smuggler. The Smythes commissioned a survey to see if there were coal deposits in Bedminster. There were, and the first pit opened in South Liberty Lane in 1744. By 1830, there were 18 pits in Bedminster, the biggest of which was in Dean Lane. This can still be seen in Dame Emily Park (named after Sir Greville Smythe's wife), where a set of railings (and formerly a bandstand) marks the covered top of the area's biggest pit. The last Bedminster pit closed in 1924.

tobacco factories, paint and glue works. The population of Bedminster grew from 3,000 in 1801 to 78,000 in 1884.

Bedminster was an important area in the very early years of Bristol. The church of St John the Baptist (destroyed in World War Two, but not demolished until 1962) dated from 1003, and it was the mother church to St Mary Redcliffe, which was officially a chapel-of-ease to Bedminster until 1852.

Despite forming a heartland of Labour support in the city, many people from the area complain that it has been overlooked by the Labour Party when it has control of Bristol City Council and, like much of South Bristol, has seen significant inroads by the Lib Dems and Green Party. Nowadays, Bedminster is still a run-down, rough-and-ready part of town with a lot of character (and characters). It has steadfastly resisted attempts to smarten it up. However, that could all change with the completion of the massive Bedminster Green plan. This high-rise development on five big plots on land between Windmill Hill and East Street will change the face of Bedminster. As seems to be the case with all new building initiatives in Bristol, the original developers have sold on the land during the planning process, open spaces and social housing provisions have been dropped and the density of housing and height of the tower blocks have increased. There has been a popular and well organised campaign to control the high-rise and high-density aspects of Bedminster Green which has been largely ignored by the Labour-controlled council and cabinet.

Heading over Bedminster Bridge from Redcliffe, Nelson Parade becomes Bedminster Parade, which turns into East Street, the main road

Poets' Corner, North Street

If you look up at the wall of the house on the junction of Merrywood Road and North Street, you'll notice a weathered and crumbling bust and the words 'Poets Corner'. Thomas Chatterton is Bristol's most famous poet, but this memorial commemorates one of the city's worst: Alfred Daw Collard, the poet/butcher of Bedminster.

The Collards were a well known South Bristol family and provided four generations of butchers. There's still the front of a closed Collards' butchers farther up North Street. Collard was famous in the late 19th Century for his dreadful music hall-style poetry, copies of which he sold for a penny to raise money for Bristol General Hospital.

One of his works, *The Redcliffe and Bedminster Christmas Meat Show of 1885*, named all of the 26 butcher's shops between North Street and Redcliffe Hill.

through Bedminster, which supposedly follows the route of a Roman Road used to carry minerals from the Mendips to the Roman Port at Sea Mills.

Just off Bedminster Parade in Stillhouse Lane is the old Bedminster Bridge School, a Grade II listed building designed by WV Gough and built in 1895. Equally impressive is the police and fire station on Bedminster Parade. This grand castle-like building was opened in 1882 by Mr ES Robinson of the paper-bag and printing company. The tower is there for practical rather than aesthetic reasons: it was a watch tower to spot fires. The original police and fire station that once stood here was one of the three built by an Act of Parliament in 1834; the other two were at Brandon Hill and St Philip's. In 1850, Bedminster had only one street light and one flushing toilet: both were at the police station. It is currently offices.

The Asda supermarket on Bedminster Parade was built on the site of the former Wills tobacco factory after that was demolished in 1986. In the 18th Century, the site of the current Asda car park was called the Paddock and was a meeting place for Bedminster's active Methodist community – John Wesley is known to have preached there at least four times.

The shops next to Asda are in an original Wills building. Before the arrival of Asda, the lower part of East Street was home to several small greengrocers, a fishmonger and other high-street stores; these were unable

Billy Butlin of Bedminster

Billy Butlin launched his multi-million pound holiday camp empire with the takings from a hoop-la stall in Bedminster.

Having moved from South Africa to Bedminster and then Canada, after World War One, Billy Butlin worked his passage from Newfoundland to Liverpool. He arrived in England with £5 and headed for Bedminster to find his mother's fairground family. Butlin walked and hitch-hiked the entire way from Liverpool to Bristol. He was given the job of painting and re-fitting rides owned by the family and eventually his uncles set him up a small hoop-la stall at a cost of 30/- (£1.50), with prizes loaned to him by his kinsfolk. His first fair was at Axbridge, where business

was very good: Billy made £10 clear profit, far more than the more experienced stall holders.

Butlin had a different outlook to the other stallholders, who made it difficult to win prizes by making the blocks too wide for the hoops to easily fit over. Bill made his blocks smaller so that the hoops went over more easily. He therefore got rid of all his prizes and made a nice profit. He re-invested his profits and quickly moved from hoop-la stalls to amusement parks.

By 1936, he had made enough money to open his first holiday camp in Skegness. His philosophy is based on the success of his Bedminster hoop-la stall: give the punters a fair deal and they'll keep coming back.

Windmill Hill City Farm is one of the most enchanting places in the city

to compete with the supermarket and closed down leaving the Bristol end of East Street in a somewhat shabby state. There's little of note as you walk through the pedestrianised part of East Street. The site of St John's Church is about half way up on the left in a small park off Church Road.

The Albert is a famous Bedminster pub which closed in 2005. Its landlord Ian Storrer is one of the city's good guys, though you wouldn't necessarily guess it from his sometimes gruff disposition. The Albert was Bristol's best jazz venue. The lounge walls were covered with Reid Miles' superb artwork for the Old Blue Note covers, and the bar was plastered with covers from *Wire* magazine. Bristol's brilliant jazz saxophonist Andy Sheppard started out at the Albert and all of the city's jazz luminaries have played there including Adrian Utley of Portishead fame. In the mid 1980s and early 1990s, Ian gave the Ashton Court Festival free use of a room for meetings. Bristol owes a lot to Ian Storrer. The Albert re-opened in 2007, sadly without Ian.

The Steam Crane on the junction with North Street (although it's changed names so much in recent years it may now be called something else) dates back to the 18th Century when it was called The Bull. In 1827 Mr Martin, the publican, bought a tiger and put it on show inside a cage in the pub. He paid a man, Joseph Kiddle, to get inside the cage with it. The tiger mauled Mr Kiddle to death. Opposite Bristol South Swimming Baths, you'll find the Magnet Chip Shop. This was voted the best chippy in Bristol in the mid 1990s. The Argus in North Street is also famous for its fish and chips. Just before Dean Lane joins Coronation Road, there's a Blue Plaque on the house which was home to the famous 1960s ivory tinkler Russ Conway (real name Trevor Herbert Stanford). Strangely, the house just a few doors down where Bear Hackenbush, Skate Muties, the Bugs 'n' Drugs crew and Chaos UK used to live has not been accorded such civic recognition.

Heading up North Street towards Southville, you'll find many relatively new and interesting shops and bars including the North Street Standard bar, Friendly Records vinyl emporium and bar, StorySmith bookshop, Corks off licence, the Leveret pub, Zero Green, Bristol's first zero waste shop, the Old Bookshop bistro, Spotted Cow pub and Jasper's Jamaican Diner which is run by ex-squaddie Jasper Thompson founder of Help Bristol's Homeless. Jasper came up with the idea of offering homeless people accommodation in converted containers after living in similar ones himself while serving in the Army in Afghanistan and Iraq.

WD & HO Wills

There were already several other tobacco manufacturers in Bristol when Henry Overton Wills arrived in the city from Salisbury in 1786 and went into partnership with Samuel Watkins. Their first shop was in Castle Street but by 1791, the firm had moved to 112 Redcliffe Street.

The company quickly established a reputation for integrity and quality. The firm made steady progress and in 1871 entered the cigarette market with the original Bristol brand. This was followed in 1874 by Passing Clouds, in 1878 by Three Castles and in 1888 by one of the most famous cigarette brands in the UK, Woodbines, at a price of five for 1d.

In 1886, the firm moved to Bedminster and expanded its operation throughout South Bristol with sites in Southville, Ashton and Hartcliffe. In 1901, the Imperial Tobacco Company was formed to resist an attempt by a powerful association of American tobacco manufacturers to capture the British market; WD & HO Wills took a leading part in its formation. The tobacco industry dominated South Bristol for much of the 20th Century.

In 1969, the Wills' Redcliffe Street premises were demolished and in 1974 production started at the new Hartcliffe Factory. Production was gradually phased out on the East Street and Southville sites and the whole operation was moved to Hartcliffe. In 1986, the original factory buildings at the bottom of East Street were demolished and an Asda supermarket was built on the site.

In 1989, the Hartcliffe head office building was vacated and in 1990 the Hartcliffe factory ceased cigarette production. All Imperial Tobacco cigarette production moved to Nottingham, though cigar production stayed in Bristol until the Hartcliffe factory was demolished in 1999.

Southville

Southville is the residential area between Bedminster and Ashton. It's the poshest part of South Bristol and estate agents periodically try to rename it Lower Clifton or Clifton View. Southville was largely built on tobacco money from the Wills family, who were teetotal. It is for this reason that there isn't a single pub in Southville, but there are many on the boundaries including the Hen & Chicken, which became Bristol's first theatre pub in 1989 when it was home to the Show of Strength theatre company.

North Street is the main shopping street in Southville. It has always been a busy high street and in recent years, it has helped Southville become Bristol's coolest neighbourhood.

The impetus for Southville becoming so trendy is the Tobacco Factory project. The Tobacco Factory is housed in the last remaining part of the 1906 old Wills Number 3 factory site on Raleigh Road. It contains a cafe bar, a theatre and various media-related enterprises. The building was saved from demolition by architect George Ferguson (who became Bristol's first elected Mayor in 2012) and is the centre of a movement for urban regeneration inspired by the Manchester Independents Campaign. The campaign philosophy is to encourage independent outlets and businesses and support local character and enterprise.

It certainly seems to be working in North Street: since the Tobacco Factory opened, the area has attracted many new bars, restaurants and shops while retaining its greengrocer, butcher's shops, bakeries (including the fabulous Mark's Bread) the mighty Lions hardware store and the Upfest gallery from where Steve and Emma Hayles organise the brilliant Upfest South Bristol street art festival. Other notable places this end of North Street include the lovely Tincan Coffee shop, Southville Deli, Bristol's original Lounge Bar and Souk Kitchen.

If you follow North Street down towards Ashton Park, where it becomes Ashton Road, you'll find Al's Tikka Grill. This is a cafe by day and BYO curry bistro and take-away by night, and is regarded as one of Bristol's best curry houses.

BS5 Easton to Redfield and St George

For centuries this area has had a streak of radicalism running through its terraced streets, once the homes of miners, weavers, leather and railway workers and it retains a strong sense of community and expression despite the creeping threat of gentrification...

At face value, there may seem little to recommend a visit to the East Bristol inner-city areas bordered by the M32 and the A420. But here you'll find one of Bristol's most pleasant walks (along the banks of the Frome at Snuff Mills), a fantastic shopping street (St Mark's Road), a dub reggae and techno paradise (the Black Swan), the home of Bristol's radical sports club the Easton Cowboys and Cowgirls in the Plough.

Easton

There is little evidence of it now, but Easton was built on coal. The earliest mining area in Bristol was further east in Kingswood where coal was produced from the 17th century to fuel the soap-making, glass, brewing and pottery industries. The first Easton mines were developed in the late 18th Century and the industry boomed in the 19th century.

Today Easton is a buzzing, run-down inner-city area alongside Stapleton

Looking down St Mark's Road towards the Easton Jamia Mosque

Road and home to the city's largest ethnic population. It has a history of political activism dating back to the weavers' riots in 1728; there were miners' strikes in the 18th and 19th centuries and it was the birthplace of Ben Tillett, one of the founders of the Labour movement and the creator of the first unions for unskilled workers.

It is currently a base for the Bristol Anarchist Solidarity Easton (BASE) anarchist centre in Robertson Road (see Underground and Radical Bristol). It's where the anti-car lobby park their bicycles and is the area of choice for a sizeable gay (particularly lesbian) community.

Bristol elected Mayor Marvin Rees was brought up in Easton and right-wing Tory Home Secretary Savid Javid's family moved from Rochdale to Stapleton Road where they lived above the family clothing shop for most of Javid's childhood before he left home for Exeter University. Javid has painted a picture of Stapleton Road being full of crime, drug dealers and prostitution which has angered community leaders. Some people have even suggested that Javid is a Tory tosspot playing to the far right of his party as he prepared a leadership challenge.

Every visitor to Bristol should take a stroll down St Mark's Road, where you'll find Moroccan cafes, a Bangladeshi restaurant, a Thali cafe, an African-Caribbean clothes store, a sari shop and the mighty Bristol Sweet Mart. The Sugar Loaf on St Mark's Road is a well-known and busy pub **91** that has merited an entry in the Good Beer Guide. It's a good spot to sit outside and watch the Easton world go by – there's regular live music in the evenings.

The Chelsea on Chelsea Road attracts Easton's radical community with regular punk and hardcore gigs and the Plough on Easton Road, once a quiet back street boozer is now a leading venue specialising in all things bass-heavy.

The Black Swan opposite the junction of St Mark's Road and Stapleton Road was the headquarters of Bristol Rovers FC between 1897 and 1910. The original building is thought to date back to 1640, although it was rebuilt in the 19th Century. It's now famous for evenings of heavyweight drum 'n' bass and is home to the mighty Bristol Dub Club hosted by DJ Bliss Zion.

Eastville Park

Eastville Park was created as a result of public pressure to tackle the problems of overcrowding and poor health in the parish of St Philip's. After much lobbying, 70 acres of land were purchased in 1889 for £30,000 on estate land owned by Heath House and Ridgeway House. At the time the land was on the outskirts of the growing city and many people were against the idea of a park at Eastville because they thought the area was too remote.

Easton Colliery, Felix Road

The Easton Colliery in Felix Road was opened in 1830 and closed in 1911 and was at its peak production in 1870. In common with mines everywhere, conditions were terrible. Children and women worked in the mines because they were able to squeeze through the narrow passageway. At the coalface, miners worked with pickaxes and spades in a choking atmosphere.

The underground workings spread for miles. The Easton Pit was linked to Whitehall pit by an underground railway two miles long.

In his memoirs, Ben Tillett recalls how he was persuaded not to become a miner: 'One of my relatives cured me of my plan to go down the pit.

He took me down into the seemingly bottomless pit and terrified me.

I saw awesome blackness: spluttering candles on greasy caps, dirt and mud, pools of filthy water, stifling heat, the rush and tempest of everyone pushing, bawling, shouting and cursing.'

On 19 February 1886, eight Easton colliers died in an explosion at the pit. A relief fund was set up and each widow received £5 towards the funeral and 5 shillings (25p) a week for herself and one child under 13, and a further 2/6d (12.5p) if there were other children. The inquest into the disaster was held at Lebeq's Tavern on Stapleton Road.

Some mature trees already growing there were kept, the existing boundary walls were repaired and paths were laid out with 100 seats and several small wooden shelters. Walks were created by planting an avenue of lime trees (now partly replaced by horse chestnuts) and London planes. The grass was managed with both sheep-grazing and mowing. The outdoor swimming pool followed in 1905, the bowling greens in 1907, and finally the lake in 1908 to 1909.

The lake is one of the best public park lakes in England; it is designed in a serpentine shape so that wherever you stand you cannot see how big it is. It is bordered by lawns, specimen trees and a hanging wood.

The park has now lost most of its original features; the bandstand and little kiosks had gone by 1950; only the plinth and footings of the octagonal drinking fountain by the Fishponds Road entrance still survive, with a stand pipe which no longer supplies water.

The Crimean War cannon which stood on a plinth near the bowling green was removed during World War Two to be melted down to make weapons. Almost all the grand entrances to the park have been lost to road-building. The widening of Fishponds Road in 1909 involved cutting back the Park for nearly the whole of its edge by the road. The M32 took away the lower entrance, with its walls, gates and drinking fountain, back in the 1960s. The best entrance is the original one up in the north-west corner, right under the remains of a clump of London plane trees. The pennant wall and gateway are both listed buildings.

You can join the 20km Frome Valley Walkway to Old Sodbury at Eastville Park.

Eastville

Eastville used to be home to Bristol Rovers Football Club but now people only go to Eastville (or Eastgate as it's been renamed) to shop at Tesco and IKEA, which was built despite a vociferous campaign by locals who objected to the increase in traffic (among other things) that the store would bring. Their arguments were dismissed by the planners, but guess what? Yep, the M32 to IKEA is solid with cars every single weekend.

Distressingly for Bristol Rovers fans, the IKEA store is almost exactly the dimensions of the old Eastville pitch. This is because the site was developed piecemeal and the pitch was the last bit to go. Bizarrely, a floodlight from the Muller Road end of the old ground was left standing in the Tesco's car park as a memorial to Rovers' home. It stayed there until 2003 when it was removed because it was becoming unstable. As is the way with these things, **93** the lights were auctioned to grateful supporters. Rovers, strangely, plunged into the darkness of the bottom division of the football league for the first time in their history just about the same time as the floodlight was taken down. What does that tell you?

The arrival of IKEA meant the loss of a Bristol institution, Eastville Market, which used to be held in the old Rovers' car park. To be honest, other than shopping at IKEA, there's not a great deal going on in Eastville. The area sits between Easton and Fishponds and marks the transition from inner city to suburban Bristol.

Fishponds

Fishponds is a suburb on the border with South Gloucestershire close to Eastville Park, Oldbury Court Estate (locals call it Vassalls Park) and the River Frome where there is a pleasant walk down to Snuff Mills. Standing at the Cross Hands pub with Downend and Staple Hill at your back you have in front of you the whole wonder of Fishponds. The high street starts at the recently updated Straits Parade, goes past historical St Mary's church and on down Fishponds road past the local Conservative Club (which was vandalised during Thatcher's funeral preparations). Shortly after the

A brief history of Fishponds

The area's name comes from two quarries filled with water named the New Pools that were used as fish ponds for the estates in the Kings Wood. John Leech of the *Bristol Times* said in 1847 "Fishponds is a most miserable looking place – so cold and cheerless, indeed, that a man instinctively buttons his coat and quickens his pace as he passes through it." It's improved a bit since then.

Once home to Fishponds Asylum and a notorious prison for French prisoners from the Napoleonic War (1803-1815). According to A Braine in *The History of Kingswood Forest* (1891): "Many hundreds of prisoners were confined in this place on one occasion that, it is said during the hot summer weather, the prisoners poked

nearly all the tiles off the roof in order to get fresh air".

The population increased after the Stapleton Enclosure act in 1781 until in 1821 St Mary's church was consecrated, and mainly served the Stapleton workhouse, when a chapelry was granted in 1869 Fishponds became an official district. In 1897 the whole area was taken out of the County of Gloucestershire to become an integral part of the City and County of Bristol where it remains to this day. Fishponds has an industrial past, being first settled by quarrymen and once home to a large shoe factory and although there is still some industry, including Bristol Tile and Travis Perkins, it is now suburban with mainly Victorian housing.

The River Frome flows through a wooded valley in Stapleton

junction with Lodge Causeway the shops peter out and are replaced by large houses.

Fishponds has two hospitals, one of which, Blackberry Hill, started out as a prison for the French during the Napoleonic wars.

Increasingly Fishponds has become an overspill for families from Easton looking for more space and that's had the effect of connecting the area more with the city whereas before it looked outwards to Staple Hill and Downend. The new population has resulted in a more modern eating and drinking options alongside the traditional boozers and take-aways. The new arrivals include, Snuffy Jack's micropub and the Porto Lounge on Fishponds Road and the Kingfisher Cafe on Straits Parade while the Cross Hands and Star pubs have had a refurb.

Stapleton

Stapleton has a village feel, despite being right next to the M32 and on the main road from Eastville to Frenchay. The peculiar impression of being time-warped from IKEA into rural England is strongest if you stroll down Colston Hill between Holy Trinity Church and Colston's School. The lane leads to the Frome Valley and Snuff Mills, a riverside walk that is one of the unspoilt gems of Bristol.

The impressive Stapleton parish church, Holy Trinity, is a particularly fine building. The first record of a church on this site goes back to 1438, but this one was built by Bristol architect John Norton in 1857 – the only other surviving example of Norton's religious architecture in the city is St Mary's in Stoke Bishop. Holy Trinity is built in the Victorian Gothic style with an elaborately carved door and a huge 170-foot tower. It is usually floodlit at night, so it is one of the first buildings you see when you enter Bristol via the M32 after dark.

The square font, which now sits in the west porch, has been dated to about 1000AD. It was sold to a bishop's butler at one point in its history; the butler went on to become landlord of the Bell pub opposite the church and took the font with him to use as a geranium pot. It was later discovered and returned to the church sometime in the late 19th century. Colston's School, next to Holy Trinity, is for stripy-blazer posh kids. The nearby Masons Arms has a pleasant garden which offers fine views over the Frome Valley. And that, my friends, is Stapleton.

Whitehall to St George

Bob Hope (yes, that Bob Hope) lived at 326 Whitehall Road and at 14 Clouds Hill Avenue, St George when he was a nipper. Like many people, Bob (or Leslie as he was called then) passed through Whitehall and St George on his way to somewhere better.

St George's Park, which has a lake and skateboard park, lies between Whitehall and St George, where Tony Benn used to have his Labour Party office on Church Road. The monument on the 'fountain' junction of Church Road, Clouds Hill Road and Summerhill Road is the Don John Cross, which is more than 400 years old and once marked the beginning

Snuff Mills

One of the best things about living in Bristol is that you don't have to head out of town to find pleasant walks. The Downs and Arnos Vale cemetery are both fantastic green spaces, but if you want to discover a riverside walk near the centre of town, head down to Snuff Mills. Take a picnic, or, even better, a dog.

Snuff Mills is the area between Blackberry Hill and Eastville Park and despite its name, as far as anyone has been able to ascertain, there has never actually been a mill there that ground snuff.

The mill that used to stand on the Frome here in the 19th Century was called Whitwood Mill but there's evidence of a mill on this site from 1297. It's thought that Snuff Mills got its name from a local character called Snuffy Jack who worked in a snuff mill further upstream and whose smock was always covered in snuff. He may also have worked in or lived near Whitwood Mill.

of the Kingswood Forest. It's said to have taken its name from when the funeral bier bearing the body of a Spanish nobleman rested at the cross for a while before resuming its journey. It's probably not called after the grubby little boozer of the same name that used to be just down the road past the Fountain Cafe.

Redfield

For many years Redfield had little to recommend it. It was a traffic-snarled enclave between two main commuter routes into town (Church Road and Whitehall Road) with a remarkable number of take-aways and no good pubs. On the other hand, it's right next to St George's Park, there's a station nearby at Lawrence Hill, it's close to the cycle path and near the Feeder at Netham Park and the River Avon at Crew's Hole. St George looked outwards towards Kingswood rather than towards Bristol, but in recent years it's become far more cosmopolitan as renters and first-time buyers are forced out of the wealthy city centre by spiralling property prices.

So, Redfield and St George are on the up. They must be because there's a Grounded cafe, a good fruit and veg shop (Dig In), a Southville Deli, several foodie destinations (the Dark Horse and the Lock Up) and its own art and music festival (Redfest).

In 2011, Weng Chin Ng of the China Garden/Peking Dynasty on Church Road was sentenced to eight months in prison suspended for 18 months for selling bags of weed from the takeaway. The case resulted in the excellent headline 'Chinese Tokeaway'.

BS6
Cotham to Westbury Park

The area on the left as you go up Gloucester Road is sandwiched between the multi-cultural alternative vibe of Montpelier and St Paul's and the more staid environment of Whiteladies Road. But rather than mixing these two distinct flavours, BS6 has a character all of its own...

Cotham

Cotham can be confusing to the first-time visitor. It's a compact, bohemian kind of district, it's full of students, but a one-bedroom flat around here will set you back a tidy wedge. The first recorded resident of this area, then known as Codd Down, was a careless snuffmaker called William Hulme. Why careless? Well, he only decided to live in a windmill – not the most sensible thing to do with all that snuff lying around. Needless to say, his business was blown away and he was declared bankrupt soon afterwards.

Cotham is dominated by elegant old houses and occasional speciality shops, pubs and restaurants. Cotham Hill, the road that runs off Whiteladies Road at Clifton Down, is easily the most vibrant area. By day it buzzes with the coffee bar crowd and shoppers, by night Cotham Hill comes into its own as a foodie hotspot with some of Bristol's finest eateries including Pasta Loco (www.pastaloco.co.uk), Bravas (www.bravas.co.uk), Falafel King (www.falafelkingbristol.com) Chai Pani (www.chaipanionline.com)

and Bellita (www.bellita.co.uk), a laid-back cocktail bar and Mediterranean-inspired restaurant founded by the team behind Bell's Diner in Montpelier who first worked together many years ago at the legendary Rocinantes tapas bar just round the corner on Whiteladies Road – one of the key meeting places at the beginning of what became the Bristol Sound.

On the other side of Cotham, on Cotham Road South, is the Cotham Porter Stores, once a famous Bristol cider house. It's now a pleasant Wickwar Brewery local. Legend has it that John Lennon sketched the picture in the bar when the Beatles came for a pint of the rough stuff following their first appearance in Bristol in 1963. Next door is the Michelin-starred Bulrush restaurant.

Kingsdown

According to a Civic Society report published in the 1980s, of all the architectural crimes that were committed in Bristol in the 1960s, 'the destruction of Bristol's most important Georgian suburb' was the most despicable. If you want to see what they mean, take a look up at Kingsdown from the city centre. Interrupting the elegantly distressed original houses are the harsh, slab-like faces of some multi-storey council blocks. However, the sideroads of Kingsdown are relatively traffic free because Bristol City Council has effectively isolated Kingsdown by blocking off the handful of roads that gave vehicles access from Cheltenham Road.

Despite the best efforts of the town planners, Kingsdown has been getting more popular in recent years with drinkers looking to escape the nightmare of the naff pub experience. The Highbury Vaults at the top of St Michael's Hill is one of Bristol's best-known pubs thanks to its popularity with students. The garden at the Vaults seems to get bigger every year and has a forest of outdoor heaters to keep the regulars warm as they tuck into their pints.

Over the road, there's a friendly and traditional pub vibe in the Cotham Arms, a relatively new arrival, though it's on the site of a pub called The Highbury Park Tavern which originally opened in 1871. Further down St Michael's Hill the White Bear has had some

Past Notes

1230 Redland is namechecked in descriptions of Bristol as 'Rubea Terra' or 'La Rede Londe' because of its ruddy soil.

1737 The Montague Tavern on Montague Hill in Kingsdown is built. Its turtle soup becomes famous in the gastronomic world.

1849 An outbreak of cholera kills 444 people.

1940 Redland Church is all but destroyed by that Hitler Fellow.

interesting promotions over the years, including a gameshow-style happy-hour wheeze where you could hit a button to determine the price of your drinks from free to full price. More recently, the former coaching inn joined forces with a team of Bristol theatre and poetry producers to create a performance space upstairs which was the original home of Wardrobe Theatre which is now based at the Old Market Assembly.

Of course, you're never far from a Merchant Venturer in Bristol, particularly in this part of town, and they manage Colston's Almshouses on the left as you walk down St Michael's Hill. Slave trade supremo Edward Colston founded the almshouses in 1691 for 12 people who were expected to attend the chapel twice a day for a prayer meeting. The baroque chapel contains panels made from ship's timbers – more than likely from ships carrying enslaved Africans across the Atlantic. Today the almshouse is 12 one-bedroom flats catering for residents of Bristol over 60 years old who are 'poor and of good character'. Preference is given to members of the Church of England.

Cutting through the houses behind St Michael's Hill, you'll find the Green Man in Alfred Place and loitering just above the A-road traffic of Stokes Croft are three excellent pubs: the Hillgrove Porter Stores in Dove Street South, the nearby Hare on the Hill in Thomas Street North. The Bell down the hill in Hillgrove Street, Stokes Croft, is a local institution where

The Kingsdown story

Wealthy merchants began moving to new homes in Kingsdown early in the 19th century. Their aim was to escape the horrible grime of the city and the overwhelming stench of the foul-smelling Avon and Frome rivers.

Much of the Kingsdown area was owned by a man called Giles Greville. The open fields were known as the Montagues and Greville divided them into plots and then built the Montague Tavern. His plan was to attract Bristol's businessmen to set up home in Kingsdown. The tavern's turtle soup, said to be based on a recipe that had been created by a Lord Mayor of Bristol from the 13th Century, was

once the talk of the turtle-supping soup world.

Civic banquets were held at the Montague Hotel – it has changed its name from Tavern at some point during the 18th century – and boys from Colston School were taken there for their annual swig of grog. The fields around the Montague Hotel became the site for dawn duels and this continued well into the 19th century. Even though the area escaped any serious bomb damage in World War Two, sadly many of Kingsdown's finest houses and landmarks were lost in a wave of post-war redevelopment tantamount to civic vandalism.

One of the few remaining Banksy originals is in Kingsdown

you can find the likes of Dope on Plastic's John Stapleton and the Blow Pop DJs delving into their back catalogue in a low key kinda way on Tuesday evenings. Keep your eyes open for one of the few remaining Banksy pieces as you descend the hill – it's a Rose In A Rat Trap on Thomas Street North.

Redland

If Clifton is Bristol's Chelsea and Montpelier its Notting Hill, then Redland is its Hampstead. There are probably more slightly distressed-looking bay window shutters here than anywhere else in the West Country. It has one of the highest levels of houses in multiple occupancy in the city. Yep, Redland is home to a vast army of students, former students, dope heads, media heads, musicians, teachers and some jaded beatniks who got in before the rents went mad and have managed to stay here ever since. However, not many of these folk can remember what happened last week, let alone when the district was called Rubea Terra in the 13th Century.

Geographically, Redland stretches from Redland Green at the top of Redland Road to Cotham Park at the bottom. On either side, Chandos Road and Zetland Road are where its heart beats fastest. Chandos is a deeply cosmopolitan road that has the look and feel of a provincial European back street enhanced by the arrival of new food and drink places including the Good Measure (the Good Chemistry micro brewery's first pub) and the Chums micropub, which won the CAMRA Bristol & District Pub Of The

Year Award in 2018. A short walk via the Kensington Arms will take you past Redland Station and onto Zetland Road. The station is on the Temple Meads to Severn Beach line which opened in 1885. The station opened in 1897. On Zetland Road you will find Casa Mexicana which brings a Central American flavour to Redland's varied eating out options. For those who prefer their food in liquid form, the area has three pubs, the Shakespeare, the Kensington and the Clyde. Of these, only the Kenny has ever been anything other than a quiet place to have a drink. In the 1980s it was the home of the JNC Firepower Pinball League, the only pinball league in the UK which, at its peak, had two divisions and a women's league. Other pubs in the League included the Lansdown, Bell, Cadbury, Mardyke, Three Horseshoes (now Cider House, Old Market), Duke of York and sadly departed Montpelier Hotel.

In 2016 the Kenny was taken over by one of Bristol's leading chefs Josh Eggleton who has introduced a top-quality menu based on pub grub such as burgers and fish and chips.

Just down the road from the Kensington on the corner of Kensington Road and Fernbank Road, you'll find 'the house that smells' where artist Jane Tarr installed a large sculpture of a nose on the side of the house.

Westbury Park

Westbury Park has always been culturally split down the middle. Half the residents have an affinity with Redland; the other half side with half-witted Henleaze. Tellingly, the most interesting thing to ever happen in Westbury Park is the famous episode of the White Tree on the Downs.

According to local legend, there are a number of suspects in the frame for painting the bottom half of the tree trunk with white emulsion. All the stories date from the 1850s. The warm-hearted version has it pinned on a bloke called George Ames who lived at the nearby Cote House and did it as an act of kindness in order to stop his children's German tutor from getting lost at night when he was on his way over to teach them. The funny version blames a Mr Woodward, who did it in a last-ditch attempt to help his regularly inebriated coachman find his way home after another night on the booze. Whoever it was and whatever they meant by it, the original was dug up in the 1950s to make way for a new roundabout. The current incarnation, number three, was planted in 1974.

Westbury Park's main street, Coldharbour Road, is a revelation with a really interesting selection of shops including the Spanish Guitar Centre, the big-on-the-outside-but-not-on-the-inside Split Tin bakery, Coldharbour

The original white tree appeared on the Downs in the 1850s and there's been one there ever since

Framery and Gallery and Rainmaker, Bristol's only gallery specialising in Native American art and crafts.

The other Westbury Park shopping street, North View is equally characterful with its specialist shops such as the mighty Homevac Electrics, Max Minerva's bookshop, the Sky Blue Gallery, Smith Fish fishmongers, Gales Butchers & Game Dealers and the highly-recommended Caffe Arabica, a laid back eatery very popular with locals. It's arrival almost makes up for the loss of the weird shrunken Victoriana of the Gillian Richards' Dollshouse Shop.

The Westbury Park pub at the bottom of North View is famous for two reasons: it is one of the very few round pubs in the UK and it was the location for the Kebab and Calculator pub in 1980s TV cult classic *The Young Ones*.

BS7 Gloucester Road to Cheltenham Road

The area around the Gloucester Road is an odd mixture of the chic and the shambolic; parts of it are in decay, other bits are bursting with energy. But beware of heading too far out of town on the A38, Patchway beckons...

Ashley Down

Set between Gloucester Road, St Paul's, St Andrew's and St Werburgh's, Ashley Down is one of those places you walk through on the way to somewhere else. It wasn't always this way. A couple of centuries ago, a spring in Ashley Down provided most of Bristol with its water supply. And the ludicrously steep allotments on Ashley Hill are a reminder of the days when the area was nothing but farmland.

It wasn't until the 18th century that houses began to be built here, when a number of well-heeled gentlemen chose the site because of its panoramic views over the city. But the most significant resident was a German immigrant called George Müller after whom Muller Road is named. Indeed, Müller could be called the Patron Saint of Ashley Down. During his lifetime, he educated more than 10,000 children at his orphanage, which is now part of the City of Bristol College. He established 117 schools which offered Christian education to more than 120,000 children. He died in 1898 aged 92 and is buried at Arnos Vale Cemetery. At his funeral in 1898, thousands of people lined the streets in silent tribute.

Today, Ashley Down hums with trainee electricians and beauticians from the College on a weekday, and Rovers fans on alternate Saturdays and Sundays. The Foresters and the Lazy Dog are packed accordingly.

Bishopston

The Nobel Prize winner of 1933, Paul Dirac, began unravelling the mysteries of quantum physics from 15 Monk Road, Bishopston, but even he'd struggle to calculate the rise in house prices around here in the last few years. According to a BBC property programme, Bishopston is one of the UK's 'golden miles': one of the county's hottest areas, where average prices have more than doubled since the previous century shot its bows. It's stupid, it benefits no-one except the banks, but it's easy to see why Bishopston has become so appealing.

Close enough to the Gloucester Road to pop out for a drink at half past ten on a Tuesday night, but far enough away to ensure you don't step in any Miss Millie's Fried Chicken carcasses as you walk through your front door, Bishopston gives its residents the best of both worlds.

As well as all the shops, cafes and restaurants, it's also a home of Bristol sport. Both the Memorial Stadium, where Bristol Rovers play, and Gloucestershire County Cricket Club are located within walking distance. The Mem is the spiritual home of Bristol Rugby who moved to Ashton Gate at the start of the 2014/15 season after almost a century in BS7. The rugby club moved there in 1921 and defeated Cardiff 19-3 in the opening match. The stadium is so called because it is dedicated as a memorial to local rugby players who lost their lives in World War One. The city's oldest public swimming pool, Bristol North Baths, was in Bishopston but is now flats.

Gloucester Road

One of Bristol's longest and most interesting streets, Gloucester Road is an extraordinary mish-mash of trendy bars, spit 'n' sawdust pubs, chic restaurants and cheap cafes. It also has more charity shops per square metre than anywhere else in the South West. Cancer Research, St

Past Notes

1750 Two mounds of earth used for archery practice are named 'Horfield Butts'.

1880 Horfield Road is renamed Gloucester Road.

1921 Postmaster General FC Kellaway lends his name to the Kellaway bit of Kellaway Avenue.

1990 Despite 16,664 local objections, a Tesco store is built on Golden Hill.

Peter's Hospice, Sue Ryder, Tenovus... you name them, they're all selling terrible jumpers from the 1980s.

Daytime browsers should be prepared to lose hours and sacrifice the soles of their feet in order to fully explore Glossy Road's multitude of nook-and-cranny stores. The best place to begin is around the junction with Ashley Down Road where the Tinto Lounge shares pavement space with a reclamation yard. As you tread southwards, you'll stumble across several 1950s-style Italian barbers, hundreds of unwanted Spandau Ballet LPs, thousands of dusty Penguin novels, enough vintage furniture to decorate a castle and an entire shop devoted to the footwear of a certain Dr Marten. But you'll also find brilliant places to browse such as the Iota and Co-Lab gift shops, the Room 212 gallery, Amnesty Bookshop, Repsycho vintage clothes and the Plastic Wax second-hand vinyl store.

If you get hungry along the way, the choices are just as varied; from deep-fried chicken in a bucket to award-winning curry, pavement-fried hot-dogs to authentic pizza houses. Gloucester Road is alive with a dizzy melody of aromas from all over the world, especially after dark. Flavours such as the Lebanese offerings of Lona (www.lonagrillhouse.com) and the Turkish eaterie Bristanbul (www.bristanbul.co.uk) sit alongside Chilean-inspired café and shop La Ruca, and the Koocha vegan mezze bar on the

Three of the strangest shops on Gloucester Road

Romantica
139 Gloucester Road

A peculiar cross between a Liberace museum and the bedroom of the person with the biggest collection of greetings cards in the world. Twee cuddly toys vie for your attention alongside posters of semi-naked girls near motorbikes.

The old-school charity shops
Gloucester Road

Beware. You may find yourself drawn into these places, such is the bizarre nature of their frontages. With their original 1960s sign lettering, these are the charity shops that time forgot. The window displays are notoriously bleak. The design team drape, say, a yellow cardigan next to a snakes-and-ladders game and lean a broken tennis racket against a naked, one-eyed doll.

Brewer's Droop
36a Gloucester Road

Fermentation vessels, thermometers, hydrometers, yeasts, sterilisation equipment, dried hops, empty bottles and bizarre corking devices aplenty live in this musty and decidedly bearded cathedral of home brewing. If you've ever had the urge to make beer that tastes like old socks, this is the place to come for advice.

The Arches marks the beginning of Gloucester Road, still largely populated by independent shops and businesses

junction with Zetland Road (www.koochamezzebar.com) and an ever-increasing number of take-aways for the inebriated to stumble into after closing time.

The stylish refurbishments of familiar haunts such as the Grace (formerly the Robin Hood's Retreat) are now in the ascendancy and none of the Gloucester Road old-style boozers remain. But what really gives Gloucester Road its 'there and back again' charm is the mixture of old-established businesses and curious newcomers attracted by the cosmopolitan vibe. Butchers Stutt & Son has been trading on Gloucester Road since 1919, Pawsons the greengrocers first opened its doors in 1958 while Bishopston Harware, Romantica and Brewers' Droop are long-time residents of great character. It may be long, mainly straight and often scruffy, but Gloucester Road has got deep roots.

Horfield

When Buffalo Bill and his Wild West extravaganza came to town in September 1891, he headed for Horfield Common where a 15,000 seat stadium had been built for his twice-daily performances. It was the biggest show ever staged in Bristol: four trainloads of animals, performers and equipment arrived at Temple Meads; the parade up Gloucester Road to Horfield was a mile long. Buffalo Bill (real name Colonel William Cody) staged 12 performances over six days to a combined audience of more than

100,000 people who all paid a shilling each to attend this huge spectacle.

Horfield could attract the stars in those days, although, even 100 years ago, the residents of Horfield were so badly behaved that the area was considered a no-go zone for travellers. All manner of nasty vagrants and thieves liked to lurk in the large wood near the common and records show that one commentator believed the area was 'lawless... worse even than Filton'. Maybe it's appropriate that Bristol's main prison was dumped here.

By the 1930s, Horfield had grown into one of those solidly working-class communities where people left the doors open and no-one ever got burgled. These days the recycling bins of the two-up-two-down terraced streets are full of *Guardians* and *Observers*.

Bristol's last execution

Russell Pascoe, a 23-year-old Bristolian, was the last person to be executed in Bristol. He was hanged at Horfield Prison at 8am on Tuesday 17 December 1963 for his part in the murder of a Cornish farmer.

Dennis Whitty, convicted with Pascoe, was hanged at the same time in Winchester.

The execution was one of the last to be carried out in Britain before the abolition of capital punishment in 1965. About 70 protesters held a silent vigil outside the prison gates and the Bishop of Bristol, the Right Reverend Oliver Tomkins, who had earlier protested at the death sentence, visited Pascoe in his cell shortly before the hanging. According to the newspaper reports of the time, he emerged pale-faced and weary at the prison gates.

The Bishop asked the 70 people keeping the silent vigil to pray for the condemned man. But when he asked for 'a kind thought for the men who hate having to carry out this unpleasant task', a man shouted: 'They don't have to do it!' The Bishop replied: 'They do.'

The demonstrators had kept up a day-and-night protest vigil since the previous Saturday and were joined by Bristol South East MP Tony Benn the night before the execution.

Pascoe and Whitty, who had been living with three women in a caravan near Truro, were sentenced to death at Cornwall Assizes for the murder of 64-year-old farmer William Rowe during a robbery. Their appeals were dismissed and on the Saturday before their execution the Home Office said that the Home Secretary had found no grounds for a reprieve.

The demonstrators at Horfield included university students, lecturers and a contingent from Cornwall. The *Bristol Evening Post* reported that as the demonstrators dispersed shortly after 8am, one man shouted: 'Sickening! The people of Bristol should have torn the gates down instead of just standing around!'

The Bishop of Bristol issued a statement in which he said Pascoe's execution: 'no more justifies hanging than the fact that war may evoke heroism is a justification of war'.

St Andrew's Park in full bloom (picture: Mike Manson)

The Tinto Lounge, one of a chain of Lounge bars around the city, has brought a touch of sophistication over the road from the Royal Oak (winner of Evening Post Pub of the Year 2010) is a very good family pub and the Draper's Arms was Bristol's first micro pub, a lovely one-roomed bar serving a superb selection of ales to an early evening crowd.

The top end of Gloucester Road is overcoming its reputation as the land that time forgot as the reinvigorated Golden Lion, and Grounded cafe and new shops bring new life to the area.

St Andrew's

Most people laugh when they drive along Effingham Road because it's as close to swearing as a street name can get without someone alerting the authorities. The other famous road in St Andrew's is Sefton Park Road which is as long and straight as an inner-city road can be and has no passing points. If you are not confident enough to reverse your car for 50 yards, don't even think about driving down it.

St Andrew's is probably best known for its perfectly blended park that has a dog-free children's area with paddling pool, a conservation area with pond, a bowling green, and lots of people from all walks of life enjoying BBQs and watching the sun set over the city in the summer. Since the UK legal high ban, the hiss of hippie crack is barely audible.

Robert Del Naja out of Massive Attack was brought up in St Andrew's. **109**

University challenge

David Williams celebrates the University of the West of England and its impact on BS7...

The University of the West of England began life as Bristol Polytechnic in 1970 combining the existing colleges at Frenchay, St Matthias (Fishponds), Bower Ashton and Glenside (plus a few smaller sites). It was granted university status in 1992 following the Further and Higher Education Act that saw 'polytechnics' become 'new universities'.

In 2016, it rebranded to create a university that focuses on working more closely with students across a variety of disciplines rather than single subjects. And many of those students (and lecturers) have made north Bristol their home over the years, adding to Gloucester Road's youthful good looks and buzzing social scene.

At UWE, the Humanities rub shoulders with the Sciences (UWE is home to the largest robotics laboratory in Europe, as well as the largest library in the south west). Law has coffee with Environmental Management, Midwifery lunches with Engineering.

Notable UWE alumni include Samantha Cameron, Bear Grylls, Lady Davina Lewis, Miranda Hart and Bristol's very own Russell Howard. Hosting one of the largest employers' fairs in the UK, UWE also ranks among the highest universities in the graduate employment market.

What may strike newcomers to UWE's main campus at Frenchay is that it's not in Bristol. The hundreds of students that arrive here at the start of their university life must find it slightly bewildering when they discover just how far out of town they are. UWE has invested heavily in new campus student accommodation in recent years to provide modern communal living spaces that are a good option for those venturing away from home for the first time.

The campus provides enough amenities for students not to have to venture too far afield and UWE is on the MetroBus route meaning that it doesn't take long to be whisked down the M32 into town. The new student union is a cavernous, white-walled penthouse that resembles a super-club, a far cry from the much-loved previous SU that held the spilt beer and cheap shots of thousands of previous students in its carpets.

With 3,000 members of staff teaching more than 27,000 students from 140 countries, UWE prides itself on its level of diversity in culture and learning. The prospectus offers more than 600 courses at undergraduate, postgraduate, professional and short course level, each one carefully honed to prepare students for life outside the university. The stats don't lie and UWE is often ahead of some of the Russell Group universities for graduate employment.

Trying to compare UWE with the University of Bristol is unproductive. They are two very different universities with different sorts of student and different ambitions. You could study the Classics at UoB or you could study a vocationally directed English course at UWE that is designed to hone your skills as a well-read English graduate and prepare you for the job market in a way that a disciplined study of literature might not.

Often the two universities amalgamate. For example, the School of Architecture at UWE was once part of UoB. And the Bristol Robotics Lab involves joint research from both institutions. I'm certain there is an element of rivalry between the two. How could there not be? But I can't imagine that is extends much further than the terraces at Varsity matches. Eventually students from both institutions will don their gowns and graduate in the magnificent Bristol Cathedral and if that isn't an experience worth sharing, I don't know what is.

He attended St Bonaventure's Catholic Primary School, Sefton Park Primary and Monks Park Secondary School in Southmead. He was kicked out of the sixth form at Monks Park for repeatedly turning up with his hair dyed different colours. On the final occasion, it was blue.

In 1941 a Wellington bomber on a wartime training exercise crashed in St Andrew's park, killing three of the six crew. The accident was not reported at the time and only came to public attention when the grandson of one of the crew was researching his family history. The Friends of St Andrew's Park unveiled a memorial to the crewmen in 2011.

BS8 Clifton and Hotwells

'Protected' on three sides by Whiteladies Road, the Downs and the Avon Gorge, the once bohemian Clifton Village is now firmly established as an enclave of respectability. It's Bristol's premier postcode...

Clifton

Bristol's most affluent area sits high above the rest of the city on top of the Avon Gorge. Clifton has got it all: it has an observatory, a camera obscura, the second oldest zoo in Britain – even its very own 'designer' suspension bridge. There's more. Clifton is quiet without being boring, lively without being rowdy; it has more than its fair share of pubs and places to eat, but take-aways are few and far between. No matter where you are in Clifton, you're only a brisk stroll away from Park Street, Whiteladies Road and the City Centre. And then there's Durdham Down, Clifton's unofficial back garden; not to mention Ashton Court and Leigh Woods about a mile over the bridge. And it's not just geographically and aesthetically superior; Clifton has the edge historically too. The fact that it is mentioned in the Domesday Book means Clifton is older than Bristol itself.

There are remains of an iron-age camp near Clifton Suspension Bridge that date back to 350BC. But this being Clifton, it wasn't long before those primitive ways made way for a more refined design for living. From the late 18th century onwards, the area became a magnet for artistic types and the wealthy. Cricketing legend WG Grace bought a house in Victoria Square, Charles Dickens and Oscar Wilde paid a visit and then the bizarre camera obscura was built.

Clifton stood for culture. In 1966, the Troubadour folk club in Waterloo Street was at the epicentre of Bristol music, in 1970 the Pigsty Hill Light Orchestra became the first band to release an album on the Village Thing record label based in Clifton Village and in the giddy days of post-punk, Clifton was a hotbed of creative activity. In the daytime, the long-gone Focus Cafe was full of dangerous-looking people with long coats and connections to the Pop Group. In the evening, in the back bar of the Lion in Cliftonwood, bands were formed and the record labels Heartbeat and Fried Egg were born. From this whirr of DIY energy came the Cortinas, Social Security, the Europeans, Maximum Joy, the Spics, Jimmy Galvin, Pigbag and more. In 1979, Clifton was the only place to be.

But by the end of the 1980s, the Albion was full of tosspots and their cling-on girlfriends. They thought they were Ben from Curiosity Killed The Cat but they looked more like Huey Lewis from the News. These tragic Jeremys and Nigellas used to be known as 'sloanes'. And they're still hanging around the village now. Useless. Boring. Ignore them. But whatever you do, don't ignore Clifton. It might have lost most of its jagged bohemian edges but at least the activity in Christchurch Studios which is run by the Bristol Old Vic Theatre School and whose clients include Massive Attack and Andy Sheppard means it's not an entirely dry zone. And there's plenty of life too at the Bristol Fringe, the Clifton Arcade, the Corrie Tap and the Lansdown. But who put that supermarket right in the middle of Princess Victoria Street?

Suspension Bridge

One of the most famous landmarks in the world and the most obvious reminder of Isambard Kingdom Brunel's engineering genius, the Clifton Suspension Bridge story goes back to 1753. This was when Bristol wine merchant William Vick left a legacy to build a bridge over the Avon Gorge. In 1829, the Merchant Venturers appointed a bridge committee which announced

Past Notes
350BC An Iron Age camp is founded on the site of Observatory Hill just near the Suspension Bridge.
1080 Clifton is described in the Domesday Book as a settlement of about 30 agricultural folk.
1130 The area falls into the aristocratic hands of a certain William de Clifton.
1791 Building begins on Royal York Crescent. It takes 30 years to complete.

a bridge design competition with a first prize of 100 guineas. Brunel was 23 and recuperating in Clifton from the injuries he had received when the Thames Tunnel (on which he was working with his father, Marc Brunel) had flooded.

He submitted four plans for the competition. His favourite design involved a 91-metre tunnel which emerged from the side of the gorge and ran into another tunnel on the Leigh Woods side. In all, 22 plans were submitted. The elderly Thomas Telford, one of the best engineers of his day, dismissed all the designs, including Brunel's, and instead offered one of his own that involved two mammoth pillars being built from the foot of the gorge. The Venturers rejected this too and in 1831 Brunel's design was accepted. However, big business was reluctant to invest in Bristol following the Queen Square riots of 1831 and it was five years before work began.

In 1836, an iron bar 305 metres long was hauled across the gorge and a basket to transport men and materials slung from it. Brunel himself made the first crossing and the basket stuck at the lowest point 60 metres above the river. Brunel climbed out of the basket, up the rope and released the cable from the jammed pulley. By 1843, the two towers were completed but funds were exhausted. To save money, the committee reduced the height of the towers and scrapped the decorative sphinxes on them. Brunel died in 1859 aged 53, through overwork and 40 cigars a day, without seeing the completion of his bridge, which he referred to in his diary as: 'My first love, my darling.' The opening ceremony for the bridge was on 8 December 1864.

Bristol Lido

One of the more unusual places in Bristol is the restored Bristol Pool tucked away in Oakfield Grove next to the Victoria pub behind the Victoria Rooms. Yet it took a monumental effort to prevent this genuine oddity from being demolished and turned into yet more drab flats. The Grade II listed pool – the first electrically-heated pool in the UK in the 1930s – was built in 1849-1850 and closed in 1990 after springing a leak and falling into disrepair.

In 1997, Sovereign Homes told the City Council they wanted to demolish the 150 year-old Egyptian-themed heritage site and build some flats. 'No problem,' said the culture-blind suits at College Green. But then the Glass Boat Company (the people behind innovative eateries Glass Boat and Spyglass) bought the site and put forward ambitious plans to renovate the pool, introduce sauna, spa and massage rooms and create a restaurant and cafe. Despite the application getting gagged and bound in council red tape, the project was completed and the resulting Clifton Lido is a sophisticated urban misfit.

In 2016, new research appeared in the *Oxford Dictionary of National Biography* suggesting that Brunel had based his design on a patent filed by the great female inventor, engineer and resident of Bristol Sarah Guppy (1770-1852). There's no doubt that Guppy was a significant influence on Brunel and also communicated with Thomas Telford whose Menai Bridge was completed in 1826, but was she the designer? Who knows?

The bridge spans the Avon Gorge which geologists say was formed during the last ice age when enormous glaciers blocked the original route of the Avon, forcing it to cut a new route through the soft Carboniferous Limestone. According to medieval mythology is was formed by two giants, the brothers Goram and Vincent.

The Downs

The Downs is the large area of greenery between Clifton, Sneyd Park and Westbury Park. It's actually two separate areas divided by Stoke Road. The area to your right as you go along Stoke Road towards Sneyd Park is Durdham Down and the area to the left running towards the Avon Gorge is Clifton Down. Durdham Down is owned by Bristol City Council for the benefit of the people of Bristol. Clifton Down is owned by the Society of Merchant Venturers.

An Anglo-Saxon charter of 883 granted grazing rights over part of Durdham Down and in 1643 and 1645, during the English revolution, Royalist and Parliamentarian armies assembled on the downs.

In 1857, concerned by Victorian-built houses encroaching on the open space as the city expanded, Bristol Corporation acquired commoners' rights on the Downs, and exercised them the following year by grazing sheep. In 1861 Durdham Down was bought by the City from the Lords of the Manor of Henbury for £15,000 via an Act of Parliament. At the same time the Society of Merchant Venturers secured Clifton Down. Grazing on the down declined during the 19th century, and finally ceased in 1925.

Since 1861 the Downs have been managed by the Downs Committee, a joint committee of the council and the Venturers. The committee appoints a Downs Ranger to oversee the area.

The Downs are not only a lovely place to walk with great views over the Gorge, but they are also home to the Downs Football League which was formed in 1905 with 30 founder members. Two of the founder member clubs, St Andrews and Sneyd Park, remain in the league to this day, with Clifton St Vincents joining the league in its second season and also clocking up 100 years of membership.

Whiteladies Road

It's wrongly assumed by some newcomers to the city that the origin of the Whiteladies Road and Blackboy Hill names are a tasteless reminder of the city's shameful slave past. But it was never the case that white ladies would go up the hill to buy black boys. There was no significant domestic slave trade in Bristol, the slavers unloaded their human cargo in the Americas and brought back sugar, tobacco and cotton so there were relatively few enslaved Africans in service in Bristol.

The name Blackboy is more likely to refer to the tar-painted faces of criminals who were hanged on the gallows on the Downs. Or it could be that it takes its name from the Blackboy Tavern, or Blackamoor's Head, a name popularised at the time of the Crusades when it was used as a description of North African Muslims – many inns were given this name complete with a suitably illustrated sign. It's also possible that the name is a reference to Charles ll who was known as the Black Boy because of his swarthy complexion. Whiteladies Road is also probably called after an inn, which, in turn, could be a reference to a nearby priory where the nuns wore all-white habits.

Up until a few years ago, the long, straight stretch of road that heads down from the top of Blackboy Hill and comes to an end when it reaches the Victoria Rooms was little more than somewhere you'd pass through on your way to Park Street. But as consensus politics got comfy at the end of the 1990s, so an invasion of super-bars arrived to suck up all the affluence. Suddenly, the street was packed full of swish new drinking dens with names, such as Boom, Bar Humbug, Henry J Beans and the Fine Line and the more established haunts, such as the Vittoria, looked like an oddity from a last orders that time forgot.

Someone, somewhere in marketing, nicknamed the whole thing 'The Strip' and it became Bristol's most sellable night-time leisure mile. Yes, it was as bad as that. When the weekend came around, thousands of call centre operatives dressed up like *Blind Date* contestants so they could stand and shiver in queues. And what was it they craved so desperately? Five-deep scrums at every bar, gormless Ministry of Sound re-mixes chugging away on maximum volume and a wall of bottled alcopops that taste like piss.

Thankfully those days are behind us and almost as quickly as it became The Strip, Whiteladies Road matured into something more in keeping with its poise and grace.

Hotwells Spa

Taking the waters on the banks of the Avon...

The Hotwells area of Bristol takes its name from the hot well or spring that once made Bristol one of the most important spa towns in Britain. The spring is still there, it runs into the Avon below Hotwell Road, just south of the Suspension Bridge. The gassy water emerges at 76 degrees Fahrenheit (23C). According to an analysis carried out in 1912, the water is 170 times more radioactive than the public water supply. Hardly surprising then, that those who have taken the water say it produces a similar sensation to being drunk. The spring was once at the centre of an impressive spa and leisure complex, but today very few Bristolians would even know where to find it. The problem was that the spring was beneath the water level of the River Avon for all but one and a half hours a day.

Bristol's worldwide fame

There is some evidence that the waters were being taken as far back as the 15th century when sailors used it as a cure for scurvy and other skin conditions. Certainly, it was attracting enough publicity by 1676 for the Merchant Venturers to buy the land, along with most of Clifton. The water was held in a brick reservoir (or well) to prevent contamination from the river. By the end of the 17th century, bottled Bristol spa water was being sent all over the world.

In 1695, the Venturers leased the spring to Charles Jones and Thomas

Callow for £5 a year, on condition that they spent £500 on developing the area. By 1723, a pump room and assembly room had been built and high society flocked to Hotwells to take the waters, attend lavish balls and take river cruises on the Avon.

The restorative powers of the water attracted the medical profession to Hotwells and by the mid 18th Century, Dowry Square had become Bristol's Harley Street. In 1729, a playhouse was built at Jacobs Wells then another spring was discovered in the Avon Gorge. Another pump house and more lodging houses were built as the Hotwells boom continued. But the second spa had closed by the end of the 18th Century because access was difficult. The original hot well continued to draw worldwide visitors to take the waters and enjoy this lively resort.

Fallen from grace

A second assembly room was built and the Colonnade was constructed to house expensive shops; it's a private house now on the side of the Portway, but the distinctive columns are still standing. Then the boom economy went bust almost overnight. Samuel Powell, who took over the lease in 1790, more than doubled spa prices; at around the same time a Dr Beddoes in Dowry Square publicly questioned the healing powers of the water and the rumours began to spread that the spring was no longer effective. The boarding houses became known as

Death Row with only those desperate for a cure coming to Hotwells. The Avon was highly polluted and the area rapidly fell into decay. It's not a pretty picture: incurable consumptives, run-down houses and a river full of turds. Unsurprisingly, polite society preferred the attractions of Bath or the Continental spa towns.

Various attempts were made to revive the spa and to pump the water up to Clifton to avoid the increasing stench from the Avon. The last serious effort to re-establish Bristol as a spa town was in 1890 when the Merchant Venturers granted permission to George Newnes to build the Clifton Rocks funicular railway on condition that he pumped water to Clifton and built a spa next to the station at the top of the Gorge. In 1894, Newnes opened the Grand Pump Room; four years later he completed work on the Grand Spa Hotel next to it (now the Avon Gorge Hotel). But the spa was closed on health grounds in 1913.

By 1920, the Grand Pump Room had become a cinema and, in the 1950s, it became one of Bristol's premier rock 'n' roll dance halls. It's difficult to imagine that the area around the Portway was once one of the most fashionable resorts in the country, or that the hot spring that brought that wealth to Bristol still pours into the Avon.

Hotwells

As part of the extensive research carried out on your behalf for the purpose of writing this book, the entire publishing team descended on Hotwells to see what, if anything, had changed. And the one single most significant thing we can report about the area is that it is really, really noisy. Standing on the pavement trying to cross four lanes of traffic on Hotwell Road, the peaceful drink or two we had planned down by the Harbourside felt as if it was in another dimension. Still, it's not as if there's a shortage of ale houses around here. From the Rose of Debmark in Dowry Place to the Three Tuns in St George's Road, Hotwells has more great pubs than its status as Lower Clifton deserves.

Until 1934, there used to be an almost perpendicular railway at the foot of the gorge that could take passengers up to Clifton in 40 seconds. You can still see the facade of the Clifton Rocks funicular railway on Hotwell Road near the suspension bridge. The station at the top was next to the current Avon Gorge Hotel. There also used to be a spring that gushed out of St Vincent's Rock that drew tourists from miles around.

But back to our walk around the pubs of Hotwell Road. What places like the Bear Inn (261 Hotwell Road) offer is something a little off the cultural beaten track. Every Friday night, for example, the Bear turns into the Bebop

Club, a live jazz happening for purists. But for this gang of fume-choked investigators, it's the places that sit on the docks that beckon. Timbers well and truly shivered, we sail into the Nova Scotia (1 Nova Scotia Place), one of the city's last great 19th-Century maritime haunts. It's cosy inside, cold outside. We sit down by the water and freeze. After we hit the Pump House (Merchants Road), just on the other side of the water. It's more of a restaurant than a bar, but a good place to sit outside in the summer. Next up there is the impossibly pink Rose of Denmark (6 Dowry Place) which offers a friendly welcome and excellent food downstairs in the old cellar. Then on to the Merchants Arms (5 Merchants Road), a Bath Ales pub with an excellent selection of fine beers and the snuggest of wood-panelled snug bars.

Back on the main road, the Mardyke (126 Hotwell Road) isn't best known for its food, (although there's the Mardyke Cafe next door), but rather as one of Bristol's biker pub. On the day of our visit it was biker-free – and very empty. The Grain Barge on the opposite side of the four lanes of traffic is a great place to enjoy fantastic views of the Harbour by day and is a lively evening meeting place.

The Hope and Anchor on Jacobs Wells Road has a lovely large Victorian walled garden, a good selection of real ale, a lively atmosphere and a wide range of excellent food. The Bag 'O Nails, just down the hill, is Bristol's world-famous cat pub. About a dozen moggies roam free around the bar and that's one of the least odd things about this totally bonkers institution rightly renowned for its beer. Just round the corner the Three Tuns (78 St George's Road) has a woody and relaxed feel. A previous landlord had a Jack Russell terrier that called 'Time' by jumping on the bar and pulling a rope to ring the bell. The pub sign features Hollywood actor Nicholas Cage for reasons that are not entirely clear.

University of Bristol

Rosemary Wagg on the University and its inhabitants...

Historically, Clifton is the area most associated with the University of Bristol. It would be hard not to notice the existence of Bristol University, not because it is the Alma Mater of a hoard of chummy media folk – Sarah Montague, Will Hutton and Sue Lawley, included – but because it is literally unmissable. From its perch at the top of Park Street, the limestone Wills Memorial Building looms down on the rest of Bristol like a bumbling but severe Law Lord.

Officially born in 1909, the university mutated from the old University College, Bristol, an institution notable for admitting men and women on an equal basis (except for studying medicine). Despite the widespread belief in students being damp petals, either in bed or pretending to read poetry, the vast majority of Bristol students are enrolled in the engineering, science or medical faculties. Hidden from the city, these students spend long hours locked in labs and have contributed to Bristol's main accolades in these areas of research.

Non-medical types hope to improve their chances of either writing or making headlines by engaging in activities such as working for the student newspaper *Epigram*, or staging plays in the Winston Theatre, housed in the Student Union in Queens Road. The hidden treasures of the university frequently emerge from the music department, which supports the Contemporary Music Venture, a series of concerts showcasing new compositions by postgrad music students. Stop scoffing long enough to attend and you'll find the performers and composers to be hideously talented and perfectly ready to shoot dead the Classic FM albatross.

With a higher proportion of students privately educated than not, Bristol University might not seem like the poster child for diversity. However, it does have a big international intake which looks likely to grow, especially as links with China get continually tighter. In 2013, there were 1,340 Chinese students officially registered and the first Bristol University graduation ceremony was held in Beijing. A double-thumbs-up visit from the Chinese Ambassador, Liu Xiaoming, in which he – perhaps ambitiously – rated Bristol as better than the Massachusetts Institute of Technology, added further gold swirls to the edge of this relationship.

The first, last and only comment to often be made on Bristol University is that it is Posh. It is said with an air of revelation, when really it is hardly news enough to make an undergrad choke on their latte.

Student life

What constitutes life as a 'typical' Bristol student is highly dependent on one thing: arts or sciences? If you are unfortunate enough to come to Bristol with the aim of leaving with a qualification in Cellular and Molecular Medicine then, quite frankly, I have no idea what you do with your days because I never see you around. I am sure your special cave full of specimens is rated more highly than the stuff that gets said in the lecture theatres of Woodland Road, but I fail to envy you.

Being an Arts student gives one the freedom to mix going to lectures with going to the gym (seemingly all the time and seemingly in better and more complete make-up than most people wear to weddings). Equally it gives one the freedom to mix going to the gym with going for coffee (on the Triangle, on St. Michael's Hill, on Whiteladies). If time is ticking towards the end of term, then the coffee and gym routine may be interrupted by a more exhaustive daily activity: battling for a seat in the ASS (Arts and Social Sciences) library. Maybe at other universities, students sleep, but at Bristol they enter into a gladiatorial fight for a seat in a library, which during revision time is often full by 8am. You read that correctly.

During the holidays, Bristol University makes its exodus East. Check a few wallets and all will contain Oyster cards. This is especially useful for after graduation when the free bed and board in London with your parents can be key to your ability to accept a year's unpaid/barely-paid internship working 'in the arts' (galleries, theatres, newspapers). Despite hailing from the city all the kids who grew up in the South West want to move to, Bristol Undergrads tend to really love Bristol. Days might be spent living and moving around the Triangle, but – when asked – it is Stokes Croft, street art and Gloucester Road that are rose-tinted. 'Bristol is SUCH a nice city!' they say as, one by one, they head back to London or up to the Edinburgh Fringe.

Notable Bristol alumni

David Walliams & Matt Lucas
Double-headed comedy beast that referenced their time at Bristol by including a local accent in *Little Britain*

Krissi Murison
Coolest of all the journalists Bristol has produced, Murison was the first female editor of *NME*. She owes it all to her time as *Epigram's* Deputy Music Editor

Simon Pegg
Following graduation, instead of becoming a 20-something drop out, Pegg co-wrote and starred in *Spaced,* a TV show about 20-something dropouts

Paul Boateng
Boateng became Britain's first black cabinet minister when he was appointed Chief Secretary to the Treasury in 2002.

Angela Carter
Like almost all English Lit undergrads, Carter had a penchant for all things reinterpreted and feminism. Hurray!

Derren Brown
Most famous alumnus of Law and German departments opts for a career hypnotism and illusion.

Jemima Khan
Cut her time at Bristol short, but still managed to become Associate Editor of the *New Statesman* and *European*. and Editor-at-Large for *Vanity Fair*.

George Ferguson
Fittingly for a man who likes coloured chinos, the Bristol Mayor has two degrees (plus an honorary MA) from Bristol University.

Alastair Shuttleworth/LICE at the Louisiana © Simon Holliday

Bristol Up Close

Graffiti & street art

Richard Jones on the origins of Bristol street art and the influence of John Nation's youth project in Barton Hill...

Bristol's graffiti and street art tradition stretches back to the early 80s when the city's counter culture was heavily influenced by New York hip-hop and its four elements – DJs, breakdancers, MCs and graffiti artists. Young Bristol artists such as 3D out of Wild Bunch/Massive Attack, Crime Inc (FLX, Inkie, Nick Walker, Jinx), Chaos, Ian Dark from Z-Boys and others began creating flyers to promote hip-hop house parties and it wasn't long before the first pieces began appearing on city walls. The scene would probably have crashed and burned as the police tracked down and cautioned those early pioneers, if it wasn't for the intervention of John Nation, a reformed bad boy turned youth worker who set up a haven for writers at the Dug Out at Barton Hill Youth Club. Kids from all over town congregated here to hone their skills away from the attentions of British Transport Police who were cracking down on train painting.

The battle between the writers, taggers, bombers and British Transport Police culminated on March 20, 1989 with the Operation Anderson dawn raids on addresses in Bristol, Bath, Exeter and Cardiff. As a result 72 young writers were handed down a variety of fines and probation orders. Just a few weeks later on May 1, Inkie and Cheo from Bristol came second in the World Street Art Championships in Bridlington and Bristol's international reputation as a street art hot spot was sealed.

However, Operation Anderson had its desired effect. Most Bristol writers decided to 'go straight' leaving just a small number of crews such as Kingswood's Bad Appelz/Dry Breadz operating outside the law and prepared to face imprisonment if they were caught.

It was against this background of illegal writing that Bristol's best-known street artist emerged in the early 90s. Banksy was younger than the rest of the Dry Breadz/Bad Appelz writers who included Lokey, Cato and Soker and he was also too young to be one of the main protagonists at Barton Hill, though he undoubtedly painted there. So Banksy emerged into a vacuum. His work as a freehand artist with

'It's No Great Crime' by 3D, 1984 © Beezer

'3D' by 3D, 1984 © Frank Drake

John Nation filling in an Inkie piece at Barton Hill Youth Club circa 1985 (picture unknown)

Dry Breadz/Bad Appelz, evolved into prolific solo stencil work. In 1998 he and Inkie organized the Walls on Fire graffiti jam on the site of @Bristol and in 2000 he held a solo show at Severnshed then left Bristol for London. The Bristol street art scene continued to flourish as artists from around the world were drawn here by John Nation's reputation and by Banksy's impact.

Chris Chalkley at the People's Republic of Stokes Croft fostered a philosophy of nurturing art in the midst of urban decay and south of the

'Body Rock' by Z-Boys, 'Treach' character added by 3D, 1983 © Frank Drake

'3D' by 3D, 1985 © Beezer

river Upfest began in 2008, the same year that Felix Braun produced the magnificent book *Children of the Can: 25 Years of Bristol Graffiti*. In 2009 Braun co-curated Crimes of Passion at the Royal West of England Academy, a street art and graffiti show that became the most successful event in the RWA's history. Hot on the heels of Crimes of Passion came the remarkable Banksy vs Bristol Museum Show which was credited with bringing 10s of millions of pounds into the Bristol economy.

Bristol City Council decided that they wanted a piece of the action **127**

Banksy 'Diver' at City Hall mid 90s. This piece was buffed within hours © Pete Maginnis

and Mike Bennett (BCC Director of Placemaking), Inkie and Dave Harvey (Futureboogie) organised See No Evil which saw scores of artists paint Nelson Street in 2011 and 2012.

The Bearpit and Stokes Croft in general acted as a focal point for the street art community. But despite the City Council and Destination Bristol trying to cash in on Bristol's street art credentials, the scene remains underground, often involves illegal painting and tagging and is largely suspicious of the 'suits'.

Perhaps the most visible expression of the dilemma between graffiti writing's illegal roots and the current attempts to sell it as a commodity

'Mild Mild West' by Banksy, 1999 © Richard Jones

Banksy's first stencil, mid-90s (picture unknown)

'Well Hung Man' by Banksy, 1999 © Richard Jones

is at Temple Meads station where there were posters of John Nation advertising his street art tours. That's the same John Nation that British Transport Police tried to lock up in 1989 alleging he was the ringleader of the 'vandals' based at Barton Hill Youth Club.

Further reading: *Banksy's Bristol: Home Sweet Home; Children of the Can; Art & Sound of the Bristol Underground; Upfest; See No Evil 1* and *SNE2; Street Art & Graffiti by John D'oh* all available at www.tangentbooks.co.uk

Banksy vs Bristol Museum, 2009 © Simon Ellis

Banksy at Bridge Farm Primary School, Whitchurch, June 2016 © Richard Jones

Banksy

Filthy Lucre's inflatable installations and
Rowdy's rocks at Crimes of Passion
© Sarah Connolly

Cheo at the RWA Crimes of Passion show, 2009 © Sarah Connolly

The old Carriage Works Stokes Croft featuring work (from left by Leah Heming, FLX, Mr Jago and Dan) © Chris Chalkley

BRISTOL UPRISING (RIOTS) 183

'Queen Square Riot' by Scott Buchanan Barden © Scott Buchanan Barden

Epok at work on the 2010 'Think Local' piece opposite the Tesco store in Stokes Croft © Chris Chalkley

Stokes Croft looking towards Breakdancing Jesus by
Cosmo Sarson © Richard Jones

'Tsunami', a PRSC production in Stokes Croft
© Chris Chalkley

The 'Ursa' bear sculpture by
Jamie Gillman in the Bear Pit
© Claudio Ahlers

The Stinkfish piece in Stokes Croft was arranged
by Beth and Vince John from 1loveart

© Vince John

Tribute wall to DJ Derek on Richmond Avenue, Montpelier by Sepr, Deamz, Piro and 45rpm © Mat Kauhanen

'Noveau Ink' by Inkie, Cheltenham Road © Richard Jones

Dancing to the Bristol Beat

Music journalist **Gil Gillespie** explains how the Cortinas and Pop Group helped shape the sound of the city...

If there was any kind of music scene in Bristol before 1977, his name was Russ Conway and he liked to play the piano. It wasn't until the jagged edges of new wave began to cut the shock tactics out of the punk movement that the first serious local bands began to emerge from their Clifton and Redland hideaways. So we'll make 1977 our starting point for a tour of the Bristol music scene.

First out of the blocks were the Cortinas, four sneering teenagers in torn blazers not long out of grammar school sixth form. Fittingly, their feisty and dangerously energetic double-A-sided single *Fascist Dictator/Television Families* set the standard that others would have to follow. And sure enough, by the middle of 1979, hundreds of nervy young punk bands were popping up all over town. A fanzine called *Loaded* sprang up in support like a regional *Sniffin' Glue*. Suddenly, there were six or seven live venues. Then Heartbeat Records released the *Social Security* EP which featured four irreverent dum-dum bullets, including the immortal *I'm Addicted To Cider*. Bristol was up and running as a music town.

The fledgling label followed their debut release with another excellent single, *The Europeans*, by the Europeans. The Europeans became the first but certainly not the last Bristol band to be linked with a major record deal that never quite came off. The likes of the Pigs, the X-Certs, Joe Public and the Numbers all followed. Aggressive, confrontational upstarts all.

But from here on in, the sound of young Bristol splintered in several different directions. There was wheel-spinning R&B in the shape of 14-year-old rebel-rousers the Untouchables. There were experimental types, such as the Art Objects, Glaxo Babies and Essential Bop. Black Roots introduced the dub influence while Shoes For Industry volunteered to be ringmaster for weird circus rock and confirmed their status by getting the lead singer to wear an inside-out brain on his head. And, most controversially of all,

Melanie, the daughter of Bristol City manager 'Alan-Alan-Alan' Dicks did a pouty Wendy James type of thing for a band called Double Vision. Ashton Court Festival became a canvas for the city's eclectic range of characters. The Wurzels were not welcome.

But lording it over this newly-built sonic kingdom were the mightiest of all the pre-1990s Bristolian hollerers, the Pop Group. How good were the Pop Group? Well, when Nick Cave and his growling Birthday Party entourage first landed on these shores in 1980, they spent every night going to gigs all over the capital but were shocked and disappointed by the limp, bloodless bands they found. 'It was like being gang-banged by a pack of marshmallows,' commented Cave, savagely. Then one night he saw The Pop Group. The experience changed his life. As part of Channel 4's *Music of the Millennium* series, Cave chose *We Are All Prostitutes* as his favourite piece of music of all time. 'The beginning of the record is the greatest start of any record, ever,' claims the awesome Aussie. And you wouldn't want to disagree with him.

This is why it's the Pop Group who are cited as being one of the biggest influences on what became known as the Bristol Sound. Even if it's not all that easy to see why, or how, they laid the foundations for Massive Attack. The Pop Group, y'see, made a fearsome, chaotic noise that was always experimental and sometimes plain unlistenable. Their first single, *She Is Beyond Good And Evil*, might have been as infectious as it was deeply disturbing, but much of the *Y* album sounded like a load of out-of-time clanging and primeval hollering, interrupted by the occasional blast of raucous feedback. These elements burned on a fire already white hot with punk, funk and thunderous dub to make a protest music completely out on its own.

So what does all this have to do with the birth of the Wild Bunch and everything that followed them? Crucially, Mark Stewart's unholy Pop Group crew were the first to assimilate the city's black, or more accurately Rasta, counter-culture into their social life, their worldview, and ultimately their sound. Back then, music allowed you to define your enemies more clearly. 'With the roots worldview... the feeling of spiritual uplift was undeniable,' says singer Stewart of his dub days. As if this wasn't significant enough, the band also spent their youth going to clubs and listening to dance beats. 'We were like the Bristol funk army,' recalls Stewart. 'We'd go to clubs and dance to records by T-Connection, BT Express, Fatback Band, all this heavy bassline funk.'

And this is how the Pop Group invented the politics of dancing. Their **139** dance was a warped, out-of-shape boogie, but a boogie none the less. 'They even used to dance in the most peculiar way,' remembers one fan. Sadly, by the time they'd made their third album, titled *For How Much Longer Do We Tolerate Mass Murder?*, all the incendiary radicalism had got a bit out of control. Maybe it's best to let the band explain their style of music. 'We were creating a wall of noise for the lyrics to fight against,' sighs bass player Dan Catsis. 'We were challenging the production process, disrespecting the machines.'

Something inevitably had to give, and the six members went their separate ways. Gareth Sager formed the distinctly patchy Rip Rig & Panic, bassist Simon Underwood sought relief in the happy honking of jazz-funkers Pigbag and had a top 20 hit, and Mark Stewart sank still deeper into the well of nihilistic creativity in which he had always prospered.

They were only around for two years or so but The Pop Group cast one hell of a long shadow. There were a lot of bands who found themselves permanently stuck in the shade. Performance art, free-festival politics, second-hand clothes, a vibrant live scene and copious amounts of cheap drugs all played their part in a shift towards an artier and more off-beat order. If you can track down copies of the compilation albums *Avon Calling, Fried Egg – Bristol 1979-1981, Wavelength/Bristol Recorder 1979-1980*, or *Western Stars Vol 1 – The Bands That Built Bristol* (now on Sugar Shack – www.sugarshackrecords.co.uk) you can hear for yourself. It's from this increasingly bohemian atmosphere that Gerard Langley's first band Art Objects sprang.

What we didn't know then is that Bristol was about to rewind to a second year zero. It began down among the funk jams and scratched beats of the St Paul's cafe sound system scene. With the fragments of post-punk scattered all over the place and pulsing electronic dub everywhere, something truly remarkable emerged. The Slits made an unlikely union with Dennis Bovell, the Clash raised swords with Mikey Dread, and the Specials united black and white to fight against anyone who wanted to make something of it. Bristol had reggae collectives Talisman, Black Roots and Restriction. At the Dugout on Park Row, DJs were lining up Chaka Khan against Superfly Soul as the first blasts of urban hip-hop began to filter across the Atlantic.

Meanwhile, somewhere around town, Robert Del Naja was getting arrested for decorating walls with a spraycan. Soon, he joined Nellee Hooper, Daddy G and Milo in a hip-hop collective called the Wild Bunch. That same year, St Paul's Carnival played host to a number of heavily-amped crews such as 3 Stripe Posse, 2Bad, City Rockas, UD4 and FBI Crew. But bigger and bolder than the rest were Wild Bunch, who blocked off Campbell Street with their colossal, towering bass bins. The band's reputation spread by word of mouth and they were invited to play at London's Titanic Club. Then they set up residency on Wednesday nights at the Dugout, spinning 12-inches, rapping over the top, heads nodding eerily in time. 1986 saw Smith and Mighty produce the Wild Bunch's cover of Hal David's and Burt Bacharach's *The Look of Love*.

Hindsight has given Wild Bunch a legendary status in modern music folklore. But Milo's retrospective album, *Story of a Soundsystem*, suggested this is as much myth as reality. It's party music, full of sax burps, cheesy disco jangles and it's very much of its time. Robert Del Naja puts his own perspective on it. 'People always ask us about the Wild Bunch,' he says. 'But the truth, is it's just history to us now. I don't know why people go on about it so much.'

No, the first truly staggering thing Wild Bunch ever did was to become Massive Attack. And the first thing Massive Attack ever did was to take a giant leap ahead of anything that had come before. *Daydreaming* is one of the most original and self-assured debut singles ever made. Even now it sounds as fresh and as relevant as it did back in the early 1990s. And there was so much more to come.

From its majestic opening line – '*Midnight rockers, city slickers, gun men and maniacs*' – it was obvious the *Blue Lines* album was going to be a classic. Three hit singles – *Daydreaming, Safe From Harm* and *Unfinished Sympathy* – propelled the band right across the globe. At the same time, they redefined what dance music could be. As 3D put it at the time: 'We're not just interested in making something for people to throw their arms and legs about to on a dancefloor.'

Everything had changed. Suddenly, Bristol was being talked about as the 'coolest city on the planet'. Then someone, somewhere in the media, labelled the sound 'trip-hop' – a supposedly softer, near-ambient version of hip-hop, unique to the South West. Apparently. And within minutes, the city was overrun by gangs of A&R clowns frantically searching for the next Bristol sound sure-things. Not only was the local music mafia not talking, they were also trying to get as far away from the term as possible. 'Who in here likes trip-hop?' asked Tricky at an early live show. When the audience all raised their hands he retorted, 'Well fuck off home, then!'

Surprisingly, no staggeringly, the next giant wave in the West Country sound surf came not from the inner city but from dozy seaside town Portishead. Geoff Barrow had been a tape operator for Massive Attack and Neneh Cherry and, with the help of an Enterprise Allowance grant, he recruited jazz head Adrian Utley, drummer/programmer Dave MacDonald and Janis Joplin cover singer Beth Gibbons to form a band named after his home town. Portishead's slow-burning cinematic scores were slow to make an impact but then a press campaign involving hundreds of mannequins placed in various locations around London grabbed the attention of the public and fired the band's third single *Glory Box* straight into the UK charts at number 13. By the end of 1994, Portishead's album *Dummy* had sold more than 1.5 million copies, won the Mercury Music Prize and been voted Album of the Year by *Melody Maker, Mixmag, ID* and the *Face*. Sales in the US topped 150,000. It was no more than Portishead deserved. *Dummy* is one of the best albums of the 1990s: a faultless and seemingly effortless record to rank alongside *Blue Lines*. And, with *Blue Lines*, it is still the chosen soundtrack for any television programme dealing with crime.

For Massive Attack, meanwhile, making a follow-up to the internationally lauded *Blue Lines* was proving to be a long and difficult affair. 'If a thing's worth doing, it's worth doing slowly,' deadpanned Del Naja. But while 1994's Nellee Hooper-produced *Protection* had its moments, most notably *Karma Coma* and *Eurochild*, it was, in truth, a bit of a disappointment. The choice of Tracey Thorn from Everything But The Girl as vocalist pushed the sound closer to the coffee table and away from the barrier-breaking low temperature hip-hop of *Blue Lines*.

By now the friction between the band members was well documented. Daddy G revealed just how bad it was. 'It's a nightmare, really... we hate each other,' said the mild-mannered bass boomer. Tricky was the first to exit stage left. The only 'kiddie' from Knowle West to ever go out in public wearing a wedding dress, Tricky had always been the unhinged little hooligan of the band. He was the voice of naivety who didn't understand the impact of Thatcher's economic policy. 'Maggie this, Maggie that, Maggie means inflation,' he had observed, incorrectly, on *Daydreaming*. Nobody really expected Massive's equivalent of Sid Vicious to release an album as stunning as *Maxinquaye*. It was a deep, dark and dangerous masterpiece and the third truly great record to come out of Bristol in four years. It seemed Bristol was the coolest city on the planet after all.

Predictably, the city's beat-dependent music scene was given fuel by the successes of the 'big three'. Some attempted mimicry and failed; some folk were barking up the wrong tree entirely; others drew a line in the sand and set about pushing back the boundaries even further. And a few brave souls continued to pick up their guitars and play the old-fashioned way. It was an odd time for Strangelove to come along, but on a cold February night at The Underworld in Camden Town, they arrived with the proverbial thump. Containing two Blue Aeroplanes escapees and a singer with charisma to burn, Strangelove instantly broke the city's 'guitar jinx'. The Camden gig got them a life-long fan in *Select* magazine's Dave Cavanagh and a deal with Food Records. Within a year they had become the biggest and best 'indie' band to ever come out of Bristol. Even Radiohead later described themselves as a 'post-Strangelove band'.

But if Bristol was famous for anything in the mid 1990s, it was its love affair with slow, slacker beats. All that was about to change: Smith & Mighty's More Rockers project had already signalled the start of some serious bpm multiplication, but it was Roni Size's 1997 album *New Forms* that really whacked the turntable into overdrive and span off the scale. Drum 'n' bass was thrust into the mainstream and the innovation spotlight shone on Bristol yet again. DJ Krust, DJ Die, DJ Suv and their miniature dreadlocked leader found themselves in the news, in the charts and on stage picking up the Mercury Music Prize. Yet again, journalists wanted to know about the Bristol sound. 'I am from Bristol, and I do make music from Bristol, so I am it and it is me,' said Krust to stun one American reporter into silence. Roni Size meanwhile, prophesised to anyone who'd listen: 'I'm a junglist and jungle is the future.' Utter nonsense, of course, but at least he said it with conviction.

The activity levels at Full Cycle records might be as frantic as ever, but drum 'n' bass has faded back into the underground again of late. Krust understands this too well: 'Forget drum 'n' bass,' he says. 'This is about endless possibilities, endless configurations, endless structures and restructures – it's infinite.' He is quite right, it is infinite. As are the possibilities. We've barely scraped the surface of electronica and Bristol is sure to be at the forefront of whatever comes next.

Massive Attack continue to reinvent themselves from their Bristol hideaways, but you are far more likely to bump into Tricky in New York than Knowle West and Portishead is again just an estuary town in Somerset, but the Bristol beat made the city the coolest place on the planet for a decade or more.

It has left a legacy that a new generation of Bristol soundscapers will surely emulate. 'Some people say that Bristol is the graveyard of ambition,' Robert Del Naja once said. But ambition has now learned to dance to Bristol's tune.

Bristol Beat timeline: 1977–2003

1977-1983 *1984-1990* *199*

Rumba Lament
(Rob Smith, guitar, Nellee Hooper, drums)

Restriction
(Rob Smith, guitar, Nellee, sound engineer, Daddy G, DJ)

Sweat
(Rob Smith guitar, Ray Mighty, synths)

Wild Bunch
The original Wild Bunch crew included Nellee Hooper, Daddy G, Milo Johnson and Willie Wee

Call Is Strong
Daddy G and Smith & Mighty produce Carlton

Any Love
Massive Attack, Carlton and Smith & Mighty team up for the first MA release

Wild Bunch
3D and Mushroom join Wild Bunch

Massive Attack
3D, Daddy G, Mushroom and Tricky create the stunning Blue Lines. Much is recorded at Neneh Cherry's home studio

Pigbag
Nellee Hooper meets Simon Underwood in Pigbag

Raw Like Sushi
Massive Attack work on Neneh Cherry's debut solo album

Soul II Soul
Nellee Hooper joins Jazzie B's new project

Pop Group
The original line-up is Mark Stewart, Gareth Sager, Simon Underwood, John Waddington and Bruce Smith

Rip Rig & Panic
Gareth Sager and Bruce Smith recruit Neneh Cherry for their new band

Head
Gareth Sager forms Head with Nick Sheppard and Rich Beale

995 | 1996-2000 | 2000+

Smith and Mighty
Rob Smith and Ray Mighty form S&M and are later joined by Peter D Rose

Mark Stewart
Stewart releases Stronger The Love with Smith & Mighty

Fresh Four
S&M work with Suv, Krust, Flynn, Judge and Liz E.

More Rockers
Heavy dub offshoot of Smith & Mighty

Mad Professor
Ex Black Roots producer remixes Massive Attack's Protection

Tricky
Stewart's lodger meets Martina Topley-Bird

Full Cycle Roni Size forms Full Cycle from the Basement Project in St Paul's. He is joined by , Krust, Suv, Die, MC Dynamite, Onalee and others

Reprazent
Wins the Mercury prize for Roni Size

Sinead O'Connor
Nellee Hooper produces the Nothing Compares 2 U monster hit. He also works with Madonna, Bjork, Smashing Pumpkins, All Saints, U2 Janet Jackson and others

Gary Clail
Mark Stewart works with Gary Clail at Adrian Sherwood's On-U-Sounds

Tru Funk
Talented youngsters Jody and Sam and their mate Dan (DJ Die) persuade S&M to produce their 4am single

Portishead
Formed by Geoff Barrow, engineer on Blue lines

Massive Attack
100th Window released in 2003. Massive Attack (3D and Grant) play Queen Square

145

Sarah Records

Jane Duffus tells the story of an influential, but often overlooked Bristol record label...

If asked to define the Bristol music scene during the 1990s, names that doubtless pop into your mind might include Massive Attack, Tricky and Portishead. The more astute might add Sarah Records.

Based in a flat on Gwilliam Street overlooking Bedminster train station between 1987 and 1995, Sarah Records was the most independent of indie labels, where co-founders Clare Wadd and Matt Haynes were driven by feminism, ethics and passion to truly embrace the do-it-yourself ethos of the post-punk world.

During its eight years of activity, Sarah released 100 7-inch singles. The chunky vinyl records all had paper labels with bright cherries on and typewritten credits. The block-coloured wraparound sleeves were folded into plastic bags (to save on production costs), and inside each bag was a typewritten sheet containing musings on Bristol, love, music, anything really. These were carried by foot to the post office and sent to the global network of fans.

The pair met after Clare tried to sell Matt her fanzine at a Primal Scream gig in the Bierkeller. Before long, even though Clare was still at university and Matt was working as a car park attendant, they had established Sarah Records. Matt explains with his tongue in his cheek: "The label was in opposition to the capitalism of multi-format releases on the major labels. We were an anti-capitalist business, changing the world through the power

of the 7-inch single. CDs in 1987 were £15 and major labels wanted everyone to re-buy their record collections. While 7-inches were £1.50 so they were accessible and affordable."

Clare and Matt were not concerned with forming a capitalist monolith to rival Virgin or EMI, instead they were eschewing the posturing and vanity of the pop charts and promoting the kind of bands that the major labels would be too scared to touch: The Orchids, Heavenly, Even As We Speak, Blueboy, The Hit Parade, Ivy and The Rosaries to name just a few. Guitar-led pop with distorted feedback and reedy vocals were common traits of a Sarah single.

There was something rebellious about being a Sarah fan because the music press despised the label so vehemently. The music industry threw such venom at Clare, Matt and their bands that it almost became a blood sport. One *NME* writer was so incensed that he went so far as to describe the label as cancerous! "Getting stuff together for *The Secret World of Sarah Records* documentary meant re-reading old reviews and sometimes I'm amazed we actually kept going," Matt says. "People often say the internet has made the world a nastier place, but no one now would have to cope with the sort of vicious bullying we received from the weekly press. We were the last generation to be sneered at and told to know our place." Yet thanks to cut'n'paste fanzines, word of mouth and sheer love, Sarah's records would sell in

droves all around the world.

But Sarah was about more than just records. Alongside 100 7-inch singles, Sarah also put out a variety of long players, some compilations, a handful of CDs, a few fanzines and, the most prized item of Sarah paraphernalia, Saropoly: a board game about how to release your own Sarah Record. Perfect.

The DIY concept was so affordable that in the 1980s you could self-publish a fanzine with a two-track flexi disc on the cover, sell it for 50p and still break even. "It was part of the post-punk DIY ethos," says Matt. And even now, in an era of illegal downloads and heavy online marketing, he still thinks there's no need for bands to sign to the majors: "I don't see why any band now needs a record label, unless they're going to invest millions in you. You can do it all yourself."

The feminism of Sarah was lost on many people, yet it was one of the inciting reasons for founding the label. At the time, Sarah was one of very few labels to have a woman as its co-owner. Clare says: "We were opposed to the sexism of the music industry. It got more important to us when we realised what we were up against. It feels like feminism is at the fore at the moment, which is great but nothing has really changed. I feel like I've been whining about the same things for 20 years."

But why call a record label Sarah? "I'd just been reading *Emma* by Jane Austen," says Clare, "and thought that if you could call a book *Emma*, you could call a record label Sarah. And Matt agreed."

12 More Bristol record labels

Folk, techno, indie, reggae, punk, dubstep, hippies...

Saydisc: Bristol's first label was formed in 1965 and specialised in folk music.

Village Thing: A subsidiary of Saydisc formed around the Clifton Village folk scene at the Troubadour Club in Waterloo Street. Mainly limited edition releases, but Fred Wedlock's *The Folker* sold 20,000 copies.

Riot City: Punk offshoot of Heartbeat, released Vice Squad's 'Last Rockers' single in 1981 which sold 20,000 copies.

Heartbeat: Founded in 1978 by musician Simon Edwards and Tony Dodds of Tony's Record Shop on Park Street. The label was at the heart of Bristol's post punk scene with releases by Glaxo Babies, Art Objects, X-Certs and the Avon Calling compilation LPs.

Bristol Archive Records: A subsidiary of Mike Darby's Sugar Shack label, BAR has a mammoth back catalogue of Bristol music post-1977 remastered and released on CD and limited-edition vinyl. The Bristol Reggae Archive is particularly impressive and the website is a tremendous resource of Bristol music history: www.bristolarchiverecords.com.

3 Stripe: Smith & Mighty's label based at the legendary Ashley Road studio and responsible for some of the seminal early sounds of the Bristol Beat including 'Walk On' , 'Anyone' and 'Steppa's Delight'.

Melankolik: Massive Attack's label set up in 1996. Notable artists include Horace Andy, Alpha, Sunna, Craig Armstrong and Day One.

Nubian: Formed in 1987 by Black Roots to release their own material.

Punch Drunk: Punch Drunk was set up in 2006 by Tom Ford as a showcase for Bristol artists involved in the local dubstep scene. It has since evolved into one of the most interesting UK electronic music labels.

Idle Hands: Set up by Chris Farrell in 2009. While he was working alongside Peverelist at the now defunct Rooted Records. Idle Hands was started to represent a resurgent house scene that was beginning to take shape in the slipstream of dubstep. It is now based at Farrell's excellent Idle Hands record shop on City Road in St Paul's.

Pop God: Founded by the Moonflowers in 1990, Pop God was home to the band plus the Praise Space Electric side project and also released work by Me and Rorschach.

Invada: Formed at the Exchange club in Old Market and now based at the Old Fire Station in York Road, Bedminster, Invada was set up by Geoff Barrow (Portishead, Beak>) and Bristol music legend Paul Horlick (Fat Paul). It specialises in outsider and alternative music with no restrictions on genre.

A who's who of Bristol music

From jazz to grime... our tribute to the individuals and
bands who have helped define the sound of the city...

Acker Bilk
Born in Pensford in 1929, Bernard Stanley Bilk was nicknamed 'Acker' which is
Somerset slang for 'mate'. He released the single 'Summer Set' in 1960 (co-written
with well-known Bristol jazz pianist Dave Collett) which reached number five in
the UK Singles Chart. Four more chart singles followed, but it was the success of
'Stranger On The Shore' released in 1962 that made Acker Bilk an international star.
'Stranger On The Shore' peaked at number two and spent 55 weeks in the UK Singles
Chart. It was Number One in America making Bilk the second British artist to achieve
this landmark. Vera Lynn was the first and the Beatles the third. Acker Bilk died on
November 2, 2014 aged 85.

Adge Cutler
Alan John Cutler was born in a nursing home in Portishead, Somerset on November
12, 1931 six miles from the family home on Nailsea High Street. In 1966 he walked
into John Miles' office at 81 Whiteladies Road and persuaded the music impresario to
back his idea for a Somerset folk act called Adge Cutler And The Mangold Wurzels –
the Mangold got dropped but Miles bought into Adge's plan. Early in 1967 his debut
single 'Drink Up Thy Zider' sold 50,000 copies and made the lower reaches of the
charts. Adge Cutler died when travelling back from a gig in Hereford at about 4am on
May 4, 1974. His MGB sports car hit a patch of grass and crashed into the roundabout
at the junction of the Wye Valley Link Road (A466) and the M4.

Andy Sheppard
Jazz saxophonist Andy Sheppard only started playing music aged 19 when his life was
changed by listening to John Coltrane. His jazz style is progressive, experimental and
distinctive, partly due to him perfecting a circular breathing technique. Sheppard is an
internationally acclaimed jazz superstar, but you'll occasionally find him playing some
of Bristol's more intimate venues.

Bananarama
Former Rodway School (Mangotsfield) pupils Sara Dallin and Keren Woodward
moved to London together in 1981, met Siobhan Fahey and formed Bananarama.
They sang background vocals on Fun Boy Three's 1982 single 'It Ain't What You Do...'
which reached number four in the charts. Terry Hall and Funboy Three returned the
compliment by backing Bananarama on 'Really Saying Something' which reached
number 5 in the same year. Bananarama have sold an estimated 40 million records
and between 1982 and 2009 they had 28 singles reach the Top 50 of the UK Singles
Chart.

Black Roots were among the first wave of British reggae bands in the late 70s and reformed in 2010

Beak>

Beak are Geoff Barrow from Portishead, Billy Fuller and Will Young who replaced original member Matt Williams in 2016. They produce an electronic form of krautrock sometimes recorded live in one room.

Beth Rowley

Born in Peru in 1981, Rowley's parents moved back to Bristol when she was two. She formed her first band while still a pupil at St Mary Redcliffe School and went on to study music in Weston-super-Mare and Brighton. Rowley's vocal style covers influences from funk and soul to rock and gospel. Her debut LP *Little Dreamer* went straight into the UK Album Chart at number six.

Big Jeff

Jeffrey Johns is Bristol's premier gig-goer attending as many as 10 shows a week. He is regarded as an arbiter of taste, a walking encyclopedia of music and the unofficial ambassador of Bristol's live scene. Bands anxiously await the arrival of Big Jeff at the front of the crowd as a mark of approval.

Black Roots

Black Roots formed in 1979 and established themselves as one of the leading British reggae acts of the 1980s and early 1990s alongside the likes of Aswad, Steel Pulse and Misty in Roots. The original line-up of the band included Errol Brown (vocals), Delroy O'Gilvie (vocals), Kondwani Ngozi (congas, vocals), Jabulani Ngozi (rhythm guitar), Cordell Francis (lead guitar), Trevor Seivwright (drums), and Derrick King (bass guitar). They folded in the mid 90s but reformed in 2010.

Blue Aeroplanes

They first performed in 1981 and in 2017 released one of their finest albums, *Welcome, Stranger!* The constant factor in this remarkable history is singer and songwriter Gerard Langley who has fronted scores of musicians who have been part of the Blue Aeroplanes over four decades. The official count of permanent and supporting members since the release of debut album Bop Art in 1984 is 87.

Brilliant Corners

A bunch of lads from the Southmead and Lawrence Western estates announced their arrival with the 1983 release of the rockabilly/psychobilly stomper 'She's Got Fever'. The original line-up of Davey Woodward (vocals, guitar), Chris Galvin (bass), Winston Forbes (guitar), Bob Morris (drums) was joined by Dan Pacini on trumpet. And by the time they released their debut album *Growing Up Absurd* in 1985 the Corners had transformed into an indie band in the style of Orange Juice or the Smiths, but with a style and attitude all of their own. Davey Woodward's sometimes wistful lyrical observations and super-cool delivery combined with a rawness from those housing estate roots set the Brilliant Corners apart.

Chaos UK

Formed in 1979 in the Portishead/North Somerset area, Chaos UK are still touring. Anarchic, squat-dwelling, punks, Chaos UK were central to the UK hardcore scene in the 1980s along with Disorder and Amebix. None of the original members remain in the band, bass player/vocalist Chaos is said to be penning a memoir while guitarist Gabba who joined in the 80s is the longest-standing member.

City Rockas

Breakdancers Lui, Dizzy T and Donovan were one of Bristol's original B-boy crews who were to be found at many of the city's hip-hop jams dating back to 1983. When they started DJing they specialised in classic funk.

Claytown Troupe

Weston-super-Mare/Bristol goth rockers who were among the flurry of local bands signed to major labels in the late 80s. Frontman Christian Riou and keyboard player Richard Williams founded the band in 1984 and in 1988 they signed to Island Records and released their debut LP *Through The Veil* in 1989. Their second LP, *Out There*, was released on EMI in 1991. A loyal following, sell-out gigs (mainly outside Bristol) and prestigious support slots didn't convert into big record sales and Claytown Troupe split in 1993.

Colonel Kilgore's Vietnamese Formation Surf Team

One of Bristol's most unusual musical adventures. The Kilgores had a massive scooter boy and mod revival following in the early 80s but were also a best-kept secret. No information was ever given from the band – even when advertising gigs, their posters just showed a picture of a helmet and sunglasses (no band name), a venue, date and time. The stage-shows were based on the *Apocaypse Now* film and the band usually announced their arrival on stage with a crescendo of helicopter blades and Wagner's *Ride Of The Valkyries*. Everyone in the band was called Chuck, the backing singers were the Chuckettes and venue security dressed in US Army Military Police uniform. All that remains is one album (*U.S.M60/1/A*) and a few YouTube videos. The head Chuck went on to form, Superlube And The Engines before performing with his brother as Butch And Randy and finally taking to the stage as a three-piece band, Loud, Ugly And Crap.

Cortinas

Arguably, this is the band that marks the beginning of the process that resulted in 'The Bristol Sound'. The Cortinas were the most successful of Bristol's first-wave punk bands. They formed in 1976 with a line-up of Jeremy Valentine (vocals), Dexter Dalwood (bass), Nick Sheppard (guitar), Mike Fewins (guitar), Daniel Swan (drums) and released two singles 'Fascist Dictator'/'Television Families' and 'Defiant Pose'/'Independence' on their own Step Forward label in 1977. In 1978, the Cortinas signed to CBS released one album, *True Romances*, and split by the end of the year.

Crazy Trains

The Crazy Trains were formed in the early 80s by ex-St Bede's pupils John McLean (vocals, harmonica) and Paul Grudzinski (guitar) plus Barry Cooper (guitar), Pete Ahluwahlia (drums) and 15-year-old prodigy Jon Chilcott (bass). Influenced by the New York Dolls, Chuck Berry, the Faces, Rolling Stones and 60s garage R&B, they exploded on the Bristol scene with an astonishing energy and rock 'n' roll attitude. Former X-Certs firebrand Neil Mackie took over on drums and former Stackridge manager Mike Tobin picked up the band and signed them to new label Spellbound for a reported £250,000. Two singles were released on Spellbound but then the band fell out with the label, who held them to their four year contract, but refused to release more material. Inevitably the Crazy Trains split up.

David and Jonathan

One of the most successful songwriting partnerships ever, Roger Cook and Roger Greenaway were born in Bristol in 1940 and 1938 respectively. Cook lived at 8 Forest Road, Fishponds; Greenaway was brought up at 98 Spring Hill, Kingswood. After knocking about with various Bristol bands (such as the Kestrels), they were discovered in 1965 by Beatles producer George Martin. Martin's wife, Judy, suggested they record under the name David and Jonathan and they reached number 11 in the charts with Lennon and McCartney's 'Michelle' in 1966.

A string of other singles followed, but it is as songwriters that Cook and Greenaway made a huge impact. They've written for artists including Gene Pitney ('Something's Gotten Hold Of My Heart'), Cilla Black, Cliff Richard, Kathy Kirby, Hank Marvin, Deep Purple and the Sweet, to name but a few. Cook joined Blue Mink in 1969 and recorded Cook and Greenaway's anti-racism classic 'Melting Pot'.

But it's as the writers of the 1970 Coca-Cola jingle 'I'd Like To Buy The World A Coke', that Cook and Greenaway reached an audience of millions around the globe. This was recorded as 'I'd Like To Teach The World To Sing' by the New Seekers and released in December 1971. It brought Cook and Greenaway their first number one in January 1972. In that month, three of the top four chart songs were Cook and Greenaway creations: at number two was 'Softly Whispering I Love You' (the Congregation) and Cilla was at number four with 'Something Tells Me Something's Gonna Happen Tonight'. They were only prevented from a straight top three run by the number two sound of Benny Hill with 'Ernie: The Fastest Milkman In The West'.

Dean Prince And The Dukes

One of Bristol's favourite skiffle/rock 'n' roll bands Dennis Small aka Dean Prince founded the band in 1960 with Ronnie Roach (lead guitar), Pete Hayden (bass), Clive Saunders (rhythm guitar) and Johnny Day (drums). In May 1961, Ronnie Roach left the band and was replaced by Roger Pritchard. In the early 70s, Pritchard changed his name to Lee Sheridan, left the band and embarked on a career as a songwriter. He joined Brotherhood Of Man as a writer/performer, who enjoyed huge success with three Number One singles, including the Eurovision Song Contest winner 'Save Your Kisses For Me' in March 1976.

DJ Derek

Derek Serpell-Morris was the old bloke in the cardigan in the corner of the Star & Garter playing a cool set of obscure ska. He went on to become a leading figure in the world of dub, reggae and ska. His Trojan collection *DJ Derek Presents Sweet Memory Sounds* was released in the summer of 2006 and he was a regular at many of Europe's leading festivals. He used to be an accountant at Fry's but gave it all up to play ska and reggae. In July 2015 Derek went missing. He was last seen leaving his beloved Wetherspoons on Corn Street and the following day his bus pass was used on the 78 service to Cribbs Causeway, but it is not known if it was used by Derek. His body was found in Patchway, near Cribbs Causeway in March 2016.

DJ Die

Founder of drum and bass label Full Cycle and a member of Reprazent who won the Mercury Music Prize with Roni Size in 1997 for the album *New Forms*. Die has been at the forefront of the electronic music scene ever since through various projects and partnerships including Breakbeat Era and Gutterfunk.

Emily Breeze

Irish refugee Emily Breeze has become the first lady of the new Bristol underground scene. "Somewhere between a punch in the guts and a tender tragic caress," is how she describes her muse and the 2010 breathtaking statement of intent 'The Penny Arcade' does both beautifully. A 21st Century post-feminist icon waiting for the world to catch up. A new album, *Rituals*, is said to be in the making.

Enterprise Sound System

Enterprise sound system was one of Bristol most respected sounds during its operation, 1975-1991. Whether the sound system was basking in the glory of St Paul's Carnival or providing life to a house party, Enterprise was truly appreciated. After a 14-year hiatus, Pappa Roots evolved out of Enterprise and continues to play regular dances in Bristol.

FBI Crew

Operating between 1984-1989, FBI were one of the city's leading hip-hop crews, particularly on the house party scene. Members included Paul Cleaves, Mark Cleaves, Phil Jones, Paul Smart and Dave McCarthy.

Flatmates

One of the city's leading indie bands, the Flatmates were formed in 1985 by guitarist

Fresh 4 and Liz E made the top 10 in 1989 with the Smith & Mighty version of 'Wishing On A Star'

Martin Whitehead and Rocker (drums) and fronted by Debbie Haynes. The original bass player Kath Beach left and was replaced by Sarah Fletcher. It was this line-up that perfected the three-minute, sugar-coated pop melodies that made the Flatmates so popular. 'Happy All The Time' reached number three in the indie charts and 'You're Gonna Cry' peaked at number five in 1987. 'Shimmer' and the 'Janice Long Sessions' both reached number two in 1988 and their final single 'Heaven Knows' was number 10. The Flatmates split up in 1989.

The Flies
Some bands are born with a buzz around them. 'It's about the occasional corruption of men by women and the ease with which men are susceptible to corruption,' says vocalist and former Spiritualized and Lupine Howl frontman Sean Cook of the 2014 stunning debut album Pleasure Yourself. With its dark hypnotic jazz beats and brooding, whispered vocals, Cook – and heavyweight Insects cohorts Bob Locke and Tim Norfolk – have sculpted a shadowy soundtrack to a freak-strewn, post-midnight netherworld. Think Max Steiner doing electronica, the sharp shuffling feet narrative of a James Ellroy crime scene or William S Burroughs rattling down a sidewalk with a hatful of narcs in his head. Cook played bass and Damon Reece from Spiritualized was the drummer on Massive Attack's 2019 Mezzanine tour.

Flynn & Flora
Flynn from Fresh 4 and DJ Flora were hugely respected drum and bass producers on the underground scene and released a string of singles mainly on their own Independent Dealers label mainly between 1994 and 2001. Also influential among the city's reggae and jungle DJs. Flora passed away in 2014.

Fred Wedlock

Fred Wedlock (born 1942) was brought up in the heart of the city in his parents' pub, the York House, a George's Brewery pub at 16 Phippen Street, Redcliffe. He later claimed that his first public engagement was as a toddler singing to dockers in the bar. He became a star of the vibrant Bristol folk scene of the 60s especially at the dockside Bathurst Hotel and at the Troubadour Club in Clifton. In the 1970s he joined the likes of Billy Connelly, Jasper Carrott and Mike Harding as one of folk's leading comedy entertainers. In 1981 his single 'Oldest Swinger In Town' reached number six in the UK Singles Chart and propelled Wedlock onto the national stage. But Fred was most at home in the West Country. In 1997 he performed in ACH Smith's play *Up The Feeder And Down The Mouth* at Bristol Old Vic. He was also a popular TV presenter, in particular with co-host Sherrie Eugene on HTV's *The Good Neighbour Show*. Fred Wedlock died on March 4, 2010.

Fresh 4 (Children Of The Ghetto) and Liz E

Straight outa Knowle West, Fresh 4 were brothers Flynn and Krust plus Suv and Judge. Flynn was introduced to producers Rob Smith and Ray Mighty by DJ Flora who liked Fresh 4's idea for a reworking of the Rose Royce song 'Wishing On A Star' and Liz E (Liz Ellis) was recruited as singer. The story goes that a snatch of the tune was left on an answerphone at Virgin Records and within weeks Fresh 4 and Liz E were signed. 'Wishing On A Star' peaked at number 10 in the UK Singles Chart on October 15, 1989. The follow-up singles 'Release Yourself' and 'Compared To What' weren't as successful and following disagreements with the record company Fresh 4's debut album was never released. In 2015 Bristol Archive Records released *Fresh 4 The Lost Tapes* on limited-edition vinyl.

Gary Clail

The apocryphal story about Gary Clail is that the queue to get out of a gig at the Western Star Domino Club was as long as the queue to get in, such was the volume of Clail's bass-heavy dub soundsystem. A scaffolder and roofer by trade, Clail, from Barton Hill, discovered the delights of the Dug Out and various blues clubs at an early age. He took his love of dub reggae to Adrian Sherwood's On-U Sound collective where his soundsystem supported bands such as African Headcharge. His singles 'Human Nature' and 'Beef' (featuring Bim Sherman) were big club hits and crossed over into the mainstream charts and his most successful album was *The Emotional Hooligan* released in 1991. After almost a decade without releasing new material, Clail returned in 2014 with his *Nail It To The Mast* LP.

George Ezra

He's not from Bristol, but George Ezra moved to the city in 2011 to study at the city's British And Irish Modern Music Institute (BIMM). Within a year he had signed to Columbia Records and in 2013 his first single 'Budapest' was a hit across the world.

Gl*xo Babies

They came, they produced some brilliant post-punk tunes, they split up and then came back again in an even more experimental form. Seek out the tunes 'This Is Your Life', 'It's Irrational', and 'Who Killed Bruce Lee' if you want to know what the Gl*xo Babies are about.

Goldfrapp

Alison Goldfrapp is the notoriously sour-faced, art-house sex kitten who has purred studied perfection all over Goldfrapp's admirably oblique nu-disco. Will Gregory is the other half of the Goldfrapp duo, a classically trained multi-instrumentalist who decided to move into the arena of experimental electro pop. The results were startling. Gregory is the synth-collecting genius who gives Goldfrapp their warped, future world soundscape.

Gonga

Hairy, heavy, headbanging. Although the chords may hark back to the days when Black Sabbath were being introduced to the rock world as 'a promising young group from England', the band's sheer unrelenting ferocity takes them way beyond retro. Gonga's debut album *Stratofortress* was released on Geoff Barrow and Fat Paul's Invada label.

Gravenhurst

What's the best way to describe Gravenhurst? There have been the inevitable Nick Drake comparisons but this doesn't even begin to tell the story. Nick Talbot was a fast-fingered virtuoso of the strings and it was this, more than anything else, that separated him from what came before. A prince of scattered nostalgia. Nick Talbot died in 2014 aged 37.

Hazel Winter

A critic once described Hazel Winter's music as 'The sound of a quite unhinging ferocity... a terrific burst of whispery nastiness'. Hard rock guitar and gritty surrealism are the mainstays of Winter's music. She was once in the Blue Aeroplanes and in 2018 released some of her finest work on the *Courtesan* album with her band the Flux Capacitors.

Head

Decadent is the word that best describes Head's style of sleazy rock music. Head combined the punk roots of guitarists Nick Sheppard (Cortinas, Clash) and Gareth Sager (Pop Group, Rip Rig & Panic) with Rich Beale (vocals), Jamie Hill (drums) and Mark Taylor (bass). Despite some serious backing from Virgin Records, Head remained too leftfield to court mainstream success but released three fine albums *A Snog On The Rocks* (Demon 1987), *Tales Of Ordinary Madness* (Virgin, 1988) and *Intoxicator* (Virgin, 1989).

Idles

Political punk/art rockers who formed in 2012 and five years later released their debut album *Brutalism* to much critical acclaim. Idles are Joe Talbot (vocals), Mark Bowen (guitar), Adam Devonshire (bass), Lee Kiernan (guitar) and Jon Beavis (drums). *Brutalism* is so called because it marks the same philosophy as the brutalist architecture movement of stripping everything back to fundamental principles. In this case it's an affirmation of hi-energy punk music and sneering at middle class values and aspirations. Their second album *Joy As An Act Of Rebellion* released in 2018 stormed into the top five in the UK Album Charts making them Bristol's most **156** successful-ever guitar band.

Jackie Jackson

The voice that helped propel Smith & Mighty to the forefront of 1980s underground dance music. Jackie Jackson was the featured vocalist on the first two Smith & Mighty tunes 'Anyone' and 'Walk On' (both released in 1988).

Jaguar

Heavy metal outfit formed in 1979 with an original line-up of Garry Pepperd (guitar) Jeff Cox (bass, vocals) and Chris Lovell (drums). Jaguar did well across Europe and in Asia as one of the New Wave Of British Heavy Metal bands and in 1982 released the single 'Axe Crazy' now considered a NWOBHM classic.

Jah Lokko Sound System

Big D, founder of Jah Lokko, is one of Bristol's most illustrious sound system figures. He runs Jah Lokko alongside his two cousins, Lloyd and Snoopy. Jah Lokko was built in 1976 and it continues to be utilised regularly not only as traditional roots sound but also as a vessel for other artists to play on. As one of the founders of Bristol Dub Club, Jah Lokko can be heard regularly at the monthly sound clash events they host at the Black Swan.

John Stapleton

DJ John Stapleton moved to Bristol in the late 70s and became a regular on the decks at hip-hop parties before getting his own Friday night slot at the Western Star Domino Club and launching the electro/funk Club Foot night at the Tropic Club. But it is as the founder of the Def Con club nights (along with Ian Dark from the Z Boys graffiti crew) that Stapleton made his biggest impact. The Def Con nights at the Thekla were legendary for their progressive mix of acid house, funk and hip-hop. Stapleton also performed with the Blue Aeroplanes and is credited on three albums between 1985-88. A compulsive collector of tunes, he runs Wanted Records in St Nick's Market and hosts several club nights incuding Easton Standard Time and Go-Go Children.

Johnny Carr And The Cadillacs

Johnny Carr And The Cadillacs made their debut at The Railway Club, Temple Meads on December 15, 1959 with the line up of Dave Faye (vocals), Pete O'Connell (lead guitar), Mervyn Alexander (rhythm guitar), Gary Keller (bass) and Dave Purslow (drums). On March 11 1960 singer Cornelius 'Con' O'Sullivan replaced Dave Faye becoming the new 'Johnny Carr'. In July and August 1961, they performed at the famous Kaiser Keller club in Hamburg, Germany taking over from a Liverpool band the Silver Beatles (who later dropped Silver from their name and became rather well known). They were one of the most popular bands in Bristol and were well-known for covering the latest American songs as soon as they were released. Johnny Carr And The Cadillacs won the Best Band award in *Western Scene* magazine three years in a row between 1963-65.

Joker

Liam McLean (aka Joker) is record producer working mainly in dubstep and grime who is also credited as being the forerunner of the purple sound electronic genre distinguished by its broken beats and synthesizer effects. Best known for his single 'Digidesign' from 2009.

Jashwa Moses

Joshua Moses (he later changed the spelling of his first name) is a roots reggae singer whose family moved from St Catherine's in Jamaica to Bristol when he was a teenager. Moses won a competition at the Bamboo Club which resulted in him recording his song 'Africa' with producer Dennis Bovell in a London studio. It was released on the More Cut label and was a top 10 hit in the Black Echo reggae chart. Back in Bristol, Moses was one of the artists involved with founding the Shoc Wave label in 1979 and recorded the track 'Pretty Girl'. Fast Forward to 2012 when Bristol Archive Records released the LP *Joshua To Jashwa 30 Years In The Wilderness* as well as re-issuing 'Pretty Girl' and putting out an unreleased track from 1983 called 'Rise Up'.

Julio Bashmore

House music producer with a string of big club hits to his name most notably 'Battle For Middle You' (2011), 'Au Seve' (2012) and 'Peppermint' (2014).

K*ners

Grime and hip-hop producer who emerged around 2002 and had his biggest success with the outstanding 'Bristol Grammar' in 2013. Real name Horaine Ferguson.

Keith Christmas

He's from Essex, but pitched up on the Bristol folk scene in the 1960s when he was a student at the School of Architecture at Bath University. In a non-conventional career, Christmas was booked for the first Glastonbury Festival, played guitar on David Bowie's 'Space Oddity', set up a commune in Vobster in the Mendips, recorded with acid rock outfit Magic Muscle, signed to Emerson Lake and Palmer's Manticore label and was a music teacher at Ashton Park school. His finest work is considered to be the five folk-style albums released between 1969 and 1976 in particular *Stimulus* and *Fable Of The Wings*. In 2016 he released the album *Crazy Dancing Days*.

Keith Tippett

Tippett was born in Southmead and went to Greenway Secondary Modern School where he formed a brass band called the KT Trad Lads when he was 14 in 1961. A few years later he was playing in a modern jazz trio at the Dug Out. He moved to London in 1967, married singer Julie Driscoll ('This Wheel's On Fire'). Tippett is internationally regarded as one of the most experimental and radical jazz musicians of his generation working with musicians around the globe from his 50-piece band Centipede to King Crimson.

Kosheen

Drum and bass trio formed in 2001 by Markee Substance, Darren Decoder and Welsh singer Sian Evans who emerged from the scene around the Ruffneck Ting raves and Breakbeat Culture shop and label. Split in 2016 after releasing five albums, the first two of which made the UK Album Chart Top 10 (*Resist*, number eight and *Kopokelli* number seven). The singles 'Hide You' (2001) and 'All In My Head' (2003) both

Idles stormed into the top 5 with their 2018 album Joy As An Act Of Rebellion © Ania Shrimpton

Krust

After the demise of Fresh 4, DJ Krust and Suv teamed up with Roni Size, DJ Die, Onallee (vocals), Clive Deamer (drums), Si John (electric and upright bass) in Reprazent and was part of the collective that won the 1997 Mercury Music Prize for the album *New Forms*. He continued the drum and bass theme with the ground-breaking *Coded Language* LP featuring Saul Williams on Island Records in 1999, teamed up with DJ Die for *I Kamanchi* on Full Cycle in 2003 and *Hidden Knowledge* (Full Cycle) in 2006.

Laid Blak

Laid Blak were formed by two veterans of the rave scene DJ Bungy and MC Joe Peng. Bass player Lui traces his roots back to body popping with the City Rockas hip-hop crew from the 80s while Flex (vocals), Stacy (drums), Tim (guitar), Sam (keyboards) and Tita (vocals) complete the line-up. Their music has been described as 'street soul meets reggae'. In 2007, they released the single 'Red' on Brown Punk, a label set up by Tricky and Island Records boss Chris Backwell. The album *About Time* was released on Bristol's Sugar Shack Records in April 2018.

Lionpulse Sound System

Lionpulse emerged in early 2009 as two friends with a passion for roots, rub a dub and dancehall music. Gerard and Henry devoted years to collecting records before they decided to build the sound system which was launched in 2013. Lionpulse are associated with a new wave of sound system culture, their impact on the Bristol scene continues to be both influential and inspiring for the next generation.

Massive Attack

Grant Marshall, Andrew Vowles and Robert Del Naja changed Bristol music for ever. Without the influence of the three core members of the Massive Attack project it's unlikely that Tricky and Portishead would have emerged; there would be no such thing as the Bristol Sound or trip-hop. In fact, there's a strong case for saying that Massive Attack changed music everywhere, such was the towering originality of their debut album *Blue Lines* released in 1991.

Maximum Joy

Formed in 1981 by ex-Gl*xo Babies Tony Wrafter (saxophone, trumpet, flute), and Charlie Llewellin (drums) plus Dan Catsis (bass) and John Waddington (guitar) from the Pop Group, Maximum Joy were fronted by livewire vocalist Janine Rainforth. The sound is influenced by punk, funk, reggae and jazz with production by reggae agitators Dennis Bovell and Adrian Sherwood. They produced one album (featuring a brief appearance by Nellee Hooper on percussion and backing vocals) and several singles but Maximum Joy split in 1983. Rainforth re-formed the band in 2015 and in 2017 Idle Hands and Blackest Ever Black released a vinyl compilation of the band's singles *I Can't Stand It Here On A Quiet Night* on the new Silent Street Records label. In February 2019 Rainforth released her first new work in decades with the *Peace* album under the name MXMJoY featuring Charlie Llewellin on drums.

Me

Tight harmonies and refined pop sensibilities set Me apart from the Indie crowd when they stumbled onto the Bristol scene in the late 1980s. Underlying that clean-cut pop sound was a mischievous sense of the surreal that ensured they baffled and entertained in equal measure. They signed to the Mooonflowers' Pop God label and produced an LP in 1993 called *Harmonise or Die*. Guitarist Paul Bradley went on to form Three Cane Whale.

Mike Crawford

He's been close to many of the interesting things that have happened in Bristol since 1979 when he fronted soul covers band the Spics, whose original line up included Nick Sheppard and Johnny Britton on guitar, WOMAD co-founder Thomas Brooman (drums), John Carley (percussion), Rachel Morgan (bass) and backing singers Wendy and Sarah Partridge, Phoebe Beedell, Heidi Hutton and Jo Swan. Crawford has been behind many solo, studio and band collaborations including the Nitecaps, Apache Dropout and most recently Mike Crawford & The Various Sorrows, who also go out as John E Vistic's backing band. He is also a stage manager for Portishead.

Mike Darby

Band manager and promoter, but most of all the man behind the remarkable Bristol Archive Records label and the Bristol Reggae Archive (an off shoot of his Sugar Shack label). Surely no city in the world has such a resource. Darby devotes his musical life to tracking down and releasing lost Bristol music from 1977 onwards.

Moonflowers

Hippies. The Legendary Moonflowers took nothing seriously apart from friendship, drugs, partying and music. Their often magic-mushroom fuelled frolics were fun, naive and the music was great. Because underlying that seemingly chaotic anarcho, acid, funky rock there were some very good musicians. Fronted by the Rev Sonik Ray (Sean O'Neill), the Moonflowers included 'Jesse' Vernon (guitar), Sam Burns (keyboards, saxophone, vocals) Yoddon (Adam Pope on drums), Paul Waterworth (bass), DJ Elmo and later Gina Griffin (vocals) and drummer Toby Pascoe who passed away in 2001.

The Moonflowers formed their own Pop God label, probably because the major labels wouldn't know what to do with them, and released several EPs, singles and LPs between 1987 and 1997, most notably *We Dig Your Earth*, *Get Higher*, *Hash Smits* and *Warshag*. Several other Bristol bands released records on Pop God including Me and Praise Space Electric. In true hippy fashion, the Moonflowers eloped to set up a commune in France and gradually drifted back when the wine ran out.

Onslaught

Onslaught were formed in 1982 as a hardcore punk band on the Kingswood side of town by guitarist Nige Rockett and drummer Steve Grice. They moved in a thrash metal direction and underwent several line-up changes along the way, gaining a loyal following, especially in Europe. The albums *Power From Hell* (1985) and *The Force* (1986) reinforced the demonic fashion in thrash metal in the Eighties. Si Keeler joined as vocalist and in 1988 Onslaught signed to London Records for a reported advance of £1.25 million, but still found time to play their regular Christmas gig at the Lamb pub, on Banjo Island in Cadbury Heath. Onslaught split in the early 1990s and have reformed a few times since around Nige Rockett. In 2017 they claimed to be the first thrash metal band to play Lebanon.

Ossia

Ossia is one of the Young Echo collective of musicians and producers responsible for some of the most experimental dance sounds in Bristol. His 'Red X' single is a mix of slowed down reggae, electronica and crashing sound effects inspired by the personal taped diaries of Wailers founder and guitarist Pete Tosh.

Paul Horlick

Fat Paul is a hero of the Bristol music scene. The former Swarf Finger and Espionage labels main man is a money-where-his-mouth-is champion of experimental noiseniks everywhere. Horlick has spread his wings Down Under and is now one half of the UK arm of Aussie label Invada. He's also the boss of the Exchange club in Old Market and occasional collaborator with Julian Cope.

Peverelist

Peverelist is a reference to Hatfield Peverel Junglist Massive, Hatfield Peverell being the town of 5,500 people in the middle of Essex where Tom Ford grew up and jungle music a particular early influence. Ford moved to Bristol when he was 18 and became manager of Rooted Records on Gloucester Road which became a centre for the city's dubstep community. He went on to form the influential Punch Drunk label in 2006 to showcase dubstep artists and other forms of electronica and dance music. One of Ford's best-known tracks is' Roll With The Punches' from 2007 and in 2017 he released his third album *Tessellations*.

Gareth Sager (guitar) and Mark Stewart of the Pop Group © Paul Roberts

Pigbag

Although they were formed in Cheltenham in 1980 and had roots in Birmingham, it was when they recruited ex-Pop Group bass player Simon Underwood and Bristol saxophonist Ollie Moore that Pigbag really took shape. Through Underwood's connections with Dick O'Dell, manager of the Slits and head of Y Records (home of the Pop Group), that Pigbag landed their first gig – supporting the Slits at Romeo And Juliet's in Bristol on October 21, 1980. It was around this time that the fledgling band took the name Pigbag, a reference to founder member Chris Hamlin's cloth bag bearing a screen print of a warthog.

In 1981 Pigbag recorded the track that made their name and continues to be played across the world. 'Papa's Got A Brand New Pigbag' was released in May 1981 and reached number two in the indie charts but didn't make an impact on the mainstream charts. When it was re-issued in March 1982 it reached Number One in the indie charts and number three in the UK Singles Chart. Pigbag split up in 1983.

Pinch

Dubstep artist Pinch (aka Rob Ellis) released his first album *Underwater Dancehall* in 2007 on his own Tectonic label and established himself as one of the most influential artists on the dubstep scene. His trademark deep and spacious style references a wide range of genres from world music and dancehall. Like fellow Bristolians Gary Clail and Mark Stewart, Pinch went on to work closely with On-U Sounds bass guru Adrian Sherwood.

PJ Harvey and John Parish

Polly Jean Harvey first performed with John Parish in a band called Automatic Dlamini in 1988 contributing backing vocals, slide guitar and saxophone. Automatic Dlamini founded by Parish and Rob Ellis were avant garde adventurers driven by percussion, drums, guitar and vocals. They hailed from the Yeovil area, not far from Harvey's Bridport home, but made Bristol their base.

A few years later, Polly took centre stage and in 1991 formed the PJ Harvey Trio with Rob Ellis (drums) and one-time Automatic Dlamini bass player Ian Oliver. The albums *Dry* and *Rid Of Me* and singles including 'Sheela-Na-Gig' were critically acclaimed and commercially successful but in 1993 the PJ Harvey Trio disbanded, Polly went solo and teamed up again with John Parish to record her third studio album To Bring You My Love. She has been working with Parish as producer and part of her band ever since.

In 2001, the album *Stories From The City, Stories From The Sea* won the Mercury Music Prize and PJ Harvey repeated that feat in 2011 with *Let England Shake* thus becoming the only artist to win the best album accolade twice.

Pop Group
Formed in 1977, the Pop Group split up in 1981, but during those few years they made a massive impact on Bristol music and indeed sent shockwaves across the world. They reformed in 2010 and have toured extensively and released new material since including the excellent *Citizen Zombie* LP in 2015.

Portishead
Portishead were formed by instrumentalist and DJ Geoff Barrow and singer Beth Gibbons in 1991. Barrow was a tape operator at the Coach House studio in Clifton when Massive Attack recorded Blue Lines and the band gave him some studio time to develop his own ideas. He met singer Beth Gibbons who had moved to Bristol from Devon and along with jazz guitarist Adrian Utley and sound engineer Dave McDonald formed the Portishead project. *Dummy* was released on August 22 1994 and produced three singles 'Numb', 'Sour Times' and 'Glory Box' and won the Mercury Music Prize in 1995. In 2016 they released a haunting version of ABBA's 'SOS' as a tribute to murdered Labour MP Jo Cox.

Qualitex Sound System
Qualitex sound system was founded in 1986 by Faada Sojie, Mellow and Jimmy Swing and later joined by Kutty, Ras Baga, Skater B and Didi Skrew. With roots from the town of Yallahs in St Thomas, Jamaica, Qualitex are renowned not only for their exclusive selection but also their custom-built equipment. Crew member Kutty launched his own speaker box building business QSS, in 2010 and builds boxes for both local and international clientele.

Queen Bee
Roz Scordilis began her career as DJ Queen Bee in the Eighties on the pirate radio stations Emergency Radio and Respect FM before becoming music programmer for FEM FM, Britain's first all female radio station in 1992. Her wide-ranging selection takes in hip-hop, funk, reggae, Latin music and more, making her a popular attraction on Bristol's club scene and on the festival circuit. Queen Bee was resident DJ on the Jazz World stage at Glastonbury Festival for 10 years and has played at international WOMAD festivals and performed all over Europe with Daddy G from Massive Attack and also as Massive Attack's Tour DJ.

Restriction

Reggae band Restriction emerged from the Arts Opportunity Theatre project in St Paul's and although they were relatively short lived and only released one single, 'Action', their impact was lasting. The original line-up was Rob Smith (guitar) who went on to form Smith & Mighty with Ray Mighty; Karl Williams (vocals) who is Ronnie Size's elder brother; Mark Spence (bass); Andy Clark (drums); Charlie Clarke (saxophone); Basil Anderson (keyboards). The sound engineer was Dave McDonald who went on to work with Portishead. Jendayi Serwah and Eric 'The General' McCarthy replaced Karl Williams as lead singer in 1983. 'The General' is Carlton McCarthy's brother who was vocalist with Daddy G on 'Any Love' in 1988, a Massive Attack/Smith & Mighty production.

Rich Beale

There is a rumour going around that Rich Beale has been on the dole since 1975. For this alone, he deserves an award. Add a CV that includes Head, Pregnant and Apache Dropout and you get a true renaissance man of the Bristol underground.

Rip Rig & Panic

Guitarist Gareth Sager, drummer Bruce Smith plus occasional keyboard player Mark Springer formed Rip Rig & Panic when they left the Pop Group in 1980. Neneh Cherry joined as singer and Sean Oliver on bass to form the core of the band. They took their name from a 1965 jazz album by Roland Kirk. By the time of their demise, the Pop Group had pushed their heavy, funk reggae, noise experiment to the brink but Rip Rig & Panic were innovative in a different way, choosing to tread a free jazz, funk and sometimes surreal path. The results were sometimes patchy, but always interesting.

Rita Lynch

Rita first appeared on the Bristol scene in the early 80s with an all-woman punk combo called Rita And The Piss Artists, she moved into electronica with God Bless You but since the 1990s she's reverted to rock as either a solo artist or fronting a band – often just guitar and drums. She was allegedly taught to play guitar by nuns while at a Catholic school. The power of her playing and vocals can be breathtaking. Rita's debut album *Call Me Your Girlfriend* in 1991 perfectly captured the tenderness and ferocity that distinguishes her work. She performed with the Blue Aeroplanes between 2010-211.

Roni Size/Reprazent

When this drum and bass collective won the Mercury Music Prize in 1997 for their debut album *New Forms* they saw off competition from, among others, Radiohead (*The Bends*), Prodigy (*Fat Of The Land*), Suede (*Coming Up*) and the Spice Girls (*Spice*). That's a measure of just how groundbreaking *New Forms* was. The original Reprazent line-up included Roni Size (programming/keyboards), Onallee (vocals), Si John (electric and upright bass), DJ Die, Suv, Krust (programming production), Clive Deamer (drums), Rob Merrill (guitar), Dynamite MC (raps). A second album, New Forms, was released in 2000 following which the various members of Reprazent began working on solo projects and collaborations. Roni Size resurrected Reprazent in 2008 and played various festivals. A 20th anniversary remastered, deluxe box set of

New Forms was released in November 2017.

Russ Conway

Pianist Trevor Herbert Stanford sold an estimated 30 million records over the course of his career as Russ Conway. The boy from Dean Lane, Bedminster had 17 consecutive top-20 hits between 1957 and 1963, appeared in his own television shows and owned mansions, Bentleys and Rolls-Royces.

He had no formal musical training and left school aged 14 to work in a solicitors' office. However, he was sent to borstal for three years for theft and taught himself piano while incarcerated. After leaving the Navy he played the holiday club and pub circuit where he was spotted by the choreographer Irving Davies, who was so impressed that he asked him to play piano for stars at rehearsals. He worked for Dennis Lotis, Dorothy Squires and Gracie Fields.

But it was when Conway made it to the BBC's *Billy Cotton Band Show* in the late 1950s that his career took off. Cotton persuaded him to loosen up his playing, and helped create the disciplined freedom of the mature Conway style. His big break came by accident. A musical he had written for the comedian Frankie Howerd, *Mr Venus*, was a write-off, but it led him to writing the score for a TV musical, *Beauty And The Beast*. He had to write a last-minute tune for one brief scene and sitting in the rehearsal room, Conway wrote 16 bars and scribbled 'Side Saddle' beside it in the margin. 'Side Saddle' reached Number One in the UK Singles Chart in 1959 and became Conway's signature tune.

Conway smoked 80 cigarettes a day and suffered from nerves and anxiety. By 1971, he was drinking at a pace which reduced him to near bankruptcy. But his friends helped to pull him through and Conway's career resumed, though on a smaller scale

At 65, Conway discovered he had cancer. He died in Eastbourne aged 75 on November 15, 2000 just two weeks after his final public performance. Almost 1000 people attended his funeral service at St Mary Redcliffe church on December 6, 2000. Sir Elton John sent flowers and a card that said 'Thanks for being such an inspiration to me, Love Elton'.

Seers

Their style was like a meeting between the Monkees and the Ramones – 60s garage rock fused with psychedelia, underpinned by punk. The Seers rocked. They deserved a similar level of success as their contemporaries such as the Stones Roses, Happy Mondays and Wonder Stuff, but this was Bristol pre-Massive Attack when many outstanding acts didn't get the recognition they deserved. Formed in 1984, the Seers were Adrian 'Age' Blackmore (drums), Spider (vocals), Leigh Wildman (guitar), Kat Day (guitar) and Jason Collins (bass). A series of record company misfortunes meant they never got the major deal they deserved and the band folded in 1991 leaving us with two albums (*Psych Out* and *Peace Crazies*), a handful of singles and memories of a great live band.

Shanti Celeste

Celeste was born in Chile but moved to the United Kingdom when she was 12 with her mother who married an English man. She had her first contact to electronic music at rave parties in Lake District when she was a teenager. Celeste moved to Bristol for an illustration course at the University of the West of England and met Chris Farrell, a Bristol-based DJ and head of the label Idle Hands. Celeste and Farrell launched the label BRSTL together, on which label Celeste also released her debut single *Need Your*

Lovin' (*Baby*) in 2013. During her time in Bristol, she also set up her own club night called Housework. Celeste was nominated Best Newcomer DJ in the 2015 DJ Awards. In 2016, Celeste relocated to Berlin.

Smith & Mighty

They may not have the profile of Massive Attack, Portishead and Tricky but in terms of influence Rob Smith and Ray Mighty are their equal. Both are products of the punk generation and the fusion with reggae and hip-hop that is one of the defining qualities of the Bristol Sound. Rob Smith was guitarist in reggae band Restriction in the early 80s and when Restriction folded he joined a funk outfit called Sweat where he met Ray Mighty. By 1987 they had set up together as Smith & Mighty. In 1988 they released their first two singles on their Three Stripe label – *Walk On* and *Anyone*, reworkings of Bacharach and David's songs *Walk On By* and *Anyone Who Had A Heart* both featuring singer Jackie Jackson.

The slow beats, stripped back drums and bass-heavy treatment plus the dreamy vocals created a distinct sound full of warmth and depth. Also in 1988, Smith & Mighty were credited with production for the 'Any Love' single by Massive Attack featuring Daddy Gee and Carlton. In 1989 they produced Fresh 4's cover of the Rose Royce tune *Wishing On A Star* which made number 10 in the UK Singes Chart. In 1990 they produced Carlton McCarthy's album *The Call Is Strong* which in many ways is the 'missing link' between the Bristol hip-hop scene and the 'trip-hop' sound of Massive Attack, Portishead and Tricky. Smith & Mighty signed a five-year deal with ffrr a subsidiary of London Records and that's where it all went wrong. The label didn't like the direction of the *Bass Is Maternal* album and when Smith & Mighty refused to compromise they had to see out their deal without any material being released.

Once free of the deal, they worked together on their More Rockers dub project, Alice Perera joined Smith & Mighty as vocalist, Peter D Rose became a regular member of the crew and Tammy Payne was guest vocalist. Rob Smith went on to release the outstanding solo album *Up On The Downs* in 2003 and to record as RSD (Rob Smith Dub). Smith & Mighty still regularly DJ together. In 2018, the *Ashley Road Sessions 1988-94* was released on Punch Drunk Records.

Stackridge

Having met at The Dug Out club in 1969 where their respective bands Dawn and Griptight Thynne often played, guitarists Andy Davis, James Warren and Jim 'Crun' Walter decided to pool their resources in a new group called Stackridge Lemon. Recruiting recent arrival from Yeovil Mick 'Mutter' Slater on flute and Billy 'Sparkle' Bent on drums and dropping the Lemon from their name they made their debut at a Christmas party at the Old Granary in December 1969. Managed by Mike Tobin, they were soon gigging all over the country and in particular in London. Adding folk musician Mike Evans on violin they became popular for their combination of a madcap stage show and their broad spectrum of music with influences ranging from the Beatles, Beach Boys and Fairport Convention to Frank Zappa and The Mothers Of Invention. Mike Tobin persuaded George Martin to produce the third Stackridge album *The Man In The Bowler Hat*, which is still regarded as one of George's finest achievements outside his Beatles canon. The band released two more albums before breaking up with a final gig in Yeovil in April 1976.

In 1979 Andy Davis and James Warren formed a duo the Korgis with the intention

Ray Mighty (left) and Rob Smith: masters of the Bristol Beat

of writing and recording more pop orientated, commercial music . They had two big selling singles 'If I Had You' and 'Everybody's Got To Learn Sometime' , the latter song being covered over 20 times by numerous artists including Beck and Zuchero .

Stackridge reformed briefly in 1999 and again in 2006 and continued to perform and record another album *A Victory For Common Sense* on Helium Records, which was produced by Tears For Fears producer Chris Hughes. Finally deciding to retire, the band did one last tour between September and December 2015, which included appearances in Tokyo and a triumphant, emotional final bow at The Fiddlers, Bedminster on December 19.

Stanton Warriors
Mike Yardley and Dominic Butler have been two of the most in demand DJs and producers since the release of their award-winning *Stanton Sessions* in 2001. *Sound of Punks* in 2016 was as fresh as ever. Stanton Warriors are named after manhole cover manufacturer and (sadly) are not a reference to the village of Stanton Drew near Bristol.

Startled Insects
Now known as the Insects, these behind-the-scenes maestros have been responsible for many TV and film scores and amassed writing and production credits for some of the biggest names in the business including Massive Attack, Madonna, Goldfrapp and Alison Moyet. The Startled Insects formed around 1983 as a collective of three producers and multi-instrumentalists Bob Locke, Tim Norfolk and Richard Grassby –Lewis. They've successfully avoided all publicity but still signed to Island Records and achieved cult status with their 1987 album *Curse Of The Pheremones*. Most recently the Insects and Adrian Utley from Portishead produced the soundtrack for the 2017 film *Becoming Cary Grant*.

167

Strangelove

If the path of excess does indeed lead to the palace of enlightenment then Strangelove were some seriously enlightened gentlemen. They formed in 1991 after Levitation drummer Dave Francolini spotted Patrick Duff busking. Allegedly Francolini said: 'Get in the car, you're going to be a pop star'. Francolini then recruited guitarist Alex Lee (Blue Aeroplanes) and bass player Joe Allen (who both played with Francolini in a band called the Coltraines when they were pupils at Bristol Grammar School) plus guitarist Julian Pransky Poole (from the Jazz Butcher). Francolini stepped down as drummer after just two gigs and was replaced by John Langley from the Blue Aeroplanes.

And so the adventure began. Duff's tales of despair and sorrow struck a chord, and his impressive, emotionally charged vocals backed by a truly talented bunch of musicians brought Strangelove to the attention of the major labels and they signed to EMI's Food Records.

Tours and support slots with Radiohead, Suede and the Manic Street Preachers plus three stand-out albums brought Strangelove to the brink of greatness, but the drink and drugs took their toll particularly for singer Patrick Duff and Strangelove split up in 1998.

Talisman

Originally formed in 1977 as Revelation Rockers, the band changed their name in the early 80s to avoid confusion with a band from London called Revelation. They were still touring and releasing new material in 2019, albeit after a significant break. Talisman's brand of reggae has always had a light touch due in part to the influence of Brendan Whitmore's distinct saxophone style and Desmond (Lazarus) Taylor's vocals. Although Whitmore isn't in the reformed Talisman that sound is still in evidence on their 2017 album release *Don't Play With Fyah* (Sugar Shack Records). In 1981 Talisman released their seminal single 'Dole Age' and in 1982 they supported the Rolling Stones at Ashton Gate. Sax player Brendan Whitmore passed away in 2018.

Tarzan The High Priest Sound System

Hector Thaws was known as Tarzan, hence the name of this sound system that ran during the late 60s and early 70s. He operated the system with his sons Roy and Rupert and (Natty) Lloyd Williams. It changed its name to Studio 17 in 1974 and ran until 1984 specialising in a rasta vibe. Roy Thaws is Adrian Thaws' father and Hector his grand father, Adrian Thaws is, of course better, known as Tricky.

This Is The Kit

This Is The Kit is essentially singer songwriter Kate Stables and musicians Rozi Plain (bass), Neil Smith (guitar) and Jamie Whitby-Coles (drums). Their first album Krulle Bol in 2008 was produced by PJ Harvey collaborator John Parish. The folk-style sound and wistful lyrics have brought the band much critical acclaim from the likes of Elbow's Guy Garvey. In 2017 This Is The Kit released their fourth studio album *Moonshine Freeze*.

Thomas Brooman CBE

Drummer with the Media, the Spics and Tesco Chainsaw Massacre in the late 70s and early 80s, Brooman was also one of the founders of the *Bristol Recorder*, an innovative and influential magazine and compilation LP in gatefold sleeve. It was through the *Recorder* that Brooman met Peter Gabriel and (with others) they went on to found the Womad festival which first took place in Shepton Mallet in 1982. In 2008, Brooman was awarded the CBE for services to music and charity. A fourth edition of the Bristol Recorder was released in 2018.

Three Cane Whale

The ability of this three-piece acoustic band to create images of landscapes through their music is truly astonishing. According to an *Observer* review 'the aroma of muddy eaves and old nettles is almost tangible'. Three Cane Whale are Alex Vann (mandolin, bowed psaltery, bouzouki, zither, banjo, dulcimer), Pete Judge (trumpet, cornet, dulcitone, harmonium, lyre, glockenspiel, tenor horn) and Paul Bradley (acoustic guitar, miniature harp). Their first eponymous album was chosen by 6 Music's Cerys Matthews as one of her top five modern folk albums, second album *Holts And Hovers* was *fRoots* magazine Editor's Choice Album of 2013, one of the *Observer's* "Hidden Gems Of 2013", and one of *Acoustic Guitarist* magazine's 20 Essential Folk Albums. The band's third album, *Palimpsest*, was recorded at Real World Studios in Wiltshire, produced by Portishead's Adrian Utley, and released in January 2016.

Torment

Psychobilly stars Torment were big news on the European festival circuit and in London at venues such as the Klub Foot, but rarely played their home town. Formed by Simon Brand (guitar, vocals), Kevin Haynes (drums) and Sean Holder (slap bass) in 1985. Tony Biggs and then Simon Crowfoot replaced Sean Holder and Torment released a series of highly rated albums and EPs including Psyclops Carnival (1986), The Mystery Men EP (1987), Three's A Crowd (1987), Round The World (1989) and Hypnosis (1990). Simon Brand died in 1994.

Tricky

Tricky (Adrian Thaws) did not have a settled childhood. He's on record as saying: 'I've been through a lot. I've been moved around from family to family, never stayed in one house from when I was born to the age of 16. I'm not normal. It's got a lot to do with my upbringing. Staying somewhere for three years then going off for three years. My uncles being villains. All that stuff. I've got quite a dysfunctional family, for some reason, in my family, the mothers always give the kids to the grandmothers'. Unsettled also describes Tricky's music. Brooding, dark often full of whispered menace and alienation, it snatches lyrical and musical references from many sources and layers them around bass-heavy beats.

Tricky's roots are in the Knowle West council estate but he was soon a regular fixture at the hip-hop parties of the early 80s in St Paul's where he hung out with the Wild Bunch and later with fellow Knowle Westerners and Merrywood schoolmates Fresh 4. He rapped with Massive Attack on Blue Lines and duetted with 3D on 'Karmacoma' on the *Protection* album.

Famously, it's said that Tricky met Martina Topley-Bird when she was sitting on the wall of the house he was sharing with Mark Stewart of the Pop Group. She was having a fag break while revising for GCSEs at Clifton College and she went on to become the voice of his first album and the mother of their daughter Mazy.

That first album was *Maxinequay* – a reference to Tricky's late mother. Released

Wild Bunch circa 1985: Grant Marshall, Robert Del Naja, Claude Williams, Nellee Hooper, Miles Johnson

in 1995, it peaked at number three in the UK Album Charts and went Gold. Since then he's released 12 albums, worked on a variety of side projects including films and remained staunchly and brilliantly unsettled.

UD4 Crew

The Ultimate Dynamic 4 Crew were a leading hip-hop force on the house party scene between 1983-1988 and also played out at the Dug Out, Moon Club and Granary. They comprised Zion, Healer MC, Spider and The General (widely regarded as the best scratch DJ in town).

Unique Star Sound System

In 1989, Unique Star sound system was born, an alias of Jah Lokko. Both sounds used the same speaker boxes and the same crew but operated in different genres, with different pre-amps. Unique Star are renowned for their stage at St Paul's Carnival, they have been hosting the City Road stage for more than 30 years.

Vice Squad

Vice Squad were from the fringes of Bristol – singer Rebecca Bond (Beki Bondage) came from Frampton Cotterell and Shane Baldwin (drums), Dave Bateman (guitar) and Mark Hambly (bass) were from Kingswood/Hanham. They formed in 1978, the second generation of punk, and according to Baldwin were inspired by the moment that he and Bateman first listened to 'God Save The Queen' by the Sex Pistols in the back room of Bateman's house. Vice Squad played their first gig at Bristol University's Anson Rooms on April 12, 1979 but only played another six gigs for the next 18 months. They set up the Riot City label with Simon Edwards of Heartbeat Records and released their debut single 'Last Rockers' in 1981. John Peel famously opened

his radio show every night for a week with 'Last Rockers' and the initial pressing of

2,000 copies sold out in a week. It went on the sell 20,000 copies and spent almost 40 weeks in the UK Indie Chart, reaching number seven. The follow-up, 'Resurrection', reached number four, and the band undertook a tour supporting UK Subs. The band split during an American tour. Beki Bondage is still performing. Dave Bateman died in 2007.

Way Out West

Way Out West are producers Nick Warren and Jodie Wisternoff who previously performed as Tru Funk Posse with younger brother Sam and recorded with Smith & Mighty. Warren and Wisternoff pioneered a breakbeat/progressive house style began releasing singles in 1994. Several of these were indie and club hits and in 1996 their single 'The Gift' scored mainstream success when it reached number 15 in the UK Singles Chart. Way Out West have been releasing material ever since, most recently their fifth studio album *Tuesday Maybe* which came out in June 2017.

Wayne Hussey

Wayne Hussey is from Coalpit Heath near Yate and went to the Ridings School in Winterbourne where he played in a band called Humph. But he's better known as one of the originators of goth with Dead Or Alive, the Sisters Of Mercy and the Mission.

Wild Bunch

Hip-hop collective that went on to form Massive Attack. Wild Bunch were one of the original Bristol posses and formed in the early 80s. The key members were MC Nellee Hooper, 3D, DJ Milo, Willy Wee and Daddy G. Tricky also rapped with the Wild Bunch. They signed to 4th & Broadway and released two 12-inch singles, 'Tearin' Down The Avenue' and 'Friends And Countrymen'. They then went on a tour of Japan, but it was badly organised and 3D left early.

After recovering from the Japan experience 3D and Daddy G teamed up with Mushroom to form Massive Attack who released the seminal *Blue Lines* album in 1981 featuring Tricky. Tricky also appeared on Massive Attack's second album *Protection*

Eddie Cochran's death

Eddie Cochran played his last ever show at the Bristol Hippodrome. And when the Ford Consul taxi carrying the rebel rocker slammed into a lamp post at Rowden Hill on 17 April 1960, Chippenham got its one and only rock 'n' roll story.

One of the most defiant young voices of the 1950s, Cochran was famous for anti-establishment classics such as *Summertime Blues, C'mon Everybody* and, most brilliantly, the snarling proto-punk burn-up

Something Else. He was in Bristol with Gene Vincent for a week-long rock 'n' roll extravaganza at the Bristol Hippodrome. On the last night of their residence, the two legendary greaseballs and Cochran's squeeze, Sharon Sheeley, made the fatal decision to get a cab up to Heathrow instead of taking the late train. Vincent and Sheeley survived the crash on the A4, but sadly Eddie Cochran died later in a Bath hospital. Chippenham has been etched forever on his soul.

A Bristol Top 40

Top tunes based on a selection for the Bristol Music:
Seven Decades Of Sound exhibition at M Shed in 2018

ARTIST	TRACK	RELEASE DATE	LABEL
Acker Bilk	Stranger on the Shore	1961	Columbia Records
Andy Sheppard	May Song	2009	ECM Records
Beak>	Mono /Kenn	2012	Invada
Beth Rowley	Nobody's Fault but Mine	2008	Universal
Black Roots	Bristol Rock	1981	Nubian
Blue Aeroplanes	Jacket Hangs	1990	Ensign
Brilliant Corners	Brian Rix	1987	SS20
Cortinas	Defiant Pose/ Independence	1977	Step Forward
David And Jonathan	Lovers of the World Unite	1966	Columbia
Flynn & Flora	Dream of You	1994	Independent Dealers
Fred Wedlock	Oldest Swinger in Town	1980	Coast
Fresh 4	Wishing on a Star	1989	10
Gary Clail	Human Nature	1991	On-U-Sound
George Ezra	Budapest	2014	Columbia
Idles	Danny Nedelko	2018	Partisan
Joker	Digidesign	2009	Hyperdub
Julio Bashmore	Battle For Middle You	2011	PMR
K*ners	Bristol Grammar	2013	Forward Ever
Krust	Warhead	2007	V-Cycle
Massive Attack	Unfinished Sympathy	1991	Wild Bunch/Circa
Maximum Joy	Silent Street	1981	Y
Onslaught	Killing Peace	2007	Candlelight
Ossia	Red X	2015	Blackest Ever Black
Peverelist	Roll With The Punches	2007	Punch Drunk
Pigbag	Papa's Got A Brand New Pigbag	1981	Y
Pinch	Quawwli	2006	Planet Mu
Pop Group	She Is Beyond Good And Evil	1979	Radar
Portishead	Glory Box	1994	Go! Discs
Rip Rig & Panic	You're My Kind Of Climate	1982	Virgin
Rita Lynch	Beautiful Eyes	1991	Moles
Roni Size/Reprazent	Brown Paper Bag	1997	Talkin' Loud
Shanti Celeste	Make Time	2017	Idle Hands
Smith & Mighty	B line Fi Blow	2010	Punch Drunk Unearthed
Talisman	Dole Age	1981	Recreational
This Is The Kit	Moonshine Freeze	2017	Rough Trade
Tricky	Tricky Kid	1996	4th & Broadway
Vice Squad	Last Rockers	1981	Riot City
Way Out West	The Gift	1996	RCA
Wurzels	Combine Harvester	1976	EMI
Young Echo	Umoja	2013	Ramp

* Compiled by M Shed curators and research/advisory group.

Members of the Young Echo collective © Alex Hughes-Games

which was produced by Nellee Hooper. Hooper became one of the most sought-after producers in the business working with many major artists including Soul II Soul, Bjork, Madonna, Smashing Pumpkins, U2 and Gwen Stefani.

Yolanda Carter
Singer with country/soul outfit Phantom Limb who formed in 2005 and eventually split up in 2013. Yolanda Carter toured as a singer with Massive Attack and more recently has been exploring gospel music as a solo project.

Young Echo
This growing experimental collective of artists and producers are taking drum and bass, dub and electronic music in unusual bass-heavy directions. Contributors to the Young Echo project include Jabu, Kahn, Vessel, Bogues, Manonmars, Ishan Sound, Neek, Ossia, Chester Giles, Rider Shafique and Gorgon.

Star & Garter

Famous pub saved from being turned into flats to become
a music venue and living museum...

Significant figures from the African-Caribbean community are recalled in photographs and memorabilia

Part pub and music venue, part slice of music history and part museum/art installation, the Star & Garter on the border of St Paul's and Montpelier is an essential visit for anyone interested in Bristol's recent African-Caribbean history and the city's music heritage.

The Star & Garter reopened in June 2019 two years after the death of long-term landlord Dutty Ken. The two public faces of the new Star & Garter are landlord and legendary music promoter Malcolm Haynes and drum 'n' bass sensation Roni Size. The Bristol rumour circuit maintains that Grant Marshall (Daddy G out of Massive Attack) and Banksy are also behind the project

The pub is one of the defining institutions in Bristol's music history most famously because it's where DJ Derek started spinning discs in the 1970s when the pub was taken over by his friend, a West Indian bus driver, called Hector. From 1993 Dutty Ken was the landlord until his death in 2017.

The re-opening party on June 1, 2019 on Albany Green was immense featuring sets from Roni Size and guest

The jukebox is an archive of super-rare mixtapes which have been digitised

DJ Deerek's minidisc collection is among the 'exhibits'

Opening time on re-opening day in June 2019

appearances by David Chapelle (who did the raffle) and Damian Marley, but it's the inside of the pub that makes it a must-visit place.

There's a huge amount of memorabilia and information on the pub walls from David 'Sid' Lawrence's cricket bat to an original poster for the two Big Youth gigs at Bristol Exhibition Centre in 1977 promoted by Tony Bullimore from the Bamboo Club. There's DJ Derek's minidisc collection, a juke box featuring mix tapes by Derek, City Rockas, Henry and Louis, Ray

Mighty, Raiders, Roar, Donovan Smith and many more, plus a small lounge with archive photographs honouring St Paul's elders such as Barbara Dettering, Tony and Lalel Bullimore from the Bamboo Club, Princess Campbell and many more. Dub poet Linton Kwesi Johnson sent a pair of his 1980s trademark large-lens glasses and a note recalling his visits to St Paul's to recite poetry and perform music. Neneh Cherry sent a signed picture.

The interior of the pub is like an art installation. It's a selection of

DJ Derek has pride of place in the bar where he began spinning discs in the 1970s

pictures and mementoes, a repository of memories, character and community that you find in many pubs, but on close inspection, this is a detailed historical archive presented around the medium of pub walls, furniture, fixtures and fittings. It's the most impressive and best-presented 'museum' of African-Caribbean achievement in the city.

The legacy of the Star & Garter is essential to understanding Bristol's modern music success – the so-called Bristol Sound. Roni Size's aunt worked behind the bar and the 11-year-old Roni would sit in a corner of the pub with a can of pop and a packet of crisps and look through DJ Derek's record box searching for James Brown singles. It's where Wild Bunch, City Rockas, FBI Crew hung out, it's where everyone involved with Bristol's underground scene went for a late drink.

After Hector, the pub was taken over in 1993 by Dutty Ken (real name Louis Hayles) and continued its theme

of late-night parties. Born in 1940 in Clarendon, Jamaica, Ken left school at the age of 12, arrived in Bristol from London in 1963 and took over the Star & Garter 30 years later. He died suddenly at the age of 76 in February 2017. His family tried to keep the pub going but it eventually closed a year after Ken's death.

The changing demographic of St Paul's, Montpelier and Stokes Croft has led to the closure of almost all the West Indian/Irish pubs in the area. The Portland House, Jamaica Inn (Inkerman), Duke of Sussex, Prince of Wales, Gloucester House, British Queen, St Nicholas House, Swan Hotel and Montpelier Hotel are long gone. The Criterion is under threat of closure leaving only the Beaufort in York Road from the old days – until the rescue of the Star & Garter.

33 Brook Road, St Paul's BS6 5LR
www.starandgarterbristol.co.uk

Wild Bunch were just one of the hip-hop crews who hung out at the Star & Garter in the 1980s

Neneh Cherry sends her best wishes for the re-opening of the pub

Dutty Ken looks down on MC Dynamite at the Star & Garter re-opening party (picture Mat Kauhanen)

The dancefloor walls are decorated with original posters including one for a legendary Big Youth gigs at the Exhibition Centre on the Harbourside (now Za Za Bazaar) and a night of dub and roots reggae headlined by Prince Fari

Politics & protest

Richard Jones explains how the colour of Bristol politics has been changing to red and green...

Bristol voted resoundingly to remain in the European Union by 62-38 per cent in the 2016 referendum. Like the rest of the country, Bristol was deeply split by the referendum with the inner-city Ashley ward returning a remain vote of 85 per cent (one of the highest in England) while many of the working-class fringes voted for Brexit with the biggest leave votes in Hartcliffe and Withywood (67 per cent), Hengrove and Whitchurch Park (62 per cent), Bishopsworth (58 per cent) and Avonmouth (57 per cent).

In the 2017 General Election all four Bristol constituencies returned Labour MPs with vegan jazz saxophonist Darren Jones unseating Tory Charlotte Leslie in Bristol North West to complete the clean sweep. The other three Bristol MPs are all women – Thangam Debbonair (Bristol West), Kerry McCarthy (Bristol East) and Karin Smyth (Bristol South).

Thangam Debbonair took the seat from Lib Dem Stephen Williams in the 2015 election with a majority of 5,673. She was one of many Labour MPs who tried to depose Jeremy Corbyn as leader but stopped complaining in public when she increased her majority in the 2017 election to a huge 37,336.

Kerry McCarthy resigned from Corbyn's team as a shadow minister and supported Owen Smith's failed attempt to unseat JC as leader. In the 2017 election she increased her majority from just under 4,000 to more than 13,000.

Karin Smyth also supported Owen Smith's campaign to unseat Corbyn and saw her majority increase from 7,000 to 16,000 in the 2017 General Election under Corbyn's leadership.

But it's at a local level that politics in Bristol has been particularly interesting.

After decades of inept political leadership, Bristol elected George Robin Paget Ferguson CBE, PPRIBA, RWA as Mayor in November 2012. George (we use his first name not through familiarity but because it's how Ferguson is universally known) stood as an Independent and beat the Labour candidate Marvin Rees by 6,000 votes. Four years later, the Labour vote turned out for Marvin, he became Europe's first black elected Mayor and local politics became dreary again.

Perhaps the most notable aspect of the original Mayoral campaign was not that George won but that Bristolians voted to have an elected Mayor in the first place. In May 2012, Prime Minister David Cameron's plans to replace local council cabinets with directly elected mayors were rejected by voters in nine other English cities. Birmingham, Manchester, Newcastle, Nottingham, Sheffield, Wakefield, Coventry, Leeds and Bradford voted No to the idea. Only Bristol was in favour and Doncaster voted to keep its Mayor. Liverpool councillors voted in favour of an elected Mayor without going to a public vote. Bristol voted for an elected mayor by 53 per cent to 47 per cent (sound familiar?).

There's a credible theory that the reason Bristol voted Yes was because George announced his intention to run for Mayor well before the vote – when Bristolians voted Yes, they knew that there was a good chance that George would get the ticket. His victory added credence to the belief that Bristol's traditional political leaders had let down the city. Of course, most

Jessie Stephen, 1893–1979

Born in 1893 in Glasgow to a socialist family, Jessie Stephen left school at 14 to go into domestic service. It was as a maid in 1912 that she received her first taste of activism by organising maids in Glasgow into the Scottish Federation of Domestic Workers. Aged 16, she was Vice Chair of the Independent Labour Party in Glasgow as well as a member of the Women's Social and Political Party (WSPU).

While wearing her maid's uniform, teenage Jessie blended into the street scene, enabling her to join the suffragettes in their campaign to destroy the contents of letterboxes in protest at their voices not being heard. Jessie was soon rewarded with an invitation to work in London alongside Sylvia Pankhurst who, unlike the rest of her family, championed the working-classes.

By 1944, Jessie was appointed as the first female Area Union Organiser of the National Clerical and Administrative Workers' Union for South Wales and the West of England, and it was this role that brought her to Bristol where she would become the first-ever woman president of the Trades Union Council. Jessie was subsequently elected as a City Councillor of Bristol in 1952 and used this as an opportunity to speak widely about birth control.

In 1978, Jessie received the MBE for her trades union work. However, she died of pneumonia and heart failure at Bristol's General Hospital on 12 June 1979, aged 86, while still attending up to three feminist meetings a week. Jessie's last address on Chessel Street, Bedminster, is honoured with a blue plaque.

A who's who of radical Bristol

Some of the city's leading lefties...

Cube Cinema

The Cube building has a history of radical entertainment dating back to the 1950s when an am-dram group built the wooden theatre. In the 1970s, it was Bristol Arts Centre, home to the radical Avon Touring Company now it screens radical films and more.

4 Princess Row, Kingsdown
www.cubecinema.com

PRSC/Bristol Cable

The People's Republic of Stokes Croft building is home to several radical projects including the *Cable* website and newspaper launched in 2014 by a group of young non-aligned lefties.

35 Jamaica Street
www.thebristolcable.org

Bristol Anarchist Solidarity Easton (BASE)

Easton-based cafe/shop and anarchist collective formerly known as Kebele came into being as a squat in the mid 1990s. Bristol Anarchist Solidarity Easton (BASE) host regular vegan Sunday lunches. There is a radical library, bike workshop and it hosts film nights, exhibitions and more.

14 Robertson Road, Easton
https://network23.org/kebele2/

Acorn

National housing action group with a particularly active and militant Bristol crew who regularly turn up en masse to confront bailiffs and halt evictions.
www.acorntheunion.org.uk

Easton Cowboys & Cowgirls

A social network of football, cricket and netball teams plus a vivacious group of can-can dancers. Close links with the Zapatistas in Mexico through regular trips to Chiapas. They even played cricket in Compton, Los Angeles. Usually found in the Plough in Easton.
www.eastoncowboys.org.uk

Subvertisers

At least two crews of subvertisers have been operating in Bristol for several years. Check out their work in the excellent *Politics and Protest* book by Pete Maginnis.
www.tangentbooks.co.uk

Bristol Radical History Group

Since 2006 BRHG has organised a bewildering range of history events; staging walks, talks, gigs, reconstructions, films, exhibitions, trips through the archives and fireside story telling. They also publish a large range of pamphlets and host an archive on the website.
www.brh.org.uk

Bristol Anarchist Bookfair

Biggest UK anarchist bookfair outside London. It used to be held at Trinity and the nearby Hydra bookshop in Old Market, but more recently one element has moved the bookfair to St Werburgh's and another has put on a Radical Book Fair at M Shed. Both are worth seeking out.
www.bristolanarchistbookfair.org

people complain about their local councils, but in Bristol there's empirical evidence that the City Council has underperformed with the Audit Commission, an independent watchdog that measured local government performance, consistently criticising Bristol across a range of services.

In 2007 the Audit Commission gave Bristol a one-star rating (79 per cent of councils achieved three or four stars). Although Bristol achieved a higher rating before the Audit Commission was scrapped by the Tory government in 2010, it was still in the bottom 20 per cent of local authorities.

George inherited a £35 million cut in the city's budget and despite the central government pressure to cut services, he was credited by many Council staff with changing the culture within days of his arrival by improving communication and confidence. On day one he renamed the Council House City Hall and swiftly made his opinions very clear on a number of issues including supporting plans for a new stadium for Bristol City at Ashton Gate rather that the out-of-town proposal at Ashton Vale. He gave his complete backing to the long-standing plans to build an arena next to Temple Meads; he committed to a green and sustainable economy in the city; backed the Bristol Pound (he took his £65,000 salary in the local currency) and introduced the Make Sundays Special initiative that saw a large area of the city centre closed to cars one Sunday a month.

Political inertia and gradualism somehow matched the modern mood of the city until the arrival of George.

In the May 2016 Mayoral elections, George's vote held up with a total of 39,577 voting to give him a second term. But the Labour vote turned out for Marvin and he increased his vote from 31,259 in 2012 to 68,750 in 2016.

Marvin's administration held a financial audit as soon as they took power and discovered a missing £30 million in the council accounts. Former chief executive of the Audit Commission Steve Bundred was commissioned to find out what had happened.

The Bundred Report, published on February 9, 2017, was a damning indictment of officer culture at Bristol City Council. It revealed that the Mayor and councillors had not been supplied with accurate financial information by officers and that 'there was a prevailing culture within the Council at the time that reports should not convey bad news'. Bundred also identified a tendency to bury financial information in big reports and said that in a particular instance regarding the use of reserves senior officers' behaviour 'can best be described as artful.'

In his State Of The City speeches, Marvin has emphasised the need for better transport links but has also said he doesn't want to make life more **181** difficult for car drivers. His One City approach aims to spread benefits to the suburbs rather than concentrate them in the centre of Bristol; he says he is committed to building more homes and launched a City Fund investment programme aimed at greater community cohesion and economic inclusion.

He also intends to create a new residential area called the Western Harbour around the Cumberland Basin and wants an underground system for Bristol. Very few commentators expect either scheme to become reality.

His reputation is one of caution, commissioning studies and consultations before taking action, but the single issue that has dominated his time as Mayor is the arena (or lack of). In April 2019 the Labour Party announced that Marvin would be reselected unopposed to stand for Mayor in 2020. The power behind Marvin's throne is said to be his Strategic Advisor Kevin Slocombe who was previousy Jeremy Corbyn's head of media (though Marvin has never come out in support of Corbyn).

George Ferguson is wrongly accused as being the person who came up with the arena plan. He wasn't. The idea of an arena next to Temple Meads goes back to 2003/4 and it was supposed to open in 2008. George certainly took the shambolic plans by the scruff of the neck and marched them towards fruition. But his term of office ended before the arena was built and as soon as Marvin took over, the project went into reverse. He commissioned a value-for-money report and on the strength of it announced that Bristol couldn't afford the arena. Despite councillors voting for the arena to be built on the 'island' site off the Bath Road next to Temple Meads, Marvin pulled the plug on the area once and for all, saying that if Bristol is to have an arena it will be at Filton Airfield and will be built in partnership with the Malaysian owners of the airfield YTL.

It's highly likely that Cardiff will have built a second arena in the same timescale that it's taken Bristol to make a pig's ear of not building just one.

Green Bristol

A significant factor in Bristol politics since 2010 is the rise of the Greens. Hardly surprising perhaps in a city that has tons of lycra-clad cyclists battling the smog-hazed traffic every morning, hosts more vegan, veggie and organic eateries than any other, is home to the Soil Association, Sustrans and more sustainable eco-friendly, self-build initiatives than you can shake a tepee at.

The Green Party won its breakthrough seat on the City Council in May 2006 with the election of Charlie Bolton with a majority of seven votes. Bolton wasn't re-elected in the 2010 local elections, but Tess Green took a

Southville seat and she was joined in 2011 by Gus Hoyt who gained Ashley ward with a whopping 744 vote majority and 42.6% of the vote, taking it from the Liberal Democrats. In May 2013, Bishopston elected Green councillor Daniella Radice and Rob Telford took a second seat in Ashley. In the 2016 elections, the Greens stood 59 candidates and despite losing two seats to Labour maintained their place as the third biggest party on Bristol City Council.

The make-up of Bristol City Council after the 2016 election gave Labour a working majority of 4. Labour was the biggest party in the previous council (when a third of the seats were up for election every year), but did not have an overall majority.

The Green Party won the vote in Bristol in the 2019 European elections with 49, 126 votes (35%). Former Lord Mayor Cleo Lake missed out on becoming the secvond MEP in the South West by a fraction.

Party	Previous Council	2016 Council
Labour	30	37
Conservative	16	15
Green	13	11
Lib Dem	10	7
UKIP	1	0

Venturers and the slave trade

It's the slave trade question that has Bristol collectively on the psychiatrist's couch – which is lucky because Bristol has more counsellors per head than any other city in Europe. But even this army of dreamcatchers and rebirthers can't beat the class divide on this vexed issue. The guilt-ridden middle classes want to apologise for the slave trade whereas the feckless proletarians don't see why they should.

There's probably a strong case to be made for the Society of Merchant Venturers to apologise since they initiated the trade and still dominate the economic life of the city. Expecting an organisation that still worships arch slave trader Edward Colston's fingernail annually to apologise is not a likely winner, but in 2017 it was announced the Colston Hall would be renamed after refurbishment so perhaps that day is drawing closer.

You can't really begin to understand politics in Bristol without appreciating the role of the sinisterly-named Society of Merchant Venturers (George Ferguson was a Merchant) which is headed by 'the one they call the master'. Historically, the SOMV has dominated the economic and commercial life of Bristol for more than 450 years, profiting greatly from the slave trade. Today, it has eased up on the Masonic secret password, roll-your-trouser-leg-up connections, and puts more emphasis on its charitable work. In reality, it still functions as a clique of powerful businessmen who dominate the commercial life of Bristol in a way not found, or tolerated, in any other city in Britain.

Edward Vl granted letters patent on 18 December 1552 to form a body to protect merchants from those 'not brought up in the merchants' art'. Only those admitted to the Society of Merchant Venturers were allowed to trade by sea from Bristol. In the 16th century, the SOMV moved into property and still owns and controls the development of large swathes of Bristol.

Abolitionists

In 2006 in the run-up to national commemorations for Abolition 200, the 200th anniversary of the abolition of the slave trade, the Venturers issued a statement that said: "We all regret that the slave trade happened. Slavery was a trade in which all of Bristol was involved in..." This has been challenged by Bristol Radical History Group – is this statement really true? Even if it were so, were Bristolians willingly involved in the African slave trade? Did those involved have a choice? Did many of them benefit from the obscene wealth created? Did the majority of Bristolians have a democratic say in the running of the city? Did Bristolians condone the slave trade?

The answer to all of these questions is a pretty emphatic no. In fact, the 'plain unvarnished truth', is that many in Bristol fought against the transatlantic slave trade from as early as the 1650s and suffered persecution, imprisonment, transportation and even death in the process.

These people included early Bristol Quakers and Baptists, Bristol Methodists from the 1740s (care of John and Charles Wesley), Bristol Unitarians and even some Anglican ministers; Bristol sailors, Bristol writers (such as Chatterton, Lovell, Southey, Coleridge, Ann Yearsley and Hannah More), Bristol reformers – electoral as well as abolitionist – and many prominent Bristol families going into the 19th Century, the Estlin's, the Blackwell's and the Carpenter's amongst others.

Bristol Quakers such as Harry Gandy, Alexander Falconbridge and Truman Harford helped abolitionist hero the Reverend Thomas Clarkson on his epic six-month fact finding mission to Bristol in 1787. Here, not only did he challenge the pro-slavery merchants, he amassed a huge volume of evidence, took them to court over a sailor's murder and even freed a sailor from a voyage to almost certain death. At the end of his stay here Clarkson got his Bristol colleagues to form the first Abolition Society outside of London and put the city in the forefront of petitioning and mounting boycotts of sugar.

Not content with helping achieve the banning of the slave trade in 1807, Bristol's abolitionists entered the breach again in 1823 – with their female colleagues forming their own Bristol branch in 1827 – in order to bring about full emancipation for the 800,000 enslaved in the British West Indies. It was the women who moved the men from a 'gradualist' approach to an 'immediate' one and this proved vital.

One Baptist missionary of note sent from Bristol to Jamaica in the 1820s, William Knibb, witnessed one of many slave revolts that helped bring an end to slavery. Sam Sharpe's Christmas Rebellion of 1831, which as most were, was brutally put down. Knibb's colleagues in the Caribbean urged him to return to England and campaign on their behalf and this he did to great effect. Just weeks after Bristol's Reform Riots, the two events had a major impact on the future direction Britain would take.

After decades of battle, electoral reform was granted in 1832. The weakening of the number of pro-slavery MPs in parliament, the efforts of the Abolition societies and in particular the enslaved fighting for their own freedom, led directly to emancipation being granted the following year.

Bristol's leading abolitionists

St Wulfstan: Got the 11th Century slave trade between Bristol and Dublin banned; if it was morally wrong in 1090, surely it was even more morally wrong in 1590, 1690 and 1790?

James 'Mad Messiah' Naylor: This early Quaker was persecuted and tortured for his views, the first to speak out against 'modern day' slavery in 1649.

'Blackymore maid' Francis: Early Anabaptist, with her friend Dorothy Hazard attended Putney Debates in 1640s where all forms of slavery were denounced.

John Wesley: Founder Methodist who experienced American slavery first-hand in the 1730s, lifelong opponent of slavery, pamphleteer and petitioner.

Hannah More: 18th Century novelist and playwright who turned her talents to anti-slavery tracts and poems. Led sugar boycotts in the 1790s and 1820s/30s.

Landlord Thompson: Hosted key abolitionist Thomas Clarkson on his epic six-month fact-finding visit to Bristol in 1787, showing him how reluctant sailors were coerced into the slave trade.

Ann Yearsley: Initially a protégé of More's who clamoured for independence, her poem on African slavery was far harder hitting than her former mentor's.

Blackwell family: Samuel and his children (including daughter Elizabeth – Britain and America's first female doctor) fought slavery both in Bristol and New York.

Estlin and Carpenter families: Generations of Unitarians who fought against slavery from the turn of the 19th Century on, both Mary Estlin and Mary Carpenter hosted the great American abolitionists William Lloyd Garrison and (the formerly enslaved) Frederick Douglass on their tour of Britain in the 1840s.

Local media

Like many UK cities the local media landscape has changed dramatically in Bristol over the last three decades with the most obvious victims of this change being the print media, the *Bristol Post* and *Western Daily Press*. In the 1980s most people in Bristol would see a copy of the Evening Post every day. The daily circulation was more than 100,000, the Post printed at least three editions every weekday and a *Green 'Un* sports paper every Saturday.

The last audited circulation figures for the Post in 2017 showed sales of just over 17,000 and these were boosted by every promotion and give-away allowed under Audit Bureau of Circulation rules. Of course, print media is in decline all over the UK, but no other major British city has suffered quite like Bristol. And the reason is probably as simple as bad management and poor editors over a number of years, plus the fact that Bristol does not have the major sports teams to drive sales in the same way that you find in Manchester, Leeds, Liverpool and Newcastle.

The other architect of the Post's downfall is the BBC. Like other areas of the country, the local BBC offers a far better online news service than

Working in Bristol

Mike Manson on the city's employers

It comes to us all eventually. We have to earn some money and that probably means work. Fortunately, Bristol weathered the recent double-dip recession, though unemployment in some of the more far flung places of the city is still high.

If you are looking for a part-time job, shop-work is a popular option. Cabot Circus has all the large retail chains and if you can travel out to Cribbs Causeway there are always vacancies. Part-time work is also available in the many restaurants, cafes and hotels in Bristol – but the hours can be long and the wages poor.

Bristol houses the headquarters of more than 160 firms. It has a world-class reputation for its science, innovation, environmental and creative industries. Engineering giants Rolls Royce and BAE Systems are based at Filton. The MoD Procurement Executive – they buy stuff in bulk for the armed forces – is based at Abbeywood, Filton and employs over 10,000 people. Bristol City Council is a major employer – the range of jobs is enormous and includes: accountants; builders; childcare workers; environmental scientists; housing managers; horticulturalists; office staff; teachers and traffic engineers.

There are several hospitals is Bristol. The National Health Service (NHS) is one of the biggest employers in Europe. The health service doesn't just employ doctors and nurses – they have jobs for: ambulance drivers; builders; caterers;

engineers; IT workers; laboratory staff; receptionists; porters and so on.

Other large public sector employers include Bristol University, the University of the West of England and City of Bristol College. Bristol has the largest number of people working in banking, finance and insurance services outside London. The days of coke-sniffing yuppies – which never hit Bristol anyway – are long gone. Ethical bank Triodos has its UK headquarters in Deanery Road.

You can also do your bit for the environment. The Environment Agency has a head office in Deanery Road, cycling and cycling charity Sustrans has its HQ in Cathedral Square while the Soil Association is based in Victoria Street.

But what Bristol is really well known for is its creative industries. The BBC has its world famous Natural History Unit at Whiteladies Road, while the lovely Aardman people, the creators of Wallace and Gromit are based on Gas Ferry Road. Creative types eagerly awaited the arrival of The Arts Council of England, who relocated their regional office to the city from Exeter in 2014.

The creative industries are notoriously difficult to get into. Don't forget there's lot of other smaller creative companies. Have a look round places like Paintworks to see the range.

For anybody with the right skills and attitude, getting a job in Bristol shouldn't be difficult.

the print media websites and the Beeb is subsidised by licence fees. Local media simply cannot compete online with a state-funded news service.

Politically, the lack of an effective local print media means that institutions such as Bristol City Council can conduct their business free from public scrutiny. Whereas in the 80s a Post reporter would have been present at most council meetings, the press benches are now empty other than for full council meetings, by which time decisions have probably been made by the relevant committees. Bristol is not unusual in this respect.

The modern history of Bristol newspapers starts in 1962 when the *Bristol Evening World* merged with the *Bristol Evening Post*. The new paper was published by Bristol United Press (founded in 1939) which also published the *Western Daily Press* morning paper. BUP was overseen by an independent board of directors with strong connections with the Merchant Venturers. The Daily Mail (Northcliffe) traditionally had a substantial shareholding in BUP and in 1998 Northcliffe bought out the independent shareholders to take control of BUP.

In 2009, Northcliffe announced that the paper would no longer be printed in Bristol but at the central printing unit in Didcot. Sales of the Post at the beginning of 2011 had plummeted to just under 40,000 and Northcliffe took the decision to demolish the press hall next to the Post building in Old Market. There was now only one edition a day meaning that the Post was completely unable to react to breaking news. For example, the Stokes Croft 'Tesco' riots that started at about 9pm on a Thursday were not reported by the *Post* until the Saturday.

In 2012 Northcliffe sold its local newspaper business to a consortium called Local Media and the *Evening Post* was rebranded as *The Post*. In 2014 Local News supremo David Montgomery shared his vision for the future of the local press in a 2,000-word memo to staff which was promptly leaked to *UK Press Gazette*. Montgomery advocated getting rid of journalists and replacing them with 'content harvesters'. He said that new technology would allow weekly newspapers to be put together by one person in a "small number of sessions" by "skimming online content" and dailies would be created by a "handful" of office-based staff. He suggested giving free access to the PR and Press Offices of bodies such as the police, health authorities and local councils to place stories directly into the paper without any of that boring fact checking which journalists are expected to do.

In October 2015, Trinity Mirror acquired the Bristol Post as part of its takeover of Local World titles. By 2019 the company had rebranded as

Reach Regional Limited and has more than 120 local titles across the UK.

The decline of the Post has coincided with the rise of the *Voice* series of 17 local monthly newspapers and websites. Each *Voice* is independently edited, so the quality can vary, but they offer an excellent local news service.

To compound the misery at the *Post*, *Bristol Property Live* took a huge chunk of its property advertising revenue and then Dougal Templeton launched *Bristol 24/7* in 2014. Templeton was the roguish publisher of *Venue* magazine, a much-loved listings and so-much-more magazine that ran for 30 years from 1982-2012. He sold Venue to the Northcliffe-owned *Post* in 2000 and left to pursue other media interests (including launching *Bristol Property Live*). In 2014, Templeton and Mike Bennett (E3 Media) joined forces with former *WDP* journalist Chris Brown who had created the excellent *Bristol 24/7* online news website, and ex-Post journo Martin Booth who ran the equally good *Bristol Culture* reviews and features site. The new beast kept the name *Bristol 24/7* and is a slick news and entertainment website and monthly newspaper/magazine. The *Post's Bristol Live* website is famously terrible to navigate, particularly on a phone, whereas 24/7 is easy to use and fast. Chris Brown parted company with Templeton soon after the takeover leaving Martin Booth in editorial control of *Bristol 24/7*.

The radical media in Bristol is well served by the *Bristol Cable* (www.bristolcable.org) which operates online and in print and offers serious analysis and investigations of local and national issues. The *Bristolian* scandal sheet (www.thebristolian.net) is scurrilous and sometimes very funny. Founded in the 90s by Ian 'Class War' Bone and the Bristol Blogger, *The Bristolian* ceased publishing when Bone decamped to London. It resurfaced occasionally, but in 2013 came back with a vengeance both in printed form and as a website – probably as a consequence of a heightened interest in local politics fuelled by the election of 'Gorgeous' George Ferguson, as he is known in *The Bristolian*.

The self-styled 'Smiter of the High and Mighty' scandal sheet has retained the mock tabloid style pioneered by Bone and The Blogger. It often seems remarkably well informed suggesting that some of the contributors have access to the inner chambers of City Hall. It is a thorn in the side of the 'Great and the Good'.

If George's successor Marvin Rees thought the Bristolian would treat him more kindly, he was mistaken and is regularly lampooned in a newsletter from St Marvin Up The Creek penned by the Reverend Rees.

Away from the BBC, the two leading community radio stations are Ujima Radio which focuses on African and Caribbean culture and BCFM (Bristol Community FM).

Radical Bristolians

Ian Bone picks the leading anarchists and lefties...

Dorothy Hazzard
Early Baptist dissenter who, with 200 women, defended the Frome Gate from Prince Rupert in the Civil War. Commemorated in a painting in the city's registry office. A lotta bottle.

James Nayler
Model Army Leveller whose Quaker radicalism was disliked by the authorities who prosecuted him for blasphemy after he rode up Corn Street on a donkey in 1656 claiming he was Jesus Christ. His barbaric torture and humility suggest he may have been right!

Thomas Clarkson
Came to Bristol to expose the slave trade – a risky business given the balance of power in the city. From his base in the Seven Stars, Clarkson dug out the crucial eye witness reports. Bristolians turned against the trade because of the high mortality rates of the slave ship crews.

Kingswood Colliers
Lawless bunch who'd march on the city to wreak havoc and mayhem. Commemorated by a Wetherspoons on Kingswood High Street. Not to be confused with that equally lawless desperado crew the Cock Road Gang from Hanham. Just don't mention 'the Cainses' in Hanham High Street. Still crazy.

Blackbeard & Long John Silver
Blackbeard was born in Redcliffe and Long John Silver came to life in Bristol boozer, the Spyglass in Robert Louis Stevenson's *Treasure Island*. Shamefully there's no plaque to either but there are plans for a Long John statue. Radical? Long John was. Pirate crews were very democratic electing their leaders and sharing booty. Who stood against Blackbeard for Captain? Er, well, um... no secret ballot, so no one fancied it.

Black Hand Gang
A gang of leftie Bemmy toughs from the 1920s – sworn enemies of The Monkey Town Mob from The Dings. Again no plaque. I can't think why not!

Tony Benn
Not strictly a Bristolian cos he moved after losing his seat, but this ex-MP was first elected to represent Bristol South East in 1950. He was eventually 'got rid of' with the help of the boundary changes in 1983. Benn was a hugely committed local MP who could pack out the Colston Hall. Died March 2014.

Dr Paul Stephenson OBE
Stephenson came to prominence as one of the organisers of the Bristol Bus Boycott in 1963, a protest against Bristol Omnibus Company's openly racist policy of refusing to employ black drivers and conductors. He went on to become a leading figure in the Civil Rights movement.

Jo Wilding
Feminist, human rights activist, smuggler of banned Iraqi dates,

sanctions buster, tomato thrower at Mr Tony Blair. Wilding also travelled to Iraq to defy Bush's bombs. This lady certainly has guts!

Dr Margaret Jones
A veritable Bristol institution as the city's most arrested activist. Veteran of road and anti-war protests who regularly takes a toothbrush to Magistrates Court hearings. She once blocked Bristol University/UWE boat race with her own boat protesting for the Gandalf Three. No? You'd better ask her!

Massive Attack
They changed to 'Massive' in the Bush production Gulf War One. However, for the Bush Jnr production Gulf War Two, Massive Attack were fully on the anti-war campaign. This band have consistently refused to play at the city's Colston Hall because of the fact it is named after the notorious Bristol slave trader Edward Colston. Throughout the Gulf War, the official Massive Attack website automatically redirected thousands of its visitors through to the CND website.

Beware of Bristol the Smart City

Bristol has been named the world's leading Smart City.
Finn Dovey explains what that means and why we should
be concerned...

Smart Cities are the newest chapter in a long history of faux utopian visions, professing to lift urban space out of the chaotic fumes of a post-industrial society. The focus in recent times has shifted from the architectural planning of Corbusier's high rises and Howard's garden cities, to a digital blueprint aimed at improving efficiency and removing problem areas.

The model gathers data on cities through a network called the Internet Of Things (IOT), producing quantifiable data on locations and their productivity. It seems a fishy concept from the outset, Smart City enthusiasts claim their mission is to drive economic growth and citizen satisfaction through the monitoring of urban ebbs and flows, though how well big data can describe a section of lived space is questionable. This fetishisation of a prestigious city has led to many countries across the globe adopting smart systems in the hope of attracting more investment, under the guise of citizen care. Bristol is the frontline for Smart Cities in the UK and won a Global Mobile Award (GLOMO) for best Smart City in the world in 2018[1].

This is all down to the Bristol is Open team, who describe Bristol as an "R&D test bed" crammed full of initiatives and incentives, sure to raise the eyebrows of more sceptical members of the digital community. Some of the fairly innocent proclamations are their dedication to reducing air pollution and traffic, however the promise of a fully programmable city dedicated to efficiency improvement, in a society where the corner stone of efficient space is a glass block of offices seems more than unnerving. Bristol also hosts a Playable Cities initiative, which uses the same tools, big data and IOTs to create supposedly entertaining digital experiences, such as talking lampposts. We shall deal with this in a moment.

Smart jargon describes the model as finding "digital solutions for real world problems", a feat which sounds innocent and appealing to people who just want to get to work quicker or do their Christmas shopping with fewer flicks of the wrist. However, this causes an acceptance in the prioritisation of statistical coherence and efficiency over psychological and emotional value of urban locations. This quick fix teaches us the only things to value in a society are those which can be calculated through data and improved upon using technology. It removes the validity of emotional interactions with the landscape, reducing rhythms of the city into potential problems that can and should be flattened.

This erosion of the psychological landscape in favour of a utopian vision, of a totally coherent city, I believe is in danger of creating a homogeneous public sphere where all space has become a high street, the only place to eat is Greggs, you buy your clothes at TK Maxx and then worry about it next door at the bank. If we think about these spaces in terms of quantitatively measurable efficiency, they are off the charts, but when you stand inside these floodlit plastic structures, they feel empty, vacuous and unbearably average. We must consider whether we want to construct a generic city, filled with monochrome but lacking in substance or somewhere which makes you less nauseous than eating a bar of soap.

There is no doubt a benefit to promoting new ways of engaging with public space using technology, the values and needs of cities have changed dramatically in the last hundred years. Technology is so ingrained in society that to totally reject it from these discussions would be ludicrous. What should be scrutinised is the people who are implementing policy and deciding on what a Smart City should look like.

Faceless companies

In a society where economic efficiency is valued over all else, these people have the potential to act as specialists without spirit. Bristol Is Open's industry partners feature the NEC, Nokia and Interdigital a company that has a name for itself as a patent troll. Whilst these companies do not directly decide on what a Smart City should look like, they are private investors who likely have an agenda regarding what the future of Bristol prioritises. I use the term specialists without spirit here, as these faceless companies and initiatives are responsible for deciding what needs changing for the people of the city, with little to no engagement with them. It is laissez faire urban planning which has become the deciding face of what our space needs more of, and if smart Santander, the first initiative headed by a bank has anything to say about it, I imagine it involves strip lighting and laminate flooring. **193**

The city is no longer industry but information based, this has revolutionised many aspects of our daily lives and not least how the populous is surveyed. As technology connects the city it also dissects it in a way never before possible. The big data Smart Cities use is inextricably tied to surveillance and while passive forms of surveying such as CCTV monitor our streets, the smart ideology promises to take a more active stance in the data collection process, using the monitoring of citizen activity in the reshaping of urban experience. This is taking the panoptic gaze of government and big business into a new realm freed from the restraints of crime prevention and advertisement, now systems may present data in a format which allows authority to pounce on an area or social group due to its supposed lack of efficiency. A shocking example of citizen coercion and control can be found in China's social credit system, which uses big data to monitor citizens activities, rewarding or sanctioning individual's scores depending on a variety of factors, including what their purchase history is, who they associate with and what social activities they take part in.

Thought police

These scores then affect where citizens are allowed to spend leisure time, if they are allowed to leave the country, sets their insurance premiums and more. While this is an extreme almost Orwellian form of control, it highlights a significant issue with the language used by smart initiatives. It is suggested in the name of the model itself, the ruling of activity in the city as either 'smart' or 'dumb'. This is sure to have a profound effect on what is valued within urban space, if the specialists without spirit label something as a smart initiative, any form of dissent can be labelled as an inefficient component of the city, hindering the possibility for meaningful challenges within the framework of this pre-decided utopian vision.

In China today, if an individual criticises the government they are liable to have points deducted from their credit score, whereas any praise of the government is likely to increase it. This is the truest manifestation of the thought police to date and the same can be said for the rhetoric surrounding Bristol's smart citizenship, albeit in a slightly less obvious way. It is an authoritarian vision of what a city is supposed to look like, and you better get with it, or your existence will be marked as inefficient, the ideological equivalent of bubble wrap.

Another troubling bastion of modern city values is a piece of legislation called a Cumulative Impact Zone. This is a label stamped upon areas of the city deemed to be suffering from an excess of nightlife related disturbances which police are not sufficiently funded to control. In Bristol the impact zoning spans the entirety of the city centre, Stokes Croft, Gloucester road, Clifton, Hotwells and North Street, all central cultural hubs of the city.

These impact zones allow for a restriction of new licensing to be allocated in 'problem' areas, whilst renewal of old licences is highly contested. Since 2011, 20 per cent of Bristol music venues have closed down, undoubtedly aided heavily by this new legislation. For example, the Surrey Vaults, a hub for young artists, video makers and musicians, was forced to close as a result of noise complaints from neighbouring luxury flats and was transformed into a cafe. Hamilton House and the Brunswick Club are under threat too and likely be turned into luxury abodes by developers who no doubt called for their closure in the first place; the Carriageworks has begun its collapse, to be fitted with just ten affordable homes out of the 115 outlined. It is harrowing enough that these essential spaces are being stripped from us, but as these closures show planning permission and licensing go hand in hand, with these new glass erections will surely come more complaints and closures, due to their central locations.

Although these impact zones are not directly related to the Smart Cities scheme, their ideological bases share many similarities in what an efficient city should look like. The data collected from smart sensors has the potential in the future to aid in cases of noise pollution and crowd dispersion, making it harder to argue the case for these spaces in the face of hard statistics. These venues are not the most traditionally efficient, quantitatively they do cause some noise pollution and minor street disturbances. Qualitatively however, they are city's truest form of expression, allowing for dissent and critique of the gentry, freeing us from the utterly stale efficiency of the private sector.

Punk spirit

When the rest of the city is constantly striving for a sleeker feel, a domination of man over space, these heterologies provide a haven. The things Bristol has for so long been known for are changing, no longer do we support a cultural ecosystem heading the rejection of private public spaces, now we are Bristol is Open, the smartest space of all.

Ideologies of the smart vision are antithetical to the DIY punk spirit of Stokes Croft and Bristol in general. Since the city is smart there should be no need for dissent. There is now a methodology passed down to us by the "experts" of urban planning and they have the tools to test it. No room is left for the traditional critique of how the city is being run, because this model has removed human incompetencies and visible figures, replaced by a digital deity, which governs the intelligence of our own behaviours. The very streets with their sensors have been elevated above us, from this eagle eye view they gaze upon our dwellings and assess the value status of our local haunts, our pubs and clubs for litter and loitering. Valuable meeting grounds for organisation and protest of the ever expanding gentrification process, such as the Peoples Republic of Stokes Croft and the Brunswick Club have been subsumed under the label of smart citizen sensing.

Urban rhythms

I have no doubt that these TED Talk thinkers believe they are doing the congested streets the most saintly service, but I absolutely refute the idea that data and quantification can accommodate for all the obscure and often absurd beauty that certain spaces create which may be seen as otherwise totally inefficient. They cannot read the psychology of urban rhythms, this can only be done by people who move through a space everyday. It is a worry for the future of cities when community-led organising, as haphazard as it can be, is being torn down and replaced by top down constructions, monetary cubes. On top of all of this, the structure in place energising this breach is considered by many as radical.

Turning now to urban creativity, fear not the smart authors have created a sad template for this most sacred of exercises as well. The most insidious of these artistic endeavours is an organisation called Futurecity[2]. Their vision for this creative cult is modelling the city as a "gallery without walls", this flags concern in two departments, firstly that my experience of corporate gallery spaces have more often than not been ultra sanitised white walls, people barely talking and feeling slightly like I shouldn't be moving as fast as I am. Surely this is not the thing we should be modelling our ideal cities on, a white cube designed for the pleasure of a middle-class voyeur.

Second, the concept of using the city as a showcasing platform is not an original idea, this is probably most obvious of all when entering the streets of Bristol, with virtually all space plastered with murals and slogans in a rejection of the bourgeois snobbery of big name galleries. The Futurecity model goes on to describe the current era for cities as the "cultural city", in which "creative genius is the new trading currency", here we see under no cloak of disguise a prophecy of the culture vulture. For generations street art created by the community for the community has been thwarted repeatedly by the authorities, only to be snapped up as the poster campaign for a group of businessmen who no doubt love Damien Hirst.

Futurecity is a platform business model meaning they facilitate exchanges between groups using the city as their platform. This concept is not inherently bad, the possibility of providing a space for art in the city I agree is a necessity. The issue is that this is being headed by corporate developers who spend large amounts of money making spectacular un-engaging art devoid of all community involvement. I find the example they use of placemaking particularly abhorrent, the rhetoric again used by this group assumes that they are in charge of making this place something more than it has been, effectively disregarding the community that resides there.

The public art facilitated by them is more than a little entertaining, most recently a "multi award winning" artist who makes catwalk jewellery, buddies with Alexander McQueen made a piece of art for a new block of flats in Kensington. What this translates to is a millionaire spending millions of pounds making decorations for a multi-million pound housing development. Another work constructed for London Bridge station by Mark Titchener features a series of sculptural slogans with sayings like "Only the first step is difficult" and "The distance means nothing", this comes across almost as a satirical attempt at creating meaningful public art. A world famous artist commissioned large sums of money to plaster motivational signage all over the tubes in which regular folk are ferried off to the rat race.

Drab thinking

As of yet Futurecity seems contained largely to London, however this is the suspect creative demeanour, which smart initiatives are leading with across the country and beyond.

In Bristol we have Playable Cities, a far less formidable foe which does engage with the community more than the drab Futurecity. Unfortunately, the initiative seems to share the drab thinking of their angry older smart brother. Some examples of previous projects include Urbanimals, a series of projected creatures onto the streets of Bristol, featuring a green rabbit that looked like a packet of Walkers salt & vinegar crisps and a glitchy kangaroo. Another attempt at being fun is the HelloLamppost scheme, which uses the same style of IOT sensor as smart systems, placed into various pieces of street furniture allowing the public to have conversations with post boxes. Although these were well-funded initiatives headed by a branch of the Watershed, I know of hardly anyone who engaged with them or found them captivating in any way. It seems fair to say that these attempts to cultivate public interest consistently fall short as they are an ordered manufactured experience, created by and for middle-class creatives with a lot of spare time on their hands.

These forms of sanctioned subversion fall short because of the way they are forcibly promoted as a playful experience in the city, an urban ballpark. Surely the creative experiences we design in the city should come out of its constant flux and its contestations allowing for some form of debate to be started, rather than piecemeal attempts at being creative through business models.

The dilemma of smartness and the city is one of coherence and incoherence. As the evolution of urban space projects into the future carried first by the train and now by the chip, planners seek to transform the world into something ever more coherent, containable and easily understandable. Progress over our physical reality seems the natural answer to growing despondency and disconnection in our relationships and careers. A totally coherent city is not the answer to these issues, on the one hand it sounds like an absurdity, and if achievable at all certain to be a grey experience with monolithic recruitment agencies, artisan tapas bars and artificial graffiti.

Total sanitation

Coherence is Cabot Circus. Incoherence is the Bearpit, Stokes Croft, Old Market. The same creative feelings Playable Cities attempt to superglue to the street are abundant in these areas, happening naturally with no predetermined measurable reason. At present we seem to have lost sight of the importance of these places, their value status has become a slab of bedrock ready for the overlaying of student housing obelisks.

With this boom of quasi-public space and smart sensors all urban areas are moving towards total sanitation. A totally sanitary pre-emptive monitoring system such as Smart Cities is creating a cloud of anomie and alienation across public space. I fear we are in danger of spreading the feeling of total dissolution with our physical reality and all its imperfections, from bathing in the anomic fluid of statistical empires too long.

If the locations we treasure have been labelled inefficient where will be left for dissent and rejection of a purely aesthetic life? Certainly not the digital public sphere for that is suffering the same fate as the physical. We must have coherence to function, but we need incoherence if we are to thrive. This level of monitoring places a pervasive anxiety on the ways of the city where there were none before, the need to control perceived disorder appears to be a collective neurosis, Smart Cities is our schizophrenia. We must reconcile this split between superego and id, our efficiency and inefficiency, for we are living under urban planning neurosis in a town that prizes statistics over all else.

Finn Dovey *is a poet, community activist and Sociology graduate who completed a thesis at the University of the West of England surrounding the Smart Cities Crisis and Utopian Urban Planning.*

Endnotes

1   Bristol beat Barcelona, Dubai, New York, Singapore and Yinchuan to win the Smart City Award at the GSM Association's (GSMA) 2018 Global Mobile Awards (The GLOMOs). The GSMA is a trade body that represents the interests of mobile network operators worldwide. The award provides global recognition for Bristol as a leading Smart City of the future. The GLOMOs, regarded as the 'Oscars' of the mobile industry, recognise and celebrate all contributions made to the evolving and developing mobile industry. The award winners were announced at the international mobile industry's largest gathering – the GSMA Mobile World Congress in Barcelona in 2018. (From Bristol City Council website).

2   Futurecity is a multidisciplinary culture agency, set up to reflect the burgeoning worldwide interest in culture-driven placemaking and regeneration. Futurecity has encouraged the property sector in the UK to use art and culture as part of a toolkit for providing a contemporary narrative for our towns, cities and urban centres. (From www.futurecity.co.uk)

Bristol buildings

John Hudson checks out some of the city's more interesting brickwork...

Bristol may lack the architectural impact of its neighbouring city of Bath, but there are still a number of buildings of merit, particularly around Corn Street and up in Clifton. Sadly, many historic sites were destroyed in World War Two, but aside from the obvious architectural big names, such as St Mary Redcliffe and the Victoria Rooms, there are some unusual buildings tucked away among the modern buildings. Here we take you on our tour of some of Bristol's less obvious buildings of merit...

Art Deco

You can look long and hard for decent art deco in Bristol. It is not exactly one of our strong points. There's a pretty good Odeon building in Union Street in Broadmead, opened in 1938, not long before World War Two, but its curved corner tower has not been the same since it lost its canopy and top. Weston-super-Mare is the place to go for a classic Odeon, cinema-organ and all. But at least Bristol's has a ghost: a long-ago projectionist murdered in some steamy sex scandal. Not many people have seen him but there's always something about the layout of these old buildings, with their lonely back corridors and stairs, that makes you expect the unexpected. Not a place to go at night if you get spooked!

The hotspot for 1930s 'modern movement' buildings is in and around the Centre. At the Broadmead end of this huge traffic roundabout that replaced redundant docks is Electricity House, opened in 1938 and designed by Giles Gilbert Scott to look like an ocean liner. You can see its stepped upper decks best from the side angle in Broad Street. It was given a welcome facelift in 1990, but with so much destroyed by the War, and then the planners, it is still hard to imagine the first shock of its contrast with the medieval city around it.

After the War, a group of architects called for the whole of the Centre to be rebuilt in the same style. Some hope... But at least the ship theme was picked up on by Percy Thomas and Son when they designed the showpiece

Electricity House is one of the Bristol buildings designed to look like an ocean liner

store for Broadmead in the mid 1950s, on the corner of Haymarket and the Horsefair. It helped pioneer the new shopping centre, and there was much grumbling about it at first – until critics saw that it was a Rolls Royce of a building compared with most of what followed. It's currently occupied by Primark, though a number of chains have come and gone over the years. The cold, commercial fact is that it's not all that big, with that wedge shape hemming it in. But it was refurbished lavishly in the 1990s by the Home Counties group Bentalls, who got their fingers burned mightily for their

Building reputations

Bristol is getting bigger. Mayor Marvin Rees announced that he wanted to see taller buildings in the city and developers responded by adding several storeys to existing plans for high-rise developments across the city. The new tallest buildings in Bristol will be in Castle Park and the Redcliffe Quarter, but at the time of writing these were the gert big 'uns

Tallest buildings

- St Mary Redcliffe Church (**89m**).
- Castlemead, Old Market (**80m**).
- Wills Memorial Building, Queen's Road (**68m**).
- Harvey Nicols, Broadmead (**65m**).
- Christ Church, Clifton Down (**65m**).
- Colston Tower, Colston Avenue (**64m**).
- One Redcliffe Street, Redcliffe (**64m**).

pains, leaving the way open for Primark to move over the road from its former shop.

Back around the Centre, swish apartments now occupy the symmetrical, angular offices from which the long-lost *Evening World* once hit the streets. There's something austere and Eastern European-looking about the place, but that's the way inter-war media moguls seemed to like their buildings. Around the corner, the redevelopment of the Colston Hall has meant the loss of the old Bristol Gas Co showrooms of 1935 which were sniffed at by purists as a deco cliché, but had an unusual air of seaside pavilion tattiness about them. Just up the road, Friary House, opened in 1938, is seen by those who know as a more worthy survivor of the modern movement.

Finally, if you're out in the suburbs at posh Sneyd Park, you'll find a clutch of cubist houses from the 1930s, all following Le Corbusier's lead. And in the Ridgeway at Westbury-on-Trym, not too far away, you can see through the trees an art deco classic of a house, with its style once more hinting at the ocean liners that never did come in to Bristol. It was built in 1934, and while it looks as if it should be basking in the sunshine of Miami Beach or St Tropez, its name is a reminder that it is pretty much one of a kind down in this part of the world. It's known simply as Concrete House.

Bristol Guild

The Bristol Guild shop in Park Street really can trace its history back to the 'guilds' of the arts and crafts movement. Today it's simply a shop specialising in glass and ceramics, furniture and furnishings, kitchenware and toys, but it's still more willing than most to showcase up-and-coming talent. The William Morris Arts and Crafts Society was founded in 1883. There was a big stir when the London-based Guild of Handicrafts moved to Chipping Campden in 1902, and though the Cockneys in Arcadia experiment was short-lived, the idea of craftspeople banding together for support and marketing opportunities was not.

The Bristol Guild of Handicrafts was opened in Park Street in 1907, the forerunner of the city's Guild of Applied Arts which started in the following year. There had been earlier arts and crafts groups in the area but none with a chance to sell in posh Park Street, 'the Bond Street of the West'. The stained-glass artist Arnold Robinson became its sole owner in 1929 and moved across the road to the present premises four years later, and from then on machine-made goods were accepted, as long as they were 'original, functional and made to the highest standards'. Ceramics by Susie Cooper, Ruskin and Royal Lancastrian were among Robinson's early favourites, as well as Elton Ware, made just along the road at Clevedon. Today the shop is owned by Bristolian Ken Stradling, who joined the company when he was demobbed from the Royal Corps of Signals in 1948.

Percival Hartland Thomas

Percival Hartland Thomas was the most off-beat of Bristol's 20th Century architects. He started his career designing arts and crafts houses and ended it with gothic churches, but in the middle years, he hit on a weird style of simplified gothic, redbrick Norman and bauhaus white, which could have added up to something big if he'd been a more influential name and had given it a bit longer. His three key churches are St Oswald's, Bedminster Down (1927), St Mary's, Shirehampton (1929), which is probably his masterpiece and St Cuthbert's, Brislington (1933). Pevsner says Shirehampton Church is neo-gothic, 'but handled with so much freedom and personality and with so much of the spirit of the 20th Century that the compromise remains convincing'. Others say uncompromising is more the word, with its huge square windows and macho-looking rubble walls. He was never as adventurous again, but when it comes to ease on the eye, a lot of his fans like Brislington best. Outside, the Norman-arched brick doorways of St Cuthbert's are undeniably great works of art, while inside Thomas created a huge light space of white illuminated by windows which are gothic in shape if not in fussiness. Hartland Thomas lived on until 1960, but sadly, he was never on this kind of form again.

Ugliest buildings

Student's Union, Queens Road – Alec French and Partners, 1965. *'Perhaps Clifton's most bruising post-war intrusion.'*

New Bristol Centre, Frogmore Street – Gillinson, Barnet & Partners, 1963-1966, demolition began 2015. *'Brutalises everything around it by scale and texture.'*

Froomsgate House, Rupert Street, Broadmead – Alec French, 1971. *'The most offensive of the area's gargantuan monoliths.'*

Former Norwich Union Building, Castle Park – Wakeford, Jerram & Harris, 1962. *'Deflates one of the city's prime sites.'*

Trenchard Street Car Park, Trenchard Street – Architect unknown, 1967, demolition began 2015. *'A multi-storey monster.'*

Descriptions from Pevsner Architectural Guide to Bristol. Buildings chosen by Naked Guide to Bristol

Cathedral Characters

The misericords on the choir stalls at Bristol Cathedral date mainly from around 1520 and, being half-hidden, gave their carvers plenty of scope for fun. They include images of Adam and Eve, Samson and the Lion, a mermaid, Reynard the Fox, the bear caught in the oak tree, dancing bears, a pig being killed, the spinster leading apes in hell, a woman taking corn to a windmill and a husband and wife doing battle with broomsticks.

Fast-forward more than 400 years and on the north windows on your left, just after you've entered the cathedral, you will see a memorial to all the Home Front services who helped guard the city and the cathedral in the World War Two. It shows a policeman, firemen, WVS member, air raid warden, nurses, and so on. The windows were unveiled in 1951, replacing earlier ones blown out by bombs, and at a 50th anniversary service in 2001, there were still plenty of old-timers around who'd served in those organisations. One of them even claimed to be the original model for one of the portraits. They're not exactly great art, but there's a nice human touch to them.

Old Market and Castle Park

You need a huge leap of imagination to take on board the fact that the shopping heart of Bristol once stretched from Old Market up along the river to Bristol Bridge. The inner ring road of Temple Way and Bond Street – did you ever see a less likely looking Bond Street? – now cuts the wide Old Market off from the heart of town, while Castle Park has greened over a network of teeming little streets that had survived from the Middle Ages until the day the Luftwaffe called.

Building trivia

The Spike Island Arts Centre was originally the Brooke Bond tea-packing warehouse. It was converted in 1998.

The distinctive electric cranes outside the Industrial Museum were to be scrapped until public outrage decreed otherwise in 1975.

The Paty family were Bristol's leading architects, builders and craftsmen in the 18th Century.

Bristol Bridge was built by Thomas Paty in 1764-67 on the site of the previous 13th-Century bridge.

St James' Priory at 1 Whitson St, Bristol BS1 3NZ next to the Bus Station is Bristol's oldest building with bits of it dating back to 1129.

The remains of St Peter's Church in Castle Park, once the centre of Bristol but destroyed in the Blitz

In the middle of them there were always the last traces of the Castle, a scene of Civil War derring-do when it fell to the Roundheads in 1645 but demolished a dozen years later. In fact, at the end of the park near the Marriott Hotel there are still some much-modified remains, but the most striking sight in the park today is the bomb-ruined shell of the 14th-century St Peter's Church. Its paved areas and terraces have become quite a popular meeting place but, while it's great in a sunny lunch hour, it can be seen as a little seedy at other times. It cost £50,000 to restore it in the 1970s, which was widely derided as a scandalous waste of money then, but wouldn't buy you a garage in Clifton now.

It's more cheerful to imagine Old Market in its heyday, especially on a busy Friday evening, which was the main shopping time for many Bristolians. Most of them would take home 'tea fish' as a special treat – dried and salted and the local answer to the Manx kipper or the Arbroath smokie. You only had to leave it to soak in a pan for two days and it was just the job for Sunday tea.

Statuesque

Gil Gillespie's brief guide to some monumental figures

Ursa Bear

Location: Bearpit for now, but Mayor Marvin Rees and Deputy Mayor Asher Craig are backing legal action to have Ursa removed.

Who's she when she's at home? Ursa the Bear was built by artist Jamie Gillman at the People's Republic of Stokes Croft. She was unveiled by Bristol Mayor George Ferguson on May 10, 2013. Volunteers removed four tons of earth to create a base for Ursa on top of the gents' toilets in the Bearpit. Ursa is 12-feet tall and sits on a four-foot-tall base. She represents the spirit of community activism, bottom-up regeneration and independence, which is why Asher Craig and Marvin Rees don't like her.

Was it worth breaking the mould? No mould. She is made from recycled timber from the hoardings surrounding a luxury flat development. It took Jamie 10-months to create Ursa. The original design didn't work because, according to Jamie, "She looked more like a meercat." In a Naked Guide to Bristol Twitter poll, Ursa and Neptune were Bristol's favourite statues.

Neptune

Location: He keeps moving around Bristol, but he is currently in the pedestrianised area on the Centre.

Who's he when he's at home? Well that's just it, he hasn't had a familiar place to hang his ragged cape lately, moving all over town in the name of Harbourside regeneration. The Mer

King is made of lead and was first erected in 1723 in the Temple area, near Bristol Bridge. He then moved to Temple Street and was left on some glebe land until 1872. The statue was then moved to the junction of Temple Street and Victoria Street and was later re-erected at the Quay Head in 1949. He moved to his present site back in 2000.

Was it worth breaking the mould? The big man of the ocean has been clutching his fork of defiance for longer than he cares to remember. He's always been gnarly, shrivelled and as stubborn as a limpet and there is no more heroic ocean figure around.

Equestrian bronze of William III

Location: Queen Square.

Who's he when he's at home? An unusually heroic-looking member of the aristocracy.

Was it worth breaking the mould? Dating back to the 1700s, this impressive looking, er, lump, of bronze man-and-his-mount was once so valued it was hidden away during World War Two and only put back again in 1948. 'Has he gone yet?' whispered his caretakers. 'Who?' came the reply. 'That horrible little German fella with the funny moustache.'

Edmund Burke

Location: St Augustine's Parade.

Who's he when he's at home? MP for Bristol 1774-1780 but sadly no relation to either Solomon or the newsreader Michael.

Was it worth breaking the mould?
Two moulds, actually. There is a marble replica in St Stephen's Hall, Westminster. Bristol gets the much cheaper version. "I wish to be a member of parliament, to have my share of doing good and resisting evil," reads the inscription. Looks like he is another berk who underestimated the persuasiveness of Tony Blair then.

Rajah Rammohun Roy
Location: Outside the Central Library on College Green.
Who's he when he's at home?
Celebrated Indian social reformer whose standing, even after his death, did much to stop the bulldozers threatening to flatten Arnos Vale Cemetery where he is buried inside a mighty impressive tomb.
Was it worth breaking the mould?
Absolutely. When it was unveiled in 1997, this public monument was a long overdue acknowledgement of the closest thing Bristol has to Ghandi – even though he was only visiting the city when he died.

Sabrina, Goddess of the Severn
Location: Broad Quay House.
Who's she when she's at home?
Naked, watery nymph types in hot lesbo action. Teenagers? Yes. Witches? More like suggestive fairies really.
Was it worth breaking the mould?
Well, artist Gerald Laing calls her: "A metaphor for the triumph of life over death." We think she is nothing of the sort.

William Penn
Location: New Millennium Square.
Who's he when he's at home?
Quaker son of Bristolian Admiral

Sir William Penn and the founder of Pennsylvania. His scroll reads 'Death is but crossing the World as Friends do the seas, they live in one another still'.
Was it worth breaking the mould?
Aren't a million boxes of Quaker oats memorial enough?

Small Worlds, a tribute to physicist Paul Dirac
Location: On Anchor Road outside the We The Curious complex.
Who's he when he's at home?
Stephen Hawking reckons: 'Dirac has done more than anyone, with the exception of Einstein, to advance physics and change our picture of the universe.' He won the Nobel Prize for Quantum Mechanics in 1933.
Was it worth breaking the mould?
Apparently, the concentric cones of the sculpture represent the theoretical movements of the physicist.

Charles Wesley
Location: The courtyard on the Horsefair side of the New Room and John Wesley Chapel in Broadmead.
Who's he when he's at home?
The brother of John and the co-founder of Methodism founder, John. Charles was a prolific hymn writer and regarded by some as the hymn writing equivalent of Lennon and McCartney. His biggest 'hit' is *Hark! The Herald Angels Sing*. He lived in Stokes Croft.
Was it worth breaking the mould?
The most striking thing about this impressive 1939 tribute to one of the founders of Methodism is his extraordinary, and very ill-advised, Yeoman-about-town mullet. In bronze. Could Charles Wesley be sporting the heaviest hairstyle in history?

A brief history of Bristol

Everything you need to know about Bristol history from 55BC to the present day...

Bristol was originally a Saxon settlement called Brigstow or Bricgstoc (the place of the bridge) which was formed where the River Frome met the River Avon near the present-day site of Bristol Bridge. The Frome was later diverted and now joins the Floating Harbour in the Centre. The original settlement was in Mercia on the site adjacent to Castle Park (handy for Broadmead) while the Medieval city expanded into the area surrounding Corn Street and St Nicholas Market. Bristol was on the border of Mercia and Wessex with the Avon marking the boundary – thereby making it the original Wild West frontier town.

There is little evidence of major Roman influence in Bristol – they seem to have preferred Bath and (unusually) Keynsham, although a Roman Villa was discovered at Kings Weston during the construction of Lawrence Weston housing estate in 1947. Perhaps Bristol is jealous of Bath's Roman heritage, because since the Middle Ages various historians have fabricated a Roman past to help enhance the city's reputation. It's an equally dubious story with Bristol's founders Brennus and Belinus, whose statues are on St John's Gate (the last remaining section of the city wall) at the bottom of Broad Street.

According to A History of Bristol by John Corry, printed in 1810 and based on earlier works, Malmutius (c.483BC) – King of Cornwall, and later Monarch of Britain – and Queen Corwenna had two sons, called Brennus and Belinus. It is said that they reigned jointly as Kings of Britain following their father's death and founded a major settlement at Bristol. Many stories are heard about Brennus and Belinus, but there is no evidence that they actually existed, or even that Bristol was founded earlier than Saxon times. Saying that, some records report that the Romans referred to Bristol as Caer Bren, or City of Brennus. However, despite allegedly founding Bristol long before Christ was born, the statues of Brennus and Belinus on St

208

A sketch of Bristol believed to date from 1640 – before Cromwell destroyed Bristol Castle in 1644

John's Gate show them with crucifixes. Which is slightly odd.

In Welsh legend, Brennus and Belinus were the sons of Dyfnwal Moelmyd, who became King of Britain and built four great roads across the Kingdom, one of which ran alongside a wide gorge at a city known as Caer Odor, or The Castle at the Gap. The only remaining reference to Caer Odor appears in the name of the Bristol Welsh Society: Cymdeithas Cymry Caerodor.

Even further back in time, the Avon Gorge was said to have been hewn from the rock by two giants, the brothers Vincent and Goram. Goram, who was an idle giant, fell asleep and was tragically killed when Vincent threw a pickaxe to him and it accidentally split his skull in half. This left Vincent distraught and he subsequently left Bristol and headed to Somerset to build Stonehenge. Following this, Vincent swam across to Ireland so that he could construct the Giant's Causeway in what is now County Antrim. He then returned to Bristol and lived by the side of the Avon Gorge, which is why the area is known as Vincent Rocks.

The Bristol High Cross

A bit of medieval history in Berkeley Square

One of the few remaining links with medieval Bristol is tucked away in the corner of a small park in Berkeley Square, off Park Street. It's a replica of the Bristol High Cross, a fine piece of craftsmanship that stood at the centre of the medieval town. If you imagine that the junction of Corn Street, Broad Street, Wine Street and High Street once formed a town square, that's where the High Cross was erected to commemorate the granting of Bristol's Charter in 1373. It replaced the previous High Cross, of which there are no remaining records.

The High Cross had four niches containing the statues of King John, Henry III, Edward III and Edward IV, all of whom had contributed to Bristol's expansion by conferring important charters. The whole Cross was gilded and coloured. In 1633, the Cross was repaired and altered to include the figures of Henry VI, Elizabeth I, James I and Charles I, who had further endowed privileges on the city. The Cross was later painted vermilion, blue and gold. By the beginning of the 18th Century, the large Cross, surrounded by steps and an iron fence, was becoming an obstruction in the increasingly busy streets. In 1733, the deputy chamberlain, Mr Vaughan, who lived at the corner of High Street and Wine Street, claimed his life and house were in danger from it every time the wind blew. A petition for its removal described the Cross as 'a superstitious relick' and 'a public nuisance'. Magistrates ordered the Cross to be put away in the Guildhall.

After protests, the High Cross was re-erected on College Green. However, in 1763, the fashionable set, who walked eight or ten abreast on the Green, complained that it impeded their promenading. It was taken down again and stored in a corner of the Cathedral. In 1765, it was given away by the Dean of Bristol to his friend Henry Hoare of Stourhead to use as an estate ornament. The High Cross is still at Stourhead and, in 1973, the Lord Mayor of Bristol unveiled a plaque there as part of the celebrations for the 600th anniversary of the granting of the city's charter. In 1848, a replica High Cross was built and erected on College Green. That, too, was demolished because of vandalism; it is the top part of this replica that survives in Berkeley Square. One of the missing statues from the replica is said to be in a private garden in Bedminster.

Occasionally there are campaigns to re-site the High Cross near the top of Corn Street, but they are usually greeted with remarkable indifference. However, the plans announced in 2006 to redevelop the St Mary le Port site opposite St Nick's Church by Bristol Bridge caused such public outrage, that the future of this area and perhaps of the High Cross could well come to the fore. There was another medieval High Cross on Gallows Hill (St Michael's Hill) that marked the city boundary, but there is no record of what happened to it.

Bristol history timeline

A big list of what happened, when it happened, where it happened and why it happened...

55BC The Romans invade Britain. The Dobunni tribe who live in the Bristol area defend themselves at Blaise, Leigh Woods and Clifton Down. There is no Roman Bristol, though there is a fort and port at Sea Mills.

C10th **978** Two silver coins minted in Bristol at the beginning of the reign of Ethelred ll (978-1016) are the first evidence of Saxon Bristol as a centre of commerce and proof that it has its own mint. They carry the stamp of the coin maker 'Aelfward on Bric'.

C11th **1066** Population of Bristol thought to be somewhere between 4,000 and 5,000.

1067 Bristol surrenders to William the Conqueror without a fight. Then King Harold's sons launch an unsuccessful attack on the town from Ireland in an attempt to unseat the Normans. They are beaten back from the city gates and pillage Somerset instead.

1086 The Domesday Book, conducted in the West by Wulfstan the last Anglo-Saxon Bishop, records that Bristol is part of the Manor of Barton. The name Barton survives in the Barton Hill (pronounced 'Bart Nil') area of Bristol, famous for its multi-coloured tower blocks and the Rhubarb public house. By now Bristol is an established port

trading with Dublin. There is 400 year old evidence of a white slave trade between Bristol and Ireland and Bristol is called the "Step-mother of all England".

1090 Bishop Wulfstan gets the slave trade from Bristol to Dublin banned. In so doing the first recorded rising of the Bristol mob occurs when the populace take one of the most nefarious slavers, who won't obey Wulfstan, outside the city walls and put his eyes out.

1088 First record of the original Bristol Castle near Bristol Bridge.

C12th **1115** First church built on the present site of St Mary Redcliffe.

1120 Robert, Earl of Gloucester, begins strengthening Bristol Castle. The Castle is built of Caen stone and has a large dungeon. The foundation walls of the keep are reputed to have been 25 foot thick.

1135-1154 Bristol is at the epicentre of the civil war between Queen Matilda and King Stephen called "the Anarchy". After much hardship and bloodshed a negotiated peace grants the throne to Henry II on Stephen's death.

1140 Robert Fitzhardinge, Bristol's richest citizen, begins work on St Augustine's Abbey, later to become Bristol Cathedral.

211

1154 King Stephen dies of 'the Piles'.

1155 Bristol is granted its first Royal Charter confirming certain rights of the townspeople. No record of this charter survives.

1171 After an alleged resumption of the slave trade between Bristol and Dublin the English conquer Ireland, Henry ll gives Dublin to the people of Bristol as a colony. Many Bristolians settle there and are massacred one Easter.

1188 Date of the earliest surviving Royal Charter. King John's Charter reveals that Bristol is by now a thriving merchant town with a penchant for protectionism – a tradition carried on to this day by the Society of Merchant Venturers. According to the Royal Charter, non-Bristolians could not buy leather, corn or wool from 'foreigners', only from Bristol merchants.

C13th **1203-41** Princess Eleanor of Brittany is imprisoned in Bristol Castle for all of her life in order to prevent her producing an heir to the throne to rival the Plantagenets: King John and his son Henry lll.

1203 After a campaign by King John, Wulfstan becomes Patron Saint of Vegetarians and Peasants, his saints day is January 19.

1216 The first Mayor of Bristol is appointed.

1220 Foundation of Gaunt's Hospital, later to become the Lord Mayor's Chapel.

1239-47 River Frome is diverted, using just spades and wheelbarrows, to provide more quays to cater for the increase in trade at the port. The work costs £5,000 and the river now provides a soft muddy bottom for boats to rest on when the tide is out. The diverted Frome is 2,400 foot long, 18 foot deep and 120 foot wide. It is one of the most remarkable feats of civic engineering of its time, doubling the port's capacity. It was so remarkable that future town planners concrete over it years later.

1247 First record of a High Cross at the junction of High Street and Corn Street.

1267 Carmelite Friary set up on banks of River Frome (roughly on the site of the Colston Hall) by 'Longshanks', Prince of Wales, the future Edward I – 'Hammer of the Scots'.

C14th **1312** The Bristol Tax Riots: the earliest recorded uprisings in Bristol and the beginning of a tradition of civil disobedience that saw its most recent expression in Stokes Croft in 2011. Bristolians rise up in anger when Edward II introduces another tax on shipping. The Mayor, William Randolph, takes over control of collecting the taxes and the ship money from Bristol. Rioting starts soon after; Edward II appoints the Constable of the Castle with powers to overrule the corporation. Thomas de Berkeley is appointed to stop the riots. Twenty men are killed and the King's officers are driven into the castle by the rioters. They remain under siege until the barons call in the army. After four days, the city surrenders. Edward II pardons the rioters but fines them.

1327 Edward ll is imprisoned at Bristol Castle. He is then moved to Berkeley Castle in Gloucestershire where he is murdered by having a red-hot poker shoved up his bum.

1371 Bristol linen merchant Edward

Blanket, the (ahem) inventor of the blanket, dies. His tomb is in St Stephen's Church, just off the Centre. Blanket lived in Tucker Street and was MP for Bristol in 1362.

1373 Edward lll grants Bristol a charter on 8 April making the city the first provincial borough to be a county in its own right. Bristol pays 600 marks for the charter. Edward needs the money to fund the war against France. The first Sheriff of Bristol is appointed; a new High Cross is erected at the junction of Broad Street, Wine Street, Corn Street and High Street to commemorate the event.

1390 Work begins on Temple Church, Bristol's equivalent to the Leaning Tower of Pisa. Work on the church stops when the tower begins to lean and starts again in 1460. The sloping is partially corrected thanks to some heavy stone laying. But by the time it is hit in the Blitz, it has been tilting again for some years and isn't going to stand up straight for that Hitler fella.

C15th **1446** With rebuilding work almost complete at St Mary Redcliffe Church, the roof is struck by lightning during a violent electric storm and destroyed. The repair work is funded by merchant William Canynges who was Mayor of Bristol five times and the city's Member of Parliament twice.

1497 John Cabot sets sail from Bristol in The Matthew and discovers North America. Born Giovanni Caboto in Genoa around 1451, Cabot is thought to have arrived in Bristol in about 1480 with an ambition to look for Hy-Brasil, an island somewhere in the Atlantic, according to Celtic legend. Cabot leaves Bristol on 20 May 1497 on board The Matthew with a crew of 18. He lands on the East Coast of

The top of the replica High Cross in Berkeley Square

America on 24 June 1497. On his return to Bristol, Cabot is rewarded for his discovery with a pension of £20 a year. In 1498, he sets off for America again, this time with five ships, and is never heard of again. Cabot's new-found land is named America after the Bristol merchant Richard Amerike, or not.

C16th **1532** Foundation of Bristol Grammar School by Robert and Nicholas Thorne.

1542 Diocese or 'the See' of Bristol created by Henry Vlll. Old Augustine Abbey becomes Bristol Cathedral.

1552 Society of Merchant Venturers formed. First Governor is John Cabot's son Sebastian, just back from Spain where he's been on holiday.

1555-57 Five martyrs are burned at the stake on St Michael's Hill during the reign of Bloody Queen Mary. The prisoners

213

– all working men – were led to their deaths from the gaol up the muddy hill that is now Christmas Steps. Mary dies 'of the Dropsy' in 1558 and is buried 'unlamented'.

1568 Bristol merchant John Young began the construction of the Great House on the site of the Carmelite Priory, which had been looted and sold on during Henry VIII's Reformation. The House plays host to Queen Elizabeth on her 'progress' to Bristol in 1574.

1574 Queen Elizabeth visits Bristol and describes St Mary Redcliffe Church as 'The goodliest, fairest and most famous parish church in England'. This is the most overused quote in the history of Bristol and will not appear in this book again. At each stage of her visit, apprentice lads persistently pop out at her to perform poems, much to her annoyance. She also negotiates the 'Treaty of Bristol' with the Spanish Ambassador, peace then ensues until the Armada of 1588.

1586 Foundation of Queen Elizabeth's Hospital School by John Carr.

1597 Renaissance spy and Prebend of Bristol Cathedral, Richard Hakylut, urges that after the passing of the 'Beggars Act' England's rogues and vagrants be sentenced and transported to work on Irish and Virginian plantations in 'prisons without walls'.

C17th **1610** Bristol merchant John Guy becomes the first governor of Newfoundland.

1612–18 Merchant Robert Aldworth sets-up Bristol's first sugar refinery in St Peter's Hospital using sugar from Madeira and Brazil.

1634 Foundation of Red Maids' School. John Whitson, merchant, Mayor and Member of Parliament for Bristol, dies in 1629, bequeathing monies for a hospital for '40 poor women children' to be 'apparelled in red cloth'. The Red Maids School is originally in Denmark Street next to the present-day Hippodrome, but moved to Westbury-on-Trym in 1930. Girls from the school still celebrate Founder's Day.

1636 Slave trader Edward Colston is born in Bristol. Colston funds Almshouses and a Hospital (School) with money from the slave trade. He goes on to bequeath around a third of his wealth to the city and other 'good causes' around the country.

1642 Outbreak of the English Revolution, Bristol joins the Parliament side.

1643 Bristol is captured by Royalist forces. Religious Radical, Dorothy Hazard and around 200 women and children, shore up the defences of the Frome Gate to try and keep them out.

1645 Bristol surrenders to Cromwell's Parliamentary forces; Bristol's population had been devastated by disease and starvation.

1654 The destruction of Bristol Castle ordered by Oliver Cromwell, 'free' building stone provides a bonanza for Bristol's builders. Also in this year, the Great House becomes Bristol's second sugar refinery, one of the first in the kingdom to start importing sugar from St Kitt's.

1655 First Quaker meeting is held in Bristol at a private house in Frenchay. Bristol born Admiral William Penn captures Jamaica while undertaking Cromwell's 'Western Design' – very much a 'booby prize' – his mission was to secure the much larger and wealthier island of Hispaniola but he failed. For his pains he was slung into the Tower of London on his return to England.

1660 Bristol apprentices revolt, demanding a free Parliament and the restoration of the Monarchy. On 5 March 1660, the bellman of Bristol makes the usual Puritan proclamation banning cock-throwing and dog-tossing. The rowdy apprentices attack him and the next day (Shrove Tuesday) squail a goose and toss cats and dogs into the air outside the Mayor's Mansion House. To squail a goose is to throw sticks, weighted with lead at one end, at it. The object is to maim the bird without killing it. The authorities are able to quickly bring the apprentices under control and halt all tossing and squailing. Admiral Penn switches sides and sets sail to the Netherland's to collect King Charles II and help restore him to the throne. This is called the 'Restoration'. Oliver Cromwell's body is dug up and his head severed off just to make sure he's still dead.

1674 Ralph Ollive becomes Mayor of Bristol on an anti-Quaker ticket. Major persecution of the Society of Friends, and early Baptists, continues. Quaker James 'the Mad Messiah' Naylor and Anabaptist Dorothy Hazard had already spoken out against the slave trade in the 1650s.

1680 Edward Teach (aka Blackbeard the Pirate) is born in Bristol. Blackbeard is believed to be the inspiration for Robert Louis Stevenson's Long John Silver in Treasure Island. Edward Colston starts his 12-year tenure as a leading member of the London based Royal African Company where he's a senior manager in the company's affairs. During his time at the helm he's responsible for the transportation of some 84,500 enslaved African men, women and children across the Atlantic to the Americas. 19,300 of die en route, 14 per cent of them children under the age of ten.

1681 William Penn of Bristol establishes a Quaker community in Pennsylvania.

1685 King Charles II dies of 'a fit of apoplexy', Catholic James II assumes the throne leading directly to the Monmouth – or Pitchfork – Rebellion. Monmouth refuses to attack Bristol as the Duke of Beaufort had threatened to torch the city. Later that year Judge Jefferies arrives in Bristol to punish the rebels, finding hardly any, he switches his ire to Bristol's Aldermen and Justices accusing them of kidnapping Englishmen to serve on their plantations in the Caribbean and Virginia. Mayor William Hayman, brother-in-law of Edward Colston, is fined a massive £1,000 'for suffering a boy committed to Bridewell to go beyond the sea'.

1688 James II 'abdicates' the throne, leaving the way clear for the Prince of Orange to invade England with his Dutch army, thereby becoming King William III. This is called the 'Glorious Revolution'.

1691 Colston puts William lll 'onto a good thing' and sells him a wodge of RAC shares; he then stands down from the company the following year.

1694 Society of Merchant Venturers organises protests against the Royal African Company's London monopoly of the slave trade.

1695 William Bonny sets up Bristol's first printing press.
1698 The 'legal' transatlantic slave trade begins for Bristol and other 'outports' when the London monopoly of the

Colston and the slave trade

The history of the slave trade in Bristol from 1698 to its abolition in 1807

Built on slavery

It has been suggested that Bristol should perhaps be the site for a permanent national exhibition about the African slave trade. Perhaps it will take a gesture of that magnitude to make the city finally confront the demons of its past – there's no getting away from the fact that the wealth of modern Bristol is built on slavery.

At the height of the slave trade, in the mid 18th Century, the Bristol economy and the Society of Merchant Venturers thrived on slavery. For example, sugar was returned to the port from the plantations where the slaves were sold, so refineries were built in the city; the refineries needed power, which was provided by the coal mines of Kingswood. The rapid growth of the city and its growing prosperity in the 18th Century and beyond was significantly based on the brutality and immorality of slavery.

Colston's secret

Many of the families and institutions that still prosper and hold considerable influence in the city made their money from slavery. The legacy of Edward Colston dominates Bristol. A statue of the MP and slave trader stands in the Centre near the Colston Hall, (opposite the Colston Tower), there are at least a dozen streets named after him and, of course, there's Colston's Schools. There's even a Colston Bun.

Edward Colston was born in Bristol in 1636, the son of a wealthy merchant.

He made his money initially by trading with Spain and other Mediterranean countries. However, although he went to great lengths to keep it a secret, Colston became a member of the Royal African Company in 1680 and took an active part in the planning and financing of slaving ventures to Africa, his name appearing in the company records for 11 years.

The African slave trade began in Bristol in 1698 when the London-based Royal African Company lost its monopoly on English trade with West Africa. Between 1698 and the abolition of the slave trade in 1807, more than 2,000 ships set sail from Bristol to enslave Africans on the West African coast. It's estimated that 500,000 enslaved Africans were carried on Bristol vessels out of a total trade of 2.8 million (*The Bristol Slave Traders: A Collective Portrait,* David Richardson), although other researchers put the figure as high as 8 million (*A Shocking History of Bristol*, Derek Robinson). As many as a quarter of the slaves died or were murdered at sea. So it's possible that around two million bodies were thrown overboard from slave ships.

Liverpool and London were the other major slave ports, but half of the slave ships that left England for Africa in 1730 sailed from Bristol. The city's share of the trade had fallen to 25% by the 1750s as Liverpool became the dominant port and, by the time of abolition in 1807, Bristol had just a 2% market share.

The slave trade worked on the triangular model, making a profit on each stage of the voyage. Ships left Bristol with a cargo of cotton, brass, copper, gin or muskets, which were bartered for slaves with the West African traders. The ships then embarked on the Middle Passage to the West Indies or America where the surviving slaves were sold at a profit, often to plantation owners originally from Bristol. The ships then returned home with a cargo of sugar or tobacco which was again sold for profit. During the 18th Century, 32 of the city's leading slave traders became members of the Society of Merchant Venturers and 16 went on to become Master.

Legal jettison
Naturally, the Africans fought the traders sent to capture them and many committed suicide when they were captured; thousands more were killed in mutinies or died due to the dreadful conditions at sea. Perhaps most shocking of all, there is a body of evidence which suggests that Bristol captains drowned their entire 'cargo' of diseased Africans so that the loss could be claimed on the owners' insurance as 'legal jettison'.

Slave ships were specially converted so they could carry the maximum number of bodies. Typically, a ship would have a hold about five foot high, so the owners built two six-foot wide platforms either side of the hold to create two decks. Enslaved Africans were driven into the hold and forced to lie on the bottom in rows until it was covered. Then another layer of people were forced onto the platforms.

On some of the larger ships a second platform was added, giving a

Bristol's most prominent statue is of the notorious slave trader Edward Colston

headroom of about 20 inches for the three layers of people. The tallest were put amidships; the smaller ones and children were wedged into the stern. The space per person was very restricted. A male enslaved African was allowed a space six foot by 16 inches; a woman was allowed five foot by 16 inches; a boy five foot by 14 inches and a girl four foot by 12 inches. They lived, and died, in these conditions on the passage from Africa to the West Indies and America. They were often seasick and had no alternative but to foul themselves.

The Africans were supposed to be brought on deck every morning to be fed and cleaned, but some captains left them in the holds for the entire journey (between six weeks and three months). Bristol merchants, sea captains and crews were responsible for the most appalling and degrading treatment of human beings. This was a crime as great as the Holocaust.

In June 1787, the Rev Thomas Clarkson arrived in Bristol to begin his fact-finding tour of the slaving ports that was to lead to the abolition of the slave trade some 20 years later. However, it was not just the suffering of the Africans that began to change public opinion, but the poor treatment of the Bristol slave crews.

Naturally, the Society of Merchant Venturers did everything possible to halt Clarkson's investigations, but he persevered. He interviewed 20,000 sailors and collected equipment used on the slave ships, such as iron handcuffs, leg shackles, thumbscrews, instruments for forcing open slaves' jaws, and branding irons. Clarkson set himself up in the Seven Stars pub (which is still there, next to the Fleece and Firkin on Thomas Lane) whose owner was sympathetic to William Wilberforce's anti-slavery movement. Pub landlords played a key role in recruiting crews for the slaving ships, and the landlord of the Seven Stars explained to Clarkson the way the business worked and introduced him to the slaving underworld that inhabited Bristol's dockside taverns. He pieced together a picture of the reality of the business and discovered that crews were recruited in three ways:

- Lying: men were lured from the drinking dens of Marsh Street with promises of high wages and an exotic life at sea.
- Doping: pub landlords were bribed to spike sailors' drinks and they were abducted.
- Blackmail: the landlords encouraged men to borrow money for drink and

then threatened them with jail unless they joined a slaving crew.

Once on board, the crew was forced to sign ship's articles legalising their poor pay. Often the crew were paid in virtually worthless foreign currencies.

Clarkson managed to gain access to the Merchant Venturers' records. From their own Muster Rolls, he found that the mortality rates of Bristol slave ship crews were very heavy in comparison to those of other cities involved in the triangular trade. His interviews revealed that the crews were treated appallingly by slaving captains. Some men were murdered; sometimes a quarter of the crew died at sea from disease, ill treatment and torture. Obviously, their suffering was nothing compared to the African people, but Clarkson's revelations began to get the attentions of the Bristol public. Not surprisingly, these revelations started to disturb people.

Public Outrage

Clarkson managed to take the murder of two seamen on board a slaver to trial, despite two slave traders sitting on the bench at the initial hearing. His witnesses all mysteriously disappeared by the time the case was due to be heard, but finally the word was out and the Bristol public were shocked by what they heard about the treatment of their local sailors. It seems they cared little for the suffering of the slaves, although there was an anti-slavery movement in the city led by Quakers and Methodists. In fact, Bristol was the first city outside London to set up a committee for the abolition of the slave trade; some 800 people volunteered to sign the first

Diagram from the 18th century showing how enslaved Africans were transported in a Bristol ship

Bristol petition against the slave trade in 1788.

The Yorkshire MP William Wilberforce, the public face of the abolition campaign, came to Bristol in 1791 to encourage the local campaign. The poets Robert Southey, William Wordsworth, Hannah More, Anne Yearsley and Samuel Coleridge all wrote against the trade. John Wesley, who founded the Methodist Church, wrote against slavery and preached against the trade in the New Rooms in Broadmead. This was one of the first political campaigns in which women played an active part and, in 1787, Hannah More was instrumental in organising a boycott of West Indian slave sugar in Bristol.

Parliament first debated a motion calling for the abolition of the slave trade in 1788. The Society of Merchant Venturers and other business interests in Bristol lobbied strongly against Wilberforce and the abolitionists, claiming it would be 'ruinous in the extreme to the petitioners engaged in the manufacture, but the mischief would extend most widely throwing hundreds of common labouring people wholly out of employment'. The slave business won the day and Parliament merely passed an Act aimed at improving conditions on slave ships by limiting the numbers carried. The Bristol Corporation ordered church bells across the city to be rung in celebration.

The Society of Merchant Venturers fought against abolition to the last, even though Bristol's share of the trade was fairly insignificant by comparison at the end of the 18th Century. The merchants could make handsome profits by trading directly with the plantation owners, many of whom were from the city, rather than undertaking the far more risky triangular voyages.

The abolition movement suffered a setback in 1793 when Britain went to war with France. The slave trade was seen as the 'nursery of seamen' and abolition of the trade was postponed. Eventually, in 1807, the slave trade in the British colonies was abolished and it became illegal to carry slaves on British ships.

Royal African Company is broken after a 'truceless warfare' of 40 years by Bristol's SMVs.

C18

th **1700** The population of Bristol is estimated to have risen to around 25,000.

1702 Work begins on building Queen Square to celebrate a visit to Bristol by Queen Anne, who had taken over from William after he fell off his horse.

1702 Bristol's first newspaper, the *Bristol Postboy*, is founded. The 91st issue, published in August 1704, is the earliest surviving copy of a provincial newspaper in the world and is now at the Central Reference Library. It was produced weekly as a single sheet.

1708 Bristol privateers Duke and Duchess set out on Woodes Rogers' three year circumnavigation of the globe, they bring home a Spanish treasure ship and marooned sailor Alexander Selkirk – the proto-type of Daniel Defoe's *Robinson Crusoe* of 1719.

1709 Food riots sweep the city. 200 coal miners from Kingswood, always a rowdy bunch, march into the city and riot against a big increase in the cost of food – a bushel of wheat had doubled in price to eight shillings. The miners disperse after being promised a reduction in the price of a bushel to five shillings and sixpence.

1710 Colston School (or Hospital) is founded in the Great House; Edward Colston is elected Bristol's first Tory MP.

1714 Celebrations for the Coronation of George 1 turn into a riot and two people are killed in the violence. Edward Colston is implicated in a scurrilous pamphlet, it

also accuses him of incestuous behaviour with his sister Ann. Lifelong bachelor Colston dies in 1721 and various societies are formed and named in his honour, the 'Cult of Colston' begins.

1727-49 The introduction of tollgates on 26 June 1727 sparks off far more serious riots than those of 1709 or 1714. Two days after they are installed, the turnpikes are destroyed. Wherever they appear, the tollgates are wrecked. For a time in 1734, not a single tollgate is left standing between Bristol and Gloucester. This continues for 21 years, the length of time that the law that allows the tollgates is in force.

1728-33 Riots by Easton and Kingswood weavers, impoverished by the industrialisation of their industry, results in a mill owner shooting dead eight protesters. Two of the Easton weavers' leaders are executed.

1728 Jonathon Swift releases *Gulliver's Travels*, an anti-colonialisation riposte to Defoe's Crusoe.

1737 Bristol Royal Infirmary opens.

1739 John Wesley invents Methodism. On 2 April, Wesley gives his first open-air sermon in St Philip's. The New Room in the Horsefair is established as the world's first Methodist chapel later in the year. After witnessing slavery first hand in America both John, and later his brother Charles, begin speaking out against the slave trade.

1743 At the height of Bristol's 'Golden Age', the Exchange in Corn Street is completed by John Wood The Elder, at a the massive cost of £50,000.

1745 The original glass-roofed St Nicholas Market is built.

1749 John Wesley's brother Charles, the greatest ever hymn writer, moves to Bristol and lives in a house at 4 Charles Street, opposite the present site of the bus station.

1750 Population of Bristol about 50,000: the city has doubled in size in just 50 years.

1752 The poet Thomas Chatterton is born into an impoverished Bristol family in Redcliffe.

1753 Very bad harvests in 1752 are the cause of food riots in 1753. Despite shortages, Bristol merchants are still exporting grain for huge profits. On 21 May 1753, Kingswood miners lead a march into the city and ransack a ship, The Lamb, that was preparing to sail with 70 tons of wheat to Dublin. On 25 May, a crowd of 900, made up mostly of colliers and weavers, break into the Bridewell and release prisoners. Four rioters are killed, around 50 injured and 30 are captured.

1766 The Theatre Royal, mostly funded by West India merchants, is opened.

1774 The future Poet Laureate Robert Southey is born the son of a linen draper at 9 Wine Street on 12 August.

1780 The development of Upper Clifton begins.

1782 In order to head off any anti-slavery sentiment, the new West India Society is formed, consisting of many of Bristol's leading Merchant Venturers.

1786 Tobacco company WD & HO Wills is founded by Henry Overton Wills when he moves from Salisbury to Bristol and goes into partnership with Samuel Watkins. They start with their first shop in Castle Street but, by 1791, the firm has expanded and moved to 112 Redcliffe Street.

1787 Abolitionist the Reverend Thomas Clarkson embarks on his epic journey around Britain to investigate the vagaries of the slave trade, coming first to Bristol and staying six months. The 20-year human rights campaign finally results in the Abolition of the Slave Trade throughout the British empire in 1807. He's pushing on an open door, the Quakers, Baptists, Methodists and new-fangled Unitarians in Bristol are all anti-slavery.

1788 As a direct result of Clarkson's visit, Bristol becomes the first location outside of London to form an Abolition Committee.

1793 Bristol Bridge Riot. Eleven people are killed and 45 injured in protests against bridge tolls, no enquiry is allowed and those guilty go free.

1796 Leading Bristol writers Hannah More, Ann Yearsley, Joseph Cottle, Robert Lovell and Robert Southey are joined in their anti-slavery campaigning by Samuel Taylor Coleridge and William Wordsworth. To this end Coleridge launches his first published work, the radical newsletter the Watchman, from the Rummer in High Street.

C19th **1800** Humphry Davy works with Thomas Beddoes at his clinic in Dowry Square, Hotwells. Davy publishes the book Researches, Chemical and Philosophical: Chiefly Concerning Nitrous Oxide in which he describes inhaling nitrous oxide (laughing gas) and obtaining a degree of analgesia from a painful condition he was suffering. Davy's research into anaesthetic effect are not tested and utilised for another 45

Coleridge, Bristol and the Romantics

Tony D'Arpino explores Bristol's connections with the 18th century Romantic poets...

Great friendships and great poetry are a Bristolian tradition. The Romantics are often iconographed with the Lake District but it really all began in Bristol. The publication of *Lyrical Ballads* by Samuel Taylor Coleridge and William Wordsworth, in 1797 by Joseph Cottle in Wine Street, Bristol, is regarded as the beginning of the Romantic Movement. It was a Summer of Love.

The friendship between Coleridge and Wordsworth lasted all their lives, with some serious rock 'n' roll crash and burns. Their horoscopes would be interesting to compare: Coleridge the wildman to Wordsworth's herb tea. There were four of them at the beginning: Samuel Coleridge, William Wordsworth, Robert Southey, and Robert Lovell. Lovell and Southey were the Bristolians, born and bred.

Coleridge was lured to Bristol from Cambridge by Robert Southey. At Uni they had dreamed a scheme to found a utopian commune on the Susquehanna River in Pennsylvania to be called Pantisocracy. Not as far-fetched as it sounds. The dissenter and scientist (and inventor of soda water) Joseph Priestley, a member of the famous Lunar Society, had already moved there a few years previously.

Bristol was a centre of scientific enquiry as well as literary culture. The physician and experimenter Thomas Beddoes, former Lunar Society member and founder of the Pneumatic Institute

on Dowry Square, was a close friend of Coleridge as well as his personal physician. Beddoes' assistant, Humphry Davy, also became a great friend of Coleridge. Davy, later head of the Royal Society, wrote vast epic poems as a young man, much of his imagery drawn from his native Cornwall. Davy discovered laughing gas in Bristol and became the first addict to it. Unlike opium, physical addiction to nitrous oxide is arguable, but Davy was well-known for carrying his "green pillow," a portable gas-bag, on long walks along the Avon Gorge.

Opium Eater

Other friends and associates of the era include Thomas De Quincey, author of Confessions of An English Opium Eater; Peter Mark Roget, already working on his Thesaurus while employed at the Pneumatic Institute; and the writer Charles Lamb, Coleridge's oldest and closest friend. The three poets Coleridge, Southey and Lovell married the three Fricker sisters – Sara, Edith, and Mary Fricker. They were all married at St Mary Redcliffe (but not on the same day). Robert Lovell is forgotten today mainly because he died the next year. He was 25. He wrote a long poem called The Bristoliad, a satirical poem making fun of the commercial life of Bristol.

Robert Southey's poetry is also not read much today, but he became Poet

Laureate of England, and his biography of Nelson is still in print. Southey helped raise Coleridge's children in the Lake District because Coleridge was largely an absentee father. Coleridge's daughter Sara and son Hartley were both poets. Robert Southey edited the first collected works of Thomas Chatterton, the boy poet of Bristol. The Gothic shadow of Chatterton, just a generation before them, was a great influence on Coleridge as well as the younger generation of Keats and Shelley.

Romantic era Bristol, one of the world's busiest ports, had republican sympathies and a long tradition of dissent. Quakers, Unitarians, free-thinkers, abolitionists were not only tolerated but listened to and respected. Exciting and dangerous times. There were spies in Somerset, rumours of war, revolutionary struggles abroad, and the people were suspicious of their government. Kind of like today.

One story is that Coleridge and Wordsworth first met at the Bristol home of sugar baron John Pinney on Great George Street, now the Georgian House Museum. Pero, the namesake of Pero's Bridge in the Floating Harbour, was a servant of the Pinneys, from the island of Nevis in the Caribbean. He may have served them wine.

Coleridge and Wordsworth met again at Racedown, the Pinney's country place in Dorset, which is still there on the old road to Lyme Regis. This extended meeting sealed their friendship. Coleridge walked there from Bristol and Dorothy Wordsworth never forgot her first sight of him, jumping over a fence to cut across a field.

Coleridge published two newspapers, the Watchman (started at the Rummer Tavern, still serving thirsty merchants and poets) and the Friend. He edited much of the Watchman from a house in Kingsdown and published The Friend while living in the village of Calne in Wiltshire. Coleridge also lived near the village of Box outside Bath, and after a serious, life-threatening laudanum-induced breakdown, he recovered in a kindly merchant's home on Queen Square.

The Somerset village of Nether Stowey is the other sacred ground of the Romantics. The final destination of one of Edward Thomas' famous walks (In Pursuit of Spring) and a site of pilgrimage to this day. The Rime of The Ancient Mariner was written in Nether Stowey, at a place we now know as Coleridge Cottage. Christabel, the Conversation Poems, and the prelude of Wordsworth's Prelude were all written there. Kubla Khan was written (under famous and still mysterious waking-dream gossip circumstances) at Ash Farm near Culbone Combe and its abandoned village. It is an accessible but remote location on what is now the Coastal Path above Porlock Bay, along one of Coleridge's many habitual and epic walks.

Coleridge may have had a laudanum and poetry problem, but what he was really known for during his lifetime was for being loveable. He was evidently a very simpatico, loveable chap. Even his enemies loved him. Dorothy Wordsworth loved him and always worried about him.

Coleridge was one of the great talkers of his age – and one of the great walkers. He and the Wordsworths practically invented fell walking. Wordsworth, the straight man, was a champion ice-skater. Who knew? The Lake District soon became one of the first popular travel destinations. Wordsworth complained bitterly about tourists.

Coleridge was for a short time a Unitarian preacher. He also served as secretary to the governor of Malta, and spent time in Rome and Germany. He gave public lectures at the Corn Market Rooms and Assembly Coffeehouse on Bristol Quay. There are no recordings of Coleridge's voice of course, but it's said he never lost his Devon accent.

A little studied aspect of the Romantics is their interest in hermetic traditions. The poet and astrologer William Gilbert was friends with Coleridge, Southey and others in the Bristol years. Coleridge published an excerpt from his long poem the Hurricane in the Watchman. He was later a contributor to The Conjuror's Magazine in London before disappearing altogether. William Gilbert has been called the Syd Barrett of Romanticism.

Bristol is still the cultural capital of the West Country with a vibrant poetry scene from the BlahBlahBlah series at the Bristol Old Vic to the Milk poets at the Wardrobe Theatrea, poetry readings in many venues, the Bristol Festival of Literature, the Bristol Poetry Institute at the University of Bristol, good-looking poets, and fearless publishers.

Coleridge, Southey and Lovell married the three Fricker sisters in St Mary Redcliffe Church

years; instead, the primary use of nitrous oxide is for recreational enjoyment and public shows. So-called 'nitrous oxide capers' took place in travelling medicine shows and carnivals, where the public paid a small price to inhale a minute's worth of gas. Many dignitaries and famous individuals come to inhale Davy's purified nitrous oxide for recreational purposes, including the poets Coleridge and Southey, the potter Josiah (later Sir Josiah) Wedgwood, and Roget of Roget's Thesaurus. 'I am sure the air in heaven must be this wonder working gas of delight,' wrote Southey after a swift inhalation in Dowry Square.

1801 Population of Bristol is around 68,000.

1803 An Act of Parliament is passed to allow the construction of the Cut, a new course for the River Avon to enable the Floating Harbour to be created.

1806 Isambard Kingdom Brunel is born at Portsea, near Portsmouth, on 9 April. His mother is English; his father is the great French engineer Sir Marc Isambard Brunel.

1809 Floating Harbour finished and the promoters have a huge party to celebrate, with copious beer flowing, a huge fight breaks out between the British and Irish navvies.

1823 The Bristol Chamber of Commerce is established, much to the chagrin of the Society of Merchant Venturers.

1823 A Bristol inventor takes his Charvolant, or Flying Car, to Ascot Races to demonstrate it to George IV. This magnificent contraption, which was tested on Durdham Downs, is the brainchild of Clifton schoolmaster George Pocock, an eccentric boffin who

had already built an automatic caning machine to deal with his wayward pupils. The Charvolant is made up of a carriage for four people that is powered by two giant kites. On a good day, it can reach speeds of 25mph. After displaying his machine to the public, Pocock begins using the Charvolant as a family vehicle, tearing through towns and villages outside Bristol. His daughter marries the cricketer and doctor, W.G.Grace.

1830 Bristol's 'Slavery Election' held. Bristol abolitionists, led by the Bristol & Clifton Female Anti-slavery Society, call for immediate not gradual emancipation of the enslaved throughout the British empire.

1831 Reform Riots in Queen Square. The Mansion House, Customs House, Bishops Palace and other buildings such as those in Queen Square are destroyed – all anti-Reform targets.

1831 Brunel begins work on the Clifton Suspension Bridge. Building stops in 1836 and the project is abandoned in 1853. Work restarts in 1862 and the bridge is eventually opened on 8 December 1864. The final cost of the project is £100,000, about £45,000 over budget. Brunel does not live to see the completion of this wonderful bridge, he died in 1859, aged just 53.

1831 Bones belonging to the Bristol Dinosaur (Thecodontosaurus Antiquus, to give it its proper name) are discovered in a quarry on Durdham Downs. The dinosaur is similar in size and table manners to the Diplodocus and is thought to be one of the oldest of all the giant plant-eating reptiles dating back some 210 million years. Now scientists have even been able to pinpoint the exact spot that the big beast called home. In 1881, local geologist Charles Moore

Bristol riots of 1831

Three days of rioting in Queen Square...

The Queen Square riots began on 31 October 1831 and remain one of the most serious outbreaks of civil disobedience in the history of England. The disturbance is thought to be connected to uprisings across the country sparked by the rejection by the Lords of the Reform Act. However, there is evidence that the fighting was a local uprising in protest at a corrupt City Corporation: it was more of a revolution than a riot.

It all kicked off thanks to the arrival in town of the Recorder of Bristol, Sir Charles Wetherell, a committed opponent of reform Sir Charles pitched up on 29 October to preside over the Court of Assizes. Two days later, the centre of Bristol was in flames. The fires could be seen in Newport and Sir Charles was forced to escape from the Mansion House in disguise by clambering over rooftops.

The Bristol Riots lasted for three days and were centred on Queen Square. The Mansion House, Excise Office and Custom House were torched and the Toll House destroyed. Prisoners were released and the prisons set on fire at Bridewell, New Gaol and Gloucester County Gaol.

Private houses on two sides of Queen Square were destroyed. A watercolour of the riots by TLS Rowbotham (on show at the City Museum and Art Gallery in Queen's Road) shows the mob being attacked by soldiers from the 14th Light Dragoons, or the Bloody Blues, as they were known. The 3rd Dragoon Guards, who were based in the city, were thought to be sympathetic to the cause, which could explain why Bristol was controlled by the rioters for three days.

The arrival of Sir Charles Wetherell may have sparked the riots, but it's likely he was the catalyst for the uprising against a 'rotten' Corporation. The Corporation had become secretive, out of touch with the city and, by 1831, was as unpopular with the Tories as it was with the masses.

In 1833, a Royal Commission on Municipal Corporations investigated the Bristol Corporation and reported that: 'The ruling principle of the Corporation appears to have been, at all times, the desire of power, the watchful jealousy that nothing should be undertaken within the limits of the city over which they cannot, at pleasure, exercise their control.'

'Queen Square Riot' by Scott Buchanan Barden © Scott Buchanan Barden

identifies the dinosaur's stomping ground as being in the Belgrave Terrace area off Blackboy Hill, just a rock's throw from the Downs. The area has now been built on, so no more evidence can be found, not that any more fossils are needed. In 1975, five tonnes of Thecodontosaurus bones were found in a quarry near Bristol and the whole lot was taken to the University for further study. It took 25 years for the Bristol Dinosaur Project to secure the funding they needed to start work. In 1999, a team of palaeontologists began the laborious process of separating rock from bone. Needless to say, they're still at it.

1832 Reform Bill finally passes in parliament finally giving a whopping five per cent of (the male) population a vote.

1833 Emancipation Act finally grants freedom to the enslaved throughout the British Empire in 1834, but only after an obscene £20 million compensation is given to the slave-holders. Even then the enslaved must serve an unpaid four year 'apprenticeship'. The loan that the British government took out to pay for the compensation wasn't paid off until 2015.

1835 Corporation Act passes through parliament, finally the crooked ways of the old Bristol Corporation are addressed – an end to Corporation tyranny prevalent in Bristol since the days of Defoe. The bill for the Great Western Railway between Bristol and London also obtains Act of Parliament.

1836 Bristol Zoological Gardens opens.

1837 Brunel's Great Western steamship is launched in Bristol.
1838 Great Western Cotton Factory established in Barton Hill, the switch to slave-produced 'king cotton' is a slap in the face to Bristol's abolitionists. After

the bogus apprenticeship system, slavery finally ends throughout the British West Indies and Canada. Bristol Baptist missionary William Knibb in Jamaica leads a 'Bury the Chains' ceremony to mark the end of slavery on the night of 31 July 1838.

1841 The opening of Brunel's Great Western Railway between Bristol and London. All three 'Great Westerns' (the GWR, GW Steamship Company and GW Cotton Factory), all use slave trade emancipation money to help fund their enterprises.

1843 Prince Albert visits the Great Western Dockyard in Bristol and names Brunel's new ship the Great Britain.

1847 The Bristol chocolate factory Fry's, based in Union Street, produces its first chocolate bar. This was followed in 1866 with the world's first mass-produced chocolate bar called Fry's Chocolate Cream.

1848 Hirsute cricket legend WG Grace is born on 18 July in Clematis House, North Street, Downend, though the family lived a few doors away in Downend House.

1861 The Durdham Downs in Clifton are secured as public open spaces.

1862 Clifton College opens. Its most famous old boys are Douglas Haig, the Commander in Chief of the British Army in France in World War One and John Cleese of Monty Python and Fawlty Towers fame.

1864 On 8 December, the ceremonial opening of Clifton Suspension Bridge takes place – five years after the death of Brunel. A procession sets off from the city centre, including soldiers, sailors and groups with banners representing various trades, organisations and friendly societies of the city. At least 16 bands take part, flags fly, field gun salutes are fired and church bells are rung. After the ceremony at midday there is a banquet for invited guests in the Victoria Rooms and at night the bridge is illuminated for the first time. In 1753, Bristol wine merchant William Vick left a legacy for a bridge to be built over the Avon Gorge. After 110 years of uncertainty, Vick's vision is finally realised.

1870 Gloucestershire Cricket Club is founded.

1876 University of Bristol is founded.

1881 Population of Bristol is 266,000.

1883 Bristol Rovers Football Club is founded as the Black Arabs FC at a meeting at Collins Restaurant on Stapleton Road.

1880s The tradition of a Jack-in-the-Green is resurrected in Victorian Bristol. Jack is nine foot tall, covered from head to toe in flowers and dances like a demented Morris dancer with a firework up his trousers. On the first Saturday in May, Bristol's Jack-in-the-Green still makes his way from the Arnolfini all the way to Horfield Common followed by a colourful procession of flute-blowing vegetation. Why does he do this? In order to release the spirit of summer, of course. This bizarre Victorian tradition probably has its roots in ancient pagan rituals and has only recently been resurrected in Bristol. Crowds are encouraged to follow Jack through the streets and on to his final destination, where he eventually curls up and dies.

1881 Robert Louis Stephenson writes *Treasure Island*. The Hispaniola sets sail from Bristol and Long John Silver is the landlord of the Spyglass Inn which is based on in the book is based on the Llandoger Trow in King Street and/or the nearby Hole in the Wall in The Grove.

1888 Bristol Rugby Club founded.

1894 Bristol City Football Club is founded as Bristol South End.

1896 On a rainy night on 18 September 1896, a bankrupt grocer called Charles Brown took his two daughters, Ruby and Elsie, up to the Clifton Suspension Bridge and threw them into the muddy water below. Luckily, there was a high tide that night and as the girls plunged into the water, the crew of a passing pilot boat spotted them and dragged them away to safety. Ruby suffered injuries to her spine while Elsie had only minor leg injuries. Both girls had recovered within a couple of weeks. Charles Brown was subsequently arrested and brought to trial. 'Father caught hold of me and I began to scream,' said Ruby while giving evidence in court. 'He lifted me up on the side of the bridge and put me over.' Unsurprisingly, the judge concluded that the poor girls' old man was utterly insane and should spend a considerable amount of time in an asylum.

1897 Bristol Rovers' Eastville Stadium is officially opened on 5 April with the visit of League Champions and FA Cup holders Aston Villa. Rovers lose 5-0 to set the tone for the next 89 years at Eastville.

C20th **1901** Population of Bristol rises to an estimated 330,000.

1904 Hollywood actor Cary Grant is born at 15 Hughenden Road, Horfield on 18 January. He was christened Archibald Alexander Leach.

1908 Edward Vll opens the Royal Edward Dock in Avonmouth.

1911 Bristol miners strike for three months over pay and loss of jobs.

1911 Bristol Aeroplane Works opens in Filton.

1914–18 About 55,000 men from the Bristol area enlist for World War One. More than 7,000 men from the Bristol area died.

1917 Avonmouth becomes the centre of the British chemical warfare manufacturing drive. The plant makes 20 tons of mustard gas a day. In December 1918, the plant Medical Officer reports that in the six months it has been operational, there are 1,400 illnesses reported by its 1,100 workers – all attributable to their work. There are 160 accidents and over 1,000 burns. Three people die in accidents and another four die as a result of their illnesses. There are 30 resident patients in the factory hospital tended by a doctor and eight nurses. The gas produced at the Avonmouth plant doesn't arrive in France until September 1918, two months before the Armistice.

1920 On Sunday 11 July 1920, Charlie Stephens, a barber from Bedminster, tries to shoot Niagara Falls in an oak barrel. Sadly, Charlie's barrel is way too heavy and he crashes straight onto the jagged rocks at the bottom. The following morning, an arm is rescued from the water bearing a tattoo that reads, 'Forget me not, Annie.' Charlie has previous: when he was five years old he was pronounced dead and laid in a coffin before springing back to life; at 16 he was almost run over by a coal wagon. Then he spent three years in the trenches of World War One and came home without a scratch. As well as running a busy barber's shop and bringing up 11 children with his wife Annie, Charlie fancied himself as a bit of a stuntman. First, he began performing daring tricks in a lions' den; then he parachuted from a balloon; then he dived off the Forth Bridge head first. Niagara should have been Charlie's finest hour. Instead, Bedminster's answer to Houdini had tried his luck once too often.

1925 King George V and Queen Mary open the new University buildings.

1926 Opening of the Portway between Bristol and Avonmouth.

1930 Official opening in May of Bristol Airport at Whitchurch by Prince George. Whitchurch is only the third civil airport in the country.

1936 William Canygne's historic house in Redcliffe Street is needlessly pulled down for a road scheme that never happened.

1940 Hitler claims Bristol has been completely destroyed following a night of intensive bombing on 2 November in which 5,000 incendiary and 10,000 high explosive bombs are dropped on the centre of the old city. On 24 November, the entire area that is now Castle Park is destroyed in a bombing raid. During World War Two 1,299 people in Bristol are killed by German bombing. About 3,000 buildings are destroyed and 90,000 are damaged.

1941 The infamous Good Friday air raids on Bristol see more destruction in the centre of the city plus major damage to Knowle, Hotwells and Filton. The last air raid on Bristol is on 25 April 1941, when Brislington, Bedminster and Knowle are badly hit. Prime Minister Winston Churchill visits the devastated city on 12

April 1941 and is booed by crowds amid rumours that the city's air defences are not being properly managed.

1945 Prime Minister Winston Churchill, Chancellor of Bristol University, receives the freedom of the city.

1947 Some Bristolians begin to complain about an odd buzzing noise and the Bristol Hum is born. According to the 5% of people who can hear it, the hum sounds like the dull drone of a distant aircraft. It varies in intensity from a soft background noise to an overpowering onslaught and causes headaches, nausea, dizziness and even muscle spasms.

1949 The Bristol Brabazon, the world's largest passenger airliner, makes its maiden flight from Filton on 5 September.

1952 Following the failure of the Brabazon project, the Bristol Britannia makes its maiden flight from Filton. It goes on to become the first plane to carry 100 passengers non-stop across the Atlantic.

1956 Queen Elizabeth II opens the new Council House on College Green.

1957 The Duchess of Kent opens Bristol Airport at Lulsgate.

1958 On 5 December, Queen Elizabeth II makes the first trunk dialling call in Britain from Bristol Central Telephone Exchange. Trunk dialling is making a long-distance call without the aid of an operator. She calls the Lord Provost of Edinburgh. Her call lasts two minutes five seconds and costs 10d (4p).

1959 Bristol's first curry restaurant opens. The Taj Mahal in Stokes Croft is run by Mr Ahmed, a Bengali. It is the first Indian restaurant in the West Country. Writing in Muktodhara, Bengalis In Bristol, Mr Ahmed says: 'I put a poster in the window saying "Indian Restaurant Opening Shortly". People used to come in, push the door and say "When are you opening, I can't wait for a curry!" My second restaurant was in the Centre by the Hippodrome Theatre, called Koh-I-Noor. Every night there was a fight. We used to sell curry for 3/6d. They used to eat and then run without paying. And we used to catch up with them!'

1961 The Arnolfini is established by Jeremy and Annabel Rees above a bookshop on the Triangle, Clifton.

1963 Paul Stephenson, Roy Hackett, Guy Bailey, Owen Henry, Prince Brown and others lead anti-racist protests against Bristol Omnibus Company following the company's refusal to consider black people for jobs.

1965 The Race Discrimination Act is passed by Parliament after Bristol South East MP Tony Benn takes up the campaign started by the Bristol Bus Boycott protests.

1965 The Cumberland Basin road and bridge scheme opens.

1966 The Queen opens the £10 million Severn Bridge on 8 September.

1966 Frogmore Street leisure complex opens. It's been an entertainment centre ever since.

1967 Steve Marriot writes the Small Faces hit Itchycoo Park while staying at the Grand Hotel.

1968 The first St Paul's Carnival is held with the procession trouping past the Lord Mayor of Bristol.

1969 In April, Brian Trubshaw pilots Concorde 002 on her British maiden flight from Filton to RAF Fairford in Gloucestershire. On emerging from the cockpit he says: 'It was wizard! A cool, calm and collected operation!'

1970 On 19 July, more than 100,000 people line the banks of the River Avon to watch the SS Great Britain being towed home on the last leg of her journey from the Falkland Islands.

1971 Christine Preece becomes Bristol's first woman bus driver.

1972 Theatre Royal and Coopers' Hall restored and re-opened in King Street. A large chunk of Totterdown is swept away for a road scheme that never happened.

1974 A bomb goes off in Park Street on 18 December. 15 people are injured but amazingly there are no fatalities.

1974 Royce Creasey organises the first Ashton Court Festival, a series of four Sunday events at Ashton Court. Fred Wedlock plays one of the days, as does a band called Pussy Spasm.

1975 The Arnolfini moves from the Triangle to its current site, Bush House, a former tea warehouse on Narrow Quay.

1977 Royal Portbury Dock opens.

1978 Bristol Industrial Museum opens.

1978 Louise Joy Brown, the world's first test-tube baby is born on 25 July to Lesley and John Brown of Hassell Drive, Easton.

1980 Rioting in St Paul's following a police raid on the Black and White cafe in Grosvenor Road. It is the first of the inner city riots of the early 1980s.

1982 The Watershed, Britain's first 'media centre', opens across the water from the Arnolfini. To this day, nobody in Bristol is quite sure what makes two cinemas, a bar and a gallery a 'media centre'.

1982 Bristol City FC goes bust and is reformed as Bristol City (1982). Eight of the club's highest earners agree to tear up their contracts so the club can survive. They become known as the Ashton Gate Eight.

1982 Second uprising in St Paul's.

1986 The Dug Out club closes following a campaign by police that culminates with police solicitor Richard Crowley telling the City Council's Public Protection Committee that the club is like a 'Fagin's kitchen'. The legendary club was at the heart of the DJ scene that went on to define the Bristol Sound.

1986 On 26 April, Bristol Rovers play their last ever game at their spiritual home, Eastville. It's a 1-1 draw with Chesterfield.

1991 *Blue Lines*, the first Massive Attack album is released.

1991 New shopping centre the Galleries opens in Broadmead. It's a 'totally enclosed mall with three levels of shopping and eateries and a 950-space car park' and replaces the old concrete monstrosity, Fairfax House with a new brick monstrosity. Hurrah!

1995 Portishead win the Mercury Music Prize with their debut album *Dummy*.

1996 The second Severn crossing opens. It cost about £300 million.

Tree-ology: Bristol Forest Lore

Tony D'Arpino reflects on the remnants of Bristol's ancient forests

The ancient forest of Bristol was known as Kingswood and once extended from the Cotswolds to the Severn to all of Bristol and south almost to Bath. Originally created as a hunting-forest by the Saxon kings based in Pucklechurch, it was a royal wood for over a thousand years. Today there are still remnants of this great forest.

In Norman times a court was set up to deal summarily with thieves and debtors of the Bristol Fair which took place in Old Market, outside the Postern Gate of Bristol Castle, called the Pie-Poudre Court. The name comes from the French, 'pieds poudrés' which can be translated as 'dusty feet', and was a temporary court set up for the duration of the fair to deal with travellers who were not resident in the town. It was held in the open air under an ancient oak, now the site of the Stag and Hounds public house.

In *Flora of Bristol* (1912), J W White identifies a Bristol oak of very unusual size and age in the grounds of The Holmes in Stoke Bishop. The remnant of this tree still stands there, now the site of the University of Bristol Botanic Garden. The Botanic Garden has moved a number of times over the past 130 years, leaving a legacy of other-worldly gardens and trees across the city.

Durdham Down was still a wild place just 100 years ago. Whether owned by the Society of Merchant Venturers or the highwaymen, the Downs first appears in history in an Anglo-Saxon document in 883. The Seven Sisters group of Austrian pine trees are now reduced to three, but the latest urban myth says seven saplings are doing well not far away. The famous White Tree of Bristol has changed shape and even species over the years.

Bristol's most famous pergola, Birdcage Walk, is a public tree-tunnel through the old churchyard of St Andrew's Church, which was lost in the Blitz. The urban forest has invaded this graveyard and now includes some rare specimen trees. A woodland has also overtaken Bristol's Arnos Vale cemetery. The dramatic plane trees on Narrow Quay and elsewhere on the Harbourside are the result of a national tree-planting scheme. In historical times of course there were no trees on Bristol docks, when the harbour was described as a street full of ships and a forest of masts.

On a pagan hill above the River Avon, St Mary Redcliffe church, unarguably the loveliest parish church in England, has dozens of green men. Jacks in the green and foliate masks entwine the doors of the famous north porch, with many figures hidden in a jungle of flowers. There are Green Man roof bosses in the transept and nave, a corbel holding John Cabot's whale rib beneath the tower, and a Green Man stained-glass window in the American Chapel. There is also a Green Man on the misericord in the choir of Bristol Cathedral and on the armrests of the choir stalls in St Mark's Chapel across

The rare Bristol Whitebeam is only found in the Avon Gorge and in Leigh Woods

College Green.

Apple trees are almost human and have a human lifespan of about 80 years. (Pears, however, can live for 300 years). Bristol at one time had apple orchards everywhere from the slope of Clifton Vale down to the marsh, all over St Paul's and Stokes Croft and out into the country in every direction. Of this greenbelt of twelfth-century apple orchards there are only remnants. A contemporary orchard at Goldney Garden commemorates the Long Aston Research Station, a now vanished landmark of cider-making and an important part of the agricultural history of Bristol. For a hundred years the orchards and fields south of Long Ashton were the home of a series of world-famous research institutes. Apple Wassail, the ancient singing to the orchards, a time of great good will, still happens here in the West Country on 'Old Twelvey Night' (17 January). Orchard-visiting, the singing-awake of the apples, is an ancient rite of winter.

The oldest, largest, and arguably the most beautiful yew tree in Bristol is in the churchyard of Abbots Leigh overlooking the Bristol Channel. It is a female at least 1500 years old, and possibly twice that age. The yew tree was actually once worshipped as a deity.

The Bristol whitebeam (Sorbus bristoliensis) is one of the rarest trees in the world and is found only in the Avon Gorge and Leigh Woods. It was first identified by Miss Martha Maria Atwood in 1854 at the overlook at Stokeleigh Camp in Leigh Woods. It's still there. Bristol poet, botanist, rock-climber, and whitebeam expert, Libby Houston, has rappelled down the cliffs of the Avon Gorge to botanise and discovered a new hybrid whitebeam, which has since been named after her (Sorbus x houstoniae). In Henleaze, the 800 year old Phoenix hedgerow was rediscovered 20 years ago by local botanist Sylvia Kelly.

The riverine woodlands of Bristol along the River Avon and the River Frome are lush conductors of green energy. The Frome River Walkway is a 20-mile path from Bristol to Old Sodbury in the Cotswolds. There are over 200 named woods in Bristol and the Bristol Community Forest Path follows an inner circle through many of them for 45 miles through Bristol and environs.

May the forest be your song.

1997 Roni Size wins the Mercury Music Prize with his album New Forms.

1999 Pero's Bridge opens linking the Watershed with the Arnolfini. Designed by Irish artist Eilis O'Connell and named after a slave brought back to Bristol by John Pinney, the bridge is generally regarded as one of the better things built in Bristol in recent years.

1999 The new-look City Centre opens to the public on Millennium Eve.

C21st **2000** The £97 million At-Bristol project opens, comprising Explore, Wildwalk and the Imax cinema. The project is the first stage of a £450 million urban rejuvenation scheme, covering 11 acres of Bristol's Harbourside. The smug "Harbourside" name takes over from the historic "Docks".

2001 Tony Blair is hit by a tomato during a protest against sanctions against Iraq when he opens City of Bristol College.

2001 PJ Harvey wins the Mercury Music Prize with her album Stories From The City, Stories From The Sea.

2002 In October, Bristol is short-listed for European City of Culture 2008.

2002 Downing Street insists there was nothing wrong in Cherie Blair's purchase of two Bristol flats with the help of a convicted fraudster. She faced criticism in December after confirming Peter Foster had helped her, despite earlier denials from the Number 10 press office. The flats are in the Old AA building opposite the nice Victorian toilets on Park Row.

2003 The Labour Party is swept from power in the May local elections after the best part of 30 years running the city. No party has an overall majority and it takes the local politicians a couple of weeks to come to agreement about how to share power. Strangely, the city seems to run itself perfectly efficiently without anybody being in control.

2003 Liverpool is chosen ahead of Bristol as European City of Culture for 2008. According to the judging panel, Bristol was the most European of the nominated cities, but its road system counted against it. The judges felt that the districts were 'divided by motorways'.

2003 Massive Attack make a triumphant homecoming in August with a huge gig in Queen Square. 'Keep Bristol music progressive!' is Robert Del Naja's message to his hometown crowd. He dedicates Teardrop from the Mezzanine album to Bristol.

2003 Tens of thousands of people stare into the Bristol skies on 27 November as Concorde returns to the city for the last time. For many, it's an emotional moment as the beak-nosed supersonic jet appears out of the clouds and zooms over the Clifton Suspension Bridge.

2005 Bristol is awarded Fairtrade City status in a ceremony at the SS Great Britain during Fairtrade Fortnight in March.

2005 On the same weekend in October that Aardman Animation celebrate Curse of the Were-Rabbit breaking box office records, a fire destroys the company's warehouse in St Philip's. The blaze destroys the entire collection of Wallace and Gromit props and models plus many other artefacts from the last 30 years.

2006 At the Oscar ceremony in March Aardman's Curse of the Were-Rabbit wins the gong for the Best Animated Feature. Aardman mainman Nick Park says: 'This is a great day for Aardman and most importantly recognition for the 200-plus dedicated crew that gave up over two years of their lives to work on the film.'

2006 Labour take a predicted battering in the May local elections. The Lib Dems don't have an overall majority but take control of Bristol City Council. Charlie Bolton becomes the city's first Green Party Councillor after winning Southville from Labour by seven votes.

2006 Work is halted on the Cabot Circus redevelopment and Bristol is gridlocked after a suspected Second World War bomb is discovered under the demolished Allied Carpets shop. It turns out not to be a bomb.

2006 In July, Louise Brown announces she is pregnant. Bristol girl Louise who lives in Knowle became the world's first test-tube baby in 1978.

2007 The 200th anniversary of the passing of the Abolition of Slavery Act is commemorated in a series of Abolition 200 events.

2008 Cabot Circus opens, local wags immediately call it "Car-boot Circus". Bristol becomes the UK's first Cycling City.

2010 A second Green Party councillor, Tess Green, is elected to the City Council.

2011 The £27m M Shed museum opens on the site of the old Industrial Museum on the city's Harbourside.

2011 Riots in Stokes Croft are sparked by a heavy-handed police raid on the Telepathic Heights squat opposite the controversial Tesco store on Cheltenham Road. Tesco is trashed after rioters force police to retreat.

2011 PJ Harvey wins the Mercury Music Prize for the second time with her new album Let England Shake, co-produced by John Parish who lives in Totterdown just round the corner from Patcos on the Wells Road.

2012 Bristol is the only English city to vote Yes for a referendum to elect a Mayor. George Ferguson is elected.

2013 Bristol is awarded the title of European Green Capital for 2015.

2013 Gromit Unleashed, a major public arts trail in the summer of 2013, saw 80 giant sculptures of award-winning Aardman Animations character Gromit decorate Bristol's streets. Each sculpture was individually decorated by famous names from the worlds of animation, art, fashion, film and music – from Cath Kidston to Sir Peter Blake; Joanna Lumley to Gerald Scarfe. After making Bristol their home for ten weeks, the Gromits went to auction in October 2013, raising more than £2.3 million for Wallace & Gromit's Grand Appeal, the Bristol Children's Hospital Charity.

2014 Bristol mourns the death of socialist MP Tony Benn who was first elected to parliament as MP for Bristol South East in 1950. He was forced to give up his seat in 1961 because of his hereditary peerage but was re-elected after rule change in 1963. He represented the constituency until 1983 when boundary changes made it a marginal seat and he was defeated by Tory Jonathan Sayeed in the new constituency of Bristol East. Tony Benn (April 3, 1925-March 14, 2014).

2014 Bristol Rovers are relegated from the Football League on the last day of the season following a 1-0 home defeat by Mansfield.

2014 Bristol Rugby Club leaves the Memorial Stadium on Filton Avenue and moves into Ashton Gate for the start of the 2014/15 season. The Rugby Club had played at The Mem since 1921 (on the old "Wild Bill Field" which they called a "ground").

2014 Bristol Elected Mayor George Ferguson unveils a plaque at Bristol Bus Station commemorating victory in the Bristol Bus Boycott of 1963. The opening is attended by the three surviving leaders of the Bus Boycott Dr Paul Stephenson OBE, Roy Hackett and Guy Bailey.

2014 Brisfest is cancelled after the 2013 event failed to break even.

2014 American businessman Kris Donaldson, the man in charge of organising Bristol's year as European Green Capital in 2015, leaves his post just weeks before the title is handed to Bristol. The City Council's chief executive Nicola Yates takes charge. Mayor George Ferguson explains that Mr Donaldson had "absolutely not" been sacked, but he "did not have his contract renewed".

2014 A spectacular firework display on Clifton Suspension Bridge on December 8th marks the 150th anniversary of the opening of Brunel's iconic bridge over the Avon Gorge.

2015 Clifton Suspension Bridge is bathed in green lights to mark the beginning of Bristol's tenure as European Green Capital. At the opening ceremony at the end of January, Bristol-based Cirque Bijou perform a high-wire act between the Create Centre and the A Bond warehouse. The opening ceremony also features a light projection show on the warehouse buildings accompanied by a musical score by Dom Coyote.

2015 Shaun in the City takes place in Bristol from July 6 to August 31, Artists decorate statues of Aardman's Shaun The Sheep which are then auctioned to raise money for Bristol Children's Hospital.

2016 Hundreds of people attend the funeral of DJ Derek who went missing in July 2015. His remains were found near Cribbs Causeway in March.

2016 Labour's Marvin Rees defeats George Ferguson to become Mayor of Bristol. Marvin is the first black elected mayor in Europe.

2017 Bristol University reveals plans for a £300 million campus on the site of the derelict sorting office next to Temple Meads. They subsequently demolished the venerable Cattle Market Tavern for a building that is no longer required.

2017 It is announced that the Colston Hall will no longer be named after slave trader Edward Colston when it is re-opened in 2020 after refurbishment.

2017 Peaches Golding becomes the first black Lord Lieutenant of Bristol.

2018 Mayor Marvin Rees scraps plans for a Bristol Arena near Temple Meads despite a majority of city councillors voting in favour of the scheme. Rees favours the arena being built at Filton airfield on the site of the Brabazon hangars.

2018 Green Party councillor Cleo Lake become the first black woman Lord Mayor of Bristol and promptly removes

Bristol boundaries

Why you'll need a boat if you intend to 'perambulate' the city's official boundaries...

Technically most of Bristol is water. The city council boundaries extend into the western Severn as far as, but not including, the islands of Flat Holm and Steep Holm. The total area of Bristol is about 90 square miles: 47 square miles in respect of the Severn Estuary/Bristol Channel down to the Holmes; and 43 square miles within the 'traditional' land-based boundary. However, the latter includes all the rivers, streams and brooks within that area. Thus the 43 square miles includes the areas of the River Avon, the River Frome, the Malago, the River Trym etc. This means that the actual water area of the city is even more the 47 square miles mentioned above, probably more than 50 square miles or even more.

The vast majority of that water boundary has remained the same since the grant of the Charter of Edward III of August 8, 1373 and the first 'perambulation' Charter of September 29, 1373 establishing and verifying that boundary.

Royston Griffey did a perambulation of the water boundaries during his year as Lord Mayor on September 29, 2007, including the easternmost water boundary of the City in the vicinity of Hanham Lock on the River Avon. He visited the four northern, western, southern and eastern water boundaries of the city on that day, and left a boundary stone (suitably marked) at each. The first three were visited via a Royal Navy minehunter, and the fourth visited via a launch to Hanham Lock.

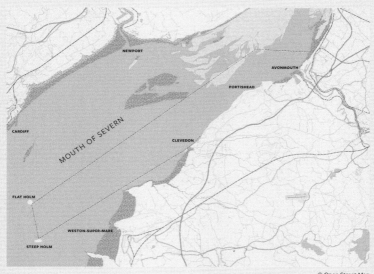

© Open Street Map

Colston's portrait from the Lord Mayor's parlour.

2019 Massive Attack play two Bristol shows on their Mezzanine tour. They build their own Steel Yard 14,000 capacity venue at Filton Airfield pretty much on the spot where Mayor Rees wants the arena to go.

2019 St Mary Redcliffe and Temple School announces that a house named after slave trader Edward Colston will instead be named after the African-American mathematician Katherine Johnson from the beginning of the new school year in September.

Compiled by Richard Jones and Mark Steeds

Made in Bristol

A tribute to our hometown heroes and sheroes, a dog and a stuffed gorilla...

Aardman Animations

Founded in 1972 by teenagers Peter Lord and David Sproxton, Aardman's first animations were for the BBC programme for deaf children *Vision On*. Nick Park joined the company in 1985 and in 1991 his short film *Creature Comforts* was the first Aardman production to win an Academy Award. Park also developed the clay modelled shorts featuring the adventures of Wallace and Gromit, a comical pair of friends: Wallace being a naive English inventor with a love of cheese, and Gromit his best friend, the intelligent but silent dog. These films include *A Grand Day Out* (1989), *The Wrong Trousers* (1993) and *A Close Shave* (1995), the latter two winning Academy Awards.

Wallace & Gromit have become two of the most recognisable characters in modern cinema. The characters are the figureheads for two major fundraising initiatives, Wallace & Gromit's Children's Foundation whoch supports UK children's hospices and hospitals and Wallace & Gromit's Grand Appeal, the charity for Bristol Children's Hospital.

Aardman are based on Spike Island near the SS Great Britain and have established Bristol as an international centre of excellence for animated film. The company name is taken from one of its early characters, a superhero created for *Vision On*. Co-founder David Sproxton has claimed that the name was a result of being unable to "find another word with more A's in it than aardvark" as a schoolboy.

Alfred the Gorilla (1928-1948)

Alfred arrived in Bristol Zoo in 1930 and quickly became one of the zoo's main attractions. His profile was further increased during World War II when visiting soldiers sent pictures of Alfred back to their home countries and articles about him appeared in the US and Australian press. After Alfred died in 1948, his taxidermic form was put on display in Bristol City Museum and Art Gallery and is still a popular attraction today.

During the Bristol University Rag Week of 1956, Alfred was stolen from the Museum. Two days later he was found by caretaker Donald Boulton in a waiting room in Bristol University's student health service building. It wasn't until 2010 that the identity of the thieves was revealed. Following the death of Ron Morgan the owner of Morgan and Sons Estate Agents in Eastville, his family and friends revealed the perpetrators were Mr Morgan, his friend Fred Hooper and another man identified only as DS who were all students at the time.

Mr Hooper, told the Bristol Post in 2010: "It was initially my idea. I was about 23 at the time and I thought it would be a great rag week jape.

"We took Alfred because he was such a big Bristol personality and he was close

239

by. It took a bit of planning, we told the museum we were making a film and that's how we got in. We knew the porter and so we were able to get a key cut to the secondary door that linked the museum to the university.

"Then we hid in the belfry until about 1am when everything was closed. It wasn't such a good idea in hindsight as the bells were still ringing and incredibly loud.

"We got into the museum and then we used the side door to get him out onto Park Row. It was very early in the morning and we stuffed him into the boot of an old Vauxhall car, that cost me £35, folded back the seats and sped off to my bedsit, in West Park, off Whiteladies Road.

"That's where he stayed for the duration and we took pictures of him in different guises. There were all sorts of stories going around, people thought Cardiff students had kidnapped him and there was a rumour he was in a cave somewhere but we never told anyone we had him.

"It was always our intention to return him and so the easiest thing was to take him to a doctor's waiting room which was just across the road. It was midday on a Saturday and we just carried him over and left him there."

Banksy (1974–)

Time was that you could hardly cross the road in Bristol without spotting a Banksy stencil. Now, there are only a few left on the city's walls and many of them are in a state of disrepair. The fact that the city's Banksy's have not been protected or preserved by the city council illustrates the Bristol's uneasy relationship with street art. On the one hand 'street art' is the most searched for term on the Destination Bristol website, on the other, Bristol City Council and Bristol Waste are clamping down on the writers.

It's the kind of hypocrisy and contradiction that has inspired some of Banksy's best work. The young Banksy started painting with the DryBreadz Crew (DBZ) also known as the BadApplez from Kingswood around 1991 and worked with graffiti writers including Tes, Kato, Lokey and Inkie. 'I started off painting graffiti in the classic New York style... but I was never good at it,' he revealed in one of his rare interviews. Not long after, he cut his first stencil.

'The ruthlessness and efficiency of it is to start revolutions and to stop wars,' he says of his weapon of choice, 'they look political just through the style'.

Easton, Bedminster, Windmill Hill and St Paul's became his canvas for images such as Mild Mild West and Abi's Wall before the international man of mystery took his art to London, Los Angeles, New York, the Israeli/Palestine security wall and elsewhere.

The first graffiti writer in Bristol was Robert Del Naja aka 3D from Wild Bunch/ Massive Attack. He was quickly followed by the Z Boyz, Inkie, FLX, Chaos, Jinx, Nick Walker and others who congregated at a Barton Hill youth centre run by youth worker John Nation. Their numbers were swelled by the likes of Cheo, Soker, Jody, Lokey and many others.

In 1989 the Barton Hill project was at the centre of a massive British Transport Police raid called Operation Anderson in which more than 70 writers were arrested and charged with criminal damage. Although none of the artists were sent to prison, they were left in no doubt that further offences would result in incarceration. Most of the artists stopped writing graffiti and those that continued flaunted the authorities knowing the consequences if they were caught would be severe. It was into this vacuum that Banksy emerged. At first, he painted freehand but moved to stencils in

Banksy: A Bristol timeline

We don't know who he is, but here's what Banksy has done in his home town...

1974: Born in Bristol area.

1991: Begins painting with DryBreadz Crew as Robin Banx. His tag appears on their work until about 1997.

1998: Paints a piece with Inkie beside the main stage at St Paul's Carnival. Collaborates with Inkie and others for the *Walls on Fire* graffiti festival at Bristol Harbourside.

1999: Mild Mild West appears in Stokes Croft. Banksy leaves Bristol for London.

2000: Returns to Bristol, to decorate the coffin of local club legend Lez Hutchinson. Solo show at Severnshed. All but three of his paintings, priced from £89 to £2,000, sold on the first day.

2001: *Banging Your Head Against A Brick Wall*, the first of Banksy's little black books, is published by Weapons of Mass Disruption.

Banksy plays in goal for the Easton Cowboys on their tour to the Chiapas region of Mexico to support the left-wing Zapatista independence movement. Because he plays in goal, there is speculation that Banksy is called after the late Gordon Banks (England's 1966 World Cup-winning goalkeeper) and therefore his real first name is Gordon.

2002: Weapons of Mass Disruption publishes *Existencilism*, Banksy's second little black book. It is dedicated to 'All people with a vicious disregard for common sense.'

Banksy tags the side of the Thekla floating nightclub. On the Thekla website, customers vote overwhelmingly to keep it, but Bristol City Council paints over it. Banksy returns to the same place soon after, and stencils an image of the Grim Reaper in a little jollyboat. The piece is now in M Shed.

2004: Banksy publishes *Cut it Out*, the third and final little black book. Greenleaf Bookshop in Bristol is selling Banksy signed prints for £40-£80.

2006: Landlord JJ Gorman removes an early Banksy stencil from the outside wall of the Full Moon pub in Stokes Croft, Bristol after several attempts to 'steal' it.

Paints Well-Hung Man, the famous window-hanging nude lover mural on Frogmore Street, Bristol. The Frogmore Street piece is allowed to stay after overwhelming support from people in the city. Nearly 500 Bristolians respond to the council survey, with 97 per cent voting to keep it.

2007: Banksy's iconic Mild Mild West mural in Stokes Croft wins BBC Radio Bristol's public poll to find an

Alternative Landmark for the city. The mural gets 47% – more than double its nearest rival, the old industrial chimney stack at Troopers Hill in St George.

2009: Banksy is credited with single-handedly saving the Bristol economy with his show Banksy vs Bristol Museum, staged at the City Museum and Art Gallery on Queen's Road. According to research carried out by the Museums Libraries and Archives Council the show (which ran from June to August) attracted 308,719 people; 106,744 visitors lived within 25 miles and 201,975 lived farther away. Visitors who stayed in Bristol generated additional income of £6,169,610 by staying visitors. Day visitors spent a total of £4,238,736. According to a leaked copy of the contract between the museum and Banksy, the artist was paid a fee of £1 to exhibit his work. Apart from taking over the two main galleries and the central space, Banksy's work was scattered around the Museum, often hidden among existing exhibits. The Paintpot Angel remains on permanent display on the plinth to the left of the central staircase.

2010 A Barcode Leopard stencil is lost from the wall of an end-of-terrace house in Pembroke Road, Clifton when a new house is built next to it. There is speculation that the piece is still there, but 'buried' under the new house.

2011: Banksy releases a limited-edition print of a Tesco Value Petrol Bomb to raise money for the defence fund for the squatters arrested in the 'Tesco Riots' that followed a raid on the Telepathic Heights squat in Stokes Croft. The 2000-edition print is sold

at the Bristol Anarchist Book Fair for £5. The proceeds are split three ways between the defence fund, the People's Republic of Stokes Croft and Coexist who run the Hamilton House project in Stokes Croft where the Bookfair took place.

2012: The Gorilla on Fishponds Road is painted over by the new owner of the building. Attempts to restore it are only partially successful.

2013: The stencil removed by landlord JJ Gorman from the wall of the Full Moon in Stokes Croft (see 2006) is sold for £26,000 at the Smile Britannia auction at the House of Commons. Half the money goes to the Bristol-based Temwa charity that supports people in northern Malawi and the other half goes towards renovation at the Full Moon.

2014: Mobile Lovers appears on a wall outside Broad Plain Boys' Club. Some of the lads arrive early at the club and realise the piece may be valuable so remove it and take it inside. It is rumoured that they were about to put the piece on eBay when youth workers arrive and realise it is a Banksy. Mobile Lovers is sold to a private collector for £403,000.

The Grim Reaper is removed from the Thekla when the boat goes into dry dock for repairs.

The 'lost' Barcode Leopard from Pembroke Road, Clifton (see 2010) is 'found' when it goes on display at an open evening at Nailsea School. The architect husband of a textile teacher at the school removed the stencil from the wall with the owner's permission and it spent four years stored under a bed.

Bristol City Council removes the

Banksy's Girl With A Pierced Eardrum is one of his few remaining pieces in Bristol

'KSY' lenticular piece on railings at the Eastville Park roundabout. Although it was never claimed by Banksy, those in the know say it was definitely his work.

Girl With A Pierced Eardrum appears on a wall at the back of a recording studio near Spike Island on Bristol's Floating Harbour. It parodies the famous Girl With A Pearl Earring by Johannes Vermeer, replacing the earring with an alarm box fixed to the wall. The piece is vandalised within hours with a splatter of dark paint.

2015: The Grim Reaper from the Thekla goes on display at the nearby M Shed museum. The piece is on long-term loan from the Thekla.

Dismaland opens at the Tropicana in Weston-super-Mare. The event is Banksy's most ambitious project to date and he claims to have completed it in six months after walking past the abandoned Tropicana site and looking inside through a gap in the fence. Banksy labels the Tropicana event as 'The UK's Most Disappointing New Visitor Attraction.' The ticket website crashes under the weight of demand although many claim the malfunction is deliberate to add to the dismal experience.

2018: Banksy offers to help save Bristol libraries from closure. At a cabinet meeting Mayor Marvin Rees confirms the artist had s been in touch. No further details are given, but plans to close 17 of the city's 27 libraries are scrapped.

order to be able to put up pieces quickly reduce the risk of apprehension. Some of the older writers remember Banksy being on the fringes of the Barton Hill scene and a faded piece bearing his tag remains there.

Tony Benn (1925-2014)

Tony Benn was a left-wing Labour politician and a Bristol MP for more than 30 years. On 1 November 1950, Tony Benn was elected to succeed Stafford Cripps as the Labour candidate for Bristol South East. However, Benn's father was created Viscount Stansgate in 1942 when Winston Churchill increased the number of Labour peers to aid political work in the House of Lords so when Stansgate died in 1960 Benn inherited his title and was automatically prevented from sitting in the House of Commons. A by-election was called in Bristol South East. Benn stood as the Labour candidate and was re-elected with an increased majority of 13,000.

An election court found that the voters were fully aware that Benn was disqualified, and declared the seat won by the Conservative runner-up, Malcolm St Clair, who was at the time also the heir presumptive to a peerage.

Within two years, though, the Conservative Government of the time, which had members in the same or similar situation to Benn's changed the law. The Peerage Act 1963, allowing lifetime disclaimer of peerages, became law shortly after 6pm on 31 July 1963. Benn was the first peer to renounce his title, doing so at 6.22 pm that day. St Clair, fulfilling a promise he had made at the time of his election, then accepted the office of Steward of the Manor of Northstead, disqualifying himself from the House (outright resignation not being possible). Benn returned to the Commons after winning a by-election on 20 August 1963, increasing his majority to 15,479.

Tony Benn remained the MP for Bristol South East until the seat was abolished for the 1983 election and replaced with Bristol East which effectively changed it from being a safe Labour seat into a more marginal constituency. Benn applied to stand in the safe Labour seat of Bristol South but Michael Cocks was chosen ahead of him so he stood in Bristol East and was defeated by 1,789 votes in the Tory's national landslide victory of that year. Benn returned to the House of Commons in 1984 when we was elected as MP for Chesterfield in a by-election. He served the Chesterfield constituency until his retirement in 2001.

Ernest Bevin (1881-1951)

A founder member of the Transport and General Workers' Union, Bevin became the Union's first Secretary in 1921. He was born in Winford near Bristol and lived at 39 Saxon Road, St Werburgh's, where there's a blue plaque in his honour. In World War Two, Churchill made Bevin Minister of Labour and National Service. He is best known for introducing a scheme for young conscripts to work in coal mines rather than join the forces – hence the term Bevin Boys. He was Foreign Secretary from 1945 to 1951.

Blackbeard (c1680-1718)

Edward Teach, better known as Blackbeard, was a Redcliffe boy who became the world's most notorious pirate. He was renowned as a shrewd tactician and established a pirate fleet that controlled many passages in the Caribbean. He was a fearsome character and placed burning tapers in his beard when going into battle. He is also said to have chewed broken glass before interrogating prisoners so blood would flow

from his mouth.

Blackbeard was killed when British naval Lieutenant Robert Maynard was sent by Virginia Governor, Alexander Spotswood, to track him down. He was tricked into boarding Maynard's ship the Jane, but Maynard had concealed his men in the hold and a terrible battle ensued when they confronted the pirates on deck. The battle ended when Blackbeard's head was cut off. It's said that his body was thrown into the sea and swam seven times around the ship before sinking. It's also claimed that the top half of Blackbeard's skull was taken to Wiiliamsburg in Virgina where it was decorated with silver and used as a puch bowl.

Elizabeth Blackwell (1821-1910)
The first woman doctor, Elizabeth Blackwell was born in Counterslip, St Thomas in 1821 and also lived in Wilson Street, St Paul's. She emigrated to America with her family where she qualified as a doctor. On eventually returning to England, she became the first woman to be enrolled on the British Medical Register and was an ardent campaigner for the reform of the medical profession.

Isambard Kingdom Brunel (1806-1859)
The great engineer's legacy to Bristol is Temple Meads railway station, the SS Great Britain and Clifton Suspension Bridge, plus various bridges and bits of railway. Strangely, there is only one monument to Brunel in Bristol: a fairly anonymous affair tucked out of the way in the Temple Quay redevelopment.

Tony Bullimore (1939-2018)
On October 28, 1966 Tony and his wife Lalel Bullimore opened the Bamboo Club, in St Paul Street, St Paul's. It was the city's first 'West Indian Entertainment Centre' and hosted many famous American and Jamaican artists including Bob Marley and Jimmy Cliff as well as being headquarters for the Bristol West Indian Cricket Club. Bullimore was also opened the Granary club on Welsh back in 1968 with Dave Bilk, Acker Bilk's brother. However, he is best known as being the round-the-world yachtsman who famously capsized 1,500 miles south west of Australia in 1997 and spent five days trapped in an air pocket in the upturned hull of his yacht before being rescued.

John Cabot (?-1500)
John Cabot set sail from Bristol in 1497 in a small ship, The Matthew, in search of the Far East. Instead, he discovered North America. Anyone who tells you that Columbus was the first European to land on the continent knows nothing. A replica of The Matthew is now moored alongside the SS Great Britain in Hotwells. The Cabot Tower on Brandon Hill was built to in 1897 to commemorate the 400th anniversary of Cabot's voyage.

Princess Campbell MBE (1939-2015)
Princess Campbell arrived in Bristol from Jamaica in 1962 and soon afterwards became the first black person to work in the Wills cigarette factory. She left Wills to become a nurse and witnessed appalling racism which led to black nurses being forced to work unfair shifts and being overlooked for promotion. Many black nurses became depressed and left the profession. When Princess Campbell applied for a position as ward sister, she was overlooked and a less qualified and inexperienced white nurse was promoted ahead of her. Eventually the hospital apologised and a

few years later Princess Campbell was made a ward sister at Glenside Hospital in Fishponds. Although it has long been recorded that Princess Campbell was the first black ward sister in Bristol, she was actually the second. May Tanner from Southmead was the first when she became a ward sister at the BRI in 1966 after qualifying as a State Registered Nurse in London. In the 1980s Princess Campbell helped set up the United Housing Association in response to the difficulties faced by black people in finding accommodation in Bristol. She was awarded an MBE in 2011 for services to the community

Princess Caraboo (1792-1864)

Mary Willcocks, a cobbler's daughter, fooled Bristol for three months in 1817 as Caraboo, Princess of Javasu. She turned up at a cottage in Almondsbury speaking in a strange tongue. Many people tried to identify her language until a Portuguese sailor, claiming comprehension, announced that she was from an island in the East Indies. He said she was brought to Bristol against her will and was a person of rank. She maintained the ruse, never lapsing from her peculiar tongue and even managed enough consistency for a dictionary to be created. Her beautiful manners and peculiar habits captivated everyone, but she was eventually found out and a benefactress quietly shipped her to America.

Mary Carpenter (1807-1877)

The 19th-Century social reformer was the daughter of the Minister of the Unitarian Church in Lewins Mead. Moved by the plight of homeless children in Bristol, she opened the Red Lodge reform school for girls in 1854 on a site which is now covered by the Colston Hall.

Thomas Chatterton (1752-1770)

He was either the Nick Drake of the 16th Century or the Dom Jolly of ecumenical prose. The story of Bristol's doomed boy poet is the stuff of rock and roll mythology. Born next door to St Mary Redcliffe Church in 1752, the teenage Chatterton was clearly one of life's more reflective souls. With time to ponder, he became obsessed with odd bits of medieval manuscript that he found stored away in Redcliffe Church. Eventually, he began writing poetry in the name of an imaginary 15th Century monk called Thomas Rowley. Rowley's challenging 'work' was at first authenticated and then universally applauded and Chatterton set off for London to pursue his literary career.

Sadly, all his attempts were greeted with indifference. Apparently crushed by the criticism, Chatterton swallowed a bottle of arsenic and was found dead at his home on 24 August 1770. This gifted, rebellious youth later became a hero to the romantic and pre-Raphaelite poets, several of whom, notably Keats and Coleridge, wrote poems about him. He became regarded as the first Romantic poet. A statue of Chatterton used to stand outside St Mary Redcliffe Church, but fell into disrepair and was removed. The house that Chatterton grew up in is on the other side of the dual carriageway from St Mary Redcliffe and is currently a café.

Chris Chalkley (1957-)

Founded the People's Republic of Stokes Croft in 2006. PRSC's aim is to make Stokes Croft the city's cultural quarter by promoting community creativity in order to
generate financial and spiritual wellbeing. It's a philosophy that has brought Chalkley

into regular conflict with the city authorities who seek to impose top-down culture in Bristol and to eradicate community expression, particularly in the form of street art. Chalkley's background is in the wholesale china trade and he founded Stokes Croft China in order to pursue his philosophy of community art and to fund the activities of PRSC through sales at the shop in Jamaica Street. (www.prsc.org.uk)

Jane Couch (1968-)

After being expelled from school in her hometown of Fleetwod, Lancashire, Jane Couch lived 'a life of booze, drugs and street fighting'. She took up boxing and moved to Bristol where she trained at Tex Woodward's Spaniorum Gym in Easter Compton. In 1998, Jane Couch became the first officially licensed female boxer and adopted the nickname name ' The Fleetwood Assassin' and the motto, 'man or woman, if you take me on, you're history'. She won five world titles.

Initially, the British Boxing Board of Control refused to grant Couch a professional licence on the sole ground that she was a woman. Fighting for gender equality, she claimed sexual discrimination and supported by the Equal Opportunities Commission, and managed to have this decision overturned in 1998. She announced her retirement on 1 December 2008, saying she intended to continue as a boxing promoter. At the time, she remarked, "Boxing has been my life for a long time and it always will be, but I'm not going to miss getting my head smashed in." She was honoured with the MBE by Prince Charles in 2007.

Sir Humphry Davy (1778-1829)

Born in Penzance in 1778, Davy pursued his scientific career in Dowry Square, Hotwells. He discovered laughing gas and invented the miners' safety lamp.

Sherrie Eugene (1964-)

TV personality Sherrie Eugene was one of Bristol's first black women role models when she appeared on the HTV local news in 1982. Sherrie's first TV job was as a signer – she learned sign language to communicate with her profoundly deaf sister Judy – and went on to become a popular TV personality co-hosting the *Good Neighbour Show* with Fred Wedlock. She is an active community campaigner and supports several organisations and charities working with deaf people. She was presented with a Lord Mayor's Medal for service in the community.

George Ferguson (1947-)

The 'Red Trousered Philanthropist' has done more to shape a creative vision of Bristol than any number of planners and developers with their mind-numbing plans for Cabot Circus or absurd justifications for uniformly bland live/work 'quarters'.

George, who is famed for wearing red trousers and being on Channel 4's Demolition programme, is one of the country's leading architects and is a passionate believer in building sustainable communities by reclaiming land and buildings. He has also been a Merchant Venturer, but we'll forgive him that. He has been in Bristol since his student days in the 1960s and has been the creative force behind many leading initiatives. George's vision is best realised in his Tobacco Factory and Bristol Beer Factory projects in Southville which paved the way for the boom of independent businesses migrating to North Street.

The Tobacco Factory was originally part of a much grander scheme under which **247**

George would have created an 'urban village' on the sites of all the former tobacco industry buildings in Southville. His Canteen bar in Stokes Croft swiftly became the focal point for the alternative movement and he tried to discourage big chains from clogging up Bordeaux Quay with Stag and Hen Parties by opening the Harbourside Bar by way of encouraging similar local businesses to reclaim the bit outside the Watershed. George was President of the Royal Institute of British Architects from 2003 to 2005 and has won numerous awards for his work. He became the first elected Mayor of Bristol in 2012.

Keith Floyd (1943-2009)
Legendary snorter of claret and one of the first TV celebrity chefs, the bon viveur's bon viveur used to have his very own restaurant on Chandos Road, in Redland. He died in 2009, aged 65.

Claudia Fragapane (1997-)
Claudia Fragapane is a British artistic gymnast who came to prominence at the 2014 Commonwealth Games, where she was the first English woman to win four gold medals since 1930. Claudia went to School in Whitchurch at St Bernadette's Catholic Secondary School and is a member of the Bristol Hawks gymnastics club in Easton. In 2015, Fragapane was part of the women's gymnastics team that won Great Britain's first-ever team medal, a bronze, at the World Artistic Gymnastics Championships. She competed at the 2016 Summer Olympics in Rio de Janeiro.

WG Grace (1848-1915)
Cricket's first ever superstar was an extremely bearded and notoriously fierce fella who annihilated bowlers and intimidated batsman for Gloucestershire and England. William Gilbert Grace was born in Downend in 1848; he played 22 times for England between 1880 and 1899, scoring 1,038 runs. He was a GP in Bristol with a surgery in Stapleton Road, Easton from 1881 to 1895.

Cary Grant (1904-1986)
Hollywood's smoothest ever leading man was born to Elias and Elsie Leach in Hughenden Road, Horfield. The small terraced house bears a blue plaque which reads, 'Archibald Alec Leach, better known as Cary Grant, was born here on 18 January 1904.' After attending Bishop Road School in Bishopston, he won a scholarship to Fairfield Grammar School in Montpelier, where there is a plaque commemorating the school's most famous pupil. It doesn't mention that Grant was expelled. The exact reason for the expulsion is unclear, but on one occasion Grant said it was because he was found in the girls' lavatory. Grant had a confused and unhappy childhood. His father was a womaniser who had a son by another relationship. When Cary Grant was 10, he left home to go to Boy Scouts one evening and on his return found his mother had disappeared. In fact, she had been placed in the Fishponds Country Home for Mental Defectives by his father. His father never told Grant what had happened to his mother, but in 1935, he learned that she was still alive in an institution. By the time he found out his mother was still alive, Grant was already on his way to becoming one of Hollywood's greatest ever leading men. He was introduced to the theatre at the Bristol Hippodrome where he worked as a caller and, in 1920, he headed for the USA along with a troupe of acrobats from the Hippodrome.

Archie Leach became Cary Grant in 1932 when Paramount purchased his contract. Part of that contract stipulated that he change his name. Paramount gave him a list of Anglo-Saxon sounding surnames, and the man known as Archie Leach became Cary Grant. Grant established himself in a series of screwball comedies such as *The Awful Truth* with Irene Dunne, *Bringing Up Baby* with Katharine Hepburn, *Girl Friday* with Rosalind Russell and *Arsenic and Old Lace* with Priscilla Lane. Alfred Hitchcock was a great admirer of Grant's smooth, charming, yet complex screen persona and once described him as: 'The only actor I ever loved in my whole life'. Grant appeared in such Hitchcock classics as *Suspicion, Notorious, To Catch a Thief* and *North by Northwest*.

Apart from being a great actor, it transpired that Grant was also a famous adventurer with LSD. During the filming of the movie *Operation Petticoat* with Tony Curtis, he told astonished reporters that his relaxed condition was due to the insights he had achieved using the then experimental mind drug on about 60 occasions. 'I have been born again,' Grant said. 'I have been through a psychiatric experience which has completely changed me.'

Grant was a proud Bristolian and returned to the city many times to visit his mother. Sometimes hundreds of fans would turn out to welcome him 'home' when they knew he was arriving in town. He continued to visit Bristol regularly, even after her death. Cary Grant died just hours before he was due on stage for *A Conversation With Cary Grant* in Iowa on 29 November 1986. A bronze statue was unveiled in Millennium Square in December 2001. Perhaps the many dilemmas in his life are best summed up by Archibald Leach himself who said: 'Everyone wants to be Cary Grant. Even I want to be Cary Grant.'

Sarah Guppy (1770-1852)

Sarah Guppy was an engineer, inventor, designer, campaigner, reformer, writer, environmentalist and businesswoman. She was born in Birmingham in 1770 and 1795 she married a Bristol merchant called Sam Guppy, and they made their home in Queen Square. In 1811, she patented a form of suspension bridge that she intended should be built at Clifton but the principle could be applied anywhere. In 2016 Sarah Guppy made the national newspapers and the *Oxford Dictionary of National Biography*. *The Independent* called her "the woman behind Britain's most famous bridge" (i.e. Clifton Suspension Bridge, which is famously attributed to Isambard Kingdom Brunel). She wasn't; they got it wrong. Although she may have offered advice to the young Brunel on his Clifton one, and to Scottish civil engineer Thomas Telford on his Menai Bridge in North Wales.

Sarah is said to have made models for Brunel although none survive. Later Sarah moved to Clifton's Richmond Hill, where her heritage plaque remains. Her son Thomas's plaque is in nearby Berkeley Square. Thomas was Brunel's business partner: he funded Brunel's projects and designed the engines for the SS Great Britain. The Guppys did a lot for Bristol and for the Brunel.

Roy Hackett (1928-)

One of the leaders of the Bristol Bus Boycott along with Paul Stephenson, Owen Henry, Prince Brown and Guy Bailey, Roy was also one of the founders of St Paul's Carnival in 1968. He arrived in the UK from Jamaica in 1952 and settled in Bristol in the late 50s. Like many black people he struggled to find anywhere to live because of the widespread policy of 'No Blacks, No Irish, No Gipsies, No Dogs'. In response, Roy and others set up the Commonwealth Co-ordinated Committee in 1962 to challenge Bristol City Council and other bodies to make changes.

Ian Holloway (1963–)

Bristol Rovers player and manager who hails from Kingswood. Ollie gained cult status for the bizarre way in which he expressed himself at press conferences when he was manager at Queens Park Rangers. There's an excellent collection of his quotes called *Let's Have Coffee: The Tao of Ian Holloway* (Toilet Books,) which contains such gems as 'Every dog has its day and today is woof day! I just want to bark!'

Bob Hope (1903–2003)

Yes, that Bob Hope. The legendary Hollywood entertainer spent his early years at 326 Whitehall Road and 14 Clouds Hill Avenue St George, next to St George's Park where he received a permanent memory of Bristol - a scar on his head. On a visit to the Colston Hall in 1952, he remembered: 'I had a little dog and one day I saw some boys ill treating it. I ran out to protect it and one of them threw a stone. It hit me on the temple. Every once in a while when I look in the mirror, I can still see the scar'

On a previous visit to Bristol in 1943, Hope met his former next-door neighbour Annie Pugh. Asked if he remembered her, Hope replied: 'Remember her? Oh sure: I was four at the time and we were going steady.'

David 'Syd' Lawrence (1964–)

Gloucestershire cricketer David Valentine Lawrence played in five Tests and one One Day International for England from 1988 to 1992. Lawrence was a popular, wholehearted if inconsistent fast bowler, whose career ended with a terrible injury in a game in New Zealand in 1992. In the middle of his delivery stride, Syd's knee cap shattered, the noise of it reaching as far as the boundary. He was never able to play for England again and was eventually forced to retire from the sport at the age of 29. Later he made a career for himself in bodybuilding.

The Mabbutts

The nearest thing that Bristol has to a football dynasty. Ray Mabbutt played almost 400 League games for Bristol Rovers between 1957 and 1969. Younger son Gary overcame diabetes to follow Ray into the Rovers first team and he played 122 League games between 1978 and 1982. He then moved to Spurs and went on to win 16 England caps. He was awarded an MBE for his services to football, but most fans will remember him as the bloke with the squeaky Bristol accent. The elder brother, Kevin, was regarded as having more potential than Gary and played for Bristol City between 1977 and 1981 before joining Crystal Palace where his career was cut short by injury. He moved to America where he owns an exclusive restaurant in Santa Fe, California. Ray Mabbutt died in October 2016 aged 80.

Kassam Majothi (1924–2002)

Kassam Majothi, his wife and six children fled persecution under Idi Amin in Uganda in 1972 and ended up in a refugee camp in Watchet, near Minehead in Somerset. Kassam visited Bristol and spotted a business opportunity for a small shop in St Mark's Road, Easton and in 1978 set up Bristol Sweetmart. Four decades later Sweetmart is still run by the Majothi family and is the centre of the buzzing community in and around one of Bristol's most interesting streets.

Paul McGann (1959-)

He will be forever remembered as the I from *Withnail & I* and the eighth *Doctor Who*. McGann lives in Clifton and tries to avoid blokes in pubs who shout 'we've come on holiday by mistake' at him. He was special guest at the opening of the Katmandu in the Colston Tower after being a regular at the take-away in Easton for 16 years.

Precious McKenzie MBE (1936-)

The little fella with the big dumbells was born in Durban, South Africa. He is the only Bristol celebrity whose father was killed while hunting crocodiles. McKenzie became a top weightlifter in South Africa, but wasn't allowed to compete because he is black. He moved to England, made Bristol his base and went on to become British and World Champion and represent Britain in three Olympic Games between 1968 and 1976. McKenzie was a hugely popular local character who worked tirelessly to promote sport, especially with youngsters. He lived in Leighton Road, Southville, trained at the Empire Gym in St Paul's and worked at the Ashton tannery. Legend has it that

World Weightlifting Champion Precious MCKenzie with World Heavyweight Champion Muhammad Ali circa 1973

the Queen was late for an official engagement because she was so determined to see Precious McKenzie win his third Commonwealth weightlifting gold medal. The 4ft 11in tall McKenzie was nicknamed the 'Pocket Rocket'. Although he now lives in New Zealand, Precious is fondly remembered as one of Bristol's finest adopted sons.

Stephen Merchant (1974-)

Former *Venue* magazine work-experience hack turned award-winning comedy writer and Ricky Gervais' lanky other half added some unmistakable touches of Bristolian weirdness to the BBC 2 sitcom *The Office*.

John Nation (1962-)

The 'Godfather of Bristol Urban Art'. John Nation, from Barton Hill, was incarcerated when he was a teenager for his part in football violence. He took his GCSEs while behind bars and used the six months to evaluate his future options. On his release, he began volunteering as a youth worker at Barton Hill Youth Club. This coincided with Nation discovering graffiti (or aerosol art as he calls it) on a visit to Amsterdam. He was profoundly affected by the art form and it has become his lifelong passion.

By 1985 he had set up street art sessions at the Barton Hill Dug Out at the youth club and young writers from across the city flocked there, inspired by the hip-hop and street art movement from New York and its expression in the form of Martha Cooper and Henry Chalfant's book *Subway Art*, films such as *Wild Style* and the music from the likes of Grandmaster Flash, Zulu Nation and Rocksteady Crew.

Nation was charged with conspiracy following the Operation Anderson raid of 1989 when more than 70 graffiti writers (most with a connection to the Barton Hill Dug Out) were arrested and charged with criminal damage and other offences. Nation was acquitted. He has continued to champion urban art in Bristol and beyond and in 2014 set up the Where The Wall street art walking tours which have won numerous awards. (www.wherethewall.com). According to Banksy "John Nation, that shouty, red-faced, little social worker who made it all happen, has had more impact on the shape of British culture over the last 20 years than anyone else to come from the city. And I bet none of the cops who arrested him can say that."

Nipper The HMV Dog (1884–1895)
The Bristol-born dog (part bull terrier with a trace of fox terrier) was bought as a pup in 1884 by flamboyant local artist Mark Barraud. Fame beckoned after Mark's death when his brother Francis painted an oil painting in 1895 of Nipper listening to an old phonograph which was chosen to be 'the loyal mutt' for the His Master's Voice advertising trademark.

Batook Pandya MBE (1945–2014)
One of the city's leading campaigners against racial discrimination, Batook Pandya was one of the founders of Stand Against Racism and Inequality (SARI) in 1988. Mr Pandya came to Britain from Kenya in 1963 when he was 17 and initially worked as an engineer for British Aerospace. Following Batook's sudden death in 2014, Mayor George Ferguson described him as "a giant in Bristol public life with a passion for fairness and cultural integration".

Colin Pillinger (1943–2014)
The son of a Kingswood gas-fitter, the world's only inter-planetary Wurzel admits he was: 'rubbish at chemistry at school and dreamt only of playing for Bristol Rovers'. Despite getting Damien Hirst and Alex James from Blur to work on the art and sound, the Mars Express orbiter and its Beagle 2 probe still haven't sent so much as a postcard. Professor Pillinger died in May 2014.

Samuel Plimsoll (1824–1898)
Born at 9 Colston Parade, Redcliffe in 1824, Plimsoll came up with the idea of putting a line on a ship's hull which would fall beneath the waterline if the vessel was overloaded. This led to the Merchant Shipping Act of 1876, which made it law for all boats to carry a Plimsoll Line.

Dave Prowse MBE (1935–)
Dave Prowse was born and raised on the Southmead council estate. Originally a weightlifter, Prowse was not only the original Green Cross Code Man, but the body of Darth Vader. Why only the body? Can you imagine hearing: 'May the force be with you, me babber' in a deep Bristolian accent? He once worked as a bouncer at Romeo and Juliet's nightclub on Nelson Street.

Sir Michael Redgrave CBE (1908–1985)
Actor, author, director, producer, great grandfather of thespianism and one half

of the couple that gave us Vanessa and Lynn Redgrave and Natasha and Joley Richardson. Born the son of a silent film actor in Bristol in 1908, this giant of stage and screen made his first professional appearance at the Liverpool Playhouse in 1934 and went on to star in movies such as Hitchcock's The Lady Vanishes, Kipps, The Dam Busters and Mourning Becomes Electra, which earned him an Oscar nomination.

Sir Tony Robinson (1946-)
Once upon a time, he was Baldrick in Blackadder and everybody loved him. Then he switched his TV career to digging up tiny fragments of iron-age flint in Channel 4's *Time Team*. Live archaeology? Whatever next? Robinson was knighted in the 2013 Birthday Honours. Supports Bristol City.

Isaac Rosenberg (1890-1918)
Arguably the greatest of the First World War poets, Rosenberg was born in Bristol in November 1890 of Russian Jewish immigrant parents. The Peugeot garage diagonally opposite Temple Meads stands on the site of his birthplace.

JK Rowling (1965-)
Joanne Kathleen Rowling was born in Chipping Sodbury near Bristol to an apprentice engineer and a French/Scottish mother. She also lived in Yate and then Winterbourne. If you'd bumped into a young JK, you would have found her (in her own words): 'A shy, snotty, swotty little kid and very insecure'. Hermione Granger is supposed to be based on her. While living in the Bristol area, she wrote her first book, *Rabbit*, at the age of six.

Richard Scudamore (1959-)
The flappy-eared, former Premier League chief executive is originally from Soundwell, Kingswood. He went to St Stephen's Primary school, where he no doubt shaped his views on supporting Bristol City. If he still lived in Soundwell, you'd probably find him in the Jolly Cobbler checking his pools coupon of a Saturday evening.

Dr Paul Stephenson OBE (1937-)
Paul Stephenson came to prominence as one of the leaders of the Bristol Bus Boycott in 1963. The Bristol Omnibus Company, backed by the leadership of the Transport and General Workers Union and the Bishop of Bristol refused to employ black drivers and conductors. Black activists Stephenson, Guy Bailey, Owen Henry, Roy Hackett and others organised a boycott of Bristol buses which was championed by Tony Benn and Harold Wilson. Eventually the company gave in. Paul Stephenson went on to become one of Britain's leading civil rights campaigners. In 2007 he became the first black person to be awarded the freedom of the city of Bristol and in 2009 he was awarded an OBE for his services to equal opportunities and to community relations in Bristol.

Randolph Sutton (1888-1969)
The music hall performer who popularised 'On Mother Kelly's Doorstep' was born in Anglesea Place, Clifton in 1888. Sutton was able to pack in his job as an accounts clerk at Robinson's packaging in Bedminster when he won a talent contest while on holiday at Burnham-on-Sea. His trademark stage outfits were pink or mauve suits and he quickly became one of Britain's most popular comedians before the Second World

Jane Duffus selects 10 influential women

Eveline Dew Blacker (1884-1956): Designed the Bristol cenotaph.

Frances Power Cobbe (1822-1904): Anti-vivisectionist who lobbied for women to receive votes and degrees.

Elsie Griffin (1895-1989): Chocolate packer who became the nation's sweetheart via her singing.

Annie Kenney (1879-1953): Northern mill worker who came to Bristol to run the South West branch of the WSPU.

Fleur Lombard (1974-1996): First female firefighter to die on of duty.

Elizabeth Pearce ?-1925): Ran the Bristol fish market and sent kippers to Bristolians on the front line in WW1.

Elizabeth Ralph (1911-2000): City archivist hid precious items during WW2 to save them from the Blitz.

Sarah Siddons (1755-1831): Popular 18th Century actor whose ghost reportedly haunts Bristol Old Vic.

Pat VT West (1938-2008): Performance poet and activist who kicked up a stink for women's liberation in the 1970s.

Susannah Winkworth (1820-1884): Social housing reformer who overhauled slum accommodation in Hotwells.

Jane Duffus is the author of The Women Who Built Bristol (Tangent Books)

War. He was offered 'On Mother Kelly's Doorstep' by a London coalman called George Stevens who was inspired to write the song by the sight of two ragged children sitting on a doorstep. Stevens sold the song for five shillings on condition that it was performed by Sutton. A few years before he died in 1969, Sutton recorded a nostalgic trip around Bristol for television with his old friend Sir John Betjeman.

Maggie Telfer OBE (1959-)

Originally from Northumberland, Maggie Telfer grew up in Durham and moved to Bristol after working on homeless projects in Swansea. She was one of the founders of Bristol Drugs project in 1986 and was still its CEO in 2019. Maggie's inspirational work has been key to building and shaping the alcohol and drug services that support thousands of people across Bristol.

Clifton Lido: Swim, eat, drink at this restored Victorian pool © Destination Bristol

Best of Bristol

Eating out

Bocabar at Paintworks: famous for its super-friendly staff

British and European

Adelina Yard
Welsh Back BS1 4SL
www.adelinayard.com

Bulrush
21 Cotham Rd South, Cotham BS6 5TZ
www.bulrushrestaurant.co.uk

Casamia
8, The General, Lower Guinea Street BS1 6FU
www.casamiarestaurant.co.uk

Cauldron
98 Mina Road, St Werburgh's BS2 9XW
www.thecauldron.restaurant

Chomp
10 St Nicholas Street BS1 1UQ
www.chompgrill.co.uk

Clifton Sausage
7 Portland Street, Clifton BS8 4JA
www.cliftonsausage.co.uk

Bristol Lido
Oakfield Place, Clifton BS82BJ
www.lidobristol.com

Glass Boat
Welsh Back BS1 4SB
www.glassboat.co.uk

Hotel du Vin
The Sugar House, Lewins Mead BS 1 2NU
www.hotelduvin.com

Ivy Clifton Brasseries
42 Caledonia Place, Clifton BS8 4DN
www.theivycliftonbrasserie.com

Jamaica Street Stores
37-39 Jamaica Street, Stokes Croft BS2 8JP
www.jamaicastreetstores.com

Lock Up
182 Church Road, St George BS5 9HX
www.thelockupbristol.com

Spiny Lobster
128 Whiteladies Road, Clifton BS8 2RS
www.thespinylobster.co.uk

International

Bauhinia
5A Boyce's Avenue, Clifton BS8 4AA
www.bauhinia-bar.co.uk
Pan-Asian bar and restaurant in Clifton with a famous downstairs dining room.

Bellita
34 Cotham Hill, Cotham BS6 6LA
www.bellita.co.uk
Spain, Morocco and the Middle East are the tapas themes. Great atmosphere.

Bravas
7 Cotham Hill, Cotham BS6 6LD
www.bravas.co.uk
Spanish food, wine and beer.

Gilan Kitchen
518 Filton Avenue, Horfield BS7 0QE
www.gilankitchen.co.uk
Former Persian restaurant Kookootoo.

La Guinguette
www.laguinguette.co.uk
243 Cheltenham Road BS6 5QP
Fantastic French restaurant in Stokes Croft. They serve Raclette, an Alsace-Lorraine speciality, which involves a little oven and cooker on your table.

Best fish & chips

Eat in	Take away
Catch 22	**Argus Fish Bar**
38 College Green BS1 5SP	**114 West Street, Bedminster BS3 3LR**
Fishers	**Bishopston Fish Bar**
35 Princess Victoria Street, Clifton BS8 4BX	**264 Gloucester Road, Bishopston BS7 8PB**
Loch Fyne	**Bristol Fryer**
51 Queen Charlotte Street BS1 4HQ	**431 Gloucester Road, Bishopston BS7 8TZ**
Rendezvous	**Farrows**
9 Denmark Street BS1 5DQ	**146 Wells Road, Totterdown BS4 2AG**
Salt and Malt	**Fishminster**
Cargo 2, Gaol Ferry Steps BS1 6WD	**267 North Street, Southville BS3 1JN**
Sea Pearl	**Kelloway Fish Bar**
73 East Street, Bedminster BS3 4HB	**4 Kellaway Avenue, Redland BS6 7XR**
Spiny Lobster	**Magnet Fish Bar**
128-130 Whiteladies Road BS8 2RS	**55 Dean Lane, Bedminster BS3 1BS**
	Reel Soul
	4a Gloucester Road, Bishopston BS7 8AE

Street food

Where to find the city's tastiest take-aways

Poet and chef Miles Chambers uses recipes handed down by his grandmother Agnes Spencer

The street food scene has taken off in recent years, with some of the finest and best-value meals in town served from a variety of specially-adapted vehicles and from stalls. Look out for **Pickled Brisket**, **Sausagenius**, **Gopal's Curry Shack**, **Smoked Vegan**, **Ah Ma's Dumplings**, **Niang's Thai Snacks** and many more at these street food hotspots.

Farmers' and Producers' Market

Corn Street/Wine Street BS1 1HT
Every Wednesday 9.30am-2.30pm
www.bristol.gov.uk/web/st-nicholas-markets
Mainly fresh and local produce with take-away food including Little Hollows

Pasta, Moist (artisan hummus), Pullins Bakers.

Finzel's Reach Market

Old Temple Street, St Thomas BS1 6BX
Every Friday 12-2pm
@FinzelsReachMarket
Regular stalls include Smoked Vegan (burgers), Wood Chop Pizza, Murray May's (kebabs), the Little Taquero (tacos) and Chef de Maison (New Orleans gumbo).

Harbourside Street Food

The Centre, BS1 5TX
Weds & Thurs 12-2.30pm, Sat & Sun 11am-4pm
www.theharboursidemarket.co.uk
Regulars include Grate (grilled cheese

sandwiches), Open Sesame (Persian wraps), Los Hermanos Combinados (fried chicken), Omar's Kitchen (Indian veggie), Pizza Bike.

St Nicholas Market Glass Arcade
Corn Street BS! 1HT
Monday-Saturday
www.bristol.gov.uk/web/st-nicholas-markets
Bristol's leading food hub. Traders include Portuguese Taste, Pieminister, Moorish Cafe, Caribbean Wrap, Big Juice Bar, Matina (Kurdish wraps and kebabs), Sausage Station, Royce Rolls, Eat-A-Pitta.

Temple Quay Market
The Square, Temple Quay BS1 6EA
@TempleQuayMarket
Every Thursday 12-2pm
Regulars include Agnes Spencer Amazing Jamaican Cuisine, She Sells Sushi, Alp Mac (mac and cheese), High Steaks (steak sandwiches), King Fin (fish wraps), Mango Hub (south Indian biryani).

Tobacco Factory Market
Raleigh Road, Southville BS3 1TF
Every Sunday 10am-2.30pm
www.tobaccofactory.com/sunday-market
Busy market with fresh produce, arts and craft, vinyl, bike repairs, plants and more. Regular street food offerings include Agnes Spencer's Amazing Jamaican Cuisine, Gopal's Curry Shack, She Sells Sushi, Pieminister, Scotch Eggsellence, Bombay Brunch.

Vegan Market
Corn Street BS1 1HT
Every Monday 10am-3pm
www.veganbristol.com
Stalls include Mel's Kindness Kitchen (vegan cheese), Miller Green

(burgers), Elspeth's Kitchen (cake and treats), Kickin' Kimchi (Korean kimchi), Thali (curry and dahl).

Wine Street Market
Wine Street BS1 1HT
Tuesdays and Fridays 11am-2.30pm
www.bristol.gov.uk/web/st-nicholas-markets
Stalls include Blue Fire Smoke and Grill (Caribbean/Cajun), DonDon (Japanese donburi), Enggi's Kitchen (Indonesian), the Italian Sausage, Momo Bar (Tibetan dumplings).

Whiteladies Road Farming & Fair Trading Market
108 Whiteladies Road BS8 2RP
Every Saturday 9am-2pm
Excellent Farmers' market specialising in fresh fruit and veg, bread and fish from the Spiny Lobster. Snowdrop Cottage does a range of scotch eggs, cakes and pies if you're peckish.

Poco
45 Jamaica Street BS2 8JP
www.pocotapasbar.com
Spanish and Moroccan-inspired tapas.

Real Habesha
146 Stapleton Road, Easton BS5 0PU
Try the injera. The national dish of Ethiopia is a sourdough flatbread made for ripping, dipping and sharing.

Salt & Pepper
139 Lawrence Hill BS5 0BT
www.saltandpepperbristol.co.uk
Proper Polish home cooking, big portions, modest prices and a very warm welcome.

Simply Thai
67 Gloucester Road, Bishopston BS7 8AD
Tiny, unpretentious, good simple cooking.

Sky Kong Kong
2, Haymarket Walk, Bearpit BS1 3LN
www.skykongkong.co.uk
Highly recommended organic Korean cafe. Great-value three-course set menu.

Thai Garden
100 West Street, Bedminster BS3 3LR
Super-cheap-and-cheerful Thai place. Good for groups and sharing meals.

Tuk Tuck
5 St Stephen's Street BS1 1EE
Asian street food cafe. Great value.

Best Sunday roasts

1766 Bar & Kitchen
Bristol Od Vic Foyer, King Street BS1 4ED
www.bristololdvic.org.uk/food-drink/bar-kitchen

Bank Tavern
8 John Street BS1 2HR
www.banktavern.com

Dark Horse
172-174 Church Road, St George BS5 9HX
www.thedarkhorse-bristol.co.uk

Glass Boat
Welsh Back BS1 4SB
www.glassboat.co.uk

Lock Up
182 Church Road, St George BS5 9HX
www.thelockupbristol.com

Love Inn
84 Stokes Croft BS1 3QY
www.theloveinn.com

Dine With I
Pop up. Frankie Loves Ava, 52 Wells Road, Totterdown BS4 2AG
@dinewithI

Pasture
2 Portwall Lane, Redcliffe BS1 6NB
www.pasturerestaurant.com

Punch Bowl
23 Old Market Street BS2 0HB
www.punchbowlbristol.com

Pump House
Merchants Road, Hotwells BS8 4BZ
www.thepumphouse.com

The Ox
43 Corn Street BS1 1HT
www.theoxbristol.com

Thanks to Bristol Sunday Roast Facebook group

Viet Kitchen
25-27 Stokes Croft, BS1 3PY
Very good pho and gyoza. Nice atmosphere, good value and down to earth.

Chinese

Beijing Cooking Pot
7 Perry Road, Park Row BS1 5BG
www.beijing-cooking-pot.business.site

Chilli Daddy
Baldwin Street and Queens Road
www.chillidaddy.com

Lucky Chef
197 Easton Road, Easton BS5 0HQ
www.luckychef.co.uk

Mayflower
1a-5a Haymarket Walk, Bearpit BS1 3LN
www.mayflowerbristol.com

Thousand Leaves
160 Muller Road, Eastville BS7 9RE

Curry

Al's Tikka Grill,
33 Ashton Road, Ashton BS3 2EG
www.alstikkagrill.com

Chilli
**The Old Ambala Sweet Centre
371 Stapleton Road, Easton BS5 6NE**
www.chilli-theoldambala.co.uk

Bandook,
Cargo 2, Wapping Wharf BS1 6ZA
www.wappingwharf.co.uk

Chai Shai
4 Jacob's Wells Road, Hotwells BS8 1EA
www.chaishaikitchen.co.uk

Devs Kerala
80 Gloucester Road, Bishopston BS7 8NU
www.devskeralabristol.com

Desi Indian Tapas
198 Wells Road, Totterdown BS4 2AX

Eastern Taste
94 St Mark's R0ad, Easton BS5 6JH
www.easterntastebristol.com

Kathmandu
Colston Tower, Colston Street BS1 4ZE
www.kathmandu-curry.com

Krishna's Inn
4 Byron Place, The Triangle, Clifton BS8 1JT
www.krishnasinn.co.uk

Nutmeg
10 The Mall, Clifton BS8 4DR
www.nutmegbristol.com

Raj
35 King Street BS1 4DZ
www.raj-bristol.co.uk

Urban Tandoor
13 Small Street, BS1 1DE
www.urban-tandoor.com

Urban Kohinoor
211 Whiteladies Road, Clifton BS8 2XS
www.urban-kohinoor.com

Italian

Bella Vista
2B Victoria St, Bristol Bridge BS1 6DT
www.bellavista-restaurant.co.uk

Bomboloni
225 Gloucester Road, Pigsty Hill BS7 8NR
www.bomboloni.net

Best breakfasts

Acapella
184C Wells Road, Totterdown BS4 2AL
www.acappellas.co.uk

Arts House
108A Stokes Croft BS1 3RU
www.theartshousecafe.co.uk

Bristolian
2 Picton Street, Montpelier BS6 5QA
www.thebristolian.co.uk

Brunel's Buttery
Wapping Wharf BS1 6UD

Cafe Britalia
111 Wick Road, Brislington BS4 4HE
www.cafebritalia.co.uk

Cafe Mocha
54 Union Street BS1 2DL

Ceres Coffee
32 Stokes Croft BS1 3QD
www.coffeeceres.com

Faraway Tree
136 Church Road, St George BS5 9FE
@thefarawaytreebristol.co.uk

Friska
Victoria Street, St Thomas BS1 6BY
(and other locations)
www.friskafood.com

Grounded
421-425 Gloucester Road, Bishopston BS7 8TZ
(and other locations)
www.cafegrounded.co.uk

Harry's Diner
Fowlers, 2-12 Bath Road, BS4 3DR
www.fowlers.co.uk/cafe

Hart's Bakery
Lower Approach Road, Temple Meads BS1 6QS
www.hartsbakery.co.uk

Kitchen
The Station, Silver Street BS1 2AG
www.thestationkitchen.co.uk

La Ruca
89 Gloucester Road, Bishopston BS7 8AS
www.laruca.co.uk

Lockside
1 Brunel Lock Road, Ashton BS1 6XS
www.lockside.net

Lounge
227-231 North Street, BS3 1JJ
(and other locations)
www.thelounges.co.uk

Mark's Cafe
291 North Street, Southville BS3 1JU
www.marksbread.co.uk

Marmalade Cafe
3 Worrall Road, Clifton BS8 2UF
@WeAreOrange

Neck Of The Woods
St Werburgh's Com Ctre, Horley Road BS2 9TJ
www.neckofthewoodscafe.co.uk

Old Book Shop
65 North Street, Bedminster BS3 1ES
www.theoldbookshop.co.uk

Olive & Fig
9 Nelson Parade, Bedminster BS3 4JA

Primrose Cafe and Bistro
Boyce's Avenue, Clifton BS8 4AA
www.primrosecafe.co.uk

Souk Kitchen
277 North Street, Southville BS3 1JP
www.soukkitchen.co.uk

Spike Island Cafe
133 Cumberland Road, BS1 6UX
www.spikeisland.org.uk

Totterdown Canteen
141 Wells Road, Totterdown BS4 2BU
www.totterdowncanteen.co.uk

Windmill Hill City Farm
Philip Street, Windmill Hill BS3 4EA
www.windmillhillcityfarm.org.uk

Zak's
92-95 St Nicholas Market BS1 1LJ

Napolita Cafe
83 Mina Road, St Werburgh's BS2 9XP
www.napolitapizza.co.uk

Pasta Ripiena
33 St Stephen's Sreet BS1 1JX
www.pastaripiena.co.uk

Vincenzo's
71A Park Street, BS1 5PB

Pizza

Acapella
184C Wells Rd, Totterdown BS4 2AL
www.acappellas.co.uk

Bosco
96 Whiteladies Road BS8 2QX and 29 Regent Street BS8 4HR
www.boscopizzeria.co.uk

G Brothers
2B High Street, Easton BS5 6DL
www.gbrotherspizza.co.uk

Franco Manca
20 Clare Street BS1 1YG
www.francomanca.co.uk

Flour & Ash
203B Cheltenham Road, Stokes Croft BS6 5QX
www.flourandash.co.uk

Mission Pizza
Pop-up at various local markets and events

Taste of Napoli
32 The Horsefair BS1 3HZ
www.tasteofnapoli.co.uk

Luna Express
107 Stokes Croft, BS1 3RW

Ray's Pizza @ Crofters' Rights
117-119 Stokes Croft, BS1 3RW

Renato's La Taverna Dell'Artista
33 King Street BS1 4DZ
www.renatosbristol.wordpress.com

Caribbean

Agnes Spencer's Amazing Jamaican Cuisine
Pop-up takeaway stall usually at Tobacco Factory Market every Sunday. Run by Miles Chambers who was Bristol's first City Poet when he was appointed to the role in 2016.

Bikkle Island
402 Stapleton Road, Easton BS5 6NQ

Cafe Cuba
69 Stokes Croft BS1 3QP

Calypso Kitchen
Unit 3, Gaol Ferry Steps Wapping Wharf BS1 6WE
www.calypsokitchen.uk

Caribbean Croft
30 Stokes Croft, BS1 3QD
www.caribbeancroft.co.uk

Caribbean Wrap
Glass Arcade, St Nicholas Market BS1 1JQ

Food
1 Nelson Parade BS3 4JA

Glen's Kitchen
St Paul's Learning Centre, 141 City Road BS2 8YH

Jaspers
22 North Street BS3 1HW
www.jamaicandiner.co.uk

King's Head
277-279 Whitehall Road BS5 7BH
www.thekingshead-bristol.co.uk

Nadine's Caribbean Cafe
131 Wilder Street, St Paul's BS2 8UT

Rice & Things
120 Cheltenham Road, Stokes Croft BS6 5RW
www.riceandthings.co.uk

Best burgers

Atomic Burger
189 Gloucester Road, Bishopston BS7 8BG
www.atomicburger.co.uk

Burger Bear
213 Gloucester Road, Bishopston BS7 8NN
www.burgerbearuk.com

Burger Joint
83 Whiteladies Road BS8 2NT, 240 North Street
BS3 1JD
www.theburgerjoint.co.uk

Ciao Burger
207a Gloucester Road, Bishopston BS7 8NN
www.ciaoburger-bristol.co.uk

Five Guys
46 Cabot Circus BS1 3BX
www.fiveguys.com

Hobgoblin
69-71 Gloucester Road, Bishopston BS7 8AS
@Hobgoblin.bristol

Honest Burgers
21 Clare Street BS1 1XA
www.honestburgers.co.uk

Oowee Diner
54 Picton Street BS6 5QA; 202 North Street, BS3
1JF; 65 Baldwin Street BS1 1QZ
www.ooweediner.com

Three Brothers
Welsh Back BS1 4SB
www.threebrothersburgers.co.uk

Yoyo Burger
6 Byron Place
www.yoyoburger.com

Greek, Turkish, North African

The Athenian
Unit 16, Cargo 2, Wapping Wharf BS1 6WD
www.theathenian.co.uk
Greek street food.

Assilah
194 Wells Road, Totterdown BS4 2AX
Well-established Moroccan bistro with occasional belly dancing events.

Biblos
62a Stokes Croft, BS1 3QU
www.biblos.co.uk
Lebanese-inspired wraps.

Lona Grill House & Juice Bar
281 Gloucester Road, Bishopston BS7 8NY
www.lonagrillhouse.com
Large Lebanese grill with big selection of freshly squeezed juice.

Cyprus Kebab House
6 St Michael's Hill, BS2 8DT
Long-established homage to Cyprus just off Park Row.

Beirut Mezze
13a Small Street BS1 1DE
www.beirutmezze.com
Atmospheric cellar restaurant in the centre of town.

Matina
The Glass Arcade, St Nick's Market BS1 1JQ
Lengthy lunchtime queues for homemade Kurdish kebabs.

Souk Kitchen
59 Apsley Road, Clifton BS8 2SW, 277 North Street, Southville BS3 1JP
www.soukitchen.co.uk
Award-winning food from north Africa and the eastern Mediterranean.

Vegetarian & Vegan

Babaganoush
81 St Nicholas' Road, St Paul's BS2 9JJ
@babaganoushbristol
Great-value middle-eastern mezze, wraps, juice bar and cakes.

Bristol Anarchist Solidarity Easton (BASE)
14 Robertson Road, Easton BS5 6JY
www.network23.org
Sunday evening vegan meal every week at 6.30pm.

Cafe Conscious
182 Avonvale Road, Barton Hill BS5 9SX
www.cafeconsciousbristol.co.uk
Jamaican diner focussed on making a social contribution by hosting local women's groups and youth workshops around music and art therapy. The vision is to enable families and communities to enjoy the benefits of a healthy lifestyle by understanding more about food education and nutritional balance.

Cafe Kino
108 Stokes Croft, BS1 3RU
www.cafekino.coop
It used to be a cosy little living-room space on Nine Tree Hill where you could chat to the chef as they whipped you up a chickpea curry. It's now the giant cafe-cum-community space at 108 Stokes Croft, permanently bustling and with more MacBooks on its tables than the Apple store. All-vegan menu includes breakfasts, burgers, salads, soup, cakes, snacks and the most excellent Kino chips.

Eat A Pita
St Nick's Mkt, Gloucester Rd, Triangle, Broadmead
www.eatapitta.co.uk

March of the vegans

Sol Wilkinson explains how Bristol has become the centre of the plant-based food universe

For the average Brit awakening from cryogenic sleep, the country must appear to have gone completely insane. There's Brexit; a crumbling government; soaring temperatures exceeding those of Spain; Old Market's becoming a nice place for a walk; and, on top of all this, people are giving up meat in favour of plants. Of course, the latter is an exaggerated generalisation but the Vegan society did confirm that Britain's vegan population had risen from 150,000 in 2006 to over 542,000 in 2016 – an astounding 350% increase – and since these stats, the UK's number of plant-based lifestyles has continued to grow like a big, beautiful aubergine. Additionally, the majority of these recent converts are young people, under the age of 34, and in 2018, Kellogg's vegan poll highlighted that over half of all 16-24 year olds had at least tried a plant-based diet in the previous 12 months.

So what's to account for this surge in herbivorous millennials? Whilst many lifestyle trends play the hare of the race, quickly seized up and squeezed dry for profit by marketing directors, vegetarianism and veganism have played the tortoise. Being a vegetarian since birth and occasional vegan, I can clarify that the journey from Sosmix and lentil soups to Pizza Hut's vegan menu has been sluggish and laboured. I endured a childhood of being the only weird, pale veggie kid in my school, the mid-summer barbeques where my friend's drunk dad would wave a greasy sausage

in my face, 'Just have a bite! No one's gonna die if you eat a bit of MEAT!', and eye-rolls from nearly everyone when asked to accommodate for my diet. It was an irritating culinary protest that eventually became accepted and has now reached an accelerating take-off in popularity.

Arguably, this is rooted in its sincere, progressive ethics that cannot be brushed off as a social fad. The plant-based diet has more in common with feminism and civil rights than it does with clean eating and spiralisers. It is a political expression railing against the prejudice and barbaric injustices inflicted upon animals. It seems only logical that in an age of #MeToo, Wokeness and LGBTQ, veganism would also stand with these cultural monoliths against the systematic persecution of minority groups.

And what of the backlash? The innovative work of Russian philosopher Sveltana Boym argues that 'nostalgia has historically coincided with revolution'; the notion being that in times of imminent, seemingly subconscious social advancement, culture retreats into its shell, gazes longingly back to the past. The suggestion here is that we are either culturally or biologically frightened of change, or at least incapable of fully coping with change as it plays out in the present. This could explain why Donald Trump and Make America Great Again exist, as well as the heights of the UKIP sentiment. It explains why confused young white males, who would have

Hywel and Babs: adventurers in plant-based cuisine at Eat Your Greens in Totterdown

identified as hardcore liberals only a decade ago, are now manifesting their frustrated angst in the backwards politics of the alt-right. It also explains the technophobic resurgence of sales in vinyl and vintage clothes.

But what does it have to do with veganism? I would argue that the 'rare meat' craze, which occurred in the early 2010s – hipsters feasting on the likes of kangaroos, zebras and crocodiles – harkened back to the decadent dining of exotic animals during the era of Colonial expansion a.k.a., the good ol' days. The hope lies in the statistics that show veganism is predominantly a practice of the youth, and not just the counter-culture either. Generally, humans feel more comfortable doing something if everybody else is already doing it, and this is maybe the simplest explanation for plant-based prevalence in the mainstream.

As well as this, the distribution of family-friendly animal rights documentaries through wide-reaching streaming platforms like Netflix, such as the immensely popular Cowspiracy, has helped ease the concept into our everyday lives. The aforementioned film has also contributed to a new factor driving the vegan switch: environmentalism.

'The only ways you can effectively reduce your carbon footprint are to go vegan, stop driving to work and stop taking foreign holidays!', my dad would angrily lecture his millennial co-workers, glaring at them, stood in his cycling shorts.

'But I use energy-saving light bulbs', one of the students feebly retorted.

I've been lucky to grow up as a vegetarian in Bristol. A pseudo-bohemian, artsy and anti-corporate vibe has always lingered in the city's air – along with the smell of weed – that runs concurrent with this Jungian mass consciousness of left-leaning politics. Logically, this has led to it becoming the Petri dish of thriving veggie and vegan eateries that you can explore today.

Eat Your Greens
156 Wells Road, Totterdown BS4 2AG
@eatyourgreensbristol
Sweet and breezy cafe that boasts an all vegan menu, evidencing the utter honesty in their humorously passive aggressive name. Renowned for their 'Beasty Breakfast', a vegan full-English that may sway devout meat-eaters to the herbivorous path.

Edna's Kitchen: Castle Park
Castle Park, Wine Street BS1 3XD
www.ednas-kitchen.com
Quality falafel, hummus, soups and salad.

Exchange Cafe
72 - 73 Old Market Street, Old Market BS2 0EJ
www.exchangebristol.com
Part of music venue. Very friendly staff.

Falafel King
6 Cotham Hill, BS6 6LF; Narrow Quay BS1 4DJ
www.falafelkingbristol.com
Established 2000, these people introduced falafel to Bristol. Also home to the sensational Abu Noor pita and flatbread bakery.

Fi Real
57 West Street, Old Market BS2 0BZ
www.fireal.co.uk
Outstanding Caribbean-style vegetarian and vegan dishes plus homemade juice and great vegan cakes.

Gopal's Curry Shack
Cargo, Wapping Wharf BS1 4RW
www.gopalscurryshack.co.uk
Vegetarian and vegan Indian street food now based at Wapping Wharf, but still return to their pop-up roots at markets.

Jeevan's Sweets
415-417 Stapleton Rd, Bristol BS5 6NE
www.jeevansweets.co.uk
Vegetarian Indian restaurant, take-away and sweet centre famous for selling the best samosas in Bristol.

Koocha Mezze Bar
10 Zetland Road, Redland BS6 7AD
www.koochamezzebar.com/
Bringing the meat-centric flavours of Persia to a vegan audience, Koocha is a family-operated mezze and cocktail bar. Exhibits a chilled-out vibe whilst maintaining the amiable vibrancy that makes it ideal for a tipsy night-out with your plant-based buddies.

Luc's
21 Midland Road, St Philip's BS2 0JT
www.lucschinesetakeaway.co.uk

Xing Wang
17 Harrowdene Road, Knowle BS4 2JL
Amidst a menu of decent Chinese food, these two obscure takeaways also provide the most exquisite fried tofu; perfect for satiating late-night munchies. Ask Xing Wang for the '159 Deep Fried Beancurd with Salt & Chilli' and Luc's for the 'Salt & Chilli Tofu'. And make sure you order a couple of pots because they are ridiculously moreish.

Matter Wholefoods
3 Greenbank Road, Easton BS5 6EZ
www.matterwholefoods.uk
Fresh & affordable organic veg boxes delivered to your door by electric powered delivery vans. Home to the Bristol Vegan Breakfast Club. Check website and FB page for details.

Miller Green
www.millergreen.co.uk
Vegan delivery offering a wide-range of plant-based dishes at a good price. Favourites include cauliflower, haricot, coconut and turmeric stew, nine jewel korma and coconut sambal. The homemade coconut yoghurt is a sensation.

Oowee Vegan
65 Baldwin Street, Bristol, BS1 1QZ
www.ooweediner.com
Totally vegan burger bar – the other two
Oowee places also serve meat. Weird
and wonderful chips. Best vegan burger
in town. Garlic waffle chips are delicious.

Pepenero
15 King Street BS1 4EF
www.pepenero.co.uk
For on-the-edge vegans, it can't be
stressed enough that Pepenero's pizzas
are the closest a vegan can get to the
real deal, without sacrificing your moral
ascendancy. They also serve a fantastic
range of vegetarian pizzas, as well as
authentic Italian starters and deserts,
all prepared with the finest family
recipes and organic ingredients. They
recently relocated to one of King Street's
underground grottos, sharing a space
with one of Bristol's best craft beer
spots, the Beer Emporium.

Resbite Cafe
27 Broad Street BS1 2HG
www.resbitecafe.com
Plant based healthy food. Very calm
space in city centre. Community project.
11am-4pm Mon to Sat.

Riverside Garden Centre Cafe
Clift House Road, Ashton BS3 1RX
www.riversidegardencentre.com
Serving a variety of heartwarming
vegetarian dishes as well as constantly
having home-made cakes and fairtrade
teas on offer. Riverside was featured
in the Telegraph as one of the top 25
"gourmet garden centres" in the country.

Royce Rolls
St Nicholas Market BS1 1JQ
Established 1979, Royce Rolls serve
healthy, good-value sandwiches, rolls and
cakes.

Shadin Indian Takeaway
70 Broad Street, Staple Hill, BS16 5NL
www.shadinbristol.co.uk
Relatively unknown outside its humble
South-Glos-border-burbs, Shadin Indian
Takeaway is a treasure trove of the
tastiest vegetarian curries in Bristol.

Suncraft
26-28 Gloucester Road, Bishopston BS7 8AL
www.suncraft.co.uk
From the team behind the Gallimaufrey.

Suyuan
Grove Avenue, Queen Square BS1 4QY
www.suyuan.co.uk
Delicious, authentic, and affordable
100% vegetarian Chinese cuisine. The
restaurant is small and the food, by
western standards, adventurous. The
staff are great and it's a BYO. Just what
the doctor ordered for a relatively cheap
but classy night out.

Taste Of Napoli
32 The Horsefair BS1 3HZ
Best vegan pizza in town? Also serves a
selection of vegan pastries and croissants
and the coffee is excellent. Usually full of
young Italians so a lively atmosphere.

VX: Vegan Junk Food
123 East Street, Bedminster BS3 4ER
www.vxbristol.com
Vegans are often associated with
frailty, clear skin and immaculate bowel
movements. VX in Bedminster, a modern
pioneer of vegan cuisine, provides the
antithesis to this stereotype. Originating
in London, VX came to Bristol with
a plant-based artillery ranging from
hotdogs and burritos to patisserie and
milkshakes. I could only have dreamed of
indulging in these greasy, saturated meals
as a kid. Truly revolutionary. Don't forget
to check out the grocery and Secret
Society of Vegan merchandise sections.

Rita's or Slix?

Evie Steen poses the eternal late-night food question and rounds up a selection of post-club take-aways

Pouring out of Lakota, Love Inn, and Crofters' Rights and making their way up Stokes Croft, wobbly club goers part like the Red Sea onto either side of the road searching for the right food to hit the spot.

Rita's or Slix? The question that divides us all.

Both places have been around since anyone can remember, feeding the 5,000 chicken and chips in the early hours of Saturday and Sunday morning. Rita's has a more expansive menu – you won't catch a kebab on the menu in Slix – and a man who looks out the window smiling at passers-by. But Slix is open until 6am and serves a good portion of fries, so it's a tough decision?

These two places remain the same in the constantly changing area of Stokes Croft. Get your Rita's T-shirt whilst you tuck into your food and try to drown out the screaming of orders and overpowering chart music once you have managed to perch on one of the two chairs available. It's all part of the experience. Slix has less of the in-flight entertainment but sometimes all you want is a quick in-and-out transaction.

Needless to say you've got all the ingredients of a late-night take-away between these two places – irritating drunk people desperate for their kebab, something greasy and over-priced mayo.

Rita's
94 Stokes Croft BS1 3RJ
Slix
89-91 Stokes Croft BS1 3RD

Dennis Kebab

Where is it: 40 Cannon Street, Bedminster BS3 1BN, just off the bottom of North Street.
What to expect: Well, Bedminster is not the most buzzing area past 2am, but after the trek from town back to your home turf across the river, reward yourself with a well-deserved kebab as Dennis makes you feel right at home.
House Speciality: Chicken kebab.
Opening hours: Sun-Thurs 4pm-12.30am; Fri-Sat 3pm-3am.

Diamond Kebab and Pizza

Where is it: 28 Park Street BS1 5JA.
What to expect: This establishment is for those University of Bristol kids who like to venture further into town for a boogie than the pop-infested Triangle and can't make it back to the top of the hill for their kebab. It's even open 24h on some Wednesdays, a bit strange, but ideal for those leaving the clubs on the Triangle late on sports society night. Catch a University of Bristol versus UWE scrap outside for entertainment with your meal.
House Speciality: Lamb donner.
Opening hours: Sun-Thurs Noon-3am; Fri-Sat Noon-5am.

Grecian Kebab House

Where is it: 2 Cromwell Rd, St Andrew's BS6 5AA, up from the arches.
What to expect: Established in 1971, the Grecian is almost as well-known as the Suspension Bridge and is far more useful at 3am. Whether it's the

wide selection of £5 pizzas or a classic donner kebab in pita bread, this buzzing shop is the place to be after a night out. You'll meet the wackiest of characters, locals and students on their ways home from a night in the boho Stokes Croft.
House Speciality: Pizza. It's hard to go wrong with a choice of 24 different combinations of toppings. From the no.1 cheese and tomato for the classic yet boring experience to their no.17 – ham, egg, courgette and aubergine – a selection of toppings more insulting than pineapple.
Opening Times: Mon-Thurs 5pm-3am; Fri-Sat 4pm-5am; Sun 3pm-2am.

Taka Taka
Where is it: 3 Queens Road, Triangle South BS8 1EZ.
What to expect: A rite of passage for University of Bristol students, based in the heart of their territory, the Clifton Triangle. Taka Taka is bold, luminous and in your face. It's rare for a kebab to taste the same before the pints or vodka lemonades kick in but this place is popular day and night, taking after-club food to a whole new level.
House speciality: The Magic Roll. Chips in a kebab? Why not?
Opening times: Mon-Sat 11am-4am; Sun noon-12am.

Jason Donervan
Where is it: Queens Road BS8 1QU
What to expect: A kebab is always more enjoyable with a pun on the side. Located right on the top of the Triangle surrounded by the likes of Gravity (previously Analog, 78, Bunker, and so on), La Rocca and Lizard Lounge, you won't be short of whining drunk girls, barefoot with their heels in their hands flirting, asking for free chicken nuggets

with their cheesy chips. Staff are good humoured. They have to be.
House Speciality: Can't go wrong with anything but you have to try their donner kebab for the sake of the name.

Quigleys
Where is it: 5 St Augustine's Parade BS1 4XG.
What to expect: It's extremely popular because it's right in the centre of town located just off the harbour and the bottom of Park Street within a clutter of kebab and pizza places. Don't be put off by the queues, they move quickly. Very friendly staff who are probably funnier than the mate you came with.
House Speciality: The best gravy in Bristol to soak your cheesy chips.
Opening times: Sun- Mon 11am–3am; Tues- Weds 11am–2am; Thurs- Fri 11am- 4am; Sat 11am- 5am.

Miss Millie's
Where is it: 91 Gloucester Road, Bristol BS7 8AT (six more shops in various locations around Bristol).
What to expect: Walking into my house after work, I found my veggie flat mate, drunk, crying in the bathroom. Was it something serious? No, she'd fallen off the meat wagon. After four years of not ingesting an animal, from what I could make out through the sobbing and mumbling, she was telling me that this was the best chicken burger she'd ever eaten. Of course, I had to try it.
House Speciality: Not often will you find me stray away from my regular chips with gravy or curry sauce but take it from the vegetarian and me, their chicken burger is definitely a winner.
Opening times: Sun-Thurs 11am- 2am; Fri-Sat 11am- 3am.

Drinking

Vince Crocker and Garvan Hicky (front left) celebrate winning CAMRA Bristol Pub Of The Year at the Drapers Arms

Old Favourite Pubs

Alma Tavern
18 Alma Vale Road, Clifton BS8 2HY
www.almatavernandtheatre.co.uk
Bristol's original pub-with-theatre has
been given a new lease of life since
becoming part of the independent Zazu
group of Bristol boozers.

Barley Mow
39 Barton Road, St Philips BS2 0LF
www.barleymowbristol.com
CAMRA Bristol Pub Of The Year 2019

Beaufort
21 York Road, Montpelier BS6 5QB
Famous old-school local. Occasional dub
reggae sessions from Generals Hi-FI.

The Bell
Hillgrove Street, Stokes Croft BS2 8JT
www.bell.butcombe.com
Tuesday night is musos' night with
informal DJ set by John Stapleton and
friends. Possibly the best pub in Bristol.

Bridge Inn
16 Passage Street, St Thomas BS2 0JF
www.bridgeinnbristol.co.uk
Proper old-favourite 'local' with huge Jimi
Hendrix mural on outside wall painted by
David Blatch.

Bristol Yard
Colston Street BS1 5BD
www.thebristolyard.co.uk

Cadbury House
68 Richmond Road, Montpelier BS6 5EW

Cat & Wheel
207 Cheltenham Road BS6 5QX
www.catandwheelbristol.cascadepubs.co.uk

Christmas Steps
2 Christmas Steps BS1 5BS
www.thechristmassteps.com
Used to be the Three Sugar Loaves, a pub that for decades delivered far less than it promised. Then, in 2014, along came *Crack* magazine and Dave Smeaton of the Spotted Cow to transform it into the Christmas Steps.

Cornubia
142 Temple Street, St Thomas BS1 6EN
www.thecornubia.co.uk
Legendary Bristol real ale pub, a beacon in a metropolis of ugly office buildings.

Coronation
18 Dean Lane, Southville BS3 1DD

Cotham Porter Stores
15 Cotham Road South, Kingsdown BS6 5TZ
www.cothamporterstores.com
Legend has it that the painting on the pub wall is the work of John Lennon who ended up on the rough cider here after the Beatles' first gig in Bristol at the Colston Hall in 1963.

Clyde Arms
129 Hampton Road, Redland BS6 6JE
@theclydeatredland

Cottage
Baltic Wharf, Cumberland Road BS1 6XG
www.butcombe.com
Fantastic harbourside setting ideal for summer al fresco drinking, yet all snug and shipshape in winter. Good home-made food. Occasional folk dancing.

Eldon House
6 Lower Clifton Hill, Clifton BS8 1BT
www.theeledonhouse.com

Duke Of York
2 Jubilee Road, St Werburgh's BS2 9RS

Gastro pubs

Albion
Boyces Avenue, Clifton BS8 4AA
www.thealbionclifton.co.uk

Grace
197 Gloucester Road, Bishopston BS7 8BG
www.thegracebristol.uk

Kensington Arms
35-37 Stanley Road, Redland BS6 6NP
www.thekensingtonarms.co.uk

Pump House
Merchants Road, Hotwells BS8 4PZ
www.the-pumphouse.com

Somerset House
11 Princess Victoria Street, Clifton BS8 4BX
www.somersethouseclifton.com

Spotted Cow
139 North Street, Bedminster BS3 1EZ
www.thespottedcowbristol.com

Victoria park
66 Raymend Road, Windmill Hill BS3 4QW
www.thevictoriapark.co.uk

Famous Royal Naval Volunteer
17-18 King Street BS1 4EF
www.navyvolunteer.co.uk
The Volley is a Bristol institution (hence the Famous bit added to its name), but was, frankly a bit dull. Then in 2014 it reinvented itself as a craft beer and cider bar in a similar style to King Street 'Beermuda Triangle' neighbours Beer Emporium and Small Bar. Hurrah!

Farm
Hopetoun Road, St Werburgh's BS2 5YL
@thefarmpub

Full Moon & Attic
1 Stokes Croft BS1 3PR
www.fmbristol.co.uk
Check out Cheba's external artwork.

Golden Guineau
19 Guineau Street, Redcliffe, BS1 6SX
www.thegoldenguinea.co.uk

Greenbank Community Pub
57 Belle Vue Road, Easton BS5 6DP
www.thegreenbankbristol.co.uk
The property developers were hovering over the Greenbank pub when in stepped

Pubs with music

Bear (Bepob Club)
261 Hotwell Road, Hotwells BS8 4SF
www.thebebopclub.co.uk

Bristol Fringe
32 Princess Victoria Street, Clifton BS8 4BZ
www.thebristolfringe.co.uk

Chelsea
60-62 Chelsea Road, Easton BS5 6AU
@TheChelseaInnBS5

Crofters' Rights
117-119 Stokes Croft, Bristol BS1 3RW
www.croftersrights.co.uk

Elmer's Arms
53 Old Market Street, Old Market BS2 0ER
@theelmersarms

Friendly Records Bar
57 North Street, Bedminster BS3 1ES
@friendlyrecordsbar

Golden Lion
244 Gloucester Rd, Bishopston BS7 8NZ
@goldenlionbristol

Gryphon
41 Colston Street BS1 5AP
@gryphonbristol

Mother's Ruin
7-9 St Nicholas Street BS1 1UE
www.mothersruinbristol.co.uk

Old Duke
45 King Street BS1 4ER
www.theoldduke.co.uk

Oxford
120 Oxford Street, Totterdown BS3 4RL
@oxford.totterdown

Plough
223 Easton Road, Easton BS5 0EG
@ThePloughEaston

Red Lion
206 Whitehall Road, Whitehall BS5 9BP
www.thelionbs5.business.site

Ropewalk
5 Nelson Parade, Bedminster BS3 4JA
www.ropewalkbristol.co.uk

Toby Bywater and his chums from Zazu's to raise this Edwardian institution from its sickbed.

Green Man
21 Alfred Place, Kingsdown BS2 8HD
www.dawkinsales.com @greenmanbristol
Country pub vibe in the heart of the city. Boasts more than 150 gins.

Hare On The Hill
41 Thomas Street North, Kingsdown BS2 8LX
Proper pub – pretension and prat-free.

Hatchet Inn
27 Frogmore Street BS1 5NA
www.butcombe.com

Highbury Vaults
164 St Michael's Hill, Kingsdown BS2 8DE
www.youngs.co.uk
One of Bristol's most celebrated drinking dens. Complete with its stark wooden flooring and stark wooden seats, the Highbury is always busy and usually full of students.

Hillgrove Porter Stores
53 Hillgrove Street North, Kingsdown BS2 8LT
www.dawkinsales.com
Laid back and modestly hip boozer that attracts a genuinely varied crowd. From real ale fans to frazzled freaks, ageing hippies to youngsters who want to avoid Stokes Croft at its busiest, the Hillgrove is more popular than ever but it somehow remains one of Kingsdown's best-kept secrets.

Hope & Anchor
38 Jacobs Wells Road, Hotwells BS8 1DR
www.hopeanchorbristol.com

Inn On The Green
2 Filton Road, Horfield BS7 0PA
www.innonthegreenbristol.com
A bit of a trek to the top of Gloucester

Road but worth it. Pub food of real quality and a great guest range of real ale and ciders. A former CAMRA Bristol pub of the year.

King's Arms
168 Whiteladies Road, Clifton BS8 2XZ
www.kingsarmsbristol.com
Epitomises the recent evolution of Whiteladies Road. Years ago this was the roughest biker boozer in town. Then Whiteladies became 'The Strip' and it morphed into 'superbars' Babushka and then Stark and now it's the Kings Arms again – a multi-floored eating and drinking experience with a roof terrace aimed at the after work and student crowd.

King's Head,
60 Victoria Street, St Thomas BS1 6DE

Kingsdown Wine Vaults
31 Kingsdown Parade, Kingsdown BS6 5UE
@TheKingsdownVaults
Lovely local pub with regular poker and quiz nights and Irish music sessions. Nice garden.

Lansdown
8 Clifton Road, Clifton BS8 1AF
www.thelansdown.com
Celebrity fact: Buster Bloodvessel used to play pool upstairs when Bad Manners were in town.

Lazy Dog
112 Ashley Down Road BS7 9JR
www.thelazydogbristol.com
Good food, large garden and regular quiz and comedy nights.

Leveret Cask House
51 North Street, Bedminster BS3 1EN
www.leveretcaskhouse.com
Elegant, small two-room pub with a surprisingly large enclosed garden.

Bristol's historic pubs

Mark Steeds reveals the historical importance of a selection of Bristol pubs

Bristol Harbour Hotel
53-55 Corn Street, BS1 1HT
www.harbourhotels.co.uk
Occupying fine 1850s bank buildings in Corn Street, the current conversion takes you back to the origins of the site when it was occupied by the world-famous coaching inn, the Bush Tavern. Late 18th Century entrepreneurial landlord Weekes transformed coaching times from Bristol to London, slashing them from three and a half days to just 16 hours, the pub was synonymous with gargantuan meals and the distribution of turtle "to all parts of the kingdom". In Dickens' *Pickwick Papers* "Mr. Pickwick walked into the coffee-room of the Bush Tavern" – the author had Mr. Winkle stay here when visiting Bristol in search of Arabella Allen.

Grand Hotel
Broad Street BS1 2EL
www.accorhotels.com
Built in the 1850s on the site of two ancient inns, the White Lion and the White Hart, the hotel has had many well-known guests, from Cary Grant to the Rolling Stones. In olden times though, the inns were at the heart of Bristol politics, with Whig and Tory societies at their heart amid much plotting and planning. These pubs, along with the Rummer and Bush were the scene of many a mini-riot at election time. The White Lion was home to the pro-slavery West India Society and the Tory Steadfast Club.

Hatchet Inn
27 Frogmore Street BS1 5NA
www.butcombe.com
A remarkable survivor, located in Frogmore Street behind the Hippodrome, this half-timbered pub of 1606 claims to be Bristol's oldest. Home to the 'Bristol Boys' of national champion bare-knuckle boxing fame, outside there's another superb narrative plaque by Mike Baker to reflect this. If you like these timbered gems Ye Shakespeare of 1636 in Victoria Street is another pub worth a try.

King's Head,
60 Victoria Street, St Thomas BS1 6DE
Just post the English Revolution of 1660, and located in the rear of bombed out Temple Church and its famous leaning tower, this pub has one of the best surviving Victorian interiors in the whole of Britain. Its 'tramways' layout and ornate fittings make it the most atmospheric pub for miles around. It's in CAMRA's National Inventory of Heritage Pubs.

Llandoger Trow
King Street BS1 4ER
www.brewersfayre.co.uk
A timbered beauty of 1664, it was originally one of five gabled houses until Mr Hitler got the two nearest the river removed in the Bristol Blitz. It was rescued after the war by the Berni Brothers who revolutionised post-war eating out in Britain and expanded the pub into all three of the

surviving gables. The Berni's were also responsible for the myth that Daniel Defoe met Alexander Selkirk here in the 1710s and Selkirk's story fortmed the basis of *Robinson Crusoe*. The pub vies with the Hole-in-the-Wall as the real home of Long John Silver's pub, the Spy-Glass, in *Treasure Island*. The Duke opposite, one of the country's last surviving great jazz pubs, the 'Bog End' is an experience.

Nova Scotia
1 Nova Scotia Place BS1 6XJ
www.novascotiabristol.co.uk
Situated at the mouth of the Floating Harbour (Cumberland Basin end) and completed at around the same time, 1807, the pub is named in honour of the 1713 Treaty of Utrecht when Nova Scotia in Canada was ceded from France to Britain. This Treaty also enabled Britain to gain control of supplying slaves to the Spanish Empire via the notorious South Seas Company.

Palace Hotel
1-2 West Street, Old Market BS2 0DF
Commonly known as the Gin Palace and dating from 1870, this magnificent edifice hides an even more spectacular interior of mirrored galleries framed by brass barley-twist columns, making it a proper 'people's palace' in a hard, working-class part of East Bristol. Originally intended to be a swanky hotel for a Midland Railway terminus that never happened.

Rummer Hotel
All Saints Lane, St Nicholas Market BS1 1JH
www.therummer.net
Bristol's oldest licensed premises dating back to 1241, the pub is currently in two halves, one thriving in St Nicholas

market and the other closed and boarded up on the High Street. Famous for hosting all manner of monarchs, it is best associated with Coleridge's short lived *Watchman* magazine which was published from here in 1796, here he covered many types of radical thought and also railed against the slave trade. Nearby is the Crown in the market with an even older pedigree – or at least an even older cellar.

Seven Stars
Thomas Lane, St Thomas BS1 6JG
www.7stars.co.uk
Opposite St Thomas's church, this is the "Pub that Changed the World" for its connections with the abolition of the slave trade. Built in the 1660s, it was owned by mayor and brewer Sir John Hawkins, one of the Merchant Venturers responsible for opening up the British slave trade in 1698. By 1787 it was being run by abolitionist landlord Thompson who helped Thomas Clarkson gather vital evidence to help get the trade banned in 1807. Outside there's a splendid narrative plaque by Mike Baker to this achievement.

Stag & Hounds
74 Old Market Street, Old Market BS2 0EJ
@TheStagandHoundsBristol
Nicknamed the 'Slag & Hounds' by nearby journos at the *Post*, this large pub in Old Market Street is well old and at times has been a brewery and a maltings. Taking its name from a pursuit in the 'kings wood' that stretched from Tog Hill to the site of nearby Bristol Castle, the pub was also a sometime host of the 600-year-old pie poudre (dusty feet) court on market days. Opposite is the traditionally tiled Punchbowl, an old Rogers pub.

Lion
Church Lane, Cliftonwood BS8 4TX
www.thelioncliftonwood.co.uk
The Lion has a mythical status – in the 1970s and 1980s, this place was as trendy as it is hard to find. More Bristol bands were formed here than in any other boozer in Bristol. Now it's a perfectly agreeable local pub.

Mall
66 The Mall, Clifton BS8 4JG
www.themallpubbristol.co.uk | Tel: 974 5318

Merchants Arms
5 Merchants Road, Hotwells BS8 4PZ
Tel: 907 0037
Mer'chant n: A Bristolian male behaving in an inappropriately lairy manner while dressed in substandard clothing. Examples: scaffolder, XR3-i racer, middle-aged slob who wants a fight. Thankfully, you won't find too many merchants in this pub. There's too much wood panelling and quiet real ale appreciation for yer lads.

Miners' Arms
136 Mina Road, St Werburgh's BS2 9YQ
www.dawkinsales.com

Nova Scotia
1 Nova Scotia Place BS1 6XJ
www.novascotiabristol.co.uk
Traditional waterside pub that's salty enough to have a Captain's Room and old enough to remember pirates. Serves legendary doorstep sandwiches.

Old England
43 Bath Buildings, Montpelier BS6 5PT
www.oldenglandbristol.co.uk
Has the Old E finally rid itself of its reputation as the pub where the crusties used to go? The answer is Yes. The only pub in Bristol with its own cricket nets.

Old Fish Market
59-63 Baldwin Street, BS1 1QZ
www.oldfishmarket.co.uk
One of only two Fullers pubs in the city (the Cambridge in Redland is the other)

Old Market Tavern
29-30 Old Market Street BS2 0HB
www.omtbristol.co.uk

Old Stillage
147 Church Road, St George BS5 9LA

Ostrich
1 Lower Guinea Street BS1 6TJ
www.butcombe.com
Thought to date back to 1775, The Ostrich is one of the largest waterside eating and drinking spots in Bristol.

Phoenix
I Wellington Buildings, St Jude's BS2 9DB
www.phoenixbristol.com

Pipe And Slippers
118 Cheltenham Road, Stokes Croft BS6 5RW
www.thepipeandslippers.com
When the Pipe and Slippers replaced rough old Irish joint the Berkeley Castle in 2004, it was the first sign that Stokes Croft was changing. Famous for its Pipe Dream cocktail pint containing four shots of rum.

Port Of Call
3 York Street, Clifton BS8 2YE
www.portofcallbristol.com
Cosy, traditional pub tucked away off Blackboy Hill. Unlikely garden.

Portcullis
3 Wellington Terrace, Clifton BS8 4LE
www.dawkinsales.com

Prince Of Wales
5 Gloucester Road BS7 8AA
www.princeofwalesbristol.co.uk

Punch Bowl
23 Old Market Street, Old Market BS2 0HB
www.punchbowlbristol.com

Quinton House
2 Park Place, Clifton BS8 1JW
www.quintonhousebristol.com
A fraternal, almost cultish experience.

Robin Hood
56 Saint Michael's Hill BS2 8DX
www.robinhoodbristol.co.uk

Rose Of Denmark
6 Dowry Place, Hotwells BS8 4QL
Wonderful boozer hidden away under
the charmless Cumberland Basin flyover.

Seamus O'Donnell's
3 St Nicholas Street BS1 1UE
@seamus.odonnells
Cool Irish bar near St Nick's Market.
Survived the Irish theme bar nonsense
because it's the real deal. Try a shot of
the poteen and you've as good as kissed
the Blarney Stone.

Shakespeare
Lower Redland Road BS6 6SS
www.theshakespearebristol.co.uk

Shakespeare
68 Prince Street BS1 4QD
www.greeneking-pubs.co.uk

Country pubs

Beaufort Arms
High Street, Hawkesbury Upton GL9 1AU
www.beaufortarms.com

Bird In Hand
17 Weston Rd, Long Ashton BS41 9LA
www.bird-in-hand.co.uk

Black Horse
Clevedon Lane, Clapton-in-Gordano BS20 7RH
www.blackhorseclapton.co.uk

Crown Inn
The Batch, Churchill, Winscombe BS25 5PP
www.the-crown-inn.co.uk

Fox & Badger
Railway Lane, Wellow, Bath BA2 8QG
www.thefoxandbadger.com

New Inn
Park Lane, Blagdon BS40 7SB
www.newinnblagdon.co.uk

Pony & Trap
Moorledge Road, Chew Magna BS40 8TQ
www.theponyandtrap.co.uk

Queen Victoria Inn
Pelting Drove, Priddy, Wells BA5 3BA
www.thequeenvicpriddy.co.uk

Red Lion
Sutton Hill Road, Bishop Sutton, BS39 5UT
www.redlionbishopsutton.co.uk

Rising Sun
Church Street, Pensford BS39 4AQ
www.risingsunpensford.com

White Hart
Littleton-upon-Severn BS35 1NR
www.whitehartbristol.com

Bag Of Nails

Tony Bolger visits Bristol's famous cat pub...

The Bag Of Nails sounds like it could be a heavy metal bar. It's not. I walk in and the entire establishment is infested with cats.

It's only a bloody cat pub!

I come from a long line of dog people that goes back to the early days of trying to convince a wolf to fetch a stick. However, much like Ross Kemp as he had a bag placed over his bald head and got shoved in the back of a van on his way to meet the Taliban, I suck it up and persevere. I see a sign on the wall declaring that **PUSSY JOKES ARE NOT FUCKING FUNNY**. There's at least one thing that I and the proprietors can agree on.

There's a terrific selection of 14 ales on tap. If there weren't as many cats, I'd be really impressed. I ask for a bottle due to obvious fur ball concerns. The cat-loving barman tells me they have more than 40 to choose from. I ask for a generic IPA. He gives me a look and disappears. At this point, I notice a sign behind the bar stating **PLEASE DO NOT ASK FOR AN IPA UNLESS YOU KNOW WHAT AN IPA ACTUALLY IS**. I know that the mysterious booze is as delicious as it is unknowable. As soon as I spot this second sign, I notice all the rest. They're everywhere. The place is plastered in pub rules. Many are just bugbears that clearly annoy the landlord. There's one beside the IPA one simply warning **NO SCIENTOLOGY**.

The petulant barman returns. I'm being as fake as I can muster but

he can clearly sense that I'm a dog person. He opens the bottle and picks up a glass and makes to pour it and my perception of the world slows down. I can't explain why there's a reality-bending personal crisis whenever I order a drink. I just wish I wasn't so constantly thirsty. As quick as I can, short of diving over the bar in slow motion, I tell him I'd rather just have the bottle. He insists on putting it in a glass. He definitely knows I'm a dog person.

Utterly defeated, I go to find somewhere to sit and spot a record player on the go with a good selection of LPs and several signs advising you to **STAY THE HELL AWAY FROM MY RECORD PLAYER**. If not for the pride of tiny lions, I'd love this. **IF YOU DON'T LIKE JOHNNY CASH, SHUT UP OR GO AWAY.**

The pub doesn't smell like you'd assume. In fact, a lot of pubs that aren't infested with cats smell a hell of a lot worse. There's a large selection of board games peppered about the place. I see a young couple in the corner trying to play _Jenga_ but with the feline saboteurs, it's like the good people of downtown Tokyo trying to build a sky scraper while Godzilla and that giant butterfly thing battle for supremacy.

I take in my surroundings **DON'T START MOVING THE DAMN FURNITURE WITHOUT ASKING OR PLUG OUT MY BLOODY LIGHTS**. The landlord's personality and presence are everywhere in this pub. **NO STILETTOS AS THEY PLAY HAVOC ON MY FLOOR BOARDS**. He's clearly an eccentric and wacky tyrant. **NO STUPID CHRISTMAS JUMPERS OR STUPID INFLATABLE ANIMALS OR FISH**.

The one about the Christmas jumpers is still up and I can't imagine the place being swarmed by inflatable fish despite there being an aquarium down the road. This place is as big as a tiny pub can be without graduating into a small pub. If a miniature, live action rendition of the power struggle in *The Lion King* wasn't going on around my ankles, I'd love this place. The landlord isn't here but he is clearly as mad as a box of frogs.

NO ANNOYING SCREECHING ALL HOLOCAUST DEBATE MUST BE FACTUALLY BASED KEITH MOON WAS THE BEST

These rules are plastered everywhere, some printed on A4, some scrawled on scraps of paper. I'd need a lab to prove that some were written in human blood. If there wasn't a truculent tabby eyeballing me, I'd be utterly charmed, and this would be my new local.

So, my boozy conclusion – If you like cats, flat shoes and Johnny Cash, give The Bag Of Nails a whirl. If you like dogs, high heels and inflatable stingrays, don't.

Shakespeare
1 Henry Street, Totterdown BS3 4UD
@shakespearetotterdown
Once the home of Mad Ern (who died in 2012) and his less chaotic partner Sane Joan, the Shakespeare used to be the most peculiar pub in Bristol. Now it's nice but normal.

Sportsman
Neville Road, Bishopston BS7 9EQ
www.the-sportsman.co.uk
Bristol's pool pub with 11 full-size eight-ball tables. The Annexe Inn next door has a further three three-quarter size tables.

Spotted Cow
139 North Street, Bedminster BS3 1EZ
www.thespottedcowbristol.com
When the Spotted Cow first rebranded as 139 North, it didn't quite work. Bringing trendy North Bristol gastro pub ideas into darkest Bedminster was too much for the locals. But a change of name back to the original and a few years down the line things have changed. Great food and drink, nice garden and one of the pubs of choice for Bristol's thriving street art community.

Stag & Hounds
74 Old Market Street, Old Market BS2 0EJ
@TheStagandHoundsBristol

Star & Garter
33 Brook Road, St Paul's BS6 5LR
Closed following the passing of lock-in legend Dutty Ken, but re-opened in June 2019 under the stewardship of Bristol's premier promoter Malcolm Haynes. DJ sets and brilliant juke box.

Three Tuns
78 St George's Road BS1 5UR
www.the3tuns.com
Once a quirky dockside pub with a menu that boasted Fish Fingers and Chips In A Basket (£2.70) and Spaghetti On Toast (£2). Now a cosy, wood-panelled local. CAMRA Bristol Pub Of The Year 2012.

Victoria
2 Southleigh Road, Clifton BS8 2BH
www.dawkinsales.com
Decent backstreet pub with a staggering selection of craft beers. Fact fans, pay attention: One of Bristol's original rock and roll promoters, Johnny Midwinter, took on the Victoria in the early 1990s. He bought John Lennon's portable jukebox at auction in 1989 for £2,500. Johnny kept the jukebox in the upstairs room at the Victoria and spent years researching the discs that Lennon took on tour with him from scribbled notes that came with the jukebox. In 2004, The South Bank Show broadcast a documentary based on Lennon's jukebox. The show was commissioned just a few days after Johnny Midwinter died.

Vittoria
57 Whiteladies Road, Clifton BS8 2LY
www.thevitt.co.uk
Lovely olde worlde pub from back in the day when brass wall hangings were the only art you could ever possibly need.

Volunteer Tavern
9 New Street, Old Market BS2 9DX
www.volunteertavern.co.uk
CAMRA Bristol Pub Of The Year 2016.

Wellington
538 Gloucester Road, Horfield BS7 8UR
www.thewellingtonbristol.co.uk
Veering dangerously close to the corporate, but brought crashing back to pub reality as a pre-match meeting place for Bristol Rovers fans on matchdays.

White Bear
133 St Michael's Hill, Kingsdown BS2 8BS
www.whitebear-bristol.co.uk
One of Bristol's oldest pubs (dating back to 1650) the White Bear has always been something of a curiosity. Multi-roomed and multi-functional, it's a pleasant, unusual place with a 50-seat theatre and comedy venue upstairs in the Room Above.

White Lion
Quay Head BS1 1EB
www.wickwarbrewing.co.uk | Tel: 925 4819
A proper pub in the middle of stiletto and theme-bar land. The White Lion's spiral staircase provides the most challenging journey to a pub toilet in Bristol.

Windmill
14 Windmill Hill, Bedminster BS3 4LU
www.thewindmillbristol.com
Laid-back community pub from the same stable as the Lazy Dog and Pipe & Slippers.

Ye Shakespeare
78 Victoria Street BS1 6DR
www.yeshakespearebristol.co.uk
One of Bristol's oldest pubs dating back to 1636.

Micropubs & Brewery taps

Arbor Ales Tap Room
181 Easton Road, Easton BS5 0HQ
www.arborales.co.uk

Bristol Beer Factory Tap Room
291 North Street, Southville BS3 1JP
www.bristolbeerfactory.co.uk

Chums
22 Chandos Road, Redland BS6 6PF
www.chumsmicropub.co.uk
CAMRA Bristol Pub Of The Year 2018

Cocksure Tap Room
Unit B, Totterdown Bridge Industrial Estate, St Philips BS2 0XH
www.cocksurebrewing.com

The craft beer city

Food and drink author **Andy Hamilton** examines
Bristol's brewing credentials...

In 1978 you could buy a pint of Courage Best for about 20p. In fact, It was difficult to get anything other than a pint of Courage Best because the brewer dominated Bristol with its huge number of tied pubs. The brewery itself towered over the Floating Harbour opposite Castle Park to the east of Bristol Bridge and the air hung heavy with the aroma of hops.

Also in 1978, two brewers began building a craft beer movement that Is now the driving force in Bristol pubs and bars. Smiles' founder John Payne (who chose the name Smiles because he didn't want Courage to take him too seriously) set up the business in Colston Yard opposite the BRI in April 1978.

Within months he had a rival in the shape of former Courage managing director Simon Whitmore, who quit the brewing giants to set up the tiny Butcombe Brewery in the North Somerset countryside. In 1991 Smiles opened the Brewery Tap pub at the Colston Yard site, but by 2005, Smiles had gone into administration, the Smiles Brewery Tap eventually became a Butcombe's pub called The Colston Yard. It's now ditched the association with slave trader Edward Colston and is called the Bristol Yard. It's the oldest craft beer pub in Bristol and possibly in Britain.

Smiles brewers Roger Jones and Richard Dempster and pub landlord Rab Oark went on to create Bath Ales in 1995 – a brewery with an identity crisis because it's situated in Kingswood on the eastern fringe of Bristol, falls under the district of South Gloucestershire and has got nothing to do with Bath.

Bath Ales is now seen as a rather establishment operation especially among those looking for something crammed with hops or made with yeast scraped off the rind of an ancient cheese found in a Sumatran cave. Yet they were one of the first on the scene back when brewing in Britain wasn't a patch on what it is now. They were also one of the first to run with the American Idea that beer should be served with food. To add to their credentials rumour had it that Roger Jones, the old MD, sometimes used his homebrew kit to create some of the new beers.

In more recent times, grumpy Vince Crocker, the anti-hipster landlord and the brains and brawn behind Ashley Down Brewery also came from the home brewing tradition. After he made a few good beers, he and his mates decided that they would start a brewery together – making good-quality traditional beers. However, in his own words he, 'was the only one stupid enough to go through with it.'

Vince still brews from his garage and he mainly supplies his own micro pub the Draper's Arms on Gloucester Road. A single-room bar with no games machines, TV screens or cocktails that closes at 9.30pm.

It's a place for beer and a good chat where phone calls and headphones are frowned upon.

With such a strong commitment to good beer, Vince has also been helping out many other brewers behind the scenes. Some even make use of the Ashley Down facilities. The debonair Michael Wiper for example used to brew Wiper And True's craft beers at Ashley Down Brewery. Their tag line is, 'no ordinary beer'. The beers are eclectic in style and epitomise the craft beer movement.

Yet if it's an eclectic mix of beer you want then Arbor Ales wins hands down. This Easton-based brewer has a weekly 'freestyle Friday'; a time to experiment with new styles or tweak old recipes, it also gives scope for countless collaborations. This approach has worked and they have continued to grow over the years, they are now big enough to supply M&S with two American-style beers.

The size of the operation at Arbor might have grown but they did start off as a oneman outfit. Unlike the massive one-man and one-woman operation of Good Chemistry brewing down in the former swamps of St Phillips Marsh. Brewer Bob Clary has to be the nicest of all of the Bristol brewers and his generous attitude is reflected in his range of beers. His aim is to create a beer for everyone. He doesn't just create hop monsters as is the current fashion, he'll have one, but "what if you came to an open day and didn't like hops?" Therefore each beer is distinctly different from the one that precedes it. Bless you Bob!

It's said in Bristol that if you turn round quickly you'll bump into a BBC Wildlife cameraman, and the same is becoming true about brewers because almost directly behind Nice Man Bob's brewery, and just beyond Temple Meads station, sits the home of Moor Beer. The brewery is owned by a short, tattooed Californian named Justin Hawke and it has attached a brewery tap with some of the biggest beer nerds in the industry serving behind the bar. Justin describes his brewery as, "a Belgian farmhouse brewery with American innovation, producing beers in the British ale tradition."

If you understand this then you are well on the way to becoming a beer nerd yourself, for everyone else it is safe to say that he makes very good, very moorish and mostly rather strong beers which are full of flavour.

Whether or not the national craft beer movement began in Bristol, we certainly have an impressive beer culture here with the likes of Bristol Beer Factory, New Bristol Brewery, Crane Beer, Towels Fine Ales, Zero Degrees, Incredible Brewing Company, Left Handed Giant and Dawkins Ales. Indeed, we would need a Naked Guide in order to properly do Bristol's beer justice, now that's an idea!

● Andy Hamilton is the author of *Booze For Free* and *Brewing Britain*.

Croft Ales Tap Room
32 Upper York Street, Stokes Croft BS2 8QN
www.croftales.com

Dawkins Tap Room
Easton Brewery, Unit 2, Industrial Units, Lawnwood Rd, Easton BS5 0EF
www.dawkinsales.com

Drapers Arms
447 Gloucester Road, Bishopston BS7 8TZ
www.thedrapersarms.co.uk
CAMRA Bristol Pub Of The Year 2017

Fierce and Noble Tap Room
25 Mina Road, St Werburgh's BS2 9TA
www.fierceandnoble.com

Good Measure
2b Chandos Road, Redland BS6 6PE
@TheGoodMeasure.Bristol

Knowle Constitutional club
162 Wells Road, Totterdown BS4 2AG
@KnowleConstitutionalClub

Lost And Grounded Tap Room
91 Whitby Road, St Philips BS4 4AR
www.lostandgrounded.co.uk

Moor Beer Tap Room
Days Road, St Philips BS2 0QS
www.moorbeer.co.uk

Snuffy Jacks
800 Fishponds Road, Fishponds BS16 3TE
@sjalehouse

Wiper and True Tap Room
2-8 York Street, St Werburgh's BS2 9XT
www.wiperandtrue.com

Wooden Walls
30 Broad Street, Staple Hill BS16 5NU
@woodenwallsmicropub

Bars

1766
Bristol Old Vic, King Street BS1 4ED
www.bristololdvic.org.uk

Alchemy 198
198 Gloucester Road, Bishopston BS7 8NU
www.alchemy198.co.uk

Beer Emporium
15 King Street BS1 4EF
www.thebeeremporium.net

Brew Dog
58 Baldwin Street, BS1 1QW
www.brewdog.com

Bristol Ram
32 Park Street BS1 5JA
www.thebristolram.co.uk

Channings
20 Pembroke Road, Clifton BS8 3BB
www.greeneking-pubs.co.uk

Friendly Records Bar
59-61 North Street, Bedminster BS3 1ES
www.friendlyrecords.co.uk

Grain Barge
Mardyke Wharf, Hotwell Road, BS8 4RU
www.grainbarge.co.uk

Leftbank
128 Cheltenham Road, Stokes Croft BS6 5RW
www.leftbankbar.co.uk

No. 1 Harbourside
1 Canon's Road, Harbourside BS1 5UH
www.no1harbourside.co.uk

No. 51 Stokes Croft
51 Stokes Croft BS1 3QP
www.51stokescroft.com

Star bars

The best bars in Bristol...

Arnolfini
16 Narrow Quay, Harbourside BS1 4QA
www.arnolfini.org.uk
Like Arnolfini (which lost its Arts Council funding in 2017 and is now operated by UWE), the Arnolfini Bar has been through difficult times as a result of some questionable commercial decisions. But since Bristol Beer Factory took over managing the cafe/bar, it's back on form providing a chilled-out Harbourside vibe. Great for sitting outside on a warm day.

Bocabar
Paintworks, Arnos Vale BS4 3EH
www.bristol.bocabar.co.uk
It's Bristol's biggest bar yet has a genuinely homely atmosphere partly because it's the 'local' for the business and residential community at the mega Paintworks 'creative quarter' but also because the staff here are super friendly, efficient and welcoming. The daytime menu is excellent offering daily specials plus a deli counter, wraps and pizzas. The evening menu is pizza and they are as good as any in Bristol. Great cocktails and a wide selection of spirits complete the winning formula which has been recognised with numerous awards.

Canteen
80 Stokes Croft BS1 3QY
www.canteenbristol.co.uk
Along with the People's Republic of Stokes Croft, Canteen is one of the institutions that both defines and reinforces the character of the area – it's independent, bohemian and ethical. The emphasis is on good affordable food, supporting local suppliers while, behind the scenes, Canteen donates 10 per cent of annual net profit into an investment fund to support local causes. It's also a very good live music venue and event space.

Gallimaufrey
26-28 The Promenade, Gloucester Road BS7 8AL
www.thegallimaufry.co.uk
When co-owner James Koch and his team took over Gloucester Road institution the Prom Wine Bar in 2012 there was always a danger the transformation wouldn't work. But James, who moved to the city to study psychology at Bristol University in 1998, took the best things about the Prom (its live music and laid-back atmosphere) and added more local beer, better food and a strong art and green/sustainable culture to create something very special. And let's face it, the Prom needed a lick of paint.

Old Market Assembly
25 West Street, Old Market, Bristol BS2 0DF
www.oldmarketassembly.co.uk
The most striking aspect of the Assembly is its magnificent setting. Housed in the old St Philips branch of the Lloyds Bank, the bar retains many of the original features on the ground floor and mezzanine levels. From the same team behind Canteen and Number 1 Harbourside (including former Mayor George Ferguson), the

Assembly works because it embraces and reflects the local character. So, like Old Market, the Assembly is slightly sleazy in its choice of decor and live music and is a mainstay of the LGBTQ community. The menu is pizza plus daily specials and local suppliers feature strongly in the wide-ranging bar selection. The business policy places equal emphasis on people, profit and planet. Out back there's the wonderful Wardrobe Theatre.

Tobacco Factory
Raleigh Road, Bristol BS3 1TF
www.tobaccofactory.com
It's that man George Ferguson again! Tobacco Factory was his first experiment in a philosophy of creating independent bars that reflect the character of an area and therefore attract like-minded independent businesses rather than franchises,

chains and multi-nationals. This large bar specialises in Bristol Beer Factory ales, brewed about 50 yards away and there's a wide-ranging menu including a pre-show selection for those attending performances at the two upstairs theatres. Outside, the yard bar serves Italian-inspired flatbreads. On Bristol City and Bristol Rugby matchdays, this place buzzes!

Watershed
Canons Road, Harbourside BS1 5TX
www.watershed.co.uk
The relentlessly popular cafe/bar of the Watershed media centre is the meeting place of choice of Bristol's creative community, particularly since the Pervasive Media Studio moved into the Watershed office space, bringing with it 90 per cent of the city's hipster community.

North Street Standard
11-13 North Street, Bedminster BS3 1EN
www.anythingbutstandard.co.uk

Racks Wine Bar
St Paul's Road BS8 1LX
www.racks-bristol.co.uk

Small Bar
31 King Street BS1 4DZ
www.smallbarbristol.com

The Social
130 Cheltenham Road, Stokes Croft BS6 5RW
www.thesocialbristol.co.uk

Steam Beer Hall
Clifton Down Station, Bs8 2Pn
www.steambristol.co.uk

Southside
172 Wells Road, Totterdown BS4 2AL
www.southsidebristol.co.uk

White Lion Cafe Bar
Avon Gorge Hotel, Sion Hill BS8 4LD
www.hotelduvin.com

Yurt Lush
Clock Tower Yard, Temple Meads BS1 6QH
www.eatdrinkbristolfashion.co.uk
Bar and cafe serving brilliant Josh Eggleton menu housed in Mongolian yurts at Temple Meads.

Zerodegrees
53 Colston Street BS1 5BA
www.zerodegrees.co.uk

Cocktails

Aluna
4 Broad Quay BS1 4DA
www.aluna.uk.com

Bar Humbug
89 Whiteladies Road, Clifton BS8 4NT
www.barhumbug.co.uk

Betty's @ The Old Bookshop
65 North Street, Bedminster BS3 1ES
www.theoldbookshop.co.uk

Browns
38 Queens Road, Clifton BS8 1RE
www.browns-restaurants.co.uk

Crying Wolf
37 Cotham Hill, Cotham BS6 6JY
www.cryingwolf.co.uk

Flipside Cocktail Club
109 Whiteladies Road BS8 2PB
www.fccbristol.com

Gold Bar
Harbour Hotel & Spa, 55 Corn Street BS1 1HQ
www.harbourhotels.co.uk

Harvey Nichols Bar
Second Floor, 27 Philadelphia Street BS1 3BZ
www.harveynichols.com

Hyde & Co
2 The Basement, Berkeley Crescent BS8 1JY
www.hydeandcobristol.net

Kinkajou
52 Upper Belgrave Road, Clifton BS8 2XP
www.kinkajoubar.co.uk

London Cocktail Club
37 Triangle West, Clifton BS8 1ER
www.londoncocktailclub.co.uk

Milk Thistle
Quay Head House, Colston Avenue BS1 1EB
www.milkthistlebristol.com

Red Light
1 Unity Street BS1 5HH
www.redlightbristol.xxx

Rummer
All Saints Lane BS1 1JH
www.therummer.net

Under The Stars
16 Narrow Quay BS1 4QA
www.underthestarsbar.co.uk

Cider

Apple
Welsh Back BS1 4SB
www.applecider.co.uk
You might be forgiven for thinking that deep water and strong cider is an alarming combination, but not at the Apple, Bristol's floating cider house moored at Welsh Back. Bristol is enjoying a craft cider renaissance and Apple is particularly popular with student admirers of the juice of the fermented apple. Excellent for al fresco drinking and for building your own Ploughman's Lunches.

Apple Tree
27 Philip Street, Bedminster BS3 4EA
One of Bristol's few remaining working-class cider houses. Dark interior, lino on the floors. Don't spill anyone's cider. A curiosity.

Avon Packet
185-187 Coronation Road, BS3 1RF
Named after a passenger steamer from the 1860s, the Packet retains the offbeat character that it shares with many of Bristol's traditional waterside boozers. The locals recommend Thatchers Taditional or Cheddar Valley cider and a home-made Scotch egg. Large garden.

Bristol Cider Shop
Unit 4, Cargo Wapping Wharf BS1 6WE
www.bristolcidershop.co.uk
The Bristol Cider Shop in Wapping Wharf is *the* place to go if you're serious about cider. It stocks more than 80 varieties of draught and bottled cider and occasionally much sought-after offerings from small-scale Bristol producers such as Totterdown Press. The Cider Shop also organises festivals, talks and events. Independent Cider Retailer of the Year 2018.

Coronation Tap
8 Sion Place BS8 4AX
www.thecoronationtap.com
Bristol's longest-serving and best-known cider pub. For well over 100 years, committed disciples of the Church Of The Fermented Apple have come here to worship, or to get 'Corried'. With a range of ciders wide enough to keep several generations of Wurzels happy, this one-room 19th-Century pub is famous all over the world. That'll be the cider talking probably. Their celebrity drinkers include 3D out of Massive Attack.

Orchard
12 Hanover Place, Harbourside BS1 6XT
www.orchardinn.co.uk
Reading the list of guest ciders on offer on the blackboard in this one-room bar tucked round the back of Spike Island, you could be forgiven for thinking that you'd died and gone to cider heaven. In fact, the Orchard probably offers the best selection of west-country ciders of any pub in the world. Sam Marriott and Steph Iles took over the pub in December 2018 and continue the tradition of previous landlord Stuart Marshall of collecting the cider and perry direct from the craft producers. The emphasis here is on proper dry cider so expect to find the finest offerings from Somerset, Herefordshire, Gloucestershire and the Wye Valley and sometimes further afield. There's also a selection of real ales served straight from the barrel.

Shopping

Liz Crawte (left) and Andrea Mahoney, purveyors of urban cool at Co-Lab

Clothes

Beast
St Nicholas Market BS1 1HQ
www.beast-clothing.com
Famous for their 'Bristolian' T-shirts and socks.

Billy Jean
208 Gloucester Road BS7 8NU
www.lovegloucesterroad.org.uk
Retro clothes and fabrics.

BS8
34 Park Street BS1 5JG
@BS8.bristol
Arcade displaying the work of young Bristol designers plus vintage.

Cooshti
57 Park Street BS1 5NU
www.cooshti.com
Designer and independent streetwear.

KBK Shoes
203 Cheltenham Road BS6 5QX
www.kbkshoes.com
Since 1910 they've been selling leather goods from the same shop and started selling Doctor Martens in 1960. Huge selection.

Loot Vintage
6 Haymarket Walk, Bear Pit BS1 3LN
www.gimmetheloot.co.uk
Vintage clothes warehouse style.

Marcruss Army Surplus
177-181 Hotwell Road, Hotwells BS8 4RY
www.marcrussoutdoors.com
Bristol's famous Army surplus and outdoors store.

No Entry
BS8, 34 Park Street BS1 5JG
New vintage outlet at the back of BS8 specialising in men's designer clothes. Set up by enthusiastic young people.

Rag Trade Boutique
2 Upper Maudlin Street BS2 8DJ
www.ragtradeboutique.co.uk
Designer recycling.

Recession
8 Jacobs Wells Road BS8 1EA
www.recessionshop.webs.com
Retro clothes shop run by Gill Loats, the first woman DJ in Bristol at the Dug Out.

Repsycho
85 Gloucester Road, Bishopston BS7 8AS
@RePsycho
Legendary vintage clothing boutique with record store downstairs.

Rhubarb Jumble
52 North Street, Bedminster, Bristol, BS3 1HJ
www.rhubarbjumble.com
Vintage clothing, furniture, jewellery and homeware.

Sobey's vintage clothing
24 Park Street BS1 5JA; 6-7 The Arcade, Broadmead, BS1 3JD
@SobeysVintageClothing
Opened second vintage store in The Arcade in 2018.

That Thing
45-47 Stokes Croft, BS1 3QP
www.thatthing.co
Streetwear and accessories from as many as 50 young Bristol designers.

Uncle Sam's
54a Park Street BS1 5JN
www.uncle-sams-vintage-clothing-store.business.site
American retro store established 1984. Vintage T-shirts, shirts, jackets, jeans and huge amounts of leather.

Urban Fox
58 Corn Street, Bristol, BS1 2AZ
www.urbanfox.me
Good range of vintage and retro clothing and accessories.

Vintage Market
15-19 Stokes Croft, BS1 3PY
Vintage furniture, clothes and second-hand vinyl.

Books

Area 51
230 Gloucester Road BS7 8NZ
www.area51online.co.uk
Comics, games, books.

Arnolfinl Book shop
16 Narrow Quay BS1 4QA
www.arnolfini.org.uk
Specialises in art, design, literature and film magazines and books.

Beware Of The Leopard
St Nicholas Market BS1 1LJ
www.bristol.gov.uk/web/st-nicholas-markets/beware-of-the-leopard-books
Bursting at the seams second-hand shop.

Bloom & Curll
74 Colston Street BS1 5BB
www.bloomandcurll.co.uk
Beautiful second-hand bookshop. Free cake and a game of chess on the go.

Books for Amnesty
103 Gloucester Rd BS7 8AT
www.booksforamnestybristol.org.uk Vast array of second-hand books.

British heart foundation
148A Whiteladies Road, Clifton BS8 2RS
www.bhf.org.uk
Great selection of second-hand books.

Dreadnought books
125 St George's Road, BS1 5UW
www.dreadnoughtbooks.co.uk
Fabulous second-hand bookshop with a broad selection but especially good for art, humanities and social sciences.

Grenville Wick
253 North Street, Southville BS3 1JN
Cards, gifts and local books.

Forbidden Planet
Units 4&5 Clifton Heights BS8 1EJ
www.forbiddenplanet.com
Sci-fi, cult comics and DVDs .

Foyles
SU21 Brigstowe Street BS1 3BH
www.foyles.co.uk
First branch of Foyles outside London.

Harbourside market
Canon's Road (outside Watershed) BS1 5TX
Second-hand stalls at weekend market.

Last Bookshop
60 Park St, Bristol BS1 5JN
Remainder specialists, most books £3.

Max Minerva's Marvellous books
39 North View, Westbury Park BS6 7PY
www.maxminervas.co.uk
Lovely new shop on site of old Durdham Down Books.

Oxfam Bookshops
1 Queen's Road BS8 1QE; 56 Cotham Hill BS6 6JX; 26 Princess Victoria Street, BS8 4BU; 1 Canford Lane BS9 3DB
www.oxfam.org.uk
Enormous stock of second-hand books plus cards and fairly traded products.

Rough Trade
3 New Bridewell, Nelson St, Bristol BS1 2QD
www.roughtrade.com
Smashing selection of music, art and humour books at keen prices.

Stanfords
29 Corn Street BS1 1HT
www.stanfords.co.uk
Specialist travel books, plus maps, globes and accessories. Lovely shop.

Storysmith
49 North Street BS3 1EN
www.storysmithbooks.com
First new bookshop in South Bristol for years. Opened 2018. Good for events.

Tangent Books
www.tangentbooks.co.uk
Online store run by the publishers of this very guide.

Waterstones
Galleries BS1 3XB; The Mall, Cribbs Causeway BS34 5GF; 37 Regent Street, Clifton BS8 4HT
www.waterstones.co.uk
The biggest selection of books in town.

Art And Gifts

Blaze
84 Colston Street BS1 5BB
www.blazestudio.co.uk
Art, gifts and ceramics from art co-op.

Bristol Guild
68-70 Park Street BS1 5JY
www.bristolguild.co.uk
Tasteful gifts, furniture and cookware.

CO-LAB
123 Gloucester Road, Bishopston BS7 8AX
Coolest gift shop in town featuring work from hip local artists and makers plus books, clothes, music all with a contemporary 'street' feel.

Eclectic Gift Shop
51c Hanham High Street, Hanham BS15 3DQ
Gifts jewellery and homeware from some of the area's finest makers.

Fig.1
Unit 9, Gaol Ferry Steps, Bristol BS1 6WE
www.fig1.co.uk
Beautiful gift and homeware shop with strong green and ethical credentials.

IOTA
167 Gloucester Road BS7 8BE
www.iotabristol.com
Eclectic mix of new and retro giftware and homeware.

Memories
St Nicholas Market BS1 1JQ
www.bristol.gov.uk/web/st-nicholas-markets/memories
Famous for its pictures of old Bristol.

Rainmaker
123 Coldharbour Road BS6 7SN
www.rainmakerart.co.uk
Bristol's only gallery featuring the work of Native American artists. It's a fascinating introduction to art from an ancient culture and tradition. Great range of jewellery

Romantica
139 and 309 Gloucester Road BS7 8BA; 77 Henleaze Road, Henleaze BS9 4JP
@RomanticaBristol
There's a bizarre quality to Romantica. OK it's only a card, poster and gift shop, but you'll probably leave wondering who shops at Romantica and feel slightly concerned when you realise it's YOU. A Bristol institution.

Room 212
212 Gloucester Road, Bishopston BS7 8NU
www.room212.co.uk
Art, crafts and gallery.

Stokes Croft China
35 Jamaica Street, Stokes Croft BS2 8JP
www.prsc.org.uk
Top of the shopping list for visitors to Bristol. The retail faction of the People's Republic of Stokes Croft sells hand-decorated, top-quality bone china fired in a kiln in the heart of Stokes Croft. There's a strong radical and local ethos in the china, prints and books stocked here.

That Art Gallery
17 Christmas Steps BS1 5BS
www.thatartgallery.com
Bijou contemporary art gallery on quirky Christmas Steps.

Upfest Gallery
198 North Street, Southville BS3 1JF
www.upfest.co.uk
Street art gallery and shop from the people behind the wonderful Upfest urban art festival.

Music

Bristol Archive Records
www.bristolarchiverecords.com
Mike Darby has been championing Bristol music for more than 30 as a manager and promoter and then he set up BAR to remaster forgotten tracks for download from bristolarchiverecords.com by local bands stretching back to the likes of the Electric Guitars, Vice Squad and Essential Bop from the late 70s.

It was the release of his Bristol Reggae Explosion collection (vinyl, CD and download) that really caught the popular imagination. The website is a remarkable resource, it's a living museum of Bristol's post-punk musical history – the digital music equivalent of M Shed, but without the squeaky chairs in the cafe or the funding.

Friendly Records
59-61 North Street, Bedminster BS3 1ES
www.friendlyrecords.co.uk
Excellent selection courtesy of former band manager and record company guy Tom Friend.

Idle hands
74 Stokes Croft BS1 5QY
www.idlehandsbristol.com
Rose from the ashes of Rooted Records. Chris Farrell's shop and Idle Hands record label is at the centre of the Bristol dance and electronica scene. And essential experience for anyone with an interest in Bristol bass culture.

Longwell Records
36 Temple Street, Keynsham BS31 1EH
www.longwellrecords.com
Brilliant shop. New and used vinyl. Runner-up in Best Small Independent Shop in UK 2018.

Payback Records
Unit 45, St Nicholas Market BS1 1LA
www.bristol.gov.uk/web/st-nicholas-marketsNew and second-hand reggae specialist.

PK Music Exchange
51 Gloucester Road, Horfield BS7 8AD
www.pk-music.co.uk
Buys, sells and trades second-hand band and DJ equipment but also has a huge collection of second-hand vinyl for sale.

Plastic Wax
222 Cheltenham Road BS6 5QU
www.plasticwaxrecords.com
Plastic Wax must have been selling second-hand music since the invention of vinyl. This is what your bedroom would look like if you'd kept all the music you'd ever bought and your mum had never made you tidy up. You'll need to invest some time in understanding the 'system' but it's worth it.

Prime Cuts
85 Gloucester Road BS7 8AS
Prime Cuts resides below the RePsycho second-hand clothes shop and deals purely in second-hand vinyl including a great selection of rare and imported music. Check out the second-hand videos, most of which you've never heard of, and some of which are worth buying on comedy value alone.

Radio/ON
First Floor 34 Park Street BS1 5JG
www.radio-on.co.uk
Specialises in DIY punk, noise-nik experimentalists, lo-fi kickers, indie-kid-politics, and especially the adventurous sounds coming from queer and feminist places.

Specialist subject records
First Floor, The Exchange72-73 Old Market Street, BS2 0EJ
www.specialistsubjectrecords.co.uk
Specialists in punk, indie, imports and hard-to-find music.

Wanted Records
Unit 1, St Nicholas Market BS1 1JQ
www.wantedrecords.co.uk
John Stapleton has been close to pretty much everything good that's come out of Bristol music for the last two decades. Although he is most associated with reggae and dance music in its many guises as Dr Jam, Blowpop, Go Go Children and various other club nights and DJ monikers, Stapleton is a walking encyclopedia of all forms of modern music.

Found a collection of obscure prog rock from the 70s? Stumbled across a stash of 60s dancehall vinyl in the attic? Head for Wanted Records to convert your vinyl treasure trove into cash and maybe pick up some new tunes from the awesome collection at St Nick's Market.

Food & Drink

Better Food Company
Sevier Street, St Werburgh's BS2 9LB; 94 Whiteladies Rd BS8 2QX
www.betterfood.co.uk
Phil Haughton's organic supermarket is the ragamuffin cousin of Clifton's posh delis. Situated on a roundabout on the Montpelier, St Paul's, St Werburgh's borders, the original BFC brought locally produced, organic food to the inner city. Now Clifton and Wapping Wharf have embraced the scruffy urchin of ethical food production, scrubbed its face, given it a smart centre parting and welcomed it to Whiteladies Road and Cargo.

Bristanbul
137 Gloucester Road BS7 8AX
www.bristanbul.co.uk
All manner of Turkish breads, pizzas and cakes are produced on the premises.

Bristol Cider Shop
Unit 4, Cargo, Wapping Wharf BS1 6WE
www.bristolcidershop.co.uk

Bristol Sweet Mart
80 St Marks Road, Easton BS5 6JH
www.sweetmart.co.uk | Tel: 951 2257
Kassam Ismail Majothi arrived penniless as a refugee from Uganda in 1972 and founded the Sweet Mart in 1978. Since then, it has become the major supplier of ethnic foods, spices and more in the south west. Sweet Mart is at the centre of the regeneration of St Mark's Road which is one of the most interesting shopping streets in Bristol.

Corks
54 Cotham Hill BS6 6JX; 79 North Street, Bedminster BS3 1ES
www.corksof.com
One of a rare breed of independent off-licenses on the high street.

Earthbound
8 Abbotsford Road, Cotham BS6 6HB
Lovely organic and wholefood store.

El Colmado
57 Gloucester Road, Bishopston BS7 8AD
www.elcolmadobristol.co.uk
Excellent Spanish deli famous for its paella on Saturdays.

Farmers' Markets
The main Farmers' Market is every Wednesday in Corn Street. Whiteladies Road market is on Saturday mornings outside 108 Whiteladies Road, BS8 2RP

Fox & West
172 Wells Rd, Bristol BS4 2AL
www.foxandwest.co.uk
Specialises in ethical and organic grocery, veg, deli and cafe.

Hart's Bakery
Temple Meads BS1 6QS
www.hartsbakery.co.uk
Very popular bakery in the tunnels next to Temple Meads. Also a small cafe.

Harvest
11 Gloucester Road, Bishopston BS7 8AA
www.harvest-bristol.coop
Retail outlet of the Essential Trading Co-op. One of the longest established wholefood co-ops in the west.

Herbert's
1 Wellington Avenue, Montpelier BS6 5HP
Founded in the 1960s, Herberts Bakery in Montpelier has a legendary status.

Hobbs House Bakery
177 Gloucester Road, Bishopston, BS7 8BE; 217 North Street, Southville BS3 1JL
www.hobbshousebakery.co.uk
This Chipping Sodbury-based family business has a closely interwoven history with Herbert's Bakery.

Eco and ethical shopping

Evie Steen checks out some of the city's green businesses...

With the increasing awareness of the need to reduce our carbon footprint, Bristol has seen a rapid increase in zero-waste shops. For around 30 years, Scoopaway led the way, serving customers nutritious and organic food and encouraging them to ditch throw-away packaging and bring reusable bags and containers to fill with staples such as rice, beans, pulses, cereals and more.

Scoop the required amounts from the food bins into your bag just like it says on the sign. This independent and friendly store also sells an impressive range of everyday grocery items and has an excellent selection of tea.

Scoopaway
113 Gloucester Road, Bishopston, BS7 8AT
www.scoopawayhealthfoods.co.uk
Take-away food often entails a handful of plastic forks, a box you will never use again and pathetic-sized ketchup and mayonnaise packets. Not to mention the amount of food wasted by making the huge eyes-bigger-than-your-stomach mistake. No need to worry, here we have some suggestions of restaurants and cafes serving up the most zero waste meals.

Friska
Park St; Here, Bath Rd; Emersons Grn; Victoria St; The Eye, Glass Wharf; Cathedral Wk, Harbourside
www.friskafood.com
Introduced to Bristol by two young entrepreneurs Griff Holland and Ed Brown in 2009, it's not just the good food that keeps people coming to Friska, it's the sustainable culture. All

of their take-away boxes and utensils are wooden, limiting the use of single use plastics means they are really doing their part. Alongside this, all unsold food is given to homeless charities and on-site waste is either re-cycled, composted or incinerated meaning nothing goes to landfill. You can't talk about Friska without mentioning their partnership with two important charities FRANK Water, who raise money for clean water projects in the developing world, and Deki (an ethical loans scheme for remote and marginalised communities).

Poco Tapas Bar
45 Jamaica Street, Stokes Croft BS2 8JP
www.pocotapasbar.com
In 2004 co-founders Tom Hunt, Jen Best and Ben Pryor took Bristol by storm, bringing even more life to the pleasure-seekers of the city by combining the acts of self-indulgence and helping the planet. With a goal of sustainability and waste reduction, this eatery has received several eco awards including most ethical restaurant in 2013 and Food Made Good Best Business Of The Year award in 2016 and 2018. Multi-talented head chef Tom Hunt defines himself as an 'Eco chef, food waste activist and a big eater', which undoubtedly creates a feeling of comfort and reassurance that you know you will be eating well in his care. All parts of the ingredients are used in some sort of funky way on your plate or in your cocktail in order to diminish waste produced from the

company. What's not to love? Check out Tom's blog and the Poco website for upcoming events in this jazzy space on the corner of Jamaica Street, hire Tom's crew out for a festival, or see how he can make your wedding day even more special (and sustainable of course). https://www.tomsfeast.com/poco-festivals/poco-bristol/

Better Food Company
Sevier Street, St Werburgh's; Whiteladies Road, Clifton; Gaol Ferry Steps, Wapping Wharf
www.betterfood.co.uk
We all know that shopping organic is important but shopping local is even better. Enter Better Food who clearly state that when it come to food shopping, the most important factors to bear in mind are organic, local and ethical. After starting off as a food box service, going against the grain of mass production in the food industry, this independent Bristol-based company has spread it wings and its territory, having shops and cafes now in three locations; St Werburgh's, Clifton and Wapping Wharf. They pride themselves on their relationships with their food providers, and on the website you are able to see a list of their suppliers so customers can be confident in what they are buying.

Boston Tea Party
Park St; Princess Victoria St, Clifton; Cheltenham Road; Gloucester Road; Whiteladies Road
www.bostonteaparty.co.uk
On 1 June 2018, the Boston Tea Party stopped using single-use coffee cups, following on from the banning of plastic straws and plastic bottles, replacing them with paper and glass bottles of water from FRANK Water. Boston Tea Party adopted the phrase 'Single use, no excuse' as part of their Make

Things Better campaign, which allows customers to bring their own cup from home, buy an Ecoffee cup for a discounted price from £4.25 in all their cafes or borrow a cup in exchange for a deposit. In 2019 the Bristol business was named Britain's Most Ethical Coffee Shop by Ethical Consumer.

Fox & West
172 Wells Road, Bristol BS4 2AL
www.foxandwest.co.uk
Deli, fresh produce and cafe run by Lucy Fox and Hannah West who commit to a minimum waster policy – no plastic, no carrier bags, refills encouraged. They also support local producers and are one of the few stockists of the excellent Sausagenius locally made sausages.

Preserve
208 Gloucester Road, Bishopston BS7 8NU
www.preservefoods.co.uk
Bring your own bag to avoid all unnecessary packaging at wholefood shop that also sells soaps, shampoo bars and other toiletries.

Smaller Footprints
9 Regent Street, Clifton BS8 4HW
www.smallerfootprints.co.uk
Following in the footsteps of Scoopaway, this store brings a zero tolerance attitude to packaging to Clifton Village.

Thali Cafes
York Rd, Montpelier, St Mark's Road, Easton; North St, Southville; Regent Street, Cliftonw
www.thethalirestaurant.co.uk
In each corner of the beloved city, Thali has planted it seeds. With its individual style of tiffin takeaway, there is no excuse for pointless waste. Purchase your funky tiffin tins from one of the

restaurants and get it filled up with a variety of tasty curry treats for £29. The local company has been awarded a three-star Sustainability Champion Rating from The Sustainable Restaurant Association (SRA) as well as winning the Cheap Eats category of the Observer Food Monthly Awards, and the Radio 4 Food & Farming Award for Best Takeaway in 2010.

Great food available all over the Bristol map with a feel-good mantra.

Zero Green
12 North Street, Bedminster BS3 1HT
www.zerogreenbristol.co.uk
Wholefood and more. No containers, no packaging means no plastic bags blowing around this part of Bedminster.

Hot Sauce Emporium
Exchange Hall, St Nick's Market BS1 1JQ
www.hotsauceemporium.co.uk
Run by Jon Finch, the affable former guitarist in punk adventuters Lunatic Fringe, the Emporium stocks a huge range of hot sauces and occasionally has limited-edition eye-burners made by Chaos out of Chaos UK.

La Ruca
83 Gloucester Road, Bishopston BS7 8AS
www.laruca.co.uk
Well-stocked wholefood shop run by a Chilean family with many fairtrade products. Nice cafe upstairs.

Licata
36 Picton Street BS6 5QA
www.licata.co.uk
Brilliant Italian deli and grocery shop run by what seems to be several generations of the same family. Licata's has been in Picton Street for as long as anyone can remember. The quality of the food and drink is excellent.

Mark's Bread
291 North Street, Southville BS3 1JU
www. marksbread.co.uk
There's a reassuring simplicity about Mark's Bread. The shop consists of a baker, an oven a till and a few tables.

That's all you need to make, display and sell fantastic organic bread. Deliveries to local shops are made by bicycle.

Pak Butchers
4 Roman Road BS5 6DH
www.pakbutchers.co.uk
Abdul Malik started out at Pak as a work experience youngster in 1990. He now runs the show and has built the business into the South West's main supplier of Halal meat and poultry. Pak also sells fish.

Rare Butchers
250 North Street, Southville BS3 1JD
@RareMeatButchersofSouthville
This used to be Bob Wherlock's butcher's shop, famous for its Saturday morning queue of carnivores. But after 35 years in North Street, Bob and his team retired and the shop reopened in 2011 as Rare.

Reg the Veg
6 Boyces Avenue, Clifton BS8 4AA
www.regtheveg.co.uk
Bristol's best-known veg shop. The original Reg was Reg Meek who ran the shop in the 1960s.

Southville Deli
262 North Street, Southville BS3 1JA
www.southvilledeli.com | Tel: 966 4507
Neighbourhood deli and cafe specialising

in organic, fairtrade and locally produced food and wine. Also has a shop in Church Road, Redfield.

T&P Murray Butchers
153 Gloucester Road, Bishopston BS7 8BA
www.murraysbristol.co.uk
This well-established butchers is a good source of organic and free range meat plus a host of salami, preserves pickles and cheeses in the deli. Saturday morning queues are sustained by a pavement barbecue.

Thatchers Cider Shop
Myrtle Farm, Sandford, Somerset BS25 5RA
www.thatcherscider.co.uk
Head out past the airport on the A38 and you'll soon be in Thatchers Cider country. The shop stocks all of the many Thatchers ciders and other locally produced products. While you're out there, take a stroll down the Strawberry Line footpath which takes you through some of the orchards.

Tobacco Factory Market
Tobacco Factory, Southville BS3 1TF
www.tobaccofactory.com/sunday-market/
Sunday morning market with fish, local veg, cheese, bread and other suppliers. Don't leave without trying a at least one Jamaican pattie from the Agnes Spencer stall.

Tony's Caribbean Food
128 Grosvenor Road BS2 8YA
If you need a matokie and some cho-cho to go with your sweet yam and ackee, you need look no further.

Toveys Seafood
198-200 Stapleton Road, Easton BS5 0NY
www.toveys.co.uk
Tovey's Seafood is a third-generation family business started in 1935 by William Tovey. Originally on Easton Road in Bristol, it moved to the current site on Stapleton Road in 1962.

Viandas Spanish Deli
5 Park Row BS1 5LJ
www.viandas.co.uk
Large selection of natural foods from organic breads to chilled and frozen foods, organic wines and beers and lots of deli fodder..

Wild Oats Natural Foods
9-11 Lower Redland Road BS6 6TB
www.woats.co.uk
Large selection of natural foods from organic breads to chilled and frozen foods, organic wines and beers and lots of deli fodder..

Culture & Entertainment

Anna Freeman host of the Blahblahblah spoken word events

© Darren Thompson

Museums And Galleries

Blaise Castle House Museum
Henbury Rd, Bristol BS10 7QS
www.bristolmuseums.org.uk

Museum and Art Gallery
Queens Road BS8 1RL
www.bristolmuseums.org.uk
From Old Masters to contemporary fine, applied and oriental art, the city has an outstanding art collection in splendid galleries on the upper floor of the museum.

Georgian House Museum
7 Great George Street BS1 5RR
www.bristolmuseums.org.uk

Here Gallery
108 Stokes Croft BS1 3RU
www.heregallery.co.uk
Small gallery primarily focused on printmaking and illustration. Shop stocks art books from illustrated children's books, to artist monographs, stylish stationery, and how-to guides. Plus, a diverse selection of magazines, graphic novels, self-published zines, underground comics, and other hard to find titles.

Lime Tree Gallery
84 Hotwell Road, Hotwells BS8 4UB
www.limetreegallery.com
Specialises in contemporary fine art and glass. Seems to have a thing about Scottish artists.

M Shed
Princes Wharf, Wapping Road BS1 4RN
www.bristolmuseums.org.uk

Outdoor Gallery
People's Republic Of Stokes Croft
35 Jamaica Street, Stokes Croft BS2 8JP
www.prsc.org.uk
Bristol's most radical gallery is essentially a wall next to the PRSC HQ on Jamaica Street. The Outdoor Gallery has displayed work by hundreds of artists and community groups since 2007 with a new design every month or so.

Red Lodge Museum
Park Row BS1 5LJ
www.bristolmuseums.org.uk

Royal West Of England Academy
Queens Road, Clifton BS8 1PX
www.rwa.org.uk
Much-respected art institution that seamlessly embraces classic and the modern age.

Spike Island
133 Cumberland Road BS1 6UX
www.spikeisland.org.uk
Spike Island is all about producing and displaying contemporary art and design. There are 70 working spaces for artists in the former tea-packing factory and a rolling programme of exhibitions in the large gallery space. Spike Island is also home to the Spike Print Studio project. For more information, take a look at www.spikeprintstudio.org.

That Art Gallery
17 Christmas Steps BS1 5BS
www.thatartgallery.com
Small, contemporary art gallery on Christmas Steps opened by the extremely well connected Andy Phipps in 2017. Attracts big-hitters from the international contemporary art scene such as David Shillinglaw, Charley Uzzell Edwards (aka Pure Evil) and James Reka.

Upfest
198 North Street, Southville BS3 1JF
www.upfest.co.uk
Urban art gallery run by Stephen and Emma Hayles with regular shows by artists from Bristol and beyond. Upfest is also the Urban Paint Festival which began life in 2008 in the Tobacco Factory car park and by 2018 was attracting more than 30,000 visitors.

Theatre

Alma Tavern & Theatre
18-20, Alma Vale Road, Clifton BS8 2HY
www.almatavernandtheatre.co.uk
50-seater venue above pub in Clifton with in-house company. Also hosts touring shows and workshops.

Bristol Old Vic
King Street BS1 4ED
www.bristol-old-vic.co.uk
The Theatre Royal was built in 1766 and has been home to the Bristol Old Vic since 1946.

Bristol Hippodrome
St Augustines Parade BS1 4UZ
www.atgtickets.com
Vast 2,000-seater theatre that has been a fixture in the city centre since 1912. Specialises in West End shows and musicals.

Redgrave Theatre
8 Percival Road, Clifton BS8 3LE
www.redgravetheatre.com
Opened by Sir Michael Redgrave in 1966.
Clifton College's purpose-built theatre
hosts plays from amateur groups and Old
Vic Theatre School.

Tobacco Factory
Raleigh Road, Southville BS3 1TF
www.tobaccofactorytheatres.com
Spielman and Factory theatres host a full
and varied programme of performances
and workshops.

WARDROBE Theatre
25 West Street, Old Market BS2 0DF
www.thewardrobetheatre.com
Fantastic 100-seater venue at the back of
the Old Market Assembly. The Wardrobe
project began is 2011 with a group of
Bristol theatre makers putting on pop-up
performances at the White Bear on St
Michael's Hill. The Wardrobe is hard-
wired into the best risk-taking artists in
town.

Cinemas

Cineworld
Hengrove Park BS14 0HR
www.cineworld.co.uk

Cube Cinema
4 Princess Row, Kingsdown BS2 8NQ
www.cubecinema.com
The most vibrant, challenging, non-
funded counter-cultural art and media
alternative in the West.

My Vue
**The Venue, Cribbs Causeway & Aspects Leisure
Park, Longwell Green**
www.myvue.com

Odeon
Union Street, Broadmead BS1 2DS
www.odeon.co.uk

Showcase Cinema/Delux
**Bath Road, Avon Meads BS2 0SP; Glass House,
Cabot Circus BS1 3BX**
www.showcasecinemas.co.uk

Watershed
Canons Road BS1 5TX
www.watershed.co.uk
Two screens offer intelligently selected
left-of-centre mainstream, arthouse and
retrospective seasons.

Westbury Park
Northumbria Drive, Henleaze BS9 4HN
www.bristolwestburypark.scottcinemas.co.uk
Used to be the Orpheus until taken over
by Scott Cinemas. The only remaining
traditional neighbourhood cinema in
Bristol.

Comedy

Comedy Box @ Hen and Chicken
Hen and Chicken, 210 North St, Bristol BS3 1JF
www.henandchicken.com | www.thecomedybox.co.uk
Comedy Box hosts upstairs venue at
south Bristol pub: the place to go for
intelligent stand-up and comics on their
way up. Also at Tobacco Factory.

Chuckle Busters @ Wardrobe
Wardrobe Theatre, 25 West Street BS2 0DF
www.chucklebusters.com
Big names, Edinburgh Fringe shows plus
emerging talents. Mainly at Wardrobe,
but also at Improv Theatre, Tobacco
Factory and Performing Arts Centre.

How Lazy Is He @ Lazy Dog
Lazy Dog, 112 Ashley Down Road BS7 9JR
www.thelazydogbristol.com
Weekly comedy hosted by Tony Chiotti.

Bristol comedy

Steve Wright on the places to go for a giggle...

Welcome to one of the funniest parts of Britain. Hell, it must be so, judging from Bristol's illustrious line of comedy exports – John Cleese (technically from Weston but we'll have him), Bill Bailey (Keynsham – but, again...), Stephen Merchant and Russell Howard, to name but a few. Bristol University can also claim a long lineage of comic talent, including the likes of Marcus Brigstocke, David Walliams, Matt Lucas and Gloucester boy Simon Pegg.

In keeping up with this illustrious heritage, Bristol has some very decent venues, ranging from bigger, dedicated spaces in the centre of town to rooms above pubs in the inner suburbs, between them offering Bristolians a tempting mix of circuit comedians, breakthrough acts and regular household names.

Bristol has its own thriving ecosystem – venues where wannabe and emerging comics can get up behind the mic, or where bigger names can drop in incognito to try out new material. Thriving promoters include Comedy Box, which programmes nights both at its own club above the Hen and Chicken pub in Southville, and a little further down the street at the Tobacco Factory Theatre; Oppo Comedy, based at the White Rabbit opposite the student union in Gordon Road, Clifton, Ashley Down's Lazy Dog pub,; This Next Act at the Kingsdown Vaults and Chuckle Busters who programme an eclectic range of established acts and emerging talent mainly at the Wardrobe Theatre, Tobacco Factory and Bristol Improv Theatre (the old Polish Club) in St Paul's Road Clifton.

Colston Hall and, more occasionally, Bristol Hippodrome will lure the big-name comics and folk you've seen on the telly: early booking always advised.

Oppo Comedy @ White Rabbit
White Rabbit, 33 Gordon Road, Clifton BS8 1AW
@OppoComedy
Regular stand-up nights for up-and-coming and established acts from

People's Comedy @ Space at PRSC
Space, PRSC, 14 Hillgrove Street, Stokes BS2 8JT
@ThePeoplesComedy
The UK's only regular socio-political comedy night.

Riproar Comedy @ Pryzm
Pryzm, Canon's Road, Harbourside BS1 5UH
www.riproarcomedy.co.uk
Saturday night comedy at Pryzm nightclub. Comedy 7.30pm-10pm. DJs till 4am.

This Next Act @ Kingsdown Vaults
31 Kingsdown Parade, BS6 5UE
@ThisNextAct
Home of This Next Act...a fortnightly Sunday night comedy show and open mic.

Clowns, fools and new circus in Bristol

A modern history of circus by **Beccy Golding**

Bristol has long been the gateway to the south west's festival scene, and a non-metropolitan haven for alternative culture. In the 1980s and 90s, a confluence of immersive festival experience groups, such as the Mutoid Waste Company, non-trad circus outfits including Archaos (French anarchists juggling chain saws), plus the back-end of time when cultural funding was still possible, somehow saw the birth of what has been called the new circus movement.

Formed in 1980, the Desperate Men are the ground-breaking granddaddies of street theatre, with a manifesto of bringing surreal, anarchic outdoor shows and happenings to the city. Still going strong, they have their own studio in Easton, at the Mivart Studios.

Fool Time, the UK's first circus school, opened in St Paul's in 1986, founded by Franki Anderson, Bim Mason, Audrey Michel and Richard Ward. It offered full-time circus and performance training as well as evening classes in circus skills.

After eight years it closed, and from its roots grew Circomedia, headed by Bim Mason and Helen Crocker. Circomedia has built its reputation ever since and draws students from across the world for their degree-level programmes in physical theatre, performance, comedy and directing.

Current players

The Invisible Circus have played a key role in shaping Bristol's circus identity. Created in 1991, they've performed internationally and at major British festivals, including Glastonbury and Boomtown. They landed in Bristol, with a site-specific show The Road to Nowhere in the old Audi garage on Stokes Croft in 2006, and toured with Beyond the Cabaret. In 2008 they created Carnyville – taking over buildings and creating site-specific circus-theatre with casts of hundreds, for audiences of thousands – a truly astonishing phenomena, people came from far and wide to witness the interactive spectacular and get involved themselves.

Arcadia are also from round these parts. Combining pyrotechnics, lighting, circus and music into large scale performance and dance spaces, they're best known for their 50-tonne spider, with flame throwers and suspended DJ booth. In 2015 the spider spent two nights in Bristol's Queen Square, performing to 24,000 people. As part of Bristol European Green Capital year, it featured the world's first pyrotechnic flame system run on recycled biofuel.

Also based in the city, Cirque Bijou make shows for stadiums, festivals and events, indoors and outdoors. Their recent work with Extraordinary Bodies – a professional circus company with disabled and non-disabled artists working equally together – created a touring show exploring the body's capacity for expression – What Am I Worth? is touring worldwide.

Sally Cookson is a renowned theatre director who lives in the city. Working with Bristol Old Vic and others, some of her shows include We're Going on a Bear Hunt, A Monster Calls, and The Lion, The Witch and The Wardrobe. Cookson is integrating more and more circus into her big theatre shows, working with local circus director, Gwen Hales.

Bristol Circus City is the biennial festival of circus, which brings high-calibre international artists in to showcase their work. Next on in 2019. bristolcircuscity.com

Clowns & fools

Previously a term coined for comedians who broke the mould in the 1980s (but are now mainstream), such as Alexi Sayle, Ben Elton and French & Saunders, these days the term alternative comedy refers to clowns, fools and physical theatre makers, who all have a strong foothold in the city.

Bristol hosts a growing population of fools – a term re-claimed in the 1980s by Fool Time co-founder Franki Anderson. Fooling is a deep form of improvisation, all about the performer standing in an empty space, with no prior plan, and seeing what happens in the moment and which masks (aspects of themselves) show up.

Clowns in Bristol may or may not wear a red nose, but they are more likely to be concerned with the ridiculousness of life, playing the flop and connecting to the audience than face painting, big shoes and custard pies. These modern forms of clowning and fooling are spear-headed by

performer, teacher and dramatherapist Holly Stoppit, herself a pupil of master-fool Franki Anderson.

2018 was billed #circus250, a UK-wide celebration of the anniversary of the first modern circus. As part of the celebration Holly Stoppit had a very sensible clown residency at Bristol Museum and Art Gallery.

Other teachers in the city are heavily influenced by internationally-renowned clown teachers Jacques Lecoq and Philippe Gaulier. As for circus skills, there is still a high-proportion of jugglers-per-head in the city, but Bristol is also well-served by classes and practitioners of silks, acrobatics, trapeze and hooping.

Seven places to learn

• **The Albany Centre**. A community venue since the 1980s, the Albany is now a dedicated rehearsal space for circus and street theatre, with training and courses particularly for aerial performers. www.albanycentre.org

• **Bristol Physical Theatre Project.** Lecoq trained Igne Barkauskaite offers ensemble, mask and movement-based workshops and courses. www.bptp.live

• **Circomedia.** Regular skills and performance classes for adults; youth circus from age 4+; full time courses to BTEC and degree level. www.circomedia.com

• **Holly Stoppit Workshops**. Start with the Introduction to Clowning weekend before joining five-day intensives or ongoing courses in aspects of clowning, fooling and inner critic inquiry. www.hollystoppit.com

• **The Island Circus Training**. Artspace Lifespace turn disused, unusual and often difficult buildings into vibrant multi-use art venues. The former Bridewell police station now has studios, gallery and dance spaces as well as classes in acro yoga, trapeze, aerial hoop, silks and more. www.theislandbristol.com

• **I want to learn circus in Bristol Facebook group**. Keep up-to-date with regular and one-off performance technique and skills-based classes and courses from Bristol-based and visiting teachers.

• **Zuma Puma**, award-winning actor, clown and workshop facilitator offers workshops, intensives and retreats internationally and in Bristol via www.clownlife.org

• **Bonus extra** - individual teachers: It's worth keeping an eye out for irregular classes and courses from Amy Rose, Dominique Fester, Brenda Waite. Out of town visiting teachers to keep an eye out for include: Jamie Wood, Jamie Catto, Franki Anderson, Lucy Hopkins, Fraser Hooper.

Six places to watch

• **Beyond The Ridiculous**. Holly Stoppit's troupe of fools create "audaciously authentic, gob-smackingly resonant, instant theatre." www.hollystoppit.com/beyond-the-ridiculous

• **Bristol Improv Theatre**. Courses and performances in the UK's first dedicated improv theatre. www.improvtheatre.co.uk

• **Circomedia** runs a programme of high quality professional performances as well as student showcases at their St Paul's site. www.circomedia.com

• **Loco Club**. A creative collaboration between The Invisible Circus and Artspace Lifespace, Loco is located in the tunnels beneath Temple Meads. There's a programme of radical, underground events and performances, including Invisible Circus productions. www.locobristol.com www.invisiblecircus.co.uk

• **Wardrobe Theatre**. Fringe venue showcasing the best in new, radical, experimental theatre & performance. Also hosts long-running improvised soap opera Closer Each Day. www.thewardrobetheatre.com

• There are countless small circus and street companies based in Bristol – you're only ever three feet away from a circus-theatre cabaret!

Spoken Word, Poetry, Prose

BlahBlahBlah @ Bristol Old Vic
Bristol Old Vic Studio, King Street BS1 4ED
www.blahbristol.com
Big, adventurous night of national spoken word hosted by the brilliant Anna Freeman.

Lines of the Mind @ Ropewalk
Ropewalk, 5 Nelson Parade, Bedminster BS3 4JA

Milk @ Wardrobe Theatre
Wardrobe Theatre, 25 West St, Old Market BS2 0DF
@MilkPoetry
Collective of exciting young poets formed by Malaika Kegode.

Novel Nights @ Square Club
Square Club, 15 Berkeley Square, Clifton BS8 1HB
www.novelnights.co.uk
Guest speakers, readings and workshops at the Square Club and other locations in Bristol and Bath. Novel Nights is an essential introduction to the Bristol literary scene.

Raise The Bar @ Arnolfini
Arnolfini, 16 Narrow Quay BS1 4QA
@RTBSpokenWord
Began life as a student night in the union bar when promoter Danny Pandolfi was at Bristol Uni. Now a big monthly show.

Spel @ Bristol Fringe
Bristol Fringe, 32 Princess Victoria Street, Clifton BS8 4BZ
Poetry and acoustic music open mic hosted by poet and musician Tim Burroughs.

Satellite of Love @ Greenbank
Greenbank, 57 Belle Vue Road, Easton BS5 6DP
Popular evening of poetry, spoken word and open mic.

Talking Tales @ Leftbank
128 Cheltenham Road, Stokes Croft BS6 5RW
@talkingtales
Short stories, flash fiction, extracts from longer pieces hosted by Stokes Croft Writers.

That's What She Said @ Club Loco
Nr Temple Meads, Clock Tower Yard BS1 6QH
www.locobristol.com
Women's spoken word night hosted by punk poet Bridget Hart.

Venues And Clubs

Anson Rooms
Queens Road, Clifton BS8 1LN
www.ubu.org.uk
Cavernous room on the first floor of the bleak 1960s-built Student Union building.

Colston Hall
Colston Street BS1 5AR
www.colstonhall.org | Tel: 0844 887 1500
Large, beautifully-refurbed venue hosting big comedy and music names. Named after slave trader Edward Colston, but that's changing in 2020.

Cosies
34 Portland Square, St Paul's BS2 8RG
www.cosies.co.uk
Bar of choice for reggae enthusiasts and dubstep devotees, Cosies' weekend club all-nighters are the stuff of legend. Yet in the daytime, this is a bistro/wine bar serving good-value grub to local office workers

Black Swan
438 Stapleton Road, Easton BS5 6NR
Heavyweight Drum 'n' Bass and Hardcore hangout. Mental. Also home to the mighty Bristol Dub Club hosted by DJ Bliss Zion.

Blue Mountain Club
2 Stokes Croft BS1 3PR
www.bluemountainclub.co.uk
Keeps threatening to revive the vibe of the mid 90s when it was one of the best clubs in town, but never seems to quite make it. Been under threat of closure and redevelopment for ages.

Bristol 02 Academy
Frogmore Street BS1 5NA
www.academymusicgroup.com
Soulless, functional venue for big names.

Dojo
12-15 Park Row BS1 5LJ
www.dojobristol.com
One of Bristol's longest-established clubs Dojo is both relaxed and ambitious.

Exchange
72-73 Old Market BS2 0EJ
www.exchangebristol.com
When Fat Paul (Paul Horlick) and his team quit The Croft in 2013, Bristol lost a shrine to grungy, loud music, experimental pop and alternative rock. But without missing a beat they decamped to The Exchange. A share issue in 2019 should ensure the future of the club in a city where club culture is threatened by housing developments.

Fiddlers
Willway Street, Bedminster BS3 4BG
www.fiddlers.co.uk
This unlikely success story has carved out a niche for itself by offering mainly earthy blues and roots with a raw live appeal.

Fleece and Firkin
12 St Thomas Street, St Thomas BS1 6JJ
www.thefleece.co.uk
Not too long ago, The Fleece was Bristol's foremost gig venue but then reverted to counterfeit Stones, pretend Blondies and several Whole Lotta Led

Zeps to fill the week, while very average soul covers get the Blues Brothers parties going at weekends. Then Blue Aeroplanes bass player Chris Sharp took over the Fleece and returned it to its former glory with an imaginative programme of new music and by telling the tribute acts to fake off.

Forty Eight
48 Park Street BS1 5JG
www.forty-eight.co.uk
Used to be The Cooler, one of Bristol's longest-established indie clubs. Now mainly student offering.

Gravity
78 Queen's Road BS8 1QU
www.gravitynightclub.com
Students welcome midweek, goes exclusive with Club Lux on Saturday. Used to be The Bunker.

Hen and Chicken
210 North Street, Southville BS3 1JF
www.henandchicken.com
Large upstairs venue that has long been known for hosting top comedy acts but also has talks, live music and theatre.

La Rocca
Triangle South BS8 1EY
www.laroccabristol.co.uk
With its original disco seating and groovy circular wall holes, La Rocca can be a cool place when the music is right.

Lakota
6 Upper York Street, St Paul's BS2 8QN
www.lakota.co.uk
The mighty Lakota has been at the forefront of Bristol club cool since the 1980s. In 2018, owners the Burgess family announced they were looking to redevelop the site as housing, but that the club would remain open for the foreseeable future.

Lizard Lounge
66 Queen's Road BS8 1QU
www.lizardloungebristol.co.uk
Caters for students in the good old fashioned pissed-off-their-heads-dancing-to-Club-Tropicana sense of the word. Cocktail nights, salsa nights, mad-for-it nights, cheap pints on Tuesday nights. This is student heaven on the Triangle.

Lola Lo
67 Queens Road BS8 1QL
www.lolalobristol.com
Students. Squeeze The Cheese nights, half-price cocktails. You get the picture.

Louisiana
Wapping Road BS1 6UA
www.thelouisiana.net
The Louisiana has pulled in some of the biggest names on the indie scene over the years. It has always been and still is one of the coolest gig venues in town.

Love inn
84 Stokes Croft BS1 3QY
www.theloveinn.com
From the team at Love Saves The Day and See No Evil. The Love Inn has regular club nights Thurs-Sat featuring a wide range of tunes from hip-hop to soul, disco and boogie.

Motion/Marble Factory
74-78 Avon Street, St Phillips BS2 0PX
www.motionbristol.com
Warehouse-style party venue round the back of Temple Meads hosting a wide range of dance styles from drum 'n' bass to rave, techno and hardcore.

Mr Wolf's
32 St Nicholas Street BS1 1TG
www.mrwolfs.com
Offering noodles, live music and a late night bar, this is a hip and vibrant hangout bang in the centre of things.

Rough Trade
3 New Bridewell, Nelson Street BS1 2QD
www.roughtrade.com
In-store performance space hosts promo performances, signings and events.

SWX
15 Nelson Street, BS1 2JY
www.swxbristol.com
There's been a club on this site for decades (Papillons, Romeo & Juliets, Odyssey, Bailey's). Actor Dave Prowse (Green Cross Code Man and Darth Vader) was a bouncer here a long time ago in a galaxy far, far away.

Thekla
The Grove, Harbourside BS1 4RB
www.theklabristol.co.uk | Tel: 929 3301
Bristol's legendary floating nightclub has always been the choice of clubbers who don't really like going to clubs.

Thunderbolt
Bath Road, Totterdown BS4 3ED
www.thethunderbolt.net
An eclectic mix of music, spoken word, film and community events is what makes The Thunderbolt special. Somehow Dave and Sophie MacDonald manage to tempt the likes of The Christians, Wayne Hussey, Dr Feelgood, Jerry Dammers and The Stranglers to play a small south Bristol pub. The 'Bolt' also has a policy of supporting new local acts as well as squeezing middle-aged blokes onto the stage.

Zed Alley
Zed Alley BS1 4UA
@zedalleybristol
Very cool underground venue in cellar of the Bristol County Sports Club on Colston Street. Created by members of the band Hooper.

Bristol LGBTQ

A banner made by Freedom Youth for Bristol Pride

Collectives and regular events

Dialogue
www.dialoguemusic.co.uk
A record label and collective which puts on techno nights that are so much more than fist-pumping to repetitive beats. *Dialogue* celebrates inclusivity and safe spaces for everyone. The event even has a low-income plan for people who genuinely cannot afford to come otherwise, their mantra being that *everyone* should be able to come and enjoy a night out once in a while. Still quite new on the block, the club nights feel a bit like the coolest house party you've ever been to. Their current home is a 250 capacity swingers' club.

Horseplay
@HorseplayClub
Has been described as "Bristol's best gay dance party". Expect to dance wildly to house and disco amid a haze of smoke and glow sticks.

Indigo
www.indigonetwork.co.uk
An all-female collective that runs networking, social and cultural events for LBTQ+ women. They help women build not only professional networks but also great friendships across Bristol. Indigo also runs the club night *Hush* once a month, hosted at *Queen Shilling* or *Basement 45* on Frogmore street.

Thorny
info@wearethorny.com
@wearethorny
A queer collective that bridges the gap between performance art and club night. Their events are so diverse it's hard to pin down exactly what genre they are. Expect drag kings and queens, punk, rock, dance and one hell of a performance.

Pubs Bars Clubs

Bank
8 John Street BS1 2HR
www.thebanktavern.com
Gay friendly. Tucked away on a lane linking the Old City with Broadmead. The Bank is a traditional pub with real ales and home-cooked food.

Bristol Bear Bar
2-3 West Street, Old Market BS2 0BH
www.bristolbears.co.uk
Britain's first bespoke Bear bar is a one-room affair for older, hairier guys. Closed Mon.

Lads' Locker Room Bar & Sauna
19-21 West Street, Old Market, BS2 0DF
www.ladslockerroom.com
Formerly the Village Sauna.

Old Market Tavern
29 Old Market Street, BS2 0HB
www.omtbristol.co.uk
Good-value lunches, friendly atmosphere, fantastic suntrap garden and cracking Sunday carvery. Popular with a mixed crowd of local office workers and LGBT regulars who eschew the campery other venues offer.

OMG Bar
4 Frogmore Street BS1 5HX
www.omgclubs.com
From the same team behind OMG: karaoke and cocktails, video jukebox. Student-friendly, cheap drink offers. Open daily (evening only). Used to be called Bent.

OMG
1-2 Frog Lane, Frogmore Street, BS1 5UX
www.omgclubs.com
Club that took over the building that housed Vibes. Just the place if your idea of fun is shaking your sequinned booty to Lady Gaga.

Palace Hotel
1 West Street, Old Market, BS2 0DF
As camp as Christmas, and as sparkly as one of Liberace's famous candelabra. Known throughout Bristol as the Gin Palace. Seems to be under constant threat of closure.

Phoenix
1 Wellington Building, Champion Square BS2 9DB
Gay friendly. Smart, contemporary free house between Old Market and Cabot Circus.

Queenshilling
9 Frogmore Street, BS1 5NA
www.queenshilling.com
It's changed hands a few times over the last few years but she's still doing the business: one of the city's longest-established gay venues.

Seamus O'Donnell's
13 Saint Nicholas St BS1 1UE
@seamus.odonnells
Gay friendly. One-roomed, old-fashioned Irish bar serving Guinness and poteen.

Shops

Glitch
49 Old Market Street, Old Market BS2 0EX
www.glitchbristol.com
A hair salon with its toes in all of the pies. Apart from amazing hair-cuts, once the sun goes down Glitch also becomes an art gallery, space for hire, music venue, plant shop, and kitchen. It would be easier to list all the things they don't do.

Nice and Naughty
45 Colston Street, BS1 5AX
Tel: 929 7666
Formerly Clone Zone, Nice and Naughty offers a range of Ann Summers-esque lingerie, sex toys, magazines, fetish wear, 'room aromas' and related tat.

Bristol LGBTQ

Eva Mason explores Bristol's thriving LGBTQ scene...

Although the scene isn't as big as in some other cities, Bristol's LGBTQ+ community is constantly growing. And just like everything in our city, we've put our own Brizzle spin on it. So, what makes Bristol's LGBTQ+ scene unique?

According to Tom, who was smoking a quick ciggie next to the *OMG Club and Bar*: "Bristol has so much more going on than the average gay club." Admittedly, this was said whilst standing outside Bristol's most average gay club, but Tom does make a good point.

From multi-coloured light-up dancefloors, old-man pub roasts, metal rock bars, cabaret nights on graffiti-tagged boats, techno and spoken word performed in swingers' clubs, queer film festivals, badass drag-king punk rock bands, to poetry, theatre, art expos, sports teams and book clubs – there's something LGBTQ+ going on for everyone. Here's a quick breakdown of what to look out for.

Frogmore Street is hidden, like the world's most fabulous troll, beneath Park Street bridge and the watchful eye of a Banksy. Home to the *Queen Shilling* and *OMG Club and Bar*, it provides a great first course for a gay night out in Bristol's West End.

The wonderful thing about these clubs is the diversity once you step through the door. If you're gay, straight, trans, male, female, fluid, furry, bronie, dom, sub, or even a Bristol City fan, everyone is welcome. When everyone is vogue-ing with cheap drinks in our hands, waving our arms to *It's Raining*

Men, there's an amazing camaraderie you don't always find on other dance floors. As another partygoer succinctly put it: "The LGBTQ+ scene can be difficult, but Bristol has some of the fiercest queens in the country. We all desire to be one... and one we are!"

For the queer women out there, in a scene that's usually still quite male dominated, the Queen Shilling also hosts *Hush*, "the biggest lesbian/LGBTQ+ night outside of London," once a month. Run by the all-female identifying collective *Indigo,* according to their website "Hush promises playful pop, dancefloor indie, electro & R 'n' B tunes from the best gal DJs in the city". It might also be one of the few nights around where a woman can go out just to dance, without being hit on by men in red chinos.

It's the collectives like *Indigo* that are really bringing Bristol's LGBTQ+ scene to life. *Thorny* is another such collective that's relatively new on the Bristol scene. Established in 2015 by Jo Bligh, they specialise in taking over spaces to put on a diverse range of events, including "music gigs, theatre/live art, club nights and spaces for discussion for the under-represented voices of Bristol."

Their nights can be legendary, such as the time they took over the Arnolfini in November 2017 for a whirlwind of slime, whipped cream and glitter. The aim was to challenge the pre-conception of galleries as mainly straight, white, middle-class spaces. If you're tired of the cheesy pop,

Sport

Bristol Bisons RFC
www.bisonsrfc.co.uk
Bristol's gay and gay-friendly rugby team, established in 2005, welcomes new players and supporters. Hosted the pan-European Union Cup in 2013.

Bristol City Panthers FC
www.bristolpanthers.com
@bristolpanthersfc
Bristol's gay and gay-friendly football team, formed in 2000.

Contacts

Bristol Pride
www.bristolpride.co.uk
Annual festival held each Jujne/July with films, live comedy, music, theatre and more culminating in Pride Day, a massive celebration for the region's LGBTQ community and friends.

Each
Freephone helpline: 0808 100 0143
(Mon-Fri 9am-4.30pm)
www.eachaction.org.uk
Charity providing support to individuals affected by homophobia and training to organisations committed to an equal and safe environment for all, regardless of sexuality, age, ethnicity or ability.

Freedom Youth
@freedomyouthlgbtq
Bristol-based LGB youth project, including a weekly drop-in offering information, advice and guidance.

Gay West
PO Box 586, Bath BA1 2YQ.
www.gaywest.org.uk
Social group for LGB people in the South West whose roots stretch back as far as 1971 and the establishment of the Bath Gay Awareness Group. The group holds a cafe/drop-in in Bath every Saturday afternoon and a monthly social in Bristol.

LGBT Bristol
www.lgbtbristol.org.uk
Formerly known as the Bristol LGB Forum, LGBT Bristol is a charity fighting for, and educating about, equality.

Switchboard LGBT
Helpline 0300 330 0630
www.switchboard.lgbt
Bristol's long-running L&G Switchboard closed in 2013: calls are now taken by their colleagues in London, who provide confidential support and information.

these are the nights for you – think experimental, political punk, subversive performance art, techno, punk, rock, rap, and a sprinkling of cabaret. It's all queer, all-inclusive and all great fun. You never know when another night might pop up so keep an eye on the *Thorny* Facebook page.

As Bristol nightlife faces closures, (Stokes Croft clubs, *Blue Moon* and *Lakota* are both set to close), it is these pop-up nights and growing collectives that will keep the Bristol nightlife and LGBTQ+ scene fresh-faced and glittery. But the best thing about a night out in one of the two LGBTQ+ areas of Bristol – West End and Old Market – is that no matter the venue, *everyone* is welcome to be their best, most authentic selves. GB, who we met strutting their stuff on the *Queen Shilling* dancefloor said: "I feel the most comfortable I've ever felt. I'm in it, and I think it's great I can be myself, unashamedly."

Children's Bristol

© Max McClure

Going aloft on the SS Great Britain

Ashton Court Estate
Long Ashton BS41 9JN
www.visitbristol.co.uk
Walking, deer park, cycling, miniature railway, golf.

Avon Valley Railway
Bitton Station, 3 Bath Road, Bitton BS30 6HD
www.avonvalleyrailway.org
Steam train rides.

Blaise Castle
Kings Weston Road BS10 7QS
www.bristolmuseums.org.uk
Adventure playground, walks, park, house and museum.

Brandon Hill/Cabot Tower
Brandon Hill Park, Park Street BS1 5RR
www.visitbristol.co.uk
Playground, park, walks.

Bristol Hawks Gymnasium
11 Roman Road, Easton BS5 6DH
www.bristolhawksgymnastics.org
Gymnastic classes.

Bristol Zoo
College Roadd, Clifton BS8 3HA
www.bristolzoo.org.uk
Adevnture playground, animals, events.

City Museum & Art Gallery
Queens Road BS8 1RL
www.bristolmuseums.org.uk
Exhibits and regular children's events.

Freedog Bristol
2A-C, Templegate Park, Mead Street BS3 4RP
www.freedogbristol.com
Indoor trampoline park.

Leigh Woods Mountain Bike Trail
Valley Road BS8 3QB
www.nationaltrust.org.uk
Download trail map from website.

M Shed
Princes Wharf, Wapping Road BS1 4RN
www.bristolmuseums.org.uk
Museum of Bristol. Regular events.

Clifton Observatory
Litfield Road, Clifton BS8 3LT
Camera Obscura and Cave above the
Avon Gorge.

Snuff Mills
River View, Stapleton BS16 1UH
www.vivitbristol.co.uk
Riverside walks.

SS Great Britain
Great Western Dockyard, Gas Ferry Road BS1 6TY
www.ssgreatbritain.org
Brunel's famous steam ship plus
museum.

Wild Place
Blackhorse Hill, Cribbs Causeway BS10 7TP
www.wildplace.org.uk
Wildlife park, giant swings, high ropes
adventure course.

We The Curious
1 Millennium Square, Anchor Road BS1 5DB
www.wethecurious.org
Hands on science and technology
exhibits.

Climbing

Redpoint Bristol Climbing centre
40 Winterstoke Road BS3 2NW
www.redpointbristol.co.uk

Undercover Rock
St Werburgh's Church, Mina Road BS2 9YT
www.theclimbingacademy.com

Bloc Indoor Climbing Wall
2 New Gatton Road BS2 9SH
www.blocclimbing.co.uk

City Farms

Windmill Hill City Farm
Philip Street BS3 4EA
www.windmillhillcityfarm.org.uk

St Werburgh's City Farm
Watercress Road BS2 9YJ
www.swcityfarm.co.uk
Play area, farmyard, events.

Active Bristol

© Rich Kenington

The popular Ashton Court Parkrun

Walks

Bristol to Keynsham along the River Avon.
12 kilometres. Waterside pubs at Hanham Lock on the way.

Avon River Trail to Pill
Walk the old towpath on the south side of the Avon to the village of Pill.

Bath Skyline
www.nationaltrust.org.uk/bath-skyline/trails/bath-skyline-walk
A 10k circular walk with stunning views of Bath and Salisbury Plain.

Portishead to Clevedon
Follow the Gordano Round footpath along the edge of the Bristol Channel.

Crook Peak to Winscombe
www.gps-routes.co.uk
Stunning views over the Bristol Channel and Somerset Levels.
Links up to the West Mendip Way.

Bike Rides

Bristol to Bath Railway Path (Sustrans Route 4)
www.bristolbathrailwaypath.org.uk
Tranquil route out of the city and into the Countryside. Cafes at Warmley and Bitton, pubs at Saltford and Bath.

The Two Tunnels Greenway (Sustrans Route 224)
www.twotunnels.org.uk
Linking together two old railway tunnels this can be turned into a circular route

by following route 24 to the Kennet and Avon Canal.

The Strawberry Line (Sustrans Route 26)
www.thestrawberryline.org.uk
11-mile, traffic-free route from Yatton to Cheddar, ideal for families.
Parking available at Yatton Station by the excellent Strawberry Line Cafe.

Mountain Biking
Beginner mountain bike routes run through Leigh Woods and Ashton Court. Mountain Bikes can be hired from Pedal Progession at Ashton Court who also run skills sessions.

Runs

Ashton Court Parkrun
http://www.parkrun.org.uk/ashton-court/
Eastville Parkrun
http://www.parkrun.org.uk/eastville/
Free weekly 5k event. 9am every Saturday morning in Eastville Park and Aston Court. All abilities welcome.

Tyntesfield 10k
www.nationaltrust.org.uk
Free monthly 10k trail run through the grounds of the Tyntesfield estate. 9am on the third Sunday of the month.

Blaise Blazer
www.westburyharriers.com
Roughly 6k route on trails around the grounds of Blaise Castle every June.

Nightingale Nightmare
www.nightingalenightmare.co.uk
Halloween themed 10k race through Leigh Woods. Costumes not compulsory but don't expect a cheer home is you're not in fancy dress! Sells out very quickly.

Water

Portishead Lido
www.portisheadopenairpool.org.uk
Heated 33-metre, open-air pool. Open from April to September each year. For the brave they also run some cold water swimming sessions out of season.

Clevedon Marine Lake
www.clevedonmarinelake.co.uk
Open year round, 250 meters long but less than 5 foot deep in many parts. Ideal for a cooling summer dip or a very refreshing winter one.

Stand Up Paddle-boarding
www.supbristol.com
SUP Bristol run regular tours on Bristol harbour evenings and weekends.

Sailing on the harbour
www.allaboardwatersports.co.uk
Harbour-based watersports.

Other

Frisbee Golf at Ashton Court
Nine "hole" woodland course is designed for beginners. Disks can be hired from the golf centre in Ashton Court. Open from 8am until dusk year round.

FootGolf at Ashton Court
www.ukfootgolf.com
By repurposing nine holes of the old golf course Ashton Court has created a fun family activity with amazing views over Bristol. Open 8am until dusk.

Climbing in the Avon gorge
www.theclimbingacademy.com
The Climbing Academy run climbing taster evenings in the Avon Gorge throughout the summer.

Compiled by Kevin Brooks

Bristol sport

Richard Jones on Bristol's relationship with sport...

Bristol is the biggest regional city in England not to have had a football team in the top division in the last 30 or so years. In fact, we've never had a team in the Premier League since its inception in 1992. Think about it – Liverpool, Manchester, Birmingham, Newcastle, Sunderland, Leess, Portsmouth, Bolton, Blackburn, Blackpool, Huddersfield Norwich, Cardiff, Brighton, Bournemouth, Reading, Swansea and Wigan are all famous for having top-flight football in recent years.

The last time a Bristol team was in the top division was when City were in Division One between 1976 and 1980. And after getting relegated, they fell straight through the divisions in successive seasons before landing bankrupt at the bottom of Division Four with one almighty thump. This resulted in the entry into Bristol folklore of the "Ashton Gate Eight" – eight players who tore up their well-paid long-term contracts to save the club from financial meltdown.

There are probably deep sociological reasons why Bristol football is as bad as it is, but the reason you'll hear trotted out most is that it's because rugby and cricket are the dominant sports. Sadly, this theory is rubbish. Although egg chasing is a popular West Country pastime, so is cheese rolling and Bristol Rugby Club have suffered poor fortunes since the advent of professionalism, while Gloucestershire County Cricket Club is hardly among the modern game's pacesetters. Besides, have you ever

heard anyone argue that football in Manchester has suffered because of the success of Lancashire CC or Sale Rugby Union?

Bristol City is the bigger of the two Bristol professional football teams and the gap has been emphasised since 2014 when Rovers were relegated to the non-League Football Conference while City were promoted to the Championship at the end of the 2014/15 season.

Nicknamed the Pirates, Rovers' highest finish was when they came within four points of promotion to the top league (then Division One) in the 1955-56 season. They finished sixth in Division Two that year... a feat they repeated in 1958-59.

But most of the time were stuck in the 3rd and 4th tiers of the football pyramid before crashing into the Conference on the final day of the 2013/14 season. They bounced back through the play-offs the next season under manager Darrell Clarke and were promoted again the following season to League One. Clarke left the club in December 2018 after a poor run of results and caretaker boss Graham Coughlan was appointed manager in January 2019 after a string of good results.

In February 2016 Rovers were taken over by the billionaire Al-Qadi family, owners of the Jordan Investment Bank. Wael Al-Qadi was appointed chairman and Gasheads (as Rovers fans are known) waited for investment in new players, the youth system and a new ground. By 2019 none of these things had happened and the new ground seemed further away than ever after a deal fell through to build a stadium on the University of the West of England's Frenchay site.

City, on the other hand, have seen very visible signs of investment by their owner, Steve Lansdown, one half of the Hargreaves Lansdown financial services juggernaut. Ashton Gate has been redeveloped into a wonderful stadium which is shared by Bristol Rugby as part of Lansdown's Bristol Sport empire. Under innovative manager Lee Johnson, City have established themselves as a force in the Championship and have genuine Premier League ambitions and the infrastructure to support it.

City's highest finish was second in the top divisio0n ion 1907 and they reached the FA Cup final in 1909, losing to Manchester United.

Bristol Rugby (Bristol Bears) never really adapted to the game going professional in 1995. Whereas neighbours Bath and Gloucester

have been a permanent fixture in the top flight since then and Exeter have come through the pyramid system to the very top of English rugby, Bristol have spent many of those years in the second division. In 2017, after the club moved from the Memorial Stadium to cement their future as part of Bristol Sport at Ashton Gate, Samoan Pat Lam took over as head coach, Bristol were promoted to the Premiership and avoided relegation playing an expansive and adventurous brand of running rugby.

The final element of Bristol Sport is the Bristol Flyers basketball club who play their home games at the South Gloucestershire and Stroud (SGS) campus in Patchway. However at the time of writing plans had been submitted for a purpose-built arena alongside Ashton Gate as part of the £100 million Ashton Gate Sports and Convention Centre development which would also include homes and two hotels on the site of a retail park next to the existing stadium.

Sports Grounds

Bristol City
Ashton Gate, Ashton BS3 2EJ
www.bcfc.co.uk

Bristol Rovers
Memorial Stadium, Filton Avenue, Horfield BS7 0BF
www.bristolrovers.co.uk

Gloucestershire County Cricket Club
County Ground, Neville Road, Bishopston BS7 9EJ
www.gloscricket.co.uk

Bristol Rugby Club
Ashton Gate, Ashton BS3 2EJ
www.bristolbearsrugby.com

Sports Centres and Swimming Pools

Bristol South Pool
Dean Lane, Bedminster BS3 1BS
www.everyoneactive.com

David Lloyd Long Aston
Ashton Road, Nr Long Ashton BS3 2HB
www.davidlloyd.co.uk

David Lloyd, Westbury
Greystoke Avenue, Westbury-on-Trym BS10 6AZ
www.davidlloyd.co.uk

Easton Leisure Centre/Pool
Thrissell Street, Easton BS5 0SW
www.everyoneactive.com

Henbury Leisure Centre/Pool
Avonmouth Way, Henbury BS10 7NG
www.everyoneactive.com

Henleaze Swimming Club
Henleaze Lake, Lake Road, Henleaze BS10 5HG
www.henleazeswimmingclub.org
A fabulous members-only lake with high diving boards. The perfect spot for a day out in the summer. Get signed in by a member if you want to try it out. Sadly, the waiting list for membership is about two years long, but worth putting your name down.

Hengrove Pool
Hengrove Park BS14 0DE
www.leisurecentre.com

Horfield Leisure Centre
Dorian Road, Horfield BS7 0XW
www.everyoneactive.com

Jubilee Pool
Jubilee Road, Knowle BS4 2LP
www.leisurecentre.com

Kingswood Leisure Centre
Church Road, Staple Hill BS16 4RH
www.activecentres.org

St Paul's Community Sports Academy
Newfoundland Road, St Paul's BS2 9NH
www.everyoneactive.com

Climbing

Redpoint Bristol Climbing Centre
40 Winterstoke Road, Ashton BS3 2NW
www.redpointbristol.co.uk

The Church
Mina Road, St Werburgh's BS2 9YT
www.theclimbingacademy.com

The Mothership
Charlton Street, Barton Hill BS5 0FD
www.theclimbingacademy.com

Athletics

Bristol and West Athletics Club
Johnsons Lane, Whitehall BS5 9AZ
www.bristolandwestac.org

Basketball

Bristol Flyers
Bristol Flyers Basketball Club
SGS College Arena, Patchway BS34 8LP
www.bristolflyers.co.uk

Fencing

Bristol Fencing Club
www.bristolfencingclub.com

Tennis

Bristol Lawn Tennis & Squash Club
Redland Green, Redland BS6 7HF
www.redlandgreen.co.uk

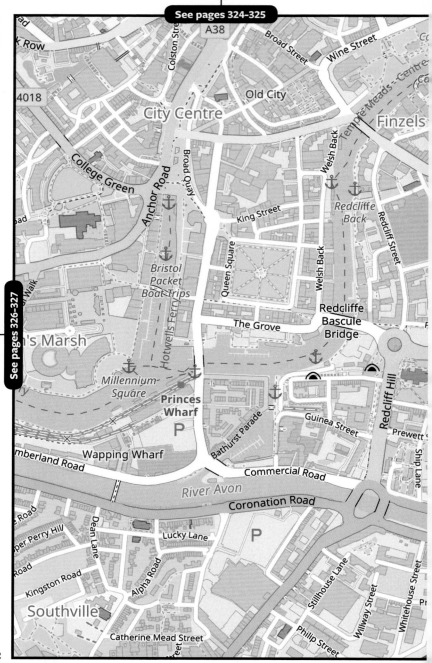

See pages 324–325

See pages 326–327

A38

Broad Street

Wine Street

Old City

City Centre

Finzels

Colston Street

4018

College Green

Anchor Road

Broad Quay

Welsh Back

Temple Meads · Centre

King Street

Redcliffe Back

Redcliff Street

Bristol Packet Boat Trips

Queen Square

Welsh Back

Redcliffe Bascule Bridge

's Marsh

The Grove

Hotwells Ferry

Walk

Millennium Square

Princes Wharf

Redcliff Hill

P

Guinea Street

Prewett

Bathurst Parade

Wapping Wharf

mberland Road

Commercial Road

Ship Lane

River Avon

Coronation Road

Road

per Perry Hill

Dean Lane

Lucky Lane

P

Road

Alpha Road

Stillhouse Lane

Willway Street

Whitehouse Street

Kingston Road

Southville

Catherine Mead Street

Philip Street

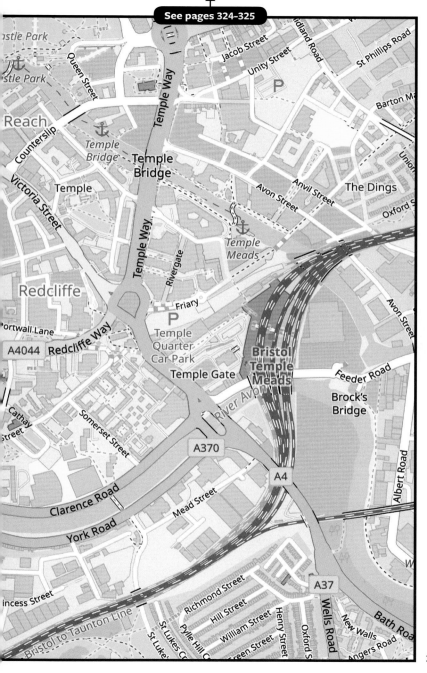

See pages 324–325

stle Park

Queen Street

stle Park

Reach

Countership

Temple Bridge

Temple Bridge

Victoria Street

Temple

Redcliffe

Portwall Lane

A4044 Redcliffe Way

Cathay Street

incess Street

Jacob Street

Unity Street

P

Temple Way

Temple Way

Rivergate

Friary

P
Temple Quarter Car Park

Temple Gate

Somerset Street

Clarence Road

York Road

Bristol to Taunton Line

Midland Road

St Phillips Road

Barton M

Avon Street

Anvil Street

The Dings

Union

Oxford S

Temple Meads

Bristol Temple Meads

River Avon

A370

Mead Street

A4

Brock's Bridge

Feeder Road

Avon Street

Albert Road

A37

A37

Richmond Street

Hill Street

William Street

Henry Street

Pyle Hill C

Green Street

St Lukes C

St Luke

Wells Road

New Walls

Oxford S

Angers Road

Bath Roa

W

The Arches

Zetland Road

Belvoir

Station Road

Redland Road

Cheltenham Road

Mo

Redland Grove

Fernbank Road

South Road

Redland

ensington Road

Meridian Road

Redland Grove

Elmgrove Road

Southfield Road

Cotham Brow

Arley Hill

Gibson Road

Sydenham Road

Sydenham Hill

Victoria Walk

Arley Hill

Sydenham Lane

Springfield Road

Sydenham Road

Bath Buildi

ton Lane

avenswood Road

Archfield Road

Cotham Grove

Cotham

Pitch Lane

Fremantle Road

Victoria Walk

rawney Road

Cotham Park

Victoria Walk

n Lawn Road

Cotham School

Cotham Road

Saint Matthews Road

Kingsdown

Somerset Street

Stokes Cro

Dove Street

High Kingsdown

Kingsdown Parade

Dove Street South

Jamaica Street

Moon Street

dall Avenue

Saint Michaels Hill

Horfield Road

Dighton Street

Charles Street

B4051

A4044

The Horsefa

Walk

Saint Michaels Hill

Broad

son Street

Fairfax St

See pages 328-329

Maps © Open Street Map

See pages 322-323

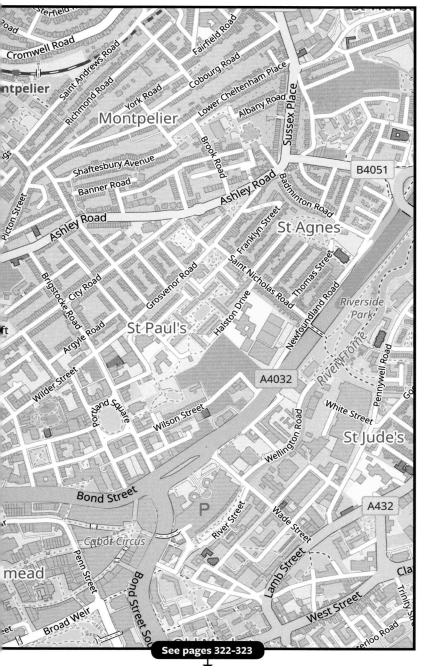

See pages 322-323

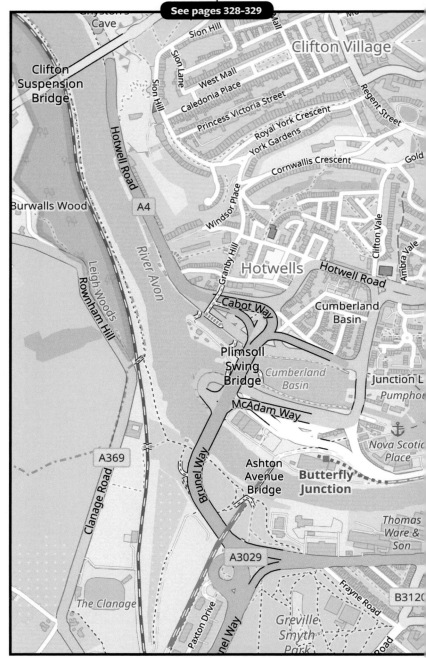

See pages 328–329

Clifton Village

Sion Hill

Mall

Clifton
Suspension
Bridge

Sion Lane

West Mall

Caledonia Place

Sion Hill

Princess Victoria Street

Royal York Crescent

Regent Street

York Gardens

Cornwallis Crescent

Gold

Hotwell Road

A4

Burwalls Wood

Windsor Place

Clifton Vale

Ambra Vale

Granby Hill

Hotwells

Hotwell Road

River Avon

Leigh Woods
Rownham Hill

Cabot Way

Cumberland
Basin

Plimsoll
Swing
Bridge

Cumberland
Basin

Junction L

Pumphoe

McAdam Way

A369

Brunel Way

Ashton
Avenue
Bridge

Butterfly
Junction

Nova Scotia
Place

Clanage Road

A3029

Thomas
Ware &
Son

Frayne Road

B3120

The Clanage

Paxton Drive

nel Way

Greville
Smyth
Park

oad

See pages 328-329

See pages 322-323

The Fosseway

Clifton Road

York Place

Berkeley Pl

Charlotte Street

Great George Street

Lower Clifton Hill

Bellevue

Jacobs Wells Road

Brandon Hill

Brandon Hill Park

Clifton Hill

ney Avenue

Constitution Hill

Goldney Hall

Clifton Wood Road

Bellevue Crescent

Saint Georges Road   Deanery R

A4

Cliftonwood

Ambrose Road

Hotwell Road

Capricorn Quay

Floating Harbour

Ca

Hotwells Ferry

Mardyke

SS Great Britain

Hotwells

ock

Bristol Marina

Spike Island

SS Great Britain

use

Baltic Wharf

Sydney Row

Cumberland Road

C

Cumberland Road

River Avon

A370   Coronation Road

Park Road

Allington Road

Islington Road

Osbor

Beauley Road

Leighton Road

Walter Street

Greenway Bush Lane

Raleigh Road

Upton Road

Hamilton Road

Birch Road

Stackpo

me Road

Road

arage Road

Milford Street

Me

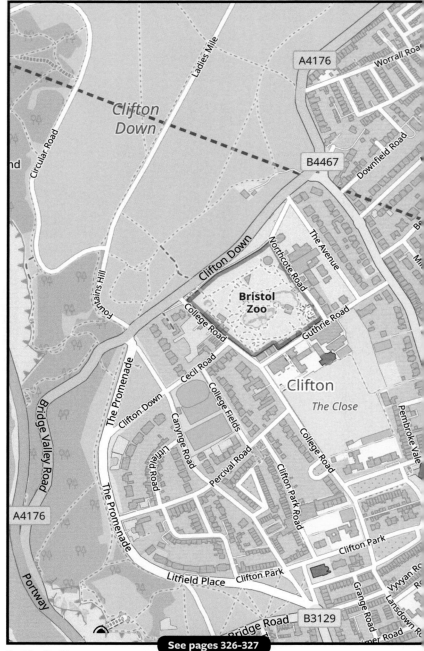

Clifton Down

Ladies Mile

A4176

Worrall Roa

Circular Road

B4467

Downfield Road

nd

Fountains Hill

Clifton Down

Northcote Road

The Avenue

Be

Mi

Bristol
Zoo

College Road

Guthrie Road

The Promenade

Cecil Road

Clifton

The Close

Bridge Valley Road

Clifton Down

College Fields

Canynge Road

Litfield Road

Percival Road

College Road

Pembroke Vale

A4176

Clifton Park Road

The Promenade

Clifton Park

Portway

Litfield Place

Clifton Park

Vyvyan Rc

Grange Road

Lansdown Re

B3129

Bridge Road

mer Road

Maps © Open Street Map

See pages 326-327

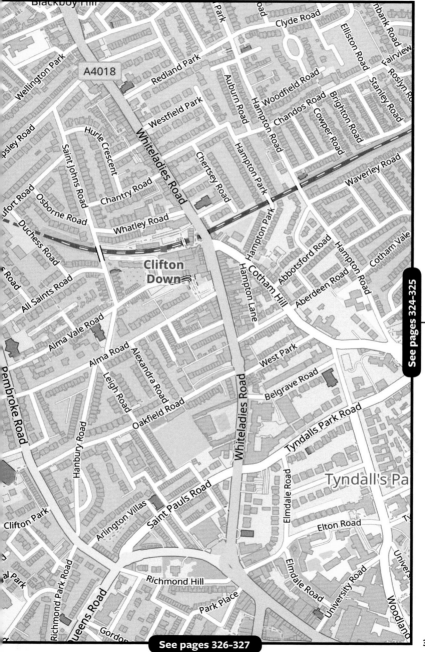

Blackboy Hill

Wellington Park

A4018

Redland Park

Clyde Road

Elliston Road

Fairview

nbank Road

Roslyn Ro

Westfield Park

Woodfield Road

Stanley Road

psley Road

Hurle Crescent

Whiteladies Road

Auburn Road

Hampton Road

Chandos Road

Brighton Road

Cowper Road

Saint Johns Road

Chersey Road

Chantry Road

Hampton Park

Waverley Road

ufort Road

Osborne Road

Whatley Road

Clifton Down

Hampton Park

Abbotsford Road

Hampton Road

Cotham Vale

Duchess Road

s Road

All Saints Road

Cotham Hill

Aberdeen Road

Alma Vale Road

Hampton Lane

Alma Road

Alexandra Road

West Park

Belgrave Road

pembroke Road

Leigh Road

Hanbury Road

Oakfield Road

Whiteladies Road

Tyndall's Park Road

Tyndall's Pa

Elmdale Road

Clifton Park

Arlington Villas

Saint Pauls Road

Elton Road

al Park

Richmond Park Road

Richmond Hill

Park Place

Elmdale Road

University Road

Ty

Univers

Queens Road

Gordo

Woodland

See pages 324-325

See pages 326-327

Notes

Notes

Notes

Notes

Notes

Notes

Notes